The Rightly Guided Caliphs

Abū Bakr, 'Umar, 'Uthmān, 'Alī

The Rightly-Guided Caliphs

Abū Bakr, ʿUmar, ʿUthmān, ʿAlī

رضي الله عنهم

by

Gibril Fouad Haddad

First edition 2023 at
Institute for Spiritual & Cultural Advancement, Fenton, MI (USA)

Published in the US by Institute for Spiritual & Cultural Advancement
17195 Silver Parkway #401, Fenton, MI 48430 USA
Tel: (888) 278-6624 Fax:(810) 815-0518
Email: info@sufilive.com
Web: http://www.sufilive.com
Purchase online at: http://www.isn1.net

Book covers and inside text designed and set by Qaf Qasyoun and ISCA.
Cover illustration: *Hilye* by Hafiz Osman, circa 1670 (detail), from Sadberk Hanim Museum, Sarıyer district, Istanbul, Turkey. Public domain.

ISBN: 978-1-938058-69-1 (pp)
978-1-938058-70-7 (ebook)

Cataloging-in-Publication Data

Haddad, Gibril Fouad, 1960-

The Rightly-Guided Caliphs: Abū Bakr, ʿUmar, ʿUthmān, ʿAlī.
327 p. 23 cm. Bibliography.
1. Muḥammad, Prophet, -632 – Successors. 2. Caliphs – Biography. 3. Rashidun Caliphate, 632–661. 4. Muḥammad, Prophet – Companions. 3. Hadith – texts. I. Author. II. Title.

بِسْمِ ٱللَّهِ ٱلرَّحْمَٰنِ ٱلرَّحِيمِ

فَسَوْفَ يَأْتِى ٱللَّهُ بِقَوْمٍ يُحِبُّهُمْ وَيُحِبُّونَهُۥٓ

then the One God shall bring forth a people whom He loves and who love Him

(Sūrat al-Māʾida 5:54)

Preamble

The foremost and first of the Emigrants and the Helpers (al-Tawba 9:100), *men who are true to what they covenanted with the One God* (al-Aḥzāb 33:23)

"Those that studiously kept his company morning and evening, received his conveyance of the Revelation, took from him the Law that became the path of the Umma, and looked to him for the ethics of Islam and to his noble traits. Those became, after him, the imams and proofs in which resides right guidance and in whose path is found right emulation and in them is safety and right belief." Al-Ḥakīm al-Tirmidhī.[1]

Praise, glory, and thanks belong to Allah Most High. Blessings and salutations of peace upon His Beloved Messenger, our Master Muḥammad, and upon his Family and Companions.

These pages were written for the most part from 1997 to 2006. Their first version was an 82-page booklet, *The Rightly-Guided Caliphs & The Four Imams*, published in 1998. It was followed in 2002 by the 140-page monograph *Abū Bakr al-Ṣiddīq*, the as-of-yet unpublished *ʿĀʾisha al-Ṣiddīqa the Mothers of the Believers* and, by the end of 2006, the 575-page *The Four Imams and Their Schools*. Their respective methods and contents are mutually complementary. All of them benefited from the blessed gaze, support and approval of our teachers Mawlana Shaykh Nazim al-Haqqani and Mawlana Shaykh Hisham Kabbani. This larger work on the Four Caliphs coming out after a quarter century is dedicated to them.

At that time I lived in Damascus, in the blessed house of Shaykh Nazim on Mount Qasyoun, thanks to the intercession of Shaykh Hisham. That house faced the mosque and *maqām* of Grandshaykh ʿAbd Allah Faʾiz al-Daghistani and hosted Shaykh Nazim's ancient library. It was equidistant, among others, from the *maqāms* of Mawlāna Khālid al-Baghdādī and the Forty *Abdāl* from above, Shaykh Muḥyī al-Dīn Ibn ʿArabī and Shaykh ʿAbd al-Ghanī al-Nābulusī from below. It was as if an extension of the niche of the lights of the inheritors of the Seal of Prophets on top of the lights of the holy land of the Prophets—upon him and them and their families blessings and peace. It received many God-sent visitors, local, regional and international shaykhs, students and families whom my family and I were privileged to serve in the course of those nine years, including Mawlana himself.

The Rightly-Guided Caliphate laid the definitive foundations and formed the accomplished archetype of what the Prophet–upon him the blessings and peace of Allah–termed *khilāfat al-Nubuwwa* in the timeline narrated

[1] Al-Ḥakīm al-Tirmidhī, *Nawādir al-Uṣūl* (*Aṣl* 222).

from him by the Companion Safīna: "**The succession of Prophetship** after me is 30 years, then Allah shall bring kingdom to whomever He wishes" (Abū Dāwūd and others). This prophesied timeline is fulfilled in the precise sum of the first five caliphates: two years and three months for Abū Bakr (Rabiʿ al-Awwal 11-Jumādā II 13); ten years and a half for ʿUmar (Jumādā II 13-Dhū al-Ḥijja 23); twelve years for ʿUthmān (Dhū al-Ḥijja 23-Dhū al-Ḥijja 35); four years and nine months for ʿAlī (Dhū al-Ḥijja 35-Ramadan 40) and six months for al-Ḥasan b. ʿAlī (Ramadan 40-Rabīʿ al-Awwal 41).

The best post-Prophetic 30-year generation to walk the earth constitutes, by consensus of *Ahl al-Sunna wal-Jamāʿa*, the most shining model of governance—and self-governance—for a just society of humble believers ever to be held up to the human ages. This glimpse in 110 chapters of their respective lives and deaths highlights the necessary qualities of true leadership which are personal sacrifice for the public welfare and dedication to the Prophetic model of trust, firm belief, constant remembrance, inspired practice and self-effaced vast mercy.

Fifteen centuries later, the lives of these first and foremost, the closest of all Companions and most intimate friends of the Seal of Messengers, still hail us. They continue to move our hearts, feed our souls, educate our spirits. *The Outrunners* (Tawba 9:100) are evoked in the prayer of everyone that says *the Path of those You have favored* (Fātiḥa 1:7) and *Peace, safety, purity is on us and on the righteous servants of Allah* (Prayer of Witnessing).

Muhammad is the Messenger of the One God. And those who are with him are severe against the unbelievers, merciful with one another. You will see them bowing down, prostrating, seeking bounty from the One God and good pleasure. Their marks are upon their faces from the effect of prostration. That is their likeness in the Torah, and their likeness in the Gospel, like a plant that sends forth its shoot then strengthens it so that it has become stout then it is firmly established on its stalks, impressing the sowers, so that He would enrage the unbelievers with them. The One God has promised those of them that believe and do the righteous deeds forgiveness and a magnificent reward (al-Fatḥ 48:29).

May Allah use this humble endeavor for the same cause that made His Beloved Prophet ﷺ happy at the sight of his Companions and at the evocation of his latter-time beloved ones. May He build up the love within the Umma in the same fashion as the Umma loves its first leaders, mould it after their states, strengthen it with their knowledge, increase it with their example. May He relent towards the *Umma* and erase its divisions. *Āmīn.*

Brunei Darussalam
Last Jumuʿa of Rajab 1444 – 17 February 2023

Contents

Abū Bakr al-Ṣiddīq

رضى الله تعالى عنه

'Atīq b. Abī Quḥāfa 'Abd Allāh b. 'Uthmān b. 'Āmir
al-Qurashī al-Taymī,
"the one and only *Shaykh al-Islam*" (Ibn al-Mubārak),
the intimate friend of the Prophet ﷺ after Allah ﷻ,
exclusive companion at his Basin and in the Cave,
greatest supporter and closest confidant,
first of the men who believed in him
and the only one who did so unhesitatingly,
first of the four Rightly-Guided Caliphs,
first of the Ten promised Paradise,
first of the Community of Islam to enter Paradise,
"the Venerable of the Community,"
"truthful, dutiful, well-guided, and following the right"
Allah Most High be well-pleased with him!

Abū Bakr al-Ṣiddīq ﷺ, 'Atīq b. Abī Quḥāfa, 'Abd Allāh b. 'Uthmān b. 'Āmir al-Qurashī al-Taymī (50BH-d. Jumāda II 13/573-August 634), the one and only *Shaykh al-Islam*, the intimate friend of the Prophet Muḥammad ﷺ after Allah ﷻ, exclusive Companion at his Basin *(ḥawḍ)* and in the Cave, greatest supporter, closest confidant, first of the men who believed in him and the only one who did so unhesitatingly, first of the four Rightly-Guided Caliphs, first of the Ten promised Paradise, first of the Community of Islam to enter Paradise, "the Venerable of the Community" (Rabī'a b. Ka'b al-Aslamī), "truthful, dutiful, well-guided, following the right" ('Umar),[2] the best of all human beings after the Prophets. He died in his bed at the same age as the Prophet when he died, 63.

[2]*Ṣādiqun bārrun rāshidun tābi'un lil-ḥaqq*. Narrated by al-Bukhārī in his Ṣaḥīḥ, book of *Farḍ al-Khumus*, and Muslim in his *Ṣaḥīḥ*, book of *al-Jihād wal-Sayr*.

1
Four Generations of Companions of the Prophet ﷺ

Imām al-Nawawī – Allah have mercy on him – wrote in *Tahdhīb al-Asmā' wal-Lughāt* that Abū Bakr's genealogical tree, alone among the Companions, regroups four successive generations of Companions of the Prophet ﷺ: his father Abū Quḥāfa, himself, his daughter Asmā', and her son 'Abd Allāh, in addition to Abū Bakr's son 'Abd al-Raḥmān and his grandson Abū 'Atīq. When his mother Umm Rūmān was buried, the Prophet ﷺ said: "Whoever wishes to see one of the women of Paradise, let him look at this woman."[3]

Imām Ja'far al-Ṣādiq said, "Whatever I hope for in the intercession of 'Alī, I hope for the same in that of Abū Bakr. Truly, Abū Bakr is twice my father!"[4] He said this in reference to Ja'far's mother, Fāṭima bint al-Qāsim b. Muḥammad b. Abī Bakr al-Ṣiddīq, and her own mother, Asmā' bint 'Abd al-Raḥmān b. Abī Bakr al-Ṣiddīq – Allah be well-pleased with all of them. 'Alī said that Abū Bakr is the only Companion to have both parents – Abū Quḥāfa and Umm al-Khayr – enter Islam.[5]

Since all Abū Bakr's children and grandchildren (see his posterity below) also accepted Islam after him, Ibn 'Abbās saw a reference to him in the verse *And We have commended unto man kindness to his parents. In pain did his mother bear him, in pain did she give him birth, and the bearing of him and the weaning of him is thirty months, till, when he attains full strength and reaches forty years, he says: My Lord! Grant me that I may give thanks for Your favor which You have bestowed upon me and upon both my parents, and that I may do right acceptable unto You. And be gracious unto me in my issue. Lo! I have turned unto You repentant, and lo! I am of those who surrender (unto You).* (46:15).[6]

[3]Narrated by Ibn Sa'd (8:267).
[4]In al-Mizzī, *Tahdhīb al-Kamāl* (5:81-82), al-Dhahabī, *Siyar* (Risāla ed. 6:255, 6:259) and *Tadhkirat al-Ḥuffāẓ* (1:167), al-Suyūṭī, *Ṭabaqāt al-Ḥuffāẓ* (p. 79), al-Sakhāwī, *al-Tuḥfat al-Laṭīfa* (1:241), and *A'yān al-Shī'a* (1:659).
[5]Narrated by al-Wāḥidī in *al-Wajīz fil-Tafsīr* (2:293), al-Baghawī in *Ma'ālim al-Tanzīl* (4:167 in his commentary on verse 46:15), and Muḥibb al-Dīn al-Ṭabarī in *al-Riyāḍ al-Naḍira* (1:399 §316).
[6]Narrated by al-Wāḥidī in *Asbāb al-Nuzūl* (p. 240), al-Baghawī in *Ma'ālim al-Tanzīl* (4:167 in his commentary on verse 46:15), Ibn 'Asākir in *Tārīkh Dimashq* (9:2), and Muḥibb al-Dīn al-Ṭabarī in *al-Riyāḍ al-Anīqa* (1:399-400 §317).

2
Abū Bakr is in Paradise

Abū Bakr is the first of the Ten Promised Paradise. The Prophet ﷺ said: "Abū Bakr is in *Janna*, 'Umar is in *Janna*, 'Uthmān is in *Janna*, 'Alī is in *Janna*, Talḥa is in *Janna*, al-Zubayr [b. al-'Awwām] is in *Janna*, 'Abd al-Raḥmān b. 'Awf is in *Janna*, Sa'd [b. Abī Waqqāṣ], Sa'īd [b. Zayd b. 'Amr] is in *Janna*, and Abū 'Ubayda b. al-Jarrāḥ is in *Janna*."[7]

There were other occasions for this glad tidings from the Prophet ﷺ. Al-Bukhārī and Muslim narrated from Abū Mūsā al-Ash'arī that the latter was standing at the gate of the enclosure of the well of Arīs inside which the Prophet ﷺ was resting, poking the muddy ground with a stick, when Abū Bakr showed up. Abū Mūsā went in and asked permission for him to enter. The Prophet ﷺ said, "Give him permission and give him the glad tidings of Paradise." Then 'Umar came and the Prophet ﷺ said the same words. Then 'Uthmān came and the Prophet ﷺ said the same but added, "after a trial that shall befall him." 'Uthmān rendered praise to Allah then said: "From Allah comes Help!" The Prophet's ﷺ legs were in the water and his thighs were uncovered. When 'Uthmān came in, he covered them. 'Uthmān sat and dangled his legs like them. At the last of that meeting the Prophet ﷺ, Abū Bakr, and 'Umar were all sitting one end of the well while 'Uthmān sat at the other end. Sa'īd b. al-Musayyab said: "I interpreted this to refer to their graves."

[7]Narrated from 'Abd al-Raḥmān b. 'Awf and Sa'īd b. Zayd by al-Tirmidhī, Abū Dāwūd, Ibn Mājah, and Aḥmad.

3
The First Rightly-Guided Caliph

Abū Bakr al-Ṣiddīq is the first of the four Rightly-Guided Caliphs of the Prophet ﷺ. The latter did not appoint anyone for his successor but pointed to Abū Bakr implicitly by ordering him to lead the prayer and becoming angry if someone else led it. It is reported by mass transmission *(tawātur)* that Abū Bakr, alone among the Companions, repeatedly led the Community in prayer in the lifetime of the Prophet ﷺ.[8]

Regarding the first Caliphate, Imām Aḥmad said: "When the Prophet ﷺ was ill he ordered Abū Bakr to pray as imām although there others were present who were more proficient in the Qur'ān *(aqra')*, but he ﷺ was pointing to the Caliphate."[9] Imām al-Shāfi'ī preceded him in this view.

Did Abū Bakr ever lead the Prophet ﷺ himself in prayer? When the Prophet ﷺ came out to pray in congregation for the last time as Abū Bakr had already begun to lead the *Ṣalāt*, the latter moved to give him his place as imām, but the Prophet ﷺ told him to stay where he was and prayed sitting to the left of Abū Bakr while the latter and the congregation remained standing. The sound ḥadīths to that effect state: "Abū Bakr followed the Prophet ﷺ who was sitting while the people followed Abū Bakr who was standing."[10] Abū Bakr continued to call *Allāhu Akbar* out loud to let the people hear.[11] This is the established account and the meaning of the report from Jābir in al-Tirmidhī *(ṣaḥīḥ)* that "the last prayer the Prophet ﷺ ever prayed was in a single garment in which he wrapped himself from head to toe, behind Abū Bakr," as opposed to the unambiguous but *mursal* report in Ibn Hishām that "the Prophet ﷺ prayed behind Abū Bakr as his imām."[12] However, al-Qasṭallānī mentioned Ibn al-Mulaqqin's citation of the two ḥadīth masters al-Ḍiyā' al-Maqdisī and Ibn Naṣir al-Salāmī as asserting that the Prophet ﷺ, in his last illness, did pray behind Abū Bakr as his imām, the latter specifying "three times" while Ibn Ḥibbān stated "twice" and provided a luminous proof:

> The reports are all sound and none of them contradicts the other. However, the Prophet ﷺ prayed two prayers in congregation during his last illness, not just one. In one of the two he was led and in the other he was the imām. The proof that they were two is that in the report of 'Ubayd Allah from 'Abd Allāh from 'Ā'isha, the Prophet ﷺ came out between two men – she meant al-'Abbās and 'Alī – while in the report

[8]As narrated from Abū Mūsā al-Ash'arī by al-Bukhārī and Muslim. This is a mass-narrated ḥadīth authentically reported also from 'Ā'isha, Ibn Mas'ūd, Ibn 'Abbās, Ibn 'Umar, 'Abd Allāh b. Zam'a, Abū Sa'īd al-Khudrī, 'Alī, and Hafṣa.
[9]Narrated from Abū Bakr al-Marwazī by Ibn al-Jawzī in *Manāqib Aḥmad* (p. 160).
[10]Narrated from 'Ā'isha by al-Bukhārī and Muslim.
[11]Narrated from Jābir by Abū Dāwūd, al-Nasā'ī, and Ibn Mājah.
[12]Cf. al-Qasṭallānī, *Mawāhib* (1:167), citing al-Suhaylī's caveat.

of Masrūq from ʿĀ'isha, the Prophet ﷺ came out between Barīra and Nawba. This shows that they were two prayers.[13]

It is established that the Prophet ﷺ prayed one prayer cycle behind ʿAbd al-Raḥmān b. ʿAwf when he joined the prayer after the Companions had already started it during the campaign of Tabūk.[14]

[13]In al-Zurqānī, *Sharḥ al-Mawāhib* (1:444-445).
[14]Narrated from al-Mughīra b. Shuʿba by Muslim and Aḥmad.

4
His Respect of the Prophet Excelled Obedience

In a previous, similar incident the Prophet ﷺ did order Abū Bakr to continue to pray as imām in front of him but Abū Bakr would not. Instead, he went backwards back in line while the Prophet ﷺ stepped up and continued the prayer. After the prayer, the Prophet ﷺ asked him: "Abū Bakr, what prevented you from standing firm when I ordered you to?" Abū Bakr excused himself with his famous word: "*Mā kāna li-Ibni Abī Quḥāfata an yataqaddama bayna yaday Rasūlillāh* – It was not fitting for the son of Abū Quḥāfa to stand ahead of the Messenger of Allah!"[15] The Prophet ﷺ approved of him.

This further allusive Prophetic confirmation of the successorship of Abū Bakr did not escape the notice of 'Umar who reminded the *Anṣār* of it at the time they lay claim to joint successorship of the Prophet ﷺ, saying to them: "Are you not aware that the Messenger of Allah ﷺ ordered Abū Bakr to pray as imām among the people?" They replied: "By Allah, yes!" He continued: "Who among you would be happy to be removed from a position in which the Messenger of Allah ﷺ put him?" They said: "We seek refuge in Allah from trying to come before Abū Bakr."[16]

The act of Abū Bakr in giving precedence to respect *(adab)* over obedience *(ṭā'a)* is the basis for the preferability of adding *Sayyidinā* to the name of the Prophet ﷺ in the *Ṣalāt Ibrāhīmiyya* during *tashahhud* in the Shāfi'ī School even if the Prophet ﷺ only said to say: *"Allāhumma Ṣalli 'alā Muḥammad..."* This fatwa was given by Ibn 'Abd al-Salām, al-Isnawī, al-Maḥallī, al-Suyūṭī, al-Fayrūzābādī, al-Ramlī, al-Sakhāwī, al-Haytamī and others such as Ibn 'Aṭā'Allah, al-Ḥaṭṭāb, al-Fāsī, Zarrūq, al-Hārūshī, etc. as reported by al-Qāḍī Yūsuf al-Nabhānī in the introduction to his *Sa'ādatu al-Dārayni fil-Ṣalāti 'alā Sayyidi al-Kawnayn* ("The Bliss of the Two Abodes in the Invocation of Blessings on the Master of the Two Universes") and again in the introduction to *al-Dilālāt al-Wāḍiḥāt Sharḥ Dalā'il al-Khayrāt*, his commentary on Imām al-Jazūlī's renowned manual of invocations of blessings on the Prophet ﷺ.[17]

Another proof for this fatwa is the statement of Ibn Mas'ūd: "When you invoke blessings on your Prophet, invoke blessings in the best possible way *(fa-aḥsinū al-ṣalāta 'alā nabiyyikum)* for – you do not know – this might be shown to him. So say: 'O Allah! Grant your *ṣalāt*, mercy, and blessings upon the Master (*sayyid*) of Messengers, the Imām of the Godfearing and the Seal of Prophets, Muḥammad your servant and Messenger, the Imām of goodness and leader of goodness and Messenger of Mercy! O Allah! Raise

[15]Narrated from Sahl b. Sa'd al-Sā'idī by al-Bukhārī, Muslim, Mālik, Abū Dāwūd, al-Nasā'ī, and Aḥmad.
[16]See below, ḥadīth at note 111.
[17]Some Ḥanafīs said such a fatwa was fit for those who have achieved the level of Abū Bakr in the faith and good manners and that, for all others, it is safest to stick to the letter and spirit of the command of the Prophet ﷺ: "Pray as you see me pray."

him to a glorious station for which the first and the last of creatures will yearn! O Allah!…"[18]

The general proofs for calling the Prophet ﷺ *sayyid* are in the verses *lordly (sayyidan), chaste, a Prophet of the righteous* (3:39) and *and they met her lord and master* (sayyidahā) *at the door* (12:42) as well as the Prophetic narrations: [1] "I am the Master *(sayyid)* of human beings";[19] [2] "This son of mine [al-Ḥasan] is a leader of men *(sayyid)*";[20] [3] "Get up to meet your chief *(qūmū ilā sayyidikum)* [Sa'd b. 'Ubāda]";[21] this ḥadīth is also narrated as *Qūmu li-sayyidikum* which means the same thing.[22] (It is noteworthy that the Prophet ﷺ specifically invoked the blessings and mercy of Allah upon the family of Sa'd b. 'Ubāda as well as Jābir b. 'Abd Allāh and the family of Ibn Abī Awfā.) [4] Sahl b. Ḥunayf said "My liege lord!" *(yā sayyidī)* when he asked the Prophet ﷺ a certain question.[23] [5] Mālik and Sufyān gave the fatwa one should not say *Yā Sayyidī* in *du'ā'* but *Yā Rabbī*.[24]

[18]Narrated from Ibn Mas'ūd by Ibn Mājah, Abū Ya'lā (9:175 §5267), al-Ṭabarānī in *al-Kabīr* (9:115 §8594), Abū Nu'aym in the *Ḥilya* (1985 ed. 4:271), and al-Bayhaqī in the *Shu'ab* (2:208 §1550), all through 'Abd al-Raḥmān b. 'Abd Allāh b. 'Utba al-Mas'ūdī who is weak although Mundhirī declared the chain fair in *al-Targhīb* (1997 ed. 2:329 §2588) cf. *Fatḥ* (11:158). Further, al-Būṣīrī in *Miṣbāḥ al-Zujāja* (1:111) said it is corroborated by an identical narration from Ibn 'Umar by Aḥmad b. Manī' in his *Musnad*. Al-Mas'ūdī is further corroborated by Abū Salama al-Mughīra b. al-Nu'mān in 'Abd al-Razzāq (2:213-214 §3109-3112) while al-Dāraquṭnī in his *'Ilal* (5:15 §682) cites yet two other chains to Ibn Mas'ūd, raising the narration to a grade of *ḥasan* at the very least, or rather *ṣaḥīḥ in shā' Allah*.

[19]Narrated from: Abū Hurayra by al-Bukhārī, Muslim, Tirmidhī *(ḥasan ṣaḥīḥ)*, Abū Dāwūd, Aḥmad, Nasā'ī in *al-Sunan al-Kubrā* (6:378), Ibn Abī Shayba (6:307, 6:317, 7:257), Ibn Sa'd (1:20), Ibn Ḥibbān (14:381), al-Bayhaqī in *al-Sunan al-Kubra* (9:4); Ḥudhayfa by al-Ḥākim (4:617) and al-Ṭabarānī in *al-Awsaṭ* cf. al-Haythamī (10:377) and others; Abū Sa'īd al-Khudrī by al-Tirmidhī *(ḥasan ṣaḥīḥ)*, Ibn Mājah, and Aḥmad; by Aḥmad and al-Dārimī; Ibn 'Abbās by Aḥmad; 'Ubāda b. al-Ṣāmit by al-Ḥākim (1990 ed. 1:83 *ṣaḥīḥ*); Ibn Mas'ūd by Ibn Ḥibbān (14:398); 'Abd Allāh b. Salām by al-Ṭabarānī and Abū Ya'lā cf. al-Haythamī (8:253) and al-Maqdisī's *al-Aḥādīth al-Mukhtāra* (9:455); and Jābir b. 'Abd Allāh by al-Ḥākim (1990 ed. 2:660 *ṣaḥīḥ al-isnād*) and al-Ṭabarānī in *al-Awsaṭ* cf. al-Haythamī (10:376); etc.

[20]Narrated from Abū Bakra by al-Bukhārī, Tirmidhī, al-Nasā'ī, Abū Dāwūd, Aḥmad.

[21]Narrated from Abū Sa'īd by al-Bukharī, Muslim, Abū Dāwūd, al-Nasā'ī, Aḥmad.

[22]Ṭaḥāwī, *Mushkil* (2:38), Ibn Kathīr, *Bidāya* (4:122), al-Zabīdī, *Itḥāf* (7:142).

[23]Narrated from Sahl b. Ḥunayf by Abū Dāwūd, Aḥmad, al-Nasā'ī, *Kubrā* (6:72 §10086, 6:256 §10873) and *'Amal al-Yawm wal-Layla* (p. 252 §257, p. 564 §1034), Ṭaḥāwī, *Ma'ānī* (4:329), Ṭabarānī, *Kabīr* (6:93 §5615), Ḥākim (4:458 *ṣaḥīḥ*).

[24]Cited by Ibn Rajab in his *Jāmi' al-'Ulum wal-Ḥikam* (Dār al-Ma'rifa ed. p. 107).

5
How the Prophet ﷺ Named Abū Bakr "the *Ṣiddīq*"

The Prophet ﷺ called him by his patronyms of Abū Bakr and Ibn Abī Quḥāfa but in many narrations gives him the attribute "Most Truthful and Trustful" *(Ṣiddīq)*; also "Freedman of Allah from the Fire" *('Atīq Allah min al-nār)*.[25]

When the Quraysh confronted the Prophet after the Night Journey, they went to Abū Bakr and said: "Do you believe what he said – that he went last night to the Hallowed House and came back before morning?" He replied: "If he said it, then I believe him! And I believe him regarding what is farther! I believe the news of heaven he brings, whether in the space of a morning or in that of an evening journey!" Because of this, Abū Bakr was named *al-Ṣiddīq*.[26] Abū Umāma al-Bāhilī ﷺ said: "Truly, the most trusting of people is the most truthful among them in his speech, and the most distrustful of people is the most untruthful among them in his speech."[27] At that time the Prophet also said to him, Jibrīl showed me the gate by which my Umma shall enter Paradise." Abū Bakr said, "Would I had been with you to see it." He said, "Behold, Abū Bakr, you will be the first of my Umma to enter it!"[28]

The Prophet ﷺ confirmed the title of *Ṣiddīq* for him in the ḥadīths of the shaking of the two mountains under their feet: Uḥud (together with 'Umar and 'Uthmān)–at which time the Prophet ﷺ said: "Keep firm *(uthbut)*, Uḥud! There is none on top of you but a Prophet, a *Ṣiddīq*, and two shahids"[29]–and Ḥirā' (together with 'Umar, 'Uthmān, 'Alī, Talḥa, and al-Zubayr), at which time he said: "Be still! There is none on top of you but a Prophet, a *Ṣiddīq*, or a shahid."[30]

[25]The Prophet's ﷺ ḥadīth "You are the freedman of Allah from the Fire" is narrated from 'Abd Allāh b. al-Zubayr by Ibn Ḥibbān (15:280 §6864), al-Ṭabarānī, and al-Bazzār, all with sound chains, and from 'Ā'isha by al-Tirmidhī, al-Ḥākim, and al-Ṭabarānī with weak chains as indicated by Shu'ayb al-Arnā'ūṭ.

[26]Narrated from 'Ā'isha by al-Ḥākim (3:62=1990 ed. 3:65, 3:76=1990 ed. 3:81) who said its chain is sound, Ibn Sa'd (1:144), Ibn Abī 'Āṣim in *al-Āḥād wal-Mathānī* (1:83 §39), al-Ṭabarānī in *al-Kabīr* (1:55 §15) and *Musnad al-Shāmiyyīn* (1:145 §232), from Anas by Ibn Abī Ḥātim in his *Tafsīr*, and from 'Alī and 'Ā'isha by Abū Nu'aym in *Ma'rifat al-Ṣaḥāba*, cf. al-Suyūṭī, *al-Durr al-Manthūr* (4:155).

[27]Narrated by Abū al-Ḥasan al-Qazwīnī in his *Amālī* cf. al-Suyūṭī, *al-Jāmi' al-Ṣaghīr* (§2202 *ḍa'īf*), *Kanz* (§6854).

[28] Narrated from Abū Hurayra by Abū Dāwūd (*Sunna, fīl-Khulafā'*) and others.

[29]Narrated from Anas by al-Bukhārī, al-Tirmidhī *(ḥasan ṣaḥīḥ)*, Abū Dāwūd, al-Nasā'ī, and Aḥmad.

[30]Narrated from Abū Hurayra by Muslim, al-Tirmidhī *(ṣaḥīḥ)*, and Aḥmad.

6
The Companions Who Entered Islam because of Abū Bakr and Those Who Narrated from Him

Allah Most High said, *And what ails you that you will not spend in the way of the One God, when to the One God belongs the inheritance of the heavens and the earth? Not equal are those of you that have spent before the conquest and have fought. Those are greater in rank than the ones that spent afterwards and fought. And to each has the One God promised the best goodness. And the One God is, of what you do, All-Aware* (57:10). Al-Bayḍāwī said, "The verse was revealed in reference to Abū Bakr[31] for he was the first to believe,[32] to spend in the way of the One God, and to oppose the unbelievers until he was beaten almost to death."

Bilāl b. Abī Rabāḥ was freed by him and was the first of the Companions Abū Bakr brought to Islam as borne out by the answer to ʿAmr b. ʿAbasa's question, "Who has followed you into this matter?" The Prophet replied, "A free man and a slave."[33] Also among the Companions who entered Islam because of him were ʿUthmān b. ʿAffān; al-Zubayr b. al-ʿAwwām; ʿAbd al-Raḥmān b. ʿAwf; Saʿd b. Abī Waqqāṣ; Ṭalḥa b. ʿUbayd Allāh; Abū Bakr's father ʿUthmān Abū Quḥāfa and his mother Salmā Umm al-Khayr; Abū ʿUbayda ʿĀmir b. ʿAbd Allāh b. al-Jarrāḥ; Abū Salama ʿAbd Allāh b. ʿAbd al-Asad; al-Arqam b. Abī al-Arqam; ʿUthmān b. Maẓʿūn and

[31] Narrated from (i) ʿAbd al-Raḥmān b. Abī Bakr by al-Wāqidī, *Futūḥ al-Shām* (2:192); (ii) al-Kalbī by al-Thaʿlabī; al-Wāḥidī (*Asbāb, Basīṭ, Wasīṭ*); al-Baghawī; (iii) "the exegetes" per Ibn al-Jawzī, *Zād*; (iv) Abū Nuʿaym, *Ḥilya* (1:28).

[32] Narrated from (i-iii) Asmāʾ bint Abī Bakr, Abū Arwā al-Dawsī and al-Nakhaʿī by Ibn Saʿd (*Ṭabaqāt al-Badriyyīn min al-Muhājirīn, wa-min Banī Taym b. Murra b. Kaʿb, Abī Bakr al-Ṣiddīq, dhikr islām Abī Bakr*); al-Nakhaʿī by Aḥmad (32:58-60 §19303, §19306); Tirmidhī (*Manāqib, manāqib Abī Bakr al-Ṣiddīq, ḥasan ṣaḥīḥ*); Ḥākim (3:136, *ṣaḥīḥ*); (iv) Anas from Abū Zakariyyā Yaḥyā b. Maʿīn b. ʿAwn al-Baghdādī, *Maʿrifat al-Rijāl* [=*Tārīkh Ibn Maʿīn*], ed. Muḥ. Kāmil Qaṣṣār, 2 vols. (Damascus: Majmaʿ al-Lughat al-ʿArabiyya, 1405/1985) 1:151; (v) Ibn ʿAbbās by Ṭabarānī, *Kabīr* (12:89 §12562); (vi-viii) Ibn ʿAbbās, Muḥ. b. Kaʿb al-Quraẓī, Muḥ. b. Sīrīn and Ismāʿīl b. Umayya by ʿAbd Allāh b. Aḥmad, *Faḍāʾil al-Ṣaḥāba* (1:133 §103, 1:226-227 §268, §272, 1:420 §656); (ix) Abū Saʿīd al-Khudrī from Abū Bakr by al-Tirmidhī (ditto); Ibn Abī ʿĀṣim, *Āḥād* (1:76 §18); al-Bazzār (1:94 §35); Ibn Ḥibbān (15:279 §6863); (x) Ibn ʿUmar by Wāsiṭī, *Tārīkh Wāsiṭ* (p. 254); Ṭabarānī, *Awāʾil* (p. 81 §55) and *Awsaṭ* (8:190 §8365); (xi-xii) Yaʿqūb al-Mājishūn and Rabīʿa by Ibn Ḥibbān, *Thiqāt* (8:130 §12577); (xiii) ʿAlī b. Abī Ṭālib by Ibn ʿAdī (2:249, Bahlūl b. ʿAbd Allāh al-Kindī); (xiv) Salama b. ʿAbd al-Raḥmān b. ʿAwf by ʿAskarī, *Awāʾil* (p. 137); (xv) Abū Umāma by al-Ṭabarī, *Tārīkh* (2:315); Thaʿlabī; al-Māwardī, *Aʿlām* (p. 162) and *Ḥāwī* (14:9); (xvi) ʿAmr b. ʿAbasa by Ibn Saʿd (4:200); Aḥmad (28:237-240 §17019); Muslim (*Ṣalāt al-musāfirīn, islām ʿAmr b. ʿAbasa*); and (xvi-xix) the sources cited in the previous note. "It is the sound position per the congregation" according to al-Ḥākim, *Maʿrifa* (Type 7) and al-Bayhaqī, *Sunan* (6:369).

[33] See previous note under (xvi).

his two full brothers Qudāma and ʿAbd Allāh; ʿUbayda b. al-Ḥārith b. al-Muṭṭalib; and many others.[34]

Among the Companions who narrated from Abū Bakr are Anas, ʿĀʾisha, Jābir, Abū Hurayra, the "four ʿAbd Allāh" (Ibn ʿAbbās, Ibn Masʿūd, Ibn ʿUmar, Ibn ʿAmr), ʿAbd Allāh b. al-Zubayr, ʿUmar, ʿUthmān, and ʿAlī ﷺ.

[34] Narrated from ʿĀʾisha by Khaythama, *Min Ḥadīth Khaythama b. Sulaymān al-Qurashī al-Aṭrābulusī*, ed. ʿUmar Tadmurī (Beirut: Dār al-Kitāb al-ʿArabī, 1400/1980) p. 125, *Faḍāʾil Abī Bakr al-Ṣiddīq*; Suhaylī, *al-Rawḍ al-Unuf* (Wakīl ed. 3:19-41).

7
His Superior Faith and Reliance

Abū Bakr surpassed all the Companions in faith-informed reliance *(tawakkul)*. When the Prophet ﷺ ordered the Companions to pay charity, ʿUmar said: "This order was given at a time when I had property, so I said: Today I shall surpass Abū Bakr if I am ever to surpass him! Then I brought half my property. The Prophet ﷺ said: 'What did you leave for your family?' I replied: 'The same amount.' Abū Bakr came and brought everything he owned. The Prophet ﷺ asked: 'Abū Bakr, what did you leave for your family?' He replied: 'I left for them Allah and His Prophet.' When I saw this I said: By Allah! I shall never ever surpass him in anything."[35]

In the time of ʿUmar's caliphate a man came to ʿUmar as the latter was in ʿArafa and said to him: "I have just left a man in Kūfa who dictates the volumes of the Qur'ān from memorization." ʿUmar became more upset than he was ever seen before. He said: "Who?" The man said, ʿAbd Allāh b. Masʿūd. ʿUmar went back to his normal state and became completely serene. He said: "Woe to you! By Allah, I know not, among the people, anyone still remaining who is entitled to do such a thing more than Ibn Masʿūd. I will tell you why. The Messenger of Allah ﷺ was always staying late at night at the house of Abū Bakr ؓ to discuss the affairs pertaining to the Muslims. One night when he was there, I was with him, and we came out together. Lo and behold! There was a man standing and praying in the Mosque. The Prophet ﷺ stood and listened to his recitation. We had almost recognized him when the Prophet ﷺ said: 'Whoever would like to recite the Qur'ān fresh and moist exactly as it was revealed, let him recite it according to the recitation of Ibn Umm ʿAbd [=ʿAbd Allāh b. Masʿūd]!' Then the latter sat and began to supplicate. At this the Messenger of Allah ﷺ began to say: 'Ask and you will receive it! Ask and you will receive it!' I [ʿUmar] said to myself: 'By Allah! I will visit him early in the morning and give him the glad tidings.' I went to see him early the next morning and found that Abū Bakr had preceded me and given him the glad tidings! By Allah, I never preceded him in anything good except he was there before me!"[36]

One time, the Prophet ﷺ told of a shepherd from whom a wolf stole a sheep. The shepherd pursued the wolf and got the sheep back. Thereupon the wolf turned around and said: "Who will save it the day of the beasts, when I will be its only shepherd?" The people exclaimed: *"Subḥān Allah!"* The Prophet ﷺ said: "I do believe this story, and so do Abū Bakr and ʿUmar!" They were absent at the time.[37]

[35]Narrated from Aslam al-ʿAdawī by al-Tirmidhī *(ḥasan ṣaḥīḥ)*, Abū Dāwūd, al-Dārimī, al-Bazzār (1:263, 1:394), al-Ḥākim (1990 ed. 1:574 *ṣaḥīḥ ʿalā sharṭ Muslim)*, al-Bayhaqī in the *Sunan* (4:190), al-Ḍyā al-Maqdisī in *al-Mukhtāra* (1:174), and others.
[36]Narrated by Aḥmad.
[37]Narrated from Anas by al-Bukhārī, Muslim, al-Tirmidhī *(ḥasan ṣaḥīḥ)*, and

The *Tābi'ī* Bakr b. 'Abd Allāh al-Muzanī said: "Abū Bakr did not surpass you for fasting or praying the most but because of something that was in his heart."[38]

There is another sign of the spiritual rank granted to Abū Bakr in the saying attributed to him on knowledge of Allah ﷻ: "Incapacity to attain comprehension is comprehension" *(al-'ajzu 'an darki al-idrāki idrākun).*[39] This statement is the essence of the committal of the meaning *(tafwīḍ al-ma'nā)* of the Divine Attributes to their Owner.

Abū Bakr applied scrupulously the instruction of the Prophet ﷺ not to rely upon the help of people even in small things. Ibn Abī Mulayka said: "If it happened that the reins fell from the hand of Abū Bakr al-Ṣiddīq ﷺ he would goad the camel's leg so as to make it kneel and would pick it up [himself]. Asked why he did not order someone to hand it to him he replied: 'My beloved, the Messenger of Allah ﷺ, commanded me not to ask anything from people.'"[40]

This command was actually issued to a very small, select group of Companions after the first pledge of loyalty *(bay'a)* and exclusively of others:[41]

'Awf b. Mālik al-Ashja'ī said: "We were a group of nine, eight, or seven with the Messenger of Allah ﷺ when he said: 'Will you not pledge loyalty to the Messenger of Allah?' We had pledged loyalty only recently, so we replied: 'We already pledged it to you, Messenger of Allah!' He said again:

Aḥmad.

38Narrated by Aḥmad in *Faḍā'il al-Ṣaḥāba* (1:141 §118) and al-Ḥakīm al-Tirmidhī in *Nawādir al-Uṣūl* (1:149, 3:55, 4:5) and *Khatm al-Awliyā'* (p. 442) cf. Ibn Rajab, *Jāmi' al-'Ulūm wal-Ḥikam* (Ma'rifa ed. p. 30). Also attributed to Abū Bakr b. 'Iyāsh cf. *Naqd al-Manqūl* and *al-Manār al-Munīf.*

39Attributed – without chain – to Abū Bakr al-Ṣiddīq by al-Sulamī in *al-Muqaddima fil-Taṣawwuf* (p. 36), al-Qushayrī's *Risāla* (p. 585, chapter on *Tawḥīd*), and subsequent Ṣūfī sources such as Ibn 'Arabī, *Futūḥāt* (2:74-75) and his commentators cf. also al-Suyūṭī's *Sharḥ Sunan al-Nasā'ī* (1:105 §169), al-Munāwī's *Fayḍ al-Qadīr* (6:181) under the ḥadīth *man 'alima anna Allāha rabbuhu wa-annī nabiyyuh,* and al-Qārī at the very beginning of his *Risāla fī Radd Waḥdat al-Wujūd* (p. 54), all without chain.

40Narrated by Aḥmad (Arnā'ūṭ ed. 1:228 §65 *ḥasan li-ghayrih*).

41Shāh Wali Allah of Delhi said in *al-Qawl al-Jamīl*: "There are nine types of pledges in the Sunna:
– The pledge of full acceptance of Islam *(bay'at qabūl al-islām)*
– The pledge to the leadership *(bay'at al-khilāfa)*
– The pledge of establishing the pillars of the Religion *(bay'at iqāmat arkān al-dīn)*
– The pledge of holding fast to the Sunna with Godwariness *(bay'at al-tamassuk bil-sunna wal-taqwā)*
– The pledge of complete avoidance of innovations *(bay'at ijtināb al-bida')*
– The pledge of emigration *(bay'at al-hijra)*
– The pledge of waging jihād *(bay'at al-jihād)*
– The pledge of hearing and obeying *(bay'at al-sam' wal-ṭā'a).*
– The pledge of love *(bay'at al-maḥabba).*"

'Will you not pledge loyalty to the Messenger of Allah?' We replied: 'We already pledged it to you, Messenger of Allah!' He said again: 'Will you not pledge loyalty to the Messenger of Allah?'[42] At this we stretched out our hands and said: 'We already pledged it to you, Messenger of Allah! To what should we pledge again?' He said: '<Pledge to me *(tubāyi'ūnī)*>[43] that you will worship Allah without associating anything with Him, <that you will accomplish *(an tuqīmū)*>[44] the Five Prayers, <that you will remit the purification-tax>'[45] – then he said something which he kept secret from others *(wa-asarra kalimatan khafiyya)*: 'and ask nothing from people!' After this I would see someone from that group, even if his camel-whip fell [from his hand while riding], he would not ask anyone to hand it back to him."[46]

[42]The triple repetition and the self-reference in the third person were pedagogical devices frequently used by the Prophet ﷺ so as (1) to draw the full attention of those present, and (2) to emphasize the gravity of what he was about to say. See Abū Ghudda's *al-Rasūl al-Mu'allim*.

[43]In Ibn Ḥibbān (8:180 §3385) only, with a sound chain as per al-Arnā'ūṭ.

[44]In Ibn Mājah and Ibn Ḥibbān only.

[45]In Ibn Ḥibbān only. These are the oaths the generality of the Companions had already pledged.

[46]Narrated from Abū Muslim al-Khawlānī by Muslim, al-Nasā'ī, Abū Dāwūd, Ibn Mājah, and Aḥmad. It is possible that the seven mentioned by 'Awf b. Mālik are the six Companions that were with the Prophet ﷺ in the ḥadīth "Be still, Ḥirā'" (cf. n. 30) together with 'Awf himself. Allah ﷻ knows best.

8
His Scrupulous Sense of Justice and Humbleness

The Prophet's ﷺ servant Rabī'a b. Ka'b al-Aslamī ؓ narrated:

> The Messenger of Allah ﷺ gave me a piece of land and he gave Abū Bakr a piece of land. The world tempted us and we began to dispute over the branch of a datepalm. I said it fell within my property and Abū Bakr said it fell within his. Words were exchanged and Abū Bakr said something for which he felt guilt and remorse. He said to me, "Rabī'a! Say something like it to me in requital." I said, "No, never!" Abū Bakr said, "You will say it or else I will seek the help of the Messenger of Allah ﷺ against you! *(aw la'asta'diyanna 'alayka Rasūlallāh)*." I said I would not do it. Abū Bakr cut short claiming the land and bolted off to the Prophet ﷺ while I followed him. People from Aslam came to me, saying, "Allah have mercy on Abū Bakr! Over what is he seeking the help of the Messenger of Allah ﷺ against you when it is he that spoke to you in the way he did?" I said, "Do you know who this is? This is Abū Bakr al-Ṣiddīq! This is *the second of two* (9:40)! This is the Venerable of the Muslims! Beware, lest he turn around and see you coming to my help against him, then become angry and come to the Messenger of Allah ﷺ who will be angry because of Abū Bakr's anger, then Allah ﷻ will be angry because of the anger of the two of them, then He will cause Rabī'a to perish!" They said, "What do you want us to do?" I said, "Leave me!" So Abū Bakr went on his way to see the Messenger of Allah ﷺ and I followed him alone until he reached the Prophet ﷺ and told him what happened. The Prophet ﷺ raised his head, looked at me, and said: "Rabī'a! What is between you and the Truthful one?" I said, Messenger of Allah! This and that took place, he said a word to me which he regretted then asked me to say the same back to him in requital, so I refused." The Messenger of Allah ﷺ said: "Good! And do not speak back to him but say, 'Allah forgive you, Abū Bakr!'" So I said: *"Ghafara Allāhu laka yā Abā Bakr."* Al-Ḥasan said that Abū Bakr left in tears.[47]

After Abū Bakr was made caliph he addressed the people thus:

> I was made your leader although I am not the best of you. However, the Qur'ān was revealed and the Prophet ﷺ practiced the Sunna and he taught us, therefore we learnt. Know, people! that the wisest of the wise – or: true guidance – is the God wary and the worst foolishness is disobedient rebellion. The strongest of you in my sight are the weak until I defend his right and the weakest of you in my sight are the strong from whom I shall take the right. People! I am but a follower and not an innovator. If I

[47]Narrated from Rabī'a b. Ka'b b. Mālik by Aḥmad with a fair to sound chain.

am correct then help me and if I err then correct me. This is all I have to say. I ask forgiveness of Allah for myself and for you.[48]

During the caliphate of Abū Bakr, Bilāl prepared to join a campaign headed for Syria. When Abū Bakr saw him equipped and geared for departure, in his gentle heart and soft nature, he said to Bilāl, "O Bilāl! I did not think that you would leave us under such circumstances. I wish you would stay here with us, and help us during these difficult times." Bilāl replied: "If you had released me from bondage for the pleasure of Allah the most exalted, then let me go to Him, but if you had bought me for your own needs, then keep me." Abū Bakr immediately gave Bilāl permission to leave, after which Bilāl joined the campaign to Syria, where he then lived the rest of his life.[49]

[48]Narrated from 'Urwa, from his father al-Zubayr b. al-'Awwām, by Ibn Sa'd (3:182-183) and others. A similar report is given by Aḥmad, al-Ṭabarānī in *al-Awsaṭ*, 'Abd al-Razzāq, and others. Al-Muḥibb al-Ṭabarī cites both in *al-Ryāḍ al-Naḍira* (2:233-234 §682-683).

[49] Narrated from Sa'īd b. al-Musayyib by Ma'mar b. Rāshid *Jāmi'* (see 'Abd al-Razzāq's *Muṣannaf* 11:234 §20412); Ibn al-Mubārak, *al-Jihād* (p. 87); Ibn Sa'd, *al-Ṭabaqāt al-Kubrā* (*al-Badriyyīn min al-Muhājirīn, Banū Taym b. Murra, Bilāl b. Rabāḥ*); and others.

9
The Prophetic Allusions to the Immediate Successions of Abū Bakr and ʿUmar

We have compiled them in our as-of-yet unpublished *Ishārāt Sayyid al-Thaqalayn ilā Awwaliyyati Khilāfati al-ʿUmarayn* (The Allusions of the Liege lord of the Humans and Jinns to the Primacy of the Successions of Abū Bakr and ʿUmar) of which this is a glimpse.

Abū Bakrat al-Thaqafī related that the Prophet ﷺ asked: "Did any of you see anything in his dream?" A man said to the Prophet ﷺ: "Messenger of Allah, I saw in my dream as if a balance came down from heaven in which you were weighed against Abū Bakr and outweighed him, then Abū Bakr was weighed against 'Umar and outweighed him, then 'Umar was weighed against 'Uthmān and outweighed him, then the balance was taken up." This displeased the Prophet ﷺ who said: "Successorship of prophethood *(khilāfa nubuwwa)*! Then Allah will give kingship to whomever He will."[50] When Abū Bakrah and others visited Mu'āwiya, the latter requested him to report something from the Prophet ﷺ. For the next several days, Abū Bakrah kept telling and re-telling this ḥadīth, to the embarrassment of his fellow travellers. In private, he would tell them: "I swear I will narrate nothing else to him until I leave!" Finally, Mu'āwiya said to him: "Kingship, you say? We are satisfied with kingship *(faqad raḍīnā bil-mulk)*!"[51]

The ḥadīth is confirmed by the narration from Safīna: "Successorship *(al-khilāfa)* after me shall last for thirty years. Afterward there will be kingship."[52] These ḥadīths are two among the dozen or so authentic allusions of the Prophet ﷺ to Abū Bakr's immediate succession after him.

Another narration to the same effect is the ḥadīth of Jābir's narration of the Prophet's ﷺ own dream that "Abū Bakr was made to latch onto the Messenger of Allah, ʿUmar was made to latch on to Abū Bakr, and ʿUthmān was made to latch on to ʿUmar." Jābir added: "As for their latching on then [it signifies] they are the ones that take charge of this affair which Allah has sent his Prophet with."[53]

[50]Narrated from Abū Bakrah by Aḥmad with three chains, Abū Dāwūd in his *Sunan*, al-Ṭayālisī (§866), Ibn Abī Shayba (11:60-61, 12:18-19), Ibn Abī 'Āṣim in *al-Sunna* (§1131-1136), al-Bazzār (§3652), al-Ṭaḥāwī in *Sharh Mushkil al-Āthār* (§3348), al-Bayhaqī in *Dalā'il al-Nubuwwa* (6:342) and *al-I'tiqād* (p. 364), and – without the last statement of the Prophet ﷺ – al-Tirmidhī who said: *ḥasan ṣaḥīḥ*; also from Safīna by Abū Dāwūd with a fair chain and al-Bazzār with a fair chain as indicated by al-Haythamī. Al-Ḥākim (3:71) narrates the latter with a chain similar to al-Tirmidhī's and graded it *ṣaḥīḥ*. It is confirmed by the identical dream of the Prophet ﷺ himself as narrated from Jābir b. 'Abd Allāh and Ibn 'Umar by Aḥmad (al-Arnā'ūṭ 23:124 §14821 and 9:338 §5469) and others.

[51]Narrated by Aḥmad (34:94-97 §20445 *ḥasan*).

[52]See the chapter on 'Alī, note 573.

[53] Aḥmad (24:124 §14821); Abū Dāwūd (*Sunna, al-khulafā'*); Ibn Abī ʿĀṣim, *Sun-*

The narration of the balance is confirmed by the ḥadīth of the Prophet ﷺ predicting the brevity of Abū Bakr's caliphate: "In a dream I saw myself drawing water from a well. Ibn Abī Quḥāfa [Abū Bakr] came and drew a large bucket *(dhanūb)* or two, but there was some weakness in his efforts – and Allah forgives him for his weakness! Then ['Umar] Ibn al-Khaṭṭāb came and the bucket turned into a huge pail *(gharab)* in his hands. I never saw any strong master of his people *('abqariyyan)* do such accomplished work as he *(yafrī fariyyahu)* – another version states: 'pull like 'Umar pulled' – until all the people drank to satiation and watered their camels."[54]

In a similar version the Prophet ﷺ said: "Last night as I dreamed I was hoisting up [water from a well] I saw a flock of black sheep and dirt-white sheep. Abū Bakr came and hoisted a bucket or two. I saw some weakness in his hoisting and Allah forgives him. Then 'Umar came and the bucket changed into a pail! He filled the drinking-basin and quenched the thirst of all that came to it. I never saw any strong master of his people hoisting water better than 'Umar! I interpreted the black [sheep] to refer to the Arabs and the dirt-white to refer to the non-Arabs." [55] In another narration the interpretation of the hoisting dream is given by Abū Bakr.[56]

Imām al-Shāfi'ī glossed the word "weakness" as referring to the short duration of Abū Bakr's caliphate and the fact that his turning to the *Ridda* wars delayed him from the conquests and expansions achieved by 'Umar during the latter's longer tenure. Al-Nawawī added that the Prophet's ﷺ expression "Allah forgives Abū Bakr" is a "discursive *du'ā'* without specific cause" while others said it is an allusion to Abū Bakr's short life-span after him ﷺ, for which Abū Bakr is guiltless.[57]

na (*dhikr khilāfat al-Rāshidīn*); al-Ṭaḥāwī, *Mushkil* (8:412 §3347); Ibn Ḥibbān, *Ṣaḥīḥ* (15:343 §6913) and *Thiqāt* (7:216 §9747); al-Ḥākim (3:71-72, 3:102); al-Bayhaqī, *Dalā'il al-Nubuwwa* (6:348) and *al-I'tiqād* (*Istikhlāf 'Uthmān*); and others.

[54]Narrated from 'Abd Allāh b. 'Umar and Abū Hurayra by al-Bukhārī, Muslim, al-Tirmidhī, and Aḥmad.

[55]Narrated from Abū al-Ṭufayl 'Āmir b. Wāthila through 'Alī b. Zayd by Aḥmad, Abū Ya'lā (2:198 §904), Ibn Abī 'Āṣim in *al-Āḥād wal-Mathānī* (2:200-201 §951), al-Bazzār (7:211 §2785) and al-Ṭabarānī "with a fair chain" per Ibn Ḥajar in the *Fatḥ* (7:39 and 12:414) and al-Haythamī (5:180, 7:183, 9:71-72) cf. also al-Muḥibb al-Ṭabarī, *al-Ryāḍ al-Naḍira* (1:350), also with a strong *mursal* chain from al-Ḥasan al-Baṣrī by Aḥmad in *Faḍā'il al-Ṣaḥāba* (1:163 §150). Some grade 'Alī b. Zayd b. Jud'ān weak cf. al-Būṣīrī in *Miṣbāḥ al-Zujāja* (2:95) but al-Tirmidhī considers him "truthful" *(ṣadūq)*, he is retained by Ibn Khuzayma in his *Ṣaḥīḥ*, Muslim in his as an auxiliary narrator *(maqrūn)*, Ibn Ḥajar grades his chain fair in the *Fatḥ* (7:39), al-Haythamī (7:183, 4:310, 9:71-72) grades him "trustworthy with a poor memory" *(thiqa sayyi' al-ḥafẓ)* and his narrations "fair," al-Dhahabī in his marginalia on al-Ḥākim (3:190=1990 ed. 3:210) grades his chain passable *(ṣāliḥ)*, and Ibn Kathīr in *al-Bidāya* (6:137-138) grades him as meeting the authenticity criteria of the *Sunan*. Cf. also al-Suyūṭī, *Khaṣā'iṣ* (2:257).

[56]See below, Ibn Abī Layla's narration of the dream of the black sheep succeeded by dirt-white sheep.

[57]In *Fatḥ al-Bārī* (7:32). See also Ibn Rajab's commentary on the same report.

Another narration to the same effect: "What a wonderful man Abū Bakr is! What a wonderful man 'Umar is! What a wonderful man Abū 'Ubayda b. al-Jarrāḥ is! What a wonderful man Usayd b. Ḥuḍayr is! What a wonderful man Thābit b. Qays b. Shammās is! What a wonderful man Mu'ādh b. Jabal is! What a wonderful man Mu'ādh b. 'Amr b. al-Jamūḥ is!"[58]

[58]Narrated from Abū Hurayra by Ibn Abī Shayba, al-Tirmidhī *(ḥasan)*, Aḥmad, al-Nasā'ī, Ibn Ḥibbān, al-Ḥākim and others.

10
'Umar's Testimony to the Superiority of Abū Bakr and 'Alī's Testimony to the Superiority of Abū Bakr and 'Umar

'Umar said: "The faith *(īmān)* of Abū Bakr's outweighs the faith of the entire *Umma*!"[59] 'Umar ﷺ was asked before he died: "Will you not appoint someone to succeed you?" He replied: "If I omit to, someone better than I omitted to – the Messenger of Allah ﷺ – and if I appoint a successor, someone better than I did appoint a successor – Abū Bakr ﷺ."[60]

When 'Alī ﷺ was asked to define who "the rightly-guided successors" were he wept and said: "Abū Bakr and 'Umar, may Allah be well-pleased with them, the two leaders of rightful guidance and the two Shaykhs of Islam, the two men of Quraysh, the two who are followed after the Messenger of Allah ﷺ! Whoever follows these two gains respect; whoever lives up to the legacy of these two is guided to a straight path; whoever sticks with these two is from the party of Allah, *and the party of Allah – these are the successful*."[61]

'Alī also said: "The best of this Community after its Prophet are Abū Bakr and 'Umar. As for myself I am only an ordinary man among the Muslims."[62] In one version he said, "I saw the Messenger of Allah ﷺ with these two eyes of mine – or else let them be struck blind! – and heard him with these two ears of mine – or else let them be struck deaf! – say: "None was

[59]Narrated from 'Umar *(mawqūf)* with a sound chain through Ibn al-Mubārak by Ibn Rāhūyah, *Musnad* (3:671-672), Ibn al-Mubārak, *al-Zuhd*, Aḥmad, *Faḍā'il al-Ṣaḥāba* (1:418 §653) and Ḥakīm al-Tirmidhī, *Nawādir al-Uṣūl* (1:280) cf. al-Dāraquṭnī, *'Ilal* (2:223), al-'Irāqī, *al-Mughnī*, Dhahabī, *Siyar* (Risāla ed. 8:405), Sakhāwī, *Maqāṣid*, and al-'Ajlūnī, *Kashf al-Khafā'*. Also narrated from 'Abd al-Raḥmān b. Sābiṭ by Ibn Sa'd (5:469) and al-Bayhaqī in the *Shu'ab* (1:79 §63). Al-Sakhāwī added: "It is narrated from Ibn 'Umar from the Prophet ﷺ *(marfū')* with a weak chain by Ibn 'Adī (4:201, 5:259) [cf. Khaṭīb, *Muwaḍḍiḥ* (2:90); *Mīzān* ('Abd Allāh b. 'Abd al-'Azīz, *Lisān* (3:310)], however, it is strengthened by other chains and is corroborated." Al-Zarkashī in *al-Tadhkira* said its import was stated in the *Sunan*. He and al-Sakhāwī are referring to the sound *(ṣaḥīḥ)* narration of Abū Bakrah and Safīna.

[60]Narrated from Ibn 'Umar by al-Bukhārī and Muslim.

[61]Muḥibb al-Dīn al-Ṭabarī, *al-Riyāḍ al-Naḍira* (1:379 §276); Zamakhsharī, *Mukhtaṣar al-Muwāfaqa* f° 23; al-Sakhāwī, *al-Jawāhir wal-Durar*, Introduction.

[62]This is a mass-narrated *(mutawātir)* saying of 'Alī according to al-Dhahabī, spoken from the pulpit in Kūfa and narrated from Muḥammad b. al-Ḥanafiyya by al-Bukhārī in his *Ṣaḥīḥ* and Abū Dāwūd with a sound chain; Wahb al-Suwā'ī, 'Alqama b. Qays, Shurayḥ, and 'Abd Khayr by Aḥmad in his *Musnad*, each through several chains; from 'Abd Allāh b. Salama by Ibn Mājah with a fair chain; and from Shurayḥ by Ibn Shādhān, al-Khaṭīb, Ibn Abī Shayba, al-Lālikā'ī, Ibn Mandah, Ibn 'Asākir, and others. See also 'Abd al-Fattāḥ Maḥmūd Surūr, *Ikmāl al-Ni'ma bi-Taṣḥīḥ Ḥadīth Khayr Hādhih al-Umma* (Riyadh: Ad}wā' al-Salaf, 1428/2007) and *Kashf al-Khafā'* under the ḥadīth: "I am the city of knowledge and 'Alī is its gate."

ever born in all Islam [other than Prophets] purer nor better than Abū Bakr then 'Umar!"[63] Ibn 'Asākir said that the more correct version is that these are the words of 'Alī.

'Alī also said: "The greatest in reward among people for the volumes of the Qur'ān is Abū Bakr, for he was the first of those who gathered the Qur'ān between two covers."[64] He was also the first to name it *muṣḥaf.* 'Alī also said: "The most courageous of people is Abū Bakr. I saw the Messenger of Allah ﷺ when the Quraysh were pouncing on him, hitting him and shoving him. Then Abū Bakr came and began to hit them right and left, saying: 'Will you kill a man just because he says, My Sovereign Lord is Allah?'" 'Alī lifted his cloak and wept. Then he continued: "I conjure you by Allah! Who is better, the secret Believer of the people of Pharaoh or Abū Bakr? You do not answer me? I swear to you that one hour of Abū Bakr outdoes the whole world filled with the Believers of Pharaoh! The Believer of Pharaoh hid his faith while Abū Bakr proclaimed it."[65]

According to 'Alī, al-Ḥasan al-Baṣrī, Qatāda, al-Daḥḥāk, and Ibn Jurayj, it is "Abū Bakr and his friends" who are the "people whom Allah loves and who love Him" meant by the verse *O you who believe! Whoso of you becomes a renegade from his religion, (know that in his stead) Allah will bring a people whom He loves and who love Him, humble toward believers, stern toward disbelievers, striving in the way of Allah and fearing not the blame of any blamer. Such is the grace of Allah which He gives to whom He will. Allah is All Embracing, All Knowing* (5:54).[66]

[63]Narrated from al-Aṣbagh b. Nabāta and al-Sha'bī by Ibn 'Asākir (44:196) cf. *Kanz* (§32685, §36732).
[64]Narrated from 'Abd Khayr by Ibn Sa'd (3:193), Abū Ya'lā, and al-Suddī with a fair chain as stated by al-Dhahabī and through seventeen chains by Ibn Abū Dāwūd in *al-Maṣāḥif.*
[65]Narrated from 'Alī by al-Bazzār (3:15) with a chain of trustworthy narrators cf. al-Haythamī (9:46-47) and al-Muḥibb al-Ṭabarī, *al-Riyāḍ al-Naḍira* (2:32 §448). The shoving episode and Abū Bakr's rescue are also narrated by al-Bukhārī and Aḥmad from 'Abd Allāh b. 'Amr b. al-'Āṣ who said this was the worst act of provocation ever committed by the idolaters against the Prophet ﷺ.
[66]Cf. al-Rāzī, *al-Tafsīr al-Kabīr* (3:427); al-Qurṭubī, *al-Jāmi' li Aḥkām al-Qur'ān*, and others.

11
The Companion-Status of Abū Bakr in the Qur'ān

Abū Bakr's high rank is indicated, among other signs, by the fact that to deny his Companionship to the Prophet ﷺ entails disbelief *(kufr)*, unlike the denial of the Companionship of 'Umar, 'Uthmān, and 'Alī to the Prophet ﷺ which "only" entails sinful innovation.[67] This is due to the mention of Abū Bakr's companionship in the Qur'ān: *The second of two when the two were in the cave, and he said unto his companion: Grieve not* (9:40) which refers, by Consensus, to the Prophet ﷺ and Abū Bakr.

Allah ﷻ further praised Abū Bakr above the rest when He said: *Those who spent and fought before the victory are not upon a level (with the rest of you)* (57:10)[68] as already discussed above.

[67]As reported from al-Ḥusayn b. al-Faḍl by al-Baghawī in his *Tafsīr* as well as al-Qurṭubī, al-Nasafī, and others, also by 'Alī al-Qārī in *Sharḥ al-Fiqh al-Akbar* cf. al-Mubārakfūrī, *Tuḥfat al-Aḥwadhī* (10:106).
[68]Cf. the *Tafsīr*s of al-Baghawī, al-Qurṭubī, al-Bayḍāwī, Ibn Kathīr, and others.

12
Sound Prophetic Hadiths on the Immense Merits of Abū Bakr

> "None knows the rank of a person in knowledge except he who is his peer and has known him personally, and he only knows him to the extent of what he himself was granted to know. None of his companions knew al-Shāfi'ī like al-Muzanī knew him, and al-Muzanī knew al-Shāfi'ī only to the extent of al-Muzanī's strength. Nor can anyone estimate the Prophet (Allah bless and greet him) as he deserves except Allah (may He be exalted), and one knows him (Allah bless and greet him) only to the extent of what one possesses. Thus the most knowledgeable in the Community about the Prophet's rank is Abū Bakr (Allah be well-pleased with him) because he was the best of the Umma, and Abū Bakr knows the Prophet (Allah bless and greet him) only according to Abū Bakr's strength."[69]

The Prophet ﷺ was asked, "Who is the most beloved of all people to you?" He replied: 'Ā'isha." He was asked, "Among the men?" He said: Her father."[70]

He ﷺ confirmed the superlative rank of Abū Bakr in many other sayings, among them:

- "Allah gave one of His servants a choice between this world and what He has with Him, and that servant chose what Allah has with Him." Abū Bakr wept profusely and we wondered why he wept, since the Prophet ﷺ had told of a servant that was given a choice. The Prophet ﷺ himself was that servant, as Abū Bakr told us later. The Prophet ﷺ continued: "Abū Bakr, do not weep! Among those most dedicated to me in his companionship and property is Abū Bakr. If I were to take an intimate friend other than my Lord, I would take Abū Bakr. But what binds us is the brotherhood of Islam and its love. Let no door [of the Prophet's ﷺ mosque] remain open except the door of Abū Bakr."[71] The latter clause is among the Prophetic allusions to Abū Bakr's immediate succession.

- "I am excused, before each of my friends, of any friendship with anyone. But if I were to take an intimate friend, I would take Ibn

[69] Narrated from Shaykh al-Islam Taqī al-Dīn Abū al-Ḥasan 'Alī b. 'Abd al-Kāfī al-Subkī by his son Tāj al-Dīn Ibn al-Subkī, *Ṭabaqāt al-Shāfi'iyyat al-Kubrā* (6:191-389 §694).
[70] Narrated from 'Amr b. al-'Āṣ by al-Bukhārī, Muslim, al-Tirmidhī, Ibn Mājah, and Aḥmad.
[71] Spoken by the Prophet ﷺ in the last days of his life and narrated from Abū Sa'īd al-Khudrī by al-Bukhārī, Muslim, al-Tirmidhī, Aḥmad, and al-Dārimī. Some versions state: "The brotherhood of Islam or its love."

Abī Quḥāfa as my intimate friend. Truly, your Companion is the intimate friend of Allah!"[72]

- "You [Abū Bakr] are my companion at the Basin and my companion in the Cave."[73]

The Prophet ﷺ relatedly specified: "I stayed with my Companion in the cave between ten and some days and we had no food other than the overripe fruit of the arack-tree *(thamr al-barīr)*."[74] Al-Muḥibb al-Ṭabarī stated that the latter report is incorrect and that the vast majority of the ḥadīth authorities said their stay in the cave was for three days, and Allah knows best.

- "Call Abū Bakr and his son ['Abd al-Raḥmān] so that I will put something down in writing, for truly I fear lest someone forward a claim or form some ambition and Allah and the believers refuse anyone other than Abū Bakr."[75] This and the next six ḥadīths are allusions to Abū Bakr's immediate succession.

Another hadith provides additional details concerning the last will the Prophet ﷺ had thought of writing:

> Ibn 'Abbās said: "The day of al-Khamīs! And what a [terrible] day was the day of al-Khamīs!" Then he wept until his tears fell on the ground. Sa'īd b. Jubayr said: "What happened that day?" Ibn 'Abbās said: "The illness of the Messenger of Allah ﷺ grew worse. He said, 'Bring me something so that I will write a writ so you will never go astray after me.' But they began to dispute. There should be no disputing in the presence of a Prophet! They even said, '[Are you saying that] the Messenger of Allah does not know what he is saying?' [And] 'Ask him yourself!' He said: 'Leave me alone! The state I am in is better [than that]! My last will for you is about three things: Expel the idolaters from the Arabian peninsula; show the same hospitality to foreign delegations which I have shown.'" Ibn 'Abbās added: "He kept silent about the third item or he might have said it then I forgot."[76]

[72]Spoken by the Prophet ﷺ in the last days of his life, as narrated from Ibn Mas'ūd by Muslim, al-Tirmidhī *(ḥasan ṣaḥīḥ)*, Ibn Mājah, and Aḥmad.
[73]Narrated from Ibn 'Umar by al-Tirmidhī who said it is *ḥasan ṣaḥīḥ*.
[74]Narrated from Ṭalḥa b. 'Amr al-Naḍrī or al-Baṣrī – he was from the *Ahl al-Ṣuffa* – by al-Bazzār, al-Ṭabarānī in *al-Kabīr* (8:310 §8160), Hannād in *al-Zuhd* (2:395), Ibn Qāni' in *Mu'jam al-Ṣaḥāba* (2:43), Ḥammād b. Isḥāq, *Tarikat al-Nabī* ﷺ, ed. Akram Ḍiyā' al-'Umarī (p. 57-58), al-Fākihī, *Akhbār Makka* (3:94-95), Ibn Ḥibbān (15:77 §6684), Abū Nu'aym (1:375), al-Taymī, *Dalā'il al-Nubuwwa* (p. 116), al-Khaṭīb, *Muwaḍḍiḥ Awhām al-Jam' wal-Tafrīq* (1:498-499), al-Ḥākim (1990 ed. 3:16 and 4:591 *isnād ṣaḥīḥ*) and in *Ma'rifat 'Ulūm al-Ḥadīth* (p. 225), and al-Bayhaqī, *Sunan* (2:445), *Shu'ab* (7:284 §10325) cf. *Iṣāba* (3:534), *Istī'āb* (3:965), *Mukhtāra* (8:146-147), and al-Muḥibb al-Ṭabarī, *al-Ryāḍ al-Naḍira* (1:459-460 §381-382) through trustworthy narrators cf. *Fatḥ al-Bārī* (7:237) and al-Haythamī (10:322).
[75]Spoken by the Prophet ﷺ in the last days of his life, as narrated from 'Ā'isha by Muslim, Abū Dāwūd, and Aḥmad in his *Musnad*.
[76]Narrated from Ibn 'Abbās by al-Bukhārī, Muslim, Abū Dāwūd, and Aḥmad.

The third item was about Abū Bakr's succession: Aḥmad narrated from ʿĀʾisha that the Prophet ﷺ had also said to her brother ʿAbd al-Raḥmān b. Abī Bakr, "Bring me a tablet so that I shall prepare for Abū Bakr something in writing over which there will be no disagreement." When ʿAbd al-Raḥmān got up to fetch it the Prophet said, "Sit. Allah has refused and the believers also, that anyone should disagree over you, O Abū Bakr!"[77] The second clause is narrated in *Ṣaḥīḥ Muslim* in the wording *yaʾbā-l-Lāhu* ⁽Allah shall refuse⁾ instead of *abā* ⁽has refused⁾, also in the *Musnad,*[78] with the addition, "I fear some claimant and some wishful thinker might say 'I am preferable!'"

- "If the people obey Abū Bakr and 'Umar they will follow the right direction!" He ﷺ said it three times.[79]

- To the woman who said: "Messenger of Allah! What if I come back but do not find you?" – as if she meant death – the Prophet ﷺ replied: "Then go to Abū Bakr!"[80]
- Anas ﷺ said: "The delegation of Banū al-Muṣṭaliq instructed me to ask the Messenger of Allah ﷺ, 'If we come next year and do not find you, to whom should we remit our [obligatory] *ṣadaqāt*?' I conveyed to him the question and he replied: 'Remit them to Abū Bakr!' I told them his answer but they said, 'What if we do not find Abū Bakr?' I conveyed to him the question and he replied: 'Remit them to 'Umar!' They asked again, 'What if we do not find 'Umar?' He said, 'Tell them, Remit them to 'Uthmān – and may you perish the day 'Uthmān is killed!'"[81]

- "It is impermissible for a people among whom is Abū Bakr, to be led by anyone other than him."[82]

[77] Narrated from ʿĀʾisha by Aḥmad (40:235-236 §24199). This is the very first of al-Suyūṭī's forty-Hadith compilation *al-Rawḍ al-Anīq fī Faḍl al-Ṣiddīq* (The Comely Grove Converning the Lofty Merit of the Most Truthful One), ed. ʿĀmir Aḥmad Ḥaydar (Beirut: Muʾassasat Nādir, 1410/1990).
[78] Narrated from ʿĀʾisha by Muslim (*Faḍāʾil al-Ṣaḥāba, faḍāʾil Abī Bakr al-Ṣiddīq*); Aḥmad (42:50 §25113).
[79]Narrated from Abū Qatāda by Muslim, Aḥmad, Abū 'Awāna, *Musnad* (2:259), al-Bayhaqī, *I'tiqād* (p. 340) and *Madkhal* (p. 122), al-Firyābī and Abū Nu'aym each in their *Dalāʾil,* and the Jahmī ḥadīth Master 'Alī b. al-Ja'd (d. 230), *Musnad* (p. 450) – al-Dhahabī calls him *al-Imām al-Ḥāfiṭ al-Ḥujja* in the *Siyar* (9:165 §1690).
[80]Narrated from Jubayr Ibn Muṭ'im by Bukhārī, Muslim al-Tirmidhī, and Aḥmad.
[81]Narrated from Anas by Abū Nu'aym, *Ḥilya* (8:358); Ibn 'Asākir (39:177); Nu'aym b. Ḥammād, *Fitan* (1:107-108 §260, 1:125 §295) cf. *Kanz* (§36333).
[82]Narrated from 'Ā'isha by Tirmidhī *(ḥasan gharīb),* a grading reiterated by Suyūṭī as cited by Mubārakfūrī in *Tuḥfat al-Aḥwadhī* (10:109) who cites Ibn Kathīr's grading of *ṣaḥīḥ* in his *Musnad al-Ṣiddīq* – although al-Tirmidhī mentions in his *'Ilal* (p. 372 §691) Bukhārī's opinion that its narrator, 'Īsā b. Maymūn al-Anṣārī, was weak *(ḍa'īf)* cf. Ibn 'Adī, *Kāmil* (5:240); Abū Ya'lā in his *Musnad* (8:228 §4798) with a very weak chain because of Yūsuf b. Khālid and Mūsā b. Dīnār al-Makkī; and Muḥibb al-Ṭabarī in *al-Ryāḍ al-Naḍira* (2:82, 2:174). Ibn al-Jawzī's claim that it is forged in his *Mawḍūʿāt* (1:318) was generally rejected by the scholars except for Dhahabī cf. Ibn al-Jawzī, *'Ilal Mutanāhiya* (1:193 §300); Suyūṭī, *Laʾāliʾ* (1:299); Dhahabī, *Tartīb al-*

- "Take for your leaders the two that come after me: Abū Bakr and 'Umar."[83] Abū Nu'aym said: "This ḥadīth is among the signs of Prophethood since he foretold that his successor would be Abū Bakr and the latter's successor would be 'Umar, and it was just as he said."[84] Ibn Rajab said: "The Messenger of Allah ﷺ therefore explicitly stipulated *(naṣṣa)* toward the end of his life those who should be followed as leaders after him."[85]
- "A man from the dwellers of Paradise is about to come into your sight." Whereupon Abū Bakr came and sat among them. The Prophet ﷺ said the same thing again and 'Umar came.[86]

The Prophet ﷺ also said of many Companions that they were among the inhabitants of Paradise, such as the rest of the Ten Promised Paradise; al-Ḥusayn b. 'Alī, his brother al-Ḥasan, their mother Fāṭima and their grandmother Khadīja; 'Ā'isha and her mother Umm Rūmān; the rest of the Mothers of the Believers; 'Abd Allāh b. Salām; all the Muslim combatants of Badr, some specifically such as 'Ammār b. Yāsir; the Pledgers of Ḥudaybiya; the slain leaders of the battle of Mu'ta: Zayd b. Ḥāritha, Ja'far al-Ṭayyār, and 'Abd Allāh b. Rawāḥa; Bilāl b. Abī Rabāḥ; the Anṣārī exempt

Mawḍū'āt (p. 87 §232); Shawkānī, *Fawā'id* (p. 359 §13); Ibn 'Arrāq, *Tanzīh al-Sharī'a* (1:372).

[83]Narrated from Ḥudhayfa by al-Tirmidhī (*ḥasan* confirmed by al-Dhahabī in the *Siyar* 1-2:512 with regard to the chain), Aḥmad (Arnā'ūṭ ed. 38:418-419 §23419 *ḥasan* and 38:280-282 §23245 *ḥasan*=al-Zayn ed. 16:566-567 §23138), Ibn Mājah, Ibn Abī Shayba (6:350), Ibn Abī 'Āṣim, *al-Sunna* (p. 531-532 §1148-1149, *ṣaḥīḥ*), Aḥmad with five chains in *Faḍā'il al-Ṣaḥāba* (1:332, 1:238, 1:359, 1:426), al-Ṭaḥāwī with six sound chains according to Arnā'ūṭ in *Mushkil al-Āthār* (3:257-259 §1227-1232), Bayhaqī, *al-Sunan al-Kubrā* (5:212 §9826, 8:153 §16353), Ibn Balbān, *Tuḥfat al-Ṣiddīq* (p. 63-64), Khalīlī who declared it sound in *al-Irshād* (1:378, 2:664-665), and Ibn 'Abd al-Barr in *al-Tamhīd* (22:126); also from Ibn Mas'ūd by al-Tirmidhī *(ḥasan)* through five chains and Aḥmad in *Faḍā'il al-Ṣaḥāba* (1:238); and from Ibn 'Umar with an erroneous chain as stated by Ibn Ḥajar in *Lisān al-Mīzān* (1:188) and *Talkhīṣ al-Ḥabīr* (4:190), cf. Ibn Kathīr, *Tuḥfa* (p. 165).

[84]Abū Nu'aym, *Dalā'il al-Nubuwwa* (1989 ed. p. 130).

[85]Ibn Rajab, *Jāmi' al-'Ulūm wa al-Ḥikam* (Zuḥaylī ed. 2:45).

[86]Narrated from Ibn Mas'ūd by al-Tirmidhī *(gharīb)* and al-Ḥākim (3:136=1990 ed. 3:146) who declared its chain sound. It is confirmed as authentic by identical narrations from **(1)** Jābir by Aḥmad with four good chains; Ṭabarāni–cf. Haythamī (9:57-58; 9:116-117)–with several chains in *al-Awsaṭs* (7:110 §7002; 8:41 §7897), *Musnad al-Shāmiyyīn* (1:375 §651), *al-Kabīr* (10:167 §10343); al-Ḥārith, *Musnad* (2:889 §961); Ṭayālisī (p. 234 §1674), Ibn Abī 'Āṣim, *Sunna* (2:624 §1453); Aḥmad in *Faḍā'il al-Ṣaḥāba* (1:209 §233; 2:577 §977); and al-Muḥibb al-Ṭabarī in *al-Riyāḍ al-Naḍira* (1:301 §146); **(2)** Abū Mas'ud by al-Ṭabarānī in *al-Mu'jam al-Kabīr* (17:250 §695); and Ibn Mas'ūd by Aḥmad in *Faḍā'il al-Ṣaḥāba* (1:104 §76). Its continuation in the latter and Tirmidhī states, "Then the Prophet ﷺ said the same thing and 'Umar came" while all the others add 'Alī third, and al-Ṭabarānī – in one narration – 'Uthmān instead. Other versions by al-Ṭabarānī mention 'Alī alone, cf. from Ibn Mas'ūd in *al-Mu'jam al-Kabīr* (10:166-167 §10342, §10344), **(3)** from Umm Marthad in *al-Āḥād wa al-Mathānī* (6:234 §3467) and *al-Kabīr* (24:301 §764) cf. Ibn 'Abd al-Barr, *al-Istī'āb* (4:1957 §4209), and from Jābir in Aḥmad's *Faḍā'il al-Ṣaḥāba* (2:608 §1038) while one version **(4)** from Ibn 'Abbās in the latter (1:454 §732) mentions 'Uthmān alone, cf. *Kanz al-'Ummāl* (§36211).

of envy; Thābit b. Qays; Mālik, Abū Sa'id al-Khudrī's father; al-Ghumayṣā' bint Milḥān – *i.e.* Umm Sulaym, Anas's mother and the Prophet's ﷺ milk-aunt[87]; Mu'āwiya; Hilāl al-Ḥabashī (Mawlā al-Mughīra b. Shu'ba); Jarīr b. 'Abd Allāh al-Bajalī; Sharīk b. Khubāsha al-Numayrī; al-Ḍaḥḥāk b. Khalīfa al-Anṣārī; Uways al-Qaranī; and others.[88]

- "'Alī! Abū Bakr and 'Umar are the leaders of the mature dwellers *(kuhūl)* of Paradise among the first and the last, except for Prophets and Messengers."[89] This is the very first of al-Suyūṭī's 40-

[87]Cf. al-Nawawī, Tahdhīb al-Asmā' wal-Lughāt (2:626).

[88]See 'Abd al-Ghanī al-Nābulusī's *Lama'ān al-Anwār fīl-Maqṭū'i lahum bil-Jannati wal-Maqṭū'i lahum bil-Nār* (The Flashes of Lights on Those Who Are Definitely in Paradise and Those Definitely in the Fire) (Cairo: Maṭba'at al-Sa'āda, 1373/1954).

[89]Al-Munāwī in his discussion of this narration in *Fayḍ al-Qadīr* (1:88-89) cited al-'Irāqī grading of *ḥasan ṣaḥīḥ.* Suyūṭī also indicated it is *ṣaḥīḥ* in *al-Jāmi' al-Saghīr* and *al-Ghurar* as did al-Nawawī in his *Fatāwā* (p. 267-268) and Arnā'ūṭ in his editions of Ibn Ḥibbān (15:330 §6904) and al-Ṭaḥāwī's *Sharḥ Mushkil al-Āthār* (5:217 §1965=Dār Ṣādir ed.2:391), a grade unaffected by the relative weakness of its chains due to their great number – from nine Companions – and corroborative force. Shaykh Aḥmad al-Ghumārī's suggestion that this ḥadīth is a forgery in *al-Burhān* (p. 81 n.) does not stand to scrutiny. Narrated from 'Alī by Aḥmad with the addition "and its youth" with a chain of sound narrators except for al-Ḥasan b. Zayd b. Ḥasan. Aḥmad Shākir in his edition of the *Musnad* (1:424 §602) said he is trustworthy *(thiqa)*, while Ibn Ḥajar, *Taqrīb* (p. 161 §1242) said of him, "truthful, but he errs" *(ṣadūq yahim)*. Ma'rūf and al-Arnā'ūṭ graded him "weak but his narrations are taken into consideration to strengthen or be strengthened by other chains [of identical or higher strength]" in *Taḥrīr Taqrīb al-Tahdhīb* (1:273 §1242). This is the case here as the ḥadīth is also narrated with the following chains:
From 'Alī by al-Tirmidhī with a very strong chain except for the *Rāfiḍī* al-Ḥārith b. 'Abd Allāh al-A'war, whose slight weakness is annulled by the other chains of this ḥadīth. Al-Ṭabarānī in *al-Awsaṭ* (2:91) narrates it through the same chain to al-Sha'bī. [The ḥadīth is also narrated from 'Alī by Ibn Mājah with a very weak chain and al-Tirmidhī with a weak, broken chain *(munqaṭi')*, also cited by al-Ṣawwāf in his *Fawā'id* (p. 35). Also from 'Alī with an entirely different chain by Ibn Abī Shayba (6:350) and Ibn Abī 'Āṣim in *al-Sunna* (p. 617). Also from 'Alī with yet another chain by al-Bazzār in his *Musnad* (3:67-68). Also from 'Alī with two chains, one of them sound according to Shaykh Ḥusayn Asad – except for a missing link which is named in other chains – by Abū Ya'lā in his *Musnad* (1:405, 1:460).]
From Anas b. Mālik by al-Tirmidhī *(ḥasan gharīb)* with a strong chain according to the narrator-evaluation of al-Ḥasan b. al-Ṣabbaḥ al-Bazzār by al-Arnā'ūṭ in *Taḥrīr al-Taqrīb* (1:275 §1251), also by Ibn Abī 'Āṣim in *al-Sunna* (p. 617), al-Ṭabarānī in *al-Awsaṭ* (7:68) and *al-Saghīr* (2:173), and al-Ḍiyā' al-Maqdisī in *al-Mukhtāra* (7:96), all with an identical chain to Muḥammad b. Kathīr. [The ḥadīth is also narrated from Anas b. Mālik with a weak chain by al-Ḍiyā' al-Maqdisī in *al-Mukhtāra* (6:244). 10 vols. Ed. 'Abd al-Mālik b. Duhaysh. Mecca: Maktabat al-Nahḍa, 1990.]
From Jābir b. 'Abd Allāh by al-Ṭabarānī in *al-Awsaṭ* (8:340) with a sound chain of narrators retained by al-Bukhārī and Muslim except for al-Ṭabarānī's shaykh, the Malikī Mufti, "learned jurist and Muḥaddith" (al-Dhahabī) Abū 'Amr Miqdām b. Dāwūd b. 'Īsā b. Talīd al-Miṣrī al-Qitbānī al-Ru'aynī (d. 283), declared weak by al-Nasā'ī [in *al-Kunā*], al-Dāraquṭnī in *Gharā'ib Mālik*, and others cf. *Siyar* (Risāla ed. 13:345), *Mīzān, Lisān*, and al-Haythamī in twenty-eight places, however, Maslama b. Qāsim accepted his narrations, al-Ḍyā' al-Maqdisī retains him as trustworthy in *al-Mukhtāra* (4:200, 7:192) as does al-Dhahabī in *Talkhīṣ al-Mustadrak* (1990 ed. 1:290, 2:66) – although elsewhere (cf. *al-Kashf al-Ḥathīth* p. 261 §782, *Siyar* 13:346) he suggests that Miqdām forged two narrations! – while al-Haythamī him-

Hadith compilation *al-Ghurar fī Faḍā'ili 'Umar* (The Shining Splendors on the Immense Merits of 'Umar).

Al-Ṭaḥāwī defined "maturity" *(al-takahhul)* as "the latter period of youth, after which one becomes a *shaykh*."[90] Abū Hurayra is called "the boy" *(al-ghulām)* in more than one narration,[91] although it is narrated from him that he was over thirty when he first came to Medina.[92] Al-Nawawī said that its meaning was that Abū Bakr and 'Umar are the leaders of all those who died in their maturity and entered Paradise, while al-Ḥasan and al-Ḥusayn are the leaders of all those who died young and entered Paradise.[93]

- The *Tābi'ī* Ismā'īl b. Abī Khālid narrated that 'Ā'isha رضي الله عنها once addressed the Prophet ﷺ, "O Master of the Arabs!" but he replied, "I am the Master of human beings and I say this without pride; but your father is the master of the mature men of the Arabs" *(sayyid kuhūl al-'arab)*.[94] One version adds, "and 'Alī is the master of the youth of the Arabs."[95]

self also said he was declared trustworthy according to Ibn Daqīq al-'Īd in *al-Imām fīl-Aḥkām*. [Also narrated from Jābir by al-Bazzār in his *Musnad* (2:132).]
From Abū Juhayfa by Ibn Mājah with a slightly weak chain that strengthens and is strengthened by other chains, and by Ibn Ḥibbān (15:330) with a chain of sound narrators except for Khunays b. Bakr b. Khunays, whom Ṣāliḥ Jazara declared weak as stated in al-Khaṭīb's *Tārīkh* (8:432), but this weakness is annulled by other, corroborative chains. Al-Ṭabarānī in *al-Awsaṭ* (4:272) and *al-Kabīr* (22:104) narrates it through the same chain to Khunays, and al-Dūlābī in *al-Kunā wa al-Asmā'* (1:120) through the same chain to Khunays's shaykh, Muḥammad b. 'Aqil.
From Abū Sa'īd al-Khudrī by al-Ṭabarānī in *al-Awsaṭ* (4:359) with a weak chain because of 'Alī b. 'Abbās as indicated by al-Haythamī (9:53).
From Ibn 'Umar by al-Jurjānī in *Tārīkh Jurjān* (p. 116) with a very weak chain because of 'Abd al-Raḥmān b. Mālik b. Mighwal. Al-Jurjānī. *Tārīkh Jurjān*. 3rd ed. Ed. Muḥammad 'Abd al-Mu'īd Khān. Beirut: 'Ālam al-Kutub, 1981.
From Ibn 'Abbās by Khaythama in *Ḥadīth Khaythama* (p. 199); al-Khaṭīb in *Tārīkh Baghdād* (14:216, 10:192 [Ibn 'Abbās from 'Alī]); and al-Ḥākim in his *Tārīkh*.
From Abū Hurayra by 'Abd Allāh b. Aḥmad in *Faḍā'il al-Ṣaḥāba* (1:188, 1:441).
From Mālik b. Rabī'a by 'Abd Allāh b. Aḥmad b. Ḥanbal in *Faḍā'il al-Ṣaḥāba* (1:377).

[90]In *Sharḥ Mushkil al-Āthār* (5:220).

[91]Cf. "The boy from Daws beat you to it!" Narrated by al-Nasā'ī in *al-Sunan al-Kubrā* (3:440 §5835) and al-Ṭabarānī in *al-Awsaṭ* with a chain of trustworthy narrators except for Qays al-Madanī who is of unknown reliability as indicated by al-Haythamī in *Majma' al-Zawā'id* (9:361), while Ibn Ḥajar declared "good" *(jayyid)* al-Nasā'ī's chain in *al-Iṣāba* (7:438 §10674) and *Tahdhīb al-Tahdhīb* (12:291). Al-Ḥākim (3:508=1990 ed. 3:582) also narrated it with a chain he declared sound *(ṣaḥīḥ)* but al-Dhahabī cited the weakness of one of its narrators, Ḥammād b. Shu'ayb. However, in the *Siyar* (4:197=al-Arnā'ūṭ ed. 2:616) he cites Qays's chain [cf. al-Mizzī in *Tahdhīb al-Kamāl* (24:94)] with al-Faḍl b. al-'Alā' in lieu of Ḥammād, adding: "Ibn al-'Alā' is truthful *(ṣadūq)*," which makes this a strong narration *in shā' Allah*, and Ibn Ḥajar cites it in his *Fatḥ* (1959 ed. 1:215).

[92]Cf. Ibn Ḥajar, *Ikmāl* (p. 34) and previous note.

[93]Al-Nawawī, *Fatāwā* (p. 268).

[94]Narrated by Ibn Abī Shayba (6:351) with a weak and broken chain.

[95]Narrated by 'Abd Allāh b. Aḥmad in *Faḍā'il al-Ṣaḥāba* (1:394 §599) with a weak and broken chain.

- "Abū al-Dardā'! Do you walk in front of your better? The sun never rose nor set over anyone, after the Prophets and Messengers, better than Abū Bakr."[96]
- "The Prophet ﷺ used to hold nightly conversations with Abū Bakr in the latter's house, discussing the affairs of Muslims, and I ['Umar] was present with them."[97] Imām al-Tirmidhī said, after narrating this ḥadīth, "Some of the people of learning among the Companions and Tābi'īn abominated night conversation after *Ṣalāt al-'Ishā'* while others permitted it on condition that it be for learning or for necessary needs. The Prophet ﷺ said: '**There are to be no late night conversations except for those who are up praying and those who are travelling.**'"[98]
- 'Umar disagreed with Abū Bakr one day and left him in anger. Abū Bakr followed after him, asking his forgiveness, but 'Umar refused and shut his door in his face. Abū Bakr then went to the Prophet ﷺ and took hold of his garment until his knee showed. The Prophet ﷺ said: "Your companion has been arguing!" Abū Bakr greeted him and said: "There was a dispute between me and 'Umar, then I felt remorse and asked him to forgive me but he would not, so I came to you." The Prophet ﷺ said, repeating three times: "Allah forgives you, Abū Bakr! Allah forgives you, Abū Bakr! Allah forgives you, Abū Bakr!" 'Umar felt remorse and went asking for Abū Bakr at his house without finding him. He came to the Prophet ﷺ and greeted him, but the Prophet's ﷺ face changed to displeasure. Seeing this, Abū Bakr sat up on his knees in fear before the Prophet ﷺ, saying twice: "Messenger of Allah! I was more at fault. Messenger of Allah! I was more at fault." The Prophet ﷺ then said to the people: "Allah sent me to you and you all said: 'You are lying!' But Abū Bakr said: 'He said the truth.' Abū Bakr gave me solace with his person and property. Will you leave my companion alone once and for all? Will you leave my companion alone once and for all?!" No-one ever insulted Abū Bakr again.[99] Another version states the

[96]Narrated with good chains from Abū al-Dardā' through Ibn Jurayj by al-Qaṭī'ī in *Zawā'id Faḍā'il al-Ṣaḥāba* (1:152-153 §135, 1:352 §508, 1:423 §662); 'Abd b. Ḥumayd, *Musnad* (p. 101 §212); Ibn Ḥibbān, *al-Thiqāt* (7:94 §9156, "Abū Bakr and 'Umar"); Abū Nu'aym, *Ḥilya* (3:325, 10:301-302); Ibn 'Asākir (30:208-209); al-Khaṭīb, *Tārīkh* (12:438), *Jāmi'* (Ma'ārif ed. 2:227), *Riḥla* (p. 181); Baḥshal, *Tārīkh Wāsiṭ* (p. 248), cf. *Kanz* (§32622); al-Muḥibb al-Ṭabarī, *al-Ryāḍ al-Naḍira* (1:320, 2:28). Abū Ḥātim considered it forged per Ibn Abī Ḥātim, *'Ilal* (2:384). Dāraquṭnī also questioned it as cited by Ibn al-Jawzī in his *'Ilal* (1:187). Aḥdab in *Zawā'id Tārīkh Baghdād* (8:582-586 §1926) said it is merely weak.

[97]Narrated from 'Umar by al-Tirmidhī and Aḥmad with sound chains as stated by Ibn Ḥajar in *Fatḥ al-Bārī*, book of Knowledge *('ilm)*, chapter entitled "Nightly Conversation Concerning Knowledge."

[98]Narrated from Ibn Mas'ūd by Aḥmad with four chains.

[99]Narrated from Abū al-Dardā' by al-Bukhārī.

Prophet ﷺ said: "People! Abū Bakr never once hurt me, so know this about him!"[100]

- "Jibrīl came to me, took me by the hand, and showed me the gate through which my Community shall enter Paradise." Abū Bakr said: "Would that I were with you to see it!" The Prophet ﷺ said: "Truly you will be the first of all my Community to enter it!"[101]

We heard our teacher Shaykh Nūr al-Dīn ʿItr mention that a man once praised his teacher in the presence of Shaykh ʿAbd Allāh Sirāj al-Dīn saying: "There is not, between him and the Prophet ﷺ, except one level!" Hearing this, Shaykh ʿAbd Allāh Sirāj al-Dīn became very angry and said: "This is the enmity! Whoever said that there is not, between him and Prophets – let alone the Prophet ﷺ – except one level, let him know that this position does not belong to anyone except Abū Bakr al-Ṣiddīq. All the rest come after him!"

[100]Narrated by Ibn Qāniʿ in *Muʿjam al-Ṣaḥāba* (3:234-235 §1216).
[101]Narrated from Abū Hurayra by al-Khaṭīb in *Tārīkh Baghdād* (5:434) and al-Ḥākim (1990 ed. 3:77) who declared it *ṣaḥīḥ*.

13
Abū Bakr Saved Islam and Humanity Twice

Abū Bakr saved Islam and humanity twice. The first time was when he led the best generation of humankind through the direst calamity that ever befell them: the death of the Prophet ﷺ. The second time was when he waged the "Apostasy War" *(ḥarb al-ridda)* against the tribes who withheld payment of the *zakāt*, after which they all returned to paying it.

When the Prophet ﷺ passed away events unfolded rapidly. Abū Bakr was away, 'Umar was in a state of shock, refusing to accept the death of the Prophet ﷺ and – ired by the gloating hypocrites – threatened to kill whoever said he died, the people were in utter confusion, 'Alī, al-Zubayr, and others confined themselves to the house of the Prophet ﷺ, while the Khazraj among the *Anṣār* were gathering with their leader to demand their share of the Caliphate. Abū Bakr arrived and, in the words of Ibn al-'Arabī al-Mālikī, "Allah ﷻ rescued Islam and humanity with Abū Bakr al-Ṣiddīq."[102] Al-Bukhārī in his *Ṣaḥīḥ* narrated from 'Ā'isha the following account of the events:

> The Messenger of Allah ﷺ died while Abū Bakr was in al-Sunh. 'Umar rose and said: "By Allah, the Messenger of Allah ﷺ did not die!" He [later] said: "By Allah, I was positively sure of it *(mā kāna yaqa'u fī nafsī illā dhāka)*, and that Allah would definitely resurrect him so that he would cut off the arms and legs of certain people!" Then Abū Bakr came, uncovered the Messenger of Allah ﷺ, kissed him, and said:
>
> <Ah! My Prophet! *(wā nabiyyāh)*
> Ah! My intimate friend! *(wā ṣafiyyāh)*
> Ah! My dearly beloved! *(wā khalīlāh)*>[103]
> My father be ransomed for you and my mother!
> Blessed are you, alive and dead! *(ṭibta ḥayyan wa mayyitā)*.[104]
> By the One in Whose Hand is my soul!
> Allah shall never make you taste the two deaths![105]

[102]Ibn al-'Arabī, al-'Awāṣim min al-Qawāṣim (p. 41).
[103]In Aḥmad's *Musnad* and al-Tirmidhī's *Shamā'il*.
[104]*Ṭibta* can also be translated "May you exude good health" as confirmed by the narration of 'Alī ؓ in Ibn Mājah's *Sunan* with a sound *(ṣaḥīḥ)* chain of trustworthy narrators according to al-Būṣīrī in his *Zawā'id* and al-Sindī in *Sharḥ Sunan Ibn Mājah*: 'Alī b. Abī Ṭālib said that when he washed the Prophet ﷺ [for burial] he prepared himself to smell whatever one smells from the dead but did not smell it. Whereupon he said: "*Bi-abī al-Ṭayyibu! Ṭibta ḥayyan wa-ṭibta mayyitā* – My father be the ransom for this fragrant one! Truly you are [always] in the bliss of health whether in life or in death."
[105]*I.e.* "His life ﷺ in the interlife *(al-barzakh)* will not be followed by death but he shall be permanently alive, and the Prophets are alive in their graves." Ibn Ḥajar,

Then he went out and said [to ʻUmar]: "O swearer of oaths, not so fast!" When Abū Bakr began to speak, ʻUmar stopped and listened. Abū Bakr rendered glory to Allah and exalted Him then he said: "Lo! Whoever used to worship Muḥammad ﷺ, then truly Muḥammad has died; and whoever used to worship Allah ﷻ, then truly Allah is living and does not die." Then he said: "*Lo! you will die, and lo! they will die* (39:30) and *Muḥammad is but a messenger, messengers (the like of whom) have passed away before him. Will it be that, when he dies or is slain, you will turn back on your heels? He who turns back does no hurt to Allah, and Allah will reward the thankful* (3:144)." Hearing this, the people burst out in tears. ʻUmar said: "I swear it by Allah, as soon as I heard Abū Bakr reciting that verse, I fell down to the ground. My legs could no longer carry me. I realized then that the Messenger of Allah had died."

Al-Qurṭubī said: "This verse is the greatest proof of the courage and strength of Abū Bakr al-Ṣiddīq. For the definition of courage and strength is the heart's firmness at the time of tests and tribulations, and they faced no greater disaster than the death of the Prophet. At that time his courage and knowledge showed for all people to see, whereas others were in denial, such as ʻUmar, and ʻUthmān was speechless, and ʻAlī kept out of sight, and things were in confusion, and all this was swept away by the Ṣiddīq through that verse [in Sūrat Āl ʻImrān] when he returned from his place in al-Sunh."

<While we were in the house of the Prophet ﷺ a man said from outside: "Come out [and talk] to me, Ibn al-Khaṭṭāb!" Whereupon he replied: "Off with you, we have other business than you!" – that is, the matter of the Messenger of Allah ﷺ. The man said: "Something has happened! The *Anṣār* gathered in the pavilion *(saqīfa)* of the Banū Sāʻida, so go and see them before they begin something which will lead to war.">[106]

The *Anṣār* had gathered around Saʻd b. ʻUbāda [al-Khazrajī] in the pavilion of the Banū Saʻīda and were saying: "Let there be a leader from among us and a leader from among you." Abū Bakr, ʻUmar b. al-Khaṭṭāb, and Abū ʻUbayda b. al-Jarrāḥ went to them. ʻUmar began to speak but Abū Bakr silenced him. [Later] ʻUmar would say: "By Allah! I meant nothing by it but had prepared a speech that seemed good to me, fearing that Abū Bakr would not speak so well."

Then Abū Bakr spoke and his speech was the most eloquent. He said in his statement: "We are the rulers and you are the ministers" *(naḥnu al-umarāʼ wa antum al-wuzarāʼ)*. But Ḥubāb b. al-Mundhir

Fatḥ al-Bārī (1959 ed. 7:29).
[106]In Ibn Ḥibbān (2:155) cf. *Fatḥ* (12:151).

said: "No, by Allah! We shall never accept! A leader from us and a leader from you!"[107] Abū Bakr said: "No. We are the rulers and you are the ministers. <By Allah! You know, Sa'd, that the Prophet ﷺ said, 'The Quraysh are the governors and rulers' *(Qurayshun wulātu hādhā al-amr)*.>[108] They [Quraysh] are the best of houses among the Arabs and the best of the Arabs in lineage and deeds. Therefore, give your pledge of allegiance to 'Umar or Abū 'Ubayda b. al-Jarrāḥ." 'Umar said: "No, we shall give our pledge to you and no other! You are our leader and the best of us and the most beloved to the Messenger of Allah ﷺ!" 'Umar took his hand and gave him his pledge then the people followed.

Someone said, "You have all killed Sa'd b. 'Ubāda [al-Anṣārī]!" 'Umar replied, "May Allah kill him <for causing this evil *fitna*>[109]!"

Ibn Mas'ūd gave the following account of the events:

When the soul of the Messenger of Allah ﷺ was taken back, the *Anṣār* said [to the *Muhājirūn*]: "Let there be a leader from us and a leader from you." <What persuaded the *Anṣār* the day of the *saqīfa Banī Sā'ida* was the argument forwarded by 'Umar ؓ.>[110] 'Umar said: "Assembly of the *Anṣār*! Are you not aware that the Messenger of Allah ﷺ ordered Abū Bakr to pray as imām among the people?" They replied: "By Allah, yes!" He continued: "Then who among you would be happy to be removed from a position in which the Messenger of Allah put him?" They said: "We seek refuge in Allah from trying to come before Abū Bakr!"[111] Another version states that 'Umar added, as he held the hand of Abū Bakr, "Who has these three merits? *When they two were in the cave*: Who are 'they two'? *When he said unto his companion*: Who is 'his companion'? *Grieve not. Lo! Allah is with us* (9:40): With whom?"[112]

107 Ḥubāb had fought at Badr. Another narration adds that he said, "For, by Allah, we are not coveting your leadership but we fear that others will follow in it whose fathers and brothers we killed in battle."

108 Narrated *mursal* from Ḥumayd b. 'Abd al-Raḥmān al-Ḥimyarī by Aḥmad, "whereupon Sa'd said, "You spoke the truth, we are the ministers and you are the leaders." Confirming it is the Prophetic narration "All people come second to Quraysh in the matter of leadership" in al-Bukhārī and Muslim.

109 In Mālik's *Muwaṭṭa'*.

110 In Ibn 'Abd al-Barr and al-Ṭabarī.

111 Narrated from Ibn Mas'ūd by Aḥmad with three fair chains per Arnā'ūṭ (1:282 §133, 6:309 §3765, 6:393 §3842), Nasā'ī in *al-Sunan* and *al-Sunan al-Kubrā* (§853), Ibn Abī Shayba (14:567), Ibn Abī 'Āṣim in *al-Sunna* (§1159), al-Ḥākim (3:67) who said its chain is sound, Bayhaqī in *al-Sunan al-Kubrā* (8:152), and Ibn Sa'd (3:178), while Ibn 'Abd al-Barr, *al-Istī'āb* (3:971) and Muḥibb al-Dīn al-Ṭabarī in *al-Riyāḍ al-Naḍira* (2:176 §649) narrate it with the phrase "None of us! We ask forgiveness of Allah" instead of "We seek refuge in Allah from ever preceding Abū Bakr."

112 Cf. *Fatḥ al-Bārī* (7:25).

Abū Bakr's caliphate lasted two years and three months in which he brought Syro-Palestine and Iraq into Islam (the "one or two bucketfuls" in the dream of the Prophet ﷺ) and suppressed apostasy among the Arab tribes in forty days. He fought the pseudo-Prophets of Najd –Ṭulayḥa al-Asadī,[113] Musaylima the Liar and his wife Sajāḥ who were killed in the devastating battle of al-Yamāma, and Fujā'at al-Sulāmī, as well as the pseudo-Prophet of Yemen, al-Aswad al-'Ansī. The harshest and most devastating of all these campaigns by far was the battle of Yamāma in which the Muslims sustained the heaviest losses and after winning which Abū Bakr went into the thanksgiving prostration.[114]

It is reported from Abū Hurayra that he said three times: "By Allah besides Whom there is no God! If Abū Bakr had not succeeded the Prophet ﷺ, Allah would no longer be worshipped!" They exclaimed, "*Mah,*[115] Abū Hurayra!" He continued:

> The Messenger of Allah had directed [20-year old] Usāma b. Zayd (d. 45) at the head of seven hundred fighters to al-Shām. When they alighted in Dhū Khushub[116] the soul of the Messenger of Allah was taken back and the Arab tribes committed apostasy all around Medina. At this the Companions of the Messenger of Allah ﷺ flocked to him, saying: "Abū Bakr! Bring those [troops] back. How can you direct them to fight the Romans when the Arabs have apostatized all around Medina?" He replied: "By the One besides Whom there is no God, even if dogs were gnawing at the legs of the wives of the Messenger of Allah ﷺ I would never bring back an army which the Messenger of Allah ﷺ sent out, nor would I ever fold up a standard deployed by the Messenger of Allah ﷺ!" So he told Usāma to continue on his way. Wherever he passed by a tribe that wanted to apostatize they would say: "If those people did not have great power, such an army would not set forth from among them! Let us but wait and see until

[113]He repented before the death of Abū Bakr and died a shahid on the Muslim side in the battle of Nahāwand in the year 21.
[114]Narrated by Ibn Abī Shayba (*Ṣalāt, Sajdat al-Shukr*, 'Awwāma ed. 5:459 §8499) and Bayhaqī, *Sunan* (2:519 §3940) through a nameless narrator; the rest are trustworthy; Mālik in the *'Utbiyya* deemed it a falsehood cf. Khalīl's *al-Tawḍīḥ Sharḥ Mukhtaṣar Ibn al-Ḥājib* (2:579) but Muḥ. b. al-Ḥasan cited it in *al-Siyar* without chain and cited the same act by 'Alī after fighting the Khawārij at Nahrawān as narrated by Bazzār (2:186) and Ibn Abī Shayba (*Ṣalāt, Sajdat al-Shukr*, 'Awwāma ed. 5:460-463 §8502-8503, §8508) cf. Sarakhsī, *Sharḥ al-Siyar al-Kabīr* (1:153-154) and Ibn Kathīr, *Bidāya* (7:300). Sarakhsī said the thanksgiving prostration, although *makrūh* according to al-Nakha'ī (cf. Ibn Abī Shayba, 'Awwāma ed. 5:462 §8507) and Abū Ḥanīfa, is a sunna according to Muḥammad and Abū Yūsuf since the Prophet is authentically related to have offered thanks with two *rak'as* at the conquest of Mecca (and on other occasions, as did his first two caliphs, see the abovementioned chapter in Ibn Abī Shayba). So did Abū Hurayra and al-Furāt b. Hayyān as mentioned in the latter's entry in Ibn Ḥajar's *Iṣāba*.
[115]*I.e.* "Stop saying this!"
[116]"A valley one night's travel from Medina." Ibn al-Athīr, *al-Nihāya*, *kh-sh-b*.

they meet the Byzantines." They met the Byzantines, routed them and returned safe. After this the tribes held fast to Islam.[117]

[117]A very weak *mawqūf* report from Abū Hurayra narrated by Abū 'Uthmān al-Ṣābūnī in his *Mi'atān* (Anthology of Two Hundred Ḥadīths), al-Bayhaqī in *al-I'tiqād* (p. 345) and Ibn 'Asākir (2:60, 30:316) cf. *Kanz* (§14066), *Sīra Ḥalabiyya* (3:229), Muḥibb al-Dīn al-Ṭabarī in *al-Riyāḍ al-Naḍira* (2:47-48 §467), Ibn Kathīr in *al-Bidāya* (Ma'ārif ed. 6:305) and al-Suyūṭī in *Tārīkh al-Khulafā'*, all through Muḥammad b. 'Alī al-Maymūnī al-Baṣrī al-Thaqafī who is discarded as a narrator [*matrūk*]).

14
Fāṭima's Displeasure and Pardon

After he was made Caliph, Abū Bakr was approached by Fāṭima and al-'Abbās for her share of her father's ﷺ inheritance out of the properties of Medina, Fadak, and Khaybar, and for his share as uncle of the Prophet ﷺ. Abū Bakr refused on the grounds that the Prophet ﷺ had said: "We [Prophets] do not bequeath anything and whatever we leave behind is charity." Ibn Ḥajar said that Fāṭima considered the statement of the Prophet ﷺ to apply generally speaking but not to the specific properties mentioned, while Abū Bakr applied it universally without exceptions. One might see this scrupulous application of the Qur'ān and ḥadīths in many of Abū Bakr's acts whether in great or small matters, such as in his repression of mass apostasy and his literal commitment never to ask anything from anyone.

The collected reports of al-Bukhārī and Muslim from 'Ā'isha state that Abū Bakr said:

> The Prophet ﷺ said: "We [Prophets] do not bequeath anything *(lā nūrathu)* and whatever we leave behind is charity *(mā taraknā ṣadaqatun)*." I am not leaving one thing the Prophet ﷺ did except I also do it. I fear perdition if I leave out one of his orders. The family of Muḥammad ﷺ may only nourish themselves out of this property and do not have the right to take from it more than their sustenance *(al-ma'kal)*. By Allah! Truly the relatives of the Messenger of Allah ﷺ are dearer to me than to keep ties with my own kin! But I will surely not change anything of the *ṣadaqāt* of the Messenger of Allah ﷺ.

Both 'Alī and al-'Abbās later witnessed before 'Umar and in the presence of 'Uthmān, 'Abd al-Raḥmān b. 'Awf, al-Zubayr, and Sa'd b. 'Ubāda[118] to the truth of the report from the Prophet ﷺ but, as narrated from 'Ā'isha in al-Bukhārī and Muslim, "Then Fāṭima was displeased with Abū Bakr for this *(fawajadat Fāṭimatu 'alā Abī Bakrin fī dhālika)* and stayed [in her house] away from him, refusing to speak to him until her death six months after the Prophet's ﷺ.[119] When she died, her husband 'Alī buried her at night and did not inform Abū Bakr of it, and he prayed over her." In al-Bukhārī alone: "Then Fāṭima became angry *(faghaḍibat Fāṭimatu)* and stayed away from Abū Bakr...."

[118]During the rule of 'Umar when the question came up publicly between 'Alī and al-'Abbās as narrated from Mālik b. Aws al-Ḥadathān by al-Bukhārī and Muslim.
[119]It was explained that this does not contradict the order of the Prophet ﷺ that "No Muslim should avoid speaking to his brother for over three days" [Narrated by] as the condition for the validity of the prohibition is to see each other and then refuse to speak, whereas Fāṭima stayed away altogether. Cf. Ibn Ḥajar, *Fatḥ* (1959 ed. 6:202).

Nevertheless, Abū Bakr visited Fāṭima in her sickness and was present at both her washing and burial. It is authentically related that she forgave him before she died. Al-Sha'bī said:

> When Fāṭima fell sick Abū Bakr al-Ṣiddīq came and asked permission to see her. 'Alī said: "Fāṭima, here is Abū Bakr al-Ṣiddīq asking permission to see you." She said: "Would you like me to give him permission?"[120] He said yes, whereupon she gave him permission. He entered to see her, seeking her good pleasure, and said: "By Allah! I did not leave my house, property, family, and tribe except to please Allah, and to please His Prophet, and to please you, the People of the House *(ahl al-bayt)*! He continued to seek her good pleasure until she was pleased.[121]

That Fāṭima forgave Abū Bakr is confirmed by the ḥadīth in which the Prophet ﷺ asked her: "Little daughter! Do you not love whomever I love?" She said yes.[122] The ḥadīth applied to 'Ā'isha and it was well-known to Fāṭima and to all the Companions that the Prophet ﷺ loved 'Ā'isha more than all other people and Abū Bakr more than all other men.

Some claim that when Fāṭima رضي الله عنها died 'Alī buried her at night "so that Abū Bakr would not be informed of it" and that "he prayed over her exclusively of Abū Bakr." Rather, as Ibn Ḥajar said, "Ibn Sa'd narrated through 'Amra bint 'Abd al-Raḥmān that al-'Abbās prayed over her... and she was buried at night according to her specific instructions for greater privacy" – the Prophetic prohibition of night funerals being lifted in case of necessity – "and it may be that ['Alī] did not inform Abū Bakr because he considered that such news would be no secret to him, as there is nothing in the ḥadīth to indicate that Abū Bakr did not know of her death or did not pray over her."[123]

Fāṭima died in the evening and was immediately washed, shrouded, and buried in a casket of palm-leaf stalks after the Abyssinian custom, which she was the first to use in Islam for greater privacy. Ibn 'Abd al-Barr said: "Fāṭima was the first to use this type of casket in Islam and, after her, Zaynab bint Jaḥsh was also buried in this fashion." Privacy was also why she asked to be buried at night in keeping with her famous statement that

[120]Dhahabī said in the *Siyar* (al-Arnā'ūṭ ed. 2:121): "She applied the Sunna by not giving permission to anyone to enter her husband's house except by his command."
[121]Narrated from 'Āmir al-Sha'bī by al-Bayhaqī in *al-Sunan al-Kubrā* (6:300-301) and *Dalā'il al-Nubuwwa* (7:273-281) who said: "It is [narrated with] a fair *(ḥasan)* chain that is missing the Successor-link *(mursal)* and is [otherwise] sound *(ṣaḥīḥ)*." Ibn Ḥajar in *Fatḥ al-Bārī* (1959 ed. 6:202) said: "Even if it is *mursal*, its chain is sound *(ṣaḥīḥ)* to al-Sha'bī. Ibn Kathīr in *al-Bidāya wa al-Nihāya* (Turāth ed. 5:310=Ma'ārif ed. 5:289) said: "This chain is good and strong, and it seems that 'Amir al-Sha'bī heard it from 'Alī or from someone who heard it from 'Alī." Muḥibb al-Dīn al-Ṭabarī cited it in *al-Riyāḍ al-Naḍira* (2:96-97 §534) and al-Dhahabī in the *Siyar* (al-Arnā'ūṭ ed. 2:121).
[122]Narrated from 'Ā'isha by al-Bukhārī and Muslim.
[123]Ibn Ḥajar, *op. cit.*.

"the best women are those who do not see men nor do men see them." 'Alī was with the Prophet ﷺ when the latter asked: "What is the best trait in women?" but no one spoke. 'Alī returned and mentioned this to Fāṭima. She said: "That they do not see men nor do the men see them." Alī mentioned this to the Prophet ﷺ and he said: "Truly, Fāṭima comes from me!"[124]

Before her death Fāṭima had stipulated to Abū Bakr's wife, Asmā' bint 'Umays al-Khath'amiyya[125] – the sister of Maymūna bint al-Ḥārith the wife of the Prophet ﷺ – that only she and 'Alī (who married Asmā' after she became widowed of Abū Bakr) should wash her. It was Asmā' who had suggested the casket, which she had seen at the time of the first *Hijra*, after Fāṭima expressed her dislike of open biers in which the shape of the woman's body was revealed even though covered. During the washing 'Ā'isha came and was turned away at the door, whereupon Abū Bakr came and asked why, then was told of Fāṭima's instructions. He said to Asmā': "Do as you were told."[126] This is another proof that Abū Bakr was aware on the spot of Fāṭima's passing away – as were his wife and daughter! – and that he was present at her funeral.

[124]Narrated from Anas through a strong chain by Abū Nu'aym in the *Ḥilya* (1985 ed. 2:40-41) and al-Dāraquṭnī in *Su'ālāt Ḥamzat al-Sahmī* (p. 280 §409) and from Alī by al-Bazzār in his *Musnad* (2:159-160 §526) and by Abū Nu'aym in the *Ḥilya* (1985 ed. 2:175) with a chain containing Qays b. al-Rabī' al-Asadī who is "truthful" *(ṣadūq)* to "weak" *(da'īf)* cf. *Taḥrīr Taqrīb al-Tahdhīb* (3:186 §5573) and 'Alī b. Zayd cf. Ibn Ḥajar, *Mukhtaṣar* (1:567 §1001), al-Haythamī (4:255; 9:203), and *Kanz* (§46012).

[125]He married her at the time of the battle of Ḥunayn after she was widowed of Ja'far b. Abī Ṭālib whom she had accompanied to Abyssinia as per Ibn Ḥajar, *al-Iṣāba* (7:473 §10803). Cf. al-Dhahabī, *Tārīkh* (*Maghāzī* p. 431).

[126]Narrated by Ibn 'Abd al-Barr in *al-Istī'āb* (4:1897-1898) and al-Dhahabī in *Tārīkh al-Islam* (1987 ed. 3:48). Cf. Abū Nu'aym, *Ḥilya*, al-Ḥākim (entries on Fāṭima) and al-Bayhaqī cf. al-Zayla'ī, *Naṣb al-Rāya* (1:339), Ibn Ḥajar, *Talkhīṣ al-Ḥabīr*, and al-Tahānawī, *I'lā' al-Sunan* (8:275-276 §2246).

15
The Delayed Pledge of 'Alī to Abū Bakr

As Abū Bakr received the pledges of allegiance, 'Alī, al-Zubayr, and others used to visit Fāṭima and consult with her, hesitating to give their allegiance. When news of this reached 'Umar he went to Fāṭima and said: "Daughter of the Messenger of Allah! None in all creation was more dearly beloved to me than your father and none is more beloved to us after him than you. However, by Allah! This will never prevent me, if that group gathers in your house, from ordering that their door be set afire!" Then 'Umar went out. The delayers came and she said: "Do you know that 'Umar came to me and swore by Allah that if you were to come back, he shall surely burn the door with you inside? By Allah! He will certainly fulfill what he swore! So go away in peace, renounce your opinion and do not come back to see me." They left her and did not return to see her until they had pledged their allegiance to Abu Bakr.[127]

'Alī, however, delayed pledging his oath of loyalty *(bay'a)* to Abū Bakr until Fāṭima died, after which he invited Abū Bakr to come to him alone – lest 'Umar be present[128] – and told him: "Truly we recognize your immense merit and what Allah gave you, and we bear no envy towards you in the great good Allah conveyed to you. However, you singled yourself out apart of us in the matter [of Caliphate] and we thought that we had a rightful claim to it because of our kinship with the Messenger of Allah ﷺ." Abū Bakr wept and said: "By the One in Whose Hand my soul is, truly the relatives of the Messenger of Allah ﷺ are dearer to me than keeping ties with my own kin. As for the matter which caused conflict between us regarding these properties, truly I left no stone unturned for the sake of truth as to it, nor did I leave out one matter I saw the Prophet ﷺ do." That same evening 'Alī came to Abū Bakr and pledged his oath to him. 'Umar gave the *ṣadaqa* of the Prophet ﷺ from Medina to 'Alī and 'Abbās, while he retained Khaybar and Fadak [for the public].[129]

[127]Narrated from Aslam by Ibn Abī Shayba (1989 al-Ḥūt ed. 7:432 §37045) through the narrators of al-Bukhārī and Muslim cf. *Kanz* (§14138). Certain forgeries depict 'Umar asking for wood at Fāṭima's door or actually bringing a burning torch there etc. None of this is true. The Prophet ﷺ had said that 'Umar was a bolt against dissension and this was exactly his role at that time.
[128]"Due to what they knew of 'Umar's forcefulness and intransigence in speech and deeds, while Abū Bakr was gentle and lenient. It seems they feared, if 'Umar had been present, too much criticism [for delaying *bay'a*], which might lead to the opposite of the resolution they had in mind." Ibn Ḥajar, *op. cit.*
[129]Part of a long mass-narrated *(mutawātir)* ḥadīth narrated with various wordings from 'Umar, 'Uthmān, 'Alī, Sa'd b. Abī Waqqāṣ, al-'Abbās, Abū Bakr, 'Abd al-Raḥmān b. 'Awf, al-Zubayr b. al-'Awwām, Abū Hurayra, 'Aisha, Talha, Ḥudhayfa, and Ibn 'Abbās by al-Bukhārī, Muslim, Mālik, al-Tirmidhī, Abū Dāwūd, al-Nasā'ī, and Aḥmad. Ibn Ḥajar in his *Amālī* declared it *mutawātir* and al-Kattānī included it

in *Naṭm al-Mutanāthir*.

16
'Ā'isha's Description of Her Father

Al-Suyūṭī cites Ibn Sa'd's report of 'Ā'isha's description of Abū Bakr: "He was a man with fair skin, thin, emaciated, with a sparse beard, a slightly hunched frame, sunken eyes and protruding forehead, and the bases of his fingers were hairless."[130] 'Ā'isha also related that both he and 'Uthmān had relinquished drinking alcohol already in the Time of Ignorance.

[130]Narrated by Ibn Sa'd (3:188) and Ṭabarī in his *Tārīkh* (2:350) cf. *Iṣāba* (4:170); al-Muḥibb al-Ṭabarī, *al-Riyāḍ al-Naḍira* (1:410); Suyūṭī, *Tārīkh al-Khulafā'* (p. 45).

17
His Expertise in Genealogy and the Interpretation of Dreams

The Prophet ﷺ described Abū Bakr as the foremost genealogist of the Quraysh.[131] He was also the best of them at interpreting dreams after the Prophet ﷺ according to Ibn Sīrīn.

The Prophet ﷺ said: "I saw in dream black sheep succeeded by dirt-white sheep. Abū Bakr! Interpret it." The latter said, "Messenger of Allah, these are the Arabs following you, then the non-Arabs succeed them until they completely engulf them in their number." The Prophet ﷺ said: "Just so did the angel interpret it [to me] before the dawn.[132]

[131] Narrated from 'Ā'isha by Muslim and others.
[132] Narrated from 'Abd al-Raḥmān b. Abī Laylā, [1] from Abū Ayyūb al-Anṣārī by al-Ḥākim (4:395= 1990 ed. 4:437) and [2] from Abū Bakr himself but al-Dāraquṭnī in his *'Ilal* (1:289) avers that this narration is more probably *mursal* from Ibn Abī Laylā cf. Ibn Abī Shayba (6:176 §30479). Also narrated *mursal* from the *Tābi'ī* Abū Maysara 'Amr b. Shuraḥbīl al-Hamdānī by al-Muḥibb al-Ṭabarī in *al-Ryāḍ al-Naḍira* (2:64 §478) cf. al-Suyūṭī, *Khaṣā'iṣ* (2:192) and something similar *mursal* from Qatāda by Ma'mar b. Rāshid in his *Majma'* ('Abd al-Razzāq 11:66).

18
Abū Bakr's Rules of War for the *Mujāhidīn*

Abū Bakr's instructions to the Muslim armies are famous in the history books. When he sent the Muslim armies to Syro-Palestine, he went out walking by the side of Yazīd b. Abī Sufyān, one of the four commanders. Yazīd said to him, "Either ride or let me walk by your side," but Abū Bakr replied, "Neither this nor that. I count my footsteps in the way of Allah." Then he said: "You will find certain people who secluded themselves purporting to worship Allah, so leave them to their purport. You will also find a people who have scraped off the hair in the midst of their heads: strike their scrapings with the swords.[133] Remember ten things: do not kill women, nor children, nor hoary elders; do not cut down fruit trees; do not ruin dwellings; do not hamstring livestock except for food; do not burn bees nor flood them; do not steal from the booty; and do not be timorous."[134]

Another version states that he said:

> Charge in the way of Allah and kill those who disbelieve in Allah! For Allah will make His way victorious. Do not be steal from the booty; do not deceive; do not be timorous; do not spread corruption in the land; do not disobey orders. When you meet the idolatrous enemy – if Allah wills – call them to three things. If they respond, accept it from them and stop fighting them. Call them to Islam. If they respond, accept it from them and stop fighting them. Then call them to move from their residence to the residence of the Emigrants. Tell them, if they do, that they have the rights and responsibilities of the Emigrants, no more and no less. If they enter Islam but prefer their own residence to the residence of the Emigrants, tell them that they have the same status as the Muslim Arabs of the desert. The Law of Allah will apply to them just as it applies to the Believers, but they will have no share in the spoils except if they fight with the Muslims. If they refuse to enter Islam then ask of them the non-Muslim duty *(al-jizya)*. If they accept, accept it from them and stop fighting them. If they refuse, seek help from Allah and fight them if Allah wills. Do not drown nor burn date orchards. Do not hamstring livestock nor cut down fruit trees nor destroy churches. Do not kill children nor elders nor women. You will find people who secluded themselves from society in monasteries. Leave

[133] *I.e.* Diocesan and other non-monastic clerics *(al-shamāmisa)* cf. Ibn Ḥabīb as quoted by al-Zurqānī in *Sharḥ al-Muwaṭṭa'* (3:17) and al-Suyūṭī in *Tanwīr al-Ḥawālik* (1:298).

[134] Narrated broken-chained *(munqaṭi')* by Mālik in the *Muwaṭṭa'*, Ibn Abī Shayba (6:484 §33134), 'Abd al-Razzāq (5:199 §9375), Sa'īd b. Manṣūr in his *Sunan* (2:181-182 §2383), and Bayhaqī in *al-Sunan al-Kubrā* (9:89). All but Mālik have "Do not drown nor burn date orchards" (نخلا)instead of "Do not drown nor burn bees.(نحلا) "

them to their seclusion. You will find others in the midst of whose heads the devil nests. When you find them, strike off their heads if Allah wills.[135]

The above were based on the instructions of the Prophet ﷺ himself, to which Abū Bakr added some stipulations. Burayda related that whenever the Prophet ﷺ sent out a military expedition he would tell its commander in private and in public to fear Allah. Then he would say:

Charge in the Name of Allah for the sake of Allah! Fight those who disbelieve in Allah! Do not steal from the booty! Do not deceive nor pretend! Do not kill children! When you meet the idolatrous enemy, call them to three things. If they accept even one of them, accept it from them and stop fighting them. Call them to Islam. If they accept, accept it from them and stop fighting them. Then call them to move from their residence to the residence of the Emigrants. Tell them, if they do, that they will have the rights and responsibilities of the Emigrants, no more and no less. If they refuse to move, tell them that they can have the status of the Muslim Arabs of the desert. The Law of Allah will apply to them just as it applies to the Believers, but they will have no share in the spoils except if they fight with the Muslims. If they refuse [both of the above] then ask of them the non-Muslim duty *(al-jizya)*. If they accept, accept it from them and stop fighting them. If they refuse, seek help from Allah and fight them. When you surround a fort and its occupants request a guarantee from you in terms honored by Allah and His Prophet, do not give a guarantee in such terms but give it in terms honored by yourself and your companions. It is easier to be the custodians of your guarantee and that of your companions than to be the custodians of the guarantee of Allah and His Prophet. When you surround a fort and its occupants request you to treat them according to the Judgment of Allah, do not grant such a request but grant that you will treat them according to your judgment. For you do not know whether you will be accurate in applying the Judgment of Allah.[136]

[135]Narrated by al-Ṭabarī in his *Tārīkh* (3:26) and Ibn al-Athīr in his (Dār Ṣādir ed. 1:227), al-Bayhaqī in his *Sunan* (9:85), and Ibn ʿAsākir in *Tārīkh Dimashq*. Cited in *Kanz al-ʿUmmāl* (§11408, §30268).
[136]Narrated from Burayda by Muslim, from Ibn ʿAbbās by Abū Dāwūd, Aḥmad, Abū Yaʿlā, al-Ṭabarānī, and others, and from Ibn ʿUmar in the *Saḥīḥayn*.

The above narrations are confirmed by the warnings reported from the Prophet ﷺ by Thawbān and Abū Hurayra as narrated by Aḥmad in his *Musnad* and Abū Dāwūd in his *Marāsīl* respectively.

19
Death and Posterity of Abū Bakr

ʿĀ'isha related that the onset of Abū Bakr's last illness began after he showered on a cold day and was taken ill for fifteen days during which he ordered ʿUmar to lead the prayers and the Companions would visit him. She said the most assiduous by his bedside was ʿUthmān.[137] The *Tābiʿī* Abū al-Safar (Sa'īd b. Yuḥmid) related that as Abū Bakr lay sick on his deathbed he was asked: "Shall we bring you a physician to examine you?" He replied: "He examined me already." "And what did he tell you?" "He said: 'I am Doer of what I will!'"[138]

'Ā'isha recited to him verses of sapiential poetry:

> *Every possessor of camels shall be inherited*
> *And every strong ravisher shall be ravished.*

Abū Bakr said: "It is not as you said, my daughter, but as Allah said: *And the agony of death comes in truth. This is that which you were wont to shun* (50:19).[139]

Abū Bakr on his deathbed summoned 'Umar and told him:

> Fear Allah, 'Umar! And be aware that Allah requires work by day which He does not accept by night, and He requires work by night which He does not accept by day! Be aware that He accepts no supererogatory work until the obligation is fulfilled! Those whose scale is heavy on the Day of Resurrection, their scale was made heavy only because they followed truth and right in the abode of the world, so they weighed down their scales. It is right and just that a scale that contains nothing but *ḥaqq* become heavy![140]

He was sixty-three years of age when he died after governing for two years and four months. His wife Asmā' bint ʿUmays washed him

[137]*Siyar* (1-2:474).
[138]Narrated by Ibn Sa'd with a chain of trustworthy narrators (3:198), Aḥmad in *al-Zuhd*, Ibn Abī Shayba, Ibn 'Asākir in *Tārīkh Dimashq* (9:2), Abū Nu'aym in the *Ḥilya*, Ibn al-Jawzī in *Ṣifat al-Ṣafwa* (1:264), Muḥibb al-Dīn al-Ṭabarī in *al-Riyāḍ al-Naḍira* (2:243-244 §694), al-Suyūṭī in *Tārīkh al-Khulafā'* as well as in the Qur'ānic commentaries (cf. al-Qurṭubī and Ibn Kathīr) for the verse *Lo! your Lord is Doer of what He will* (11:107, cf. 85:16). Ibn 'Abd al-Barr in *al-Tamhīd* (5:269) attributes the saying to Abū al-Dardā'.
[139]Narrated *mursal* from Bakr b. 'Abd Allāh al-Muzanī by Ibn Sa'd (3:197).
[140]Narrated from 'Abd al-Raḥmān b. 'Abd Allāh b. Sābāṭ by Abū Nu'aym in the *Ḥilya* (1:36) with a chain of trustworthy narrators cf. Ibn al-Jawzī in *Ṣifat al-Ṣafwa* (1:264), Muḥibb al-Dīn al-Ṭabarī in *al-Riyāḍ al-Naḍira* (2:244-245 §695).

before burial then said to the Emigrants: "I am fasting and this is a very cold day. Must I make *ghusl*?" They said no.[141]

His children are 'Abd Allāh (from his wife Qutayla or Qutla of the Banū ʿĀmir b. Lu'ay) the eldest, 'Abd al-Raḥmān Abū 'Abd Allāh – one of the knights in Jāhiliyya and Islam – (from Umm Rūmān bint al-Ḥārith), Muḥammad Abū al-Qāsim (from Asmā' bint ʿUmays al-Khathʿamiyya), 'Ā'isha the Mother of the believers (from Umm Rūmān), Asmā' (from Qutayla) his eldest daughter who lived to be a hundred, and Umm Kulthūm (from Ḥabība bint Khārija b. Zayd), who was born after he passed away, Allah be well-pleased with him and them. The only children of our liege lord Abū Bakr with posterity are ʿAbd al-Raḥmān and Muḥammad. From them descend, in the Middle East, the famous Bakrī family and the Ḥamdān family, as well as the Ṣiddīqī family in the Indian Subcontinent.

[141]Narrated through Mālik b. ʿAbd Allāh b. Abī Bakr from 'Abd Allāh b. Abī Bakr by ʿAbd al-Razzāq, *Muṣannaf* (3:409-410 §6123) and Ibn Saʿd, *Ṭabaqāt* (*al-Badriyyin min al-Muhājirīn, Banū Taym, waṣiyyat Abī Bakr*).

20
His Miraculous Foresight *(Firāsa)*

Al-Bukhārī narrated in his *Ṣaḥīḥ* that Abū Bakr was hoping to die on the same day of the week as the Prophet ﷺ – *al-ithnayn* – but he died that night, when the next day – *al-thulāthā'* – had entered. He was buried before morning. Before he died he foresaw that the child his wife Ḥabība bint Khārija b. Zayd al-Khazrajīyya bore in her womb was a girl and told 'Ā'isha that she would have to share her inheritance with "your two brothers and your two sisters." 'Ā'isha said, "Is it not just Asmā'? Who is the other one?" Abū Bakr said: "The one in the womb of Khārija's daughter. I was shown that it is a girl." Later, his daughter Umm Kulthūm was born.[142]

[142]Narrated from 'Ā'isha by Mālik in his *Muwaṭṭa'*, Ibn Sa'd (3:194-195), al-Bayhaqī in *al-Sunan al-Kubrā* (6:169-170 §11728, 6:178 §11784, 6:257 §12267), 'Abd al-Razzāq (9:101), al-Ṭaḥāwī in *Ma'ānī al-Āthār* (4:88), *Istī'āb* (4:1807), *Naṣb* (4:122), Ibn al-Jawzī in *Ṣifat al-Ṣafwa* (1:265), al-Nawawī in *Tahdhīb al-Asmā'* (2:574, 2:630), al-Lālikā'ī in *Karāmāt al-Awliyā'* (p. 117), al-Mizzī, *Tahdhīb* (35:380), and Muḥibb al-Dīn al-Ṭabarī in *al-Riyāḍ al-Naḍira* (2:122-123 §576).

21
Abū Bakr Related 142 Hadiths from the Prophet ﷺ

Imām al-Nawawī in *Tahdhīb al-Asmā' wal-Lughāt* states that only one hundred and forty-two hadiths of the Prophet ﷺ are narrated from Abū Bakr.[143] He comments: "The reason for this scarcity, despite the seniority of his companionship to the Prophet ﷺ, is that his death predated the dissemination of hadiths and the endeavor of the Successors to hear, gather, and preserve them."

It is also related that Abū Bakr had the written record of all the ḥadīths he had in his possession burnt lest a mistake slip into them. It is related that ʿĀ'isha said: "My father gathered the hadith from the Messenger of Allah ﷺ and it was five hundred hadiths. He spent one night tossing and turning and this worried me. I said, 'Are you tossing and turning because of some ailment or have you heard some bad news?" In the morning he said, "Daughter, bring me the hadiths you have with you." I brought them, then he called for fire and burnt them. He said, "I fear lest I die with those [hadiths] still in your possession and there might be among them ḥadīths from someone I trusted and believed, but it was not as he said to me, and I would have imitated him [in his error]."[144]

His care for verification is illustrated by his double-checking of even the most trustworthy transmitters of reports from the Prophet ﷺ. When he asked: "How much does the grandmother inherit?" Al-Mughīra b. Shuʿba said, "I bear witness that the Messenger of Allah ﷺ gave her one sixth." Abū Bakr said, "Does anyone else know this?" Then Muḥammad b. Salama came forward with the same report.[145]

The nonagenarian Hadith master and qadi of Homs then Damascus Abū Bakr Aḥmad b. ʿAlī b. Saʿīd al-Umawī al-Marwazī (202-292) narrated 143 Prophetic hadiths with his chain to Abū Bakr al-Ṣiddīq in his *Musnad Abī Bakr al-Ṣiddīq*.[146]

[143]*I.e.* without repetitions through various chains. Al-Suyūṭī in *Tārīkh al-Khulafā'* (p. 96-104) documents fully over a hundred of them, which he follows up with over a hundred of Abū Bakr's own sayings.
[144]Narrated by al-Ḥākim as stated by Ibn Kathīr in the *Musnad al-Ṣiddīq* inside his *Jāmiʿ al-Asānīd*.
[145]Narrated in the *Muwaṭṭa'* and *Sunan*.
[146] Ed. Shuʿayb al-Arnāʾūṭ, 4th ed. (Beirut: al-Maktab al-Islāmī, 1406/1986).

22
His *Jihād al-Nafs*, Self-Blame, Modesty and Intense Consciousness of Allah

Among Abū Bakr's sayings: "Whoever fights his ego *(nafs)* for the sake of Allah, He will protect him against what he hates."[147]

'Umar went in to see Abū Bakr one day and found him pulling out his tongue. "Stop!" 'Umar said, "Allah forgive you!" Abū Bakr said: "This thing has brought me to catastrophes."[148] Other versions state that Abū Bakr added: "The Messenger of Allah ﷺ said: "There is nothing in the body except it will complain to Allah of the tongue's sharpness."[149]

Ibn Shihāb al-Zuhrī narrated from 'Urwa b. al-Zubayr, from his father, and Ibn al-Mubārak from Yūnus, that Abū Bakr addressed the people and said, "O people, have shame before Allah Most High! For, by the One in Whose hand is my soul, verily even when I go out to pass my need in the wilderness I remain completely veiled out of shyness before my nurturing Lord."[150]

When the people of Yemen came in the time of his caliphate and heard the Qur'an they took to weeping, whereupon he said: 'Thus were we before, then the hearts hardened (*qasat al-qulūb*).'" Abū Nu'aym said: "*The hearts hardened* means they became strong and tranquil through knowledge of Allah."[151]

[147]Cited by Muḥammad b. Qudāma in *Minhāj al-Qāṣidīn*.
[148]Narrated from Aslam al-'Adawī the *mawlā* of 'Umar by Mālik in his *Muwaṭṭa'*, Abū Nu'aym in the *Ḥilya* (1985 ed. 1:33), and al-Bayhaqī in *Shu'ab al-Īmān* (4:256 §4990).
[149]Narrated from Aslam by Abū Ya'lā (1:4 and 1:17 §5) – with a chain of trustworthy narrators cf. al-Haythamī (10:302) as confirmed by al-'Irāqī in *Takhrīj Aḥādīth al-Iḥyā'* – Ibn al-Sunnī in *'Amal al-Yawm wal-Layla* (§7), Ibn Abī al-Dunyā in *al-Ṣamt wa Ādāb al-Lisān* (Gharb ed. p. 186-187 §13=p. 50-51 §13) and *al-Wara'* (p. 76 §92), al-Bayhaqī in the *Shu'ab* (4:244 §4947), and, without the incident, by al-Bazzār (1:161 §84). On the chains and wordings of this narration see al-Dāraquṭnī's *'Ilal* (Riyāḍ ed. 1:158-161) and Abū Nu'aym's monograph on the narrators from Sa'īd b. Manṣūr towards the end. Something similar to Abū Bakr's act is reported from Ibn 'Abbās cf. Ibn Rajab, *Jāmi' al-'Ulūm wal-Ḥikam* (ch. §28).
[150] Ibn al-Mubārak, *al-Zuhd* (p. 107); Ibn Abī al-Dunyā, *Makārim al-Akhlāq* (p. 40); Abū Nu'aym, *Ḥilyat al-Awliyā'* (1:34=1:68); al-Bayhaqī, *Shu'ab* (6:142).
[151]Narrated by al-Qāsim b. Sallām in *Faḍā'il al-Qur'ān* (p. 135), Ibn Abī Shayba (6:14 = 'Awwāma ed. 19:452-453 §36673 = Luḥaydān ed. 12:423 §36534), and Abū Nu'aym (1:33-34). Al-Sha'rāwī cited these reports at the end of the chapter on Abū Bakr in his *Lawāqiḥ al-Anwār fī Ṭabaqāt al-Akhyār* known as the *Ṭabaqāt al-Kubrā*.

23
Is al-Mahdī Better Than the Two Shaykhs?

Al Barzanjī wrote in *al-Ishā'a fī Akhbār al-Sā'a*:

Abū Nu'aym in his Forty Ḥadīths on the Mahdī – listed by al-Ṣuyūṭī in *al-'Arf al-Wardī fī Akhbār al-Mahdī* – related from Ibn Sīrīn that he said the Mahdī is better than Abū Bakr and 'Umar رضي الله عنهما. He was asked, "O Abū Bakr! Better than Abū Bakr and 'Umar?" He replied that some thought the Mahdī was better even than some of the Prophets. Ibn Abī Shayba related from Ibn Sīrīn that he merely said Abū Bakr and 'Umar are not better than the Mahdī. Al-Suyūṭī said in *al-'Arf al-Wardī*:

> The latter chain is sound and its wording is less momentous than the former report but the most indicated way in my view is to interpret both wordings in the same sense as the ḥadīth, "Rather, fifty of you."[152] This is because there will be severe trials in the time of the Mahdī, the *Rūm* (Christians) will be banding together against him, and the Dajjāl will be besieging him. This does not mean that he will have more reward nor a higher level [than the Two Shaykhs] in the Divine presence because **the sound ḥadīths and the Consensus state that that Abū Bakr and 'Umar are the best of all creation after Prophets and Messengers.**[153]

In addition to al-Suyūṭī's clarification, another ḥadīth clearly states that no one after the major Companions can reach the deeds of any of them on any given day of their lives even if one spent the like of Mount Uḥud in the way of Allah.[154]

[152]This is the ḥadīth that those of the Prophet's ﷺ Community that would hold fast to his Sunna at the end of time would each be given the reward of fifty of his Companions. Narrated from Abū Tha'laba al-Khushanī by al-Tirmidhī, Abū Dāwūd, Ibn Mājah and others.
[153]Al-Suyūṭī, *al-'Arf al-Wardī* in *al-Ḥāwī lil-Fatāwā* (2:73) notwithstanding the citations of Shaykh Muḥyī al-Dīn Ibn 'Arabī's *Futūḥāt* and al-Qārī's *al-Mashrab al-Wardī fī Madhhab al-Mahdī* adduced by al-Barzanjī in *al-Ishā'a li-Ashrāṭ al-Sā'a* (Kāndihlawī-Shukrī 1997 Jeddah ed. p. 238).
[154]Cf. al-Wānsharīsī, *al-Mi'yār al-Mu'rib* (11:13-15).

'Umar b. al-Khaṭṭāb

رضی اللہ تعالی عنہ

'Umar b. al-Khaṭṭāb b. Nufayl b. 'Abd al-'Uzza, *Amīr al-Mu'minīn*, Abū Ḥafs al-Qurashī al-Fārūq, the second Caliph of the Prophet ﷺ after Abū Bakr رضي الله عنه, famous for his sagacity and fierce stand for the truth, by whom Allah answered the Prophet's ﷺ supplication, "O Allah! Strengthen Islam with 'Umar b. al-Khaṭṭāb," who embraced Islam in the year 6 of the Prophethood, at age twenty-seven, after having fought it, then took up the task of Caliphate with utmost diligence, to an extent the sky never saw the like after the Prophets with regard to strength of character and perfect justice, giving all in the way of Allah as the Prophet ﷺ predicted, the skilled fighter and horseman of immense courage, the scrupulously Godfearing leader who wept much and died as a shahid as predicted by the Prophet ﷺ. Allah Most High be well-pleased with him!

'Umar b. al-Khaṭṭāb b. Nufayl b. 'Abd al-'Uzzā b. Rayyāḥ, *Amīr al-Mu'minīn*, Abū Ḥafs al-Qurashī al-'Adawī al-Fārūq ﷺ (42BH-23/581-644), the second Caliph of the Prophet ﷺ after Abū Bakr ﷺ, famous for his sagacity and fierce stand for the truth. Allah ﷻ lavished His bounty on Islam and its people by inspiring Abū Bakr to appoint 'Umar as his successor. The latter took up the task with the utmost diligence, to an extent the sky never saw the like of after the Prophets with regard to strength of character and perfection of justice. The conquest of the territories of Syro-Palestine was completed in his time as well as those of Egypt and most of Persia. He routed Chosroes and humiliated him until the latter retreated to the far end of his kingdom. He cut down Caesar to size *(qaṣṣara Qayṣara)* and left him no influence at all in Syro-Palestine until the latter retreated to Constantinople. He spent their spoils in the way of Allah just as the Messenger of Allah ﷺ had predicted and promised. The Prophet ﷺ called him "my little brother" *(ukhayya)* and asked him to pray for him.[155] Among the Companions who narrated from him: 'Alī, Ibn Mas'ūd, Ibn 'Abbās, Abū Hurayra, and especially his son Ibn 'Umar upon whose narrations Mālik relied in his *Muwaṭṭa'*.

'Umar was fair-skinned with some reddishness, tall with a large build, fast-paced, and a skilled fighter and horseman of immense courage.[156] He was one of those who wept much.

'Umar's caliphate followed that of Abū Bakr's and lasted ten years and a half, during which Islam covered all Egypt, Syria, Sijistān, most of Persia, and other regions. He died a shahid, stabbed in the back while at prayer by a disgruntled Sabean or Zoroastrian slave, at sixty-six years of age, thanking Allah that he died at the hand of someone who never once prostrated to Him in worship. Ibn Mas'ūd said: "When 'Umar died we considered that nine tenths of all learning had disappeared."[157]

[155]Ḥadīth: "My little brother, join us in your supplication and do not forget us." *(Ay ukhayya ashriknā fī du'ā'ik wa lā tansanā)*. Narrated from 'Umar by al-Tirmidhī *(ḥasan ṣaḥīḥ)*, Ibn Mājah, and al-Nasā'ī. Al-Nawawī in *al-Adhkār* and others cited it as an example of the permissibility of asking for the supplication of one less meritorious than the one who asks.

[156]Ibn Qudāma in *Ithbāt Ṣifat al-'Uluw* (p. 42) cited the report of 'Alī's courage *(shajā'a)* and knowledge *('ilm)* together with 'Umar's justice *('adl)* – in general terms – as mass-transmitted *(mutawātir)* truths that necessitate categorical assent.

[157] Narrated with sound chains by Ibn Sa'd, *Ṭabaqāt* (2:336); al-Fasawī, *al-Ma'rifa wal-Tārīkh* (1:247); al-Ṭabarānī, *Kabīr* (9:163); Ibn 'Asākir, *Tārīkh* (44:283).

1
ʿUmar's Islam

He embraced Islam after having fought it, in the year 6 of the Prophethood, at age twenty-seven according to al-Dhahabī. This came as the result of the Prophet's ﷺ explicit supplications: "Allah! Strengthen Islam with the dearest of the two to you: ʿUmar b. al-Khaṭṭāb or Abū Jahl [ʿAmr b. Hishām]."[158] Another version states: "O Allah! Strengthen Islam with ʿUmar b. al-Khaṭṭāb."[159]

Al-Suyūṭī in *al-Durar al-Muntathira* reported from Ibn ʿAsākir that the discrepancy is explained by the fact that the Prophet ﷺ first called for either of the two, then it was made clear to him that Abū Jahl's conversion was precluded and he concentrated his *tawajjuh* or spiritual concentration on ʿUmar.

Ibn Isḥāq narrated that ʿUmar entered the house of his brother-in-law Saʿīd b. Zayd b. ʿAmr b. Nufayl the husband of ʿUmar's sister Umm Jamīl Fāṭima bint al-Khaṭṭāb[160] as the two were reciting the Qurʾān and he struck both of them, whereupon his sister openly declared her faith. At this ʿUmar asked to see what they were reading and made a solemn promise to return it to them. She requested him to shower first. He did and then sat and read the beginning of the Sura of Ṭa Ha until *fa-tardā* (20:1-16). Then he read *idhā al-shamsu kuwwirat* until *ʿalimat nafsun mā aḥḍarat* (81:1-14). Then he declared his submission and went to see the Prophet ﷺ.[161] Something similar is narrated from Aslam the *mawlā* of ʿUmar but with the Sura of al-Ḥadīd from the beginning to *in kuntum muʾminīn* (57:1-8),[162] a weaker report in light of the fact that the latter Sura is Medinan by near-consensus.

Ibn Masʿūd said that the Muslims had been weak until ʿUmar joined them, at which time they were able to come out. He was the fortieth Muslim, whereupon Allah ﷻ revealed the verse *O Prophet! Allah is sufficient for you and those who follow you of the believers* (8:65).[163]

[158]Narrated from Ibn ʿUmar by Aḥmad and al-Tirmidhī who said it is *ḥasan ṣaḥīḥ gharīb*, and by him from Ibn ʿAbbās with a weaker chain.
[159]Narrated from Ibn ʿUmar, Thawbān, Ibn ʿAbbās, ʿĀʾisha, ʿAlī, and al-Zubayr b. al-ʿAwwām by Ibn Mājah, al-Ḥākim (3:83), al-Bayhaqī in his *Sunan* (6:370), al-Ṭabarānī in *al-Kabīr*, and Ibn al-Najjār. Al-Dhahabī in the *Siyar* (1/2:510) said its chains are good, and al-Haythamī (§14404-14406, 2180) indicated likewise for al-Ṭabarānī's chain, while al-Būṣīrī in *Zawāʾid Ibn Mājah* stated that the latter's narration was weak. The ḥadīth itself is weak by the criterion of al-Bukhārī, al-Haythamī, al-Būṣīrī, Abū Ḥātim al-Rāzī, and al-Nasāʾī, while it is authentic according to Ibn Maʿīn, Ibn Ḥibbān, and al-Dhahabī.
[160] Ibn Ḥajar, *Iṣāba* (8:271-272 §11594). Ibn Saʿd calls her Ramla bint al-Khaṭṭāb.
[161] Narrated by Ibn ʿAsākir, *Tārīkh* (16:538-539); cf. Ibn Ṭāhir al-Maqdisī, *al-Badʾ wal-Tārīkh* (5:88-90).
[162] ʿAbd Allāh b. Aḥmad b. Ḥanbal, *Faḍāʾil al-Ṣaḥāba* (1:285 §376); al-Bazzār, *Musnad* (1:400-403 §279); al-Ājurrī, *Sharīʿa* (*Faḍāʾil ʿUmar, ibtidāʾ islām ʿUmar*).
[163]Narrated *mursal* from Saʿīd b. Jubayr by Ibn Abī Ḥātim with a sound chain miss-

ing the Companion-link as stated by al-Ghumārī in *al-Ibtihāj* (p. 158).

2
The Great Trust of the Prophet ﷺ for 'Umar

'Umar was second only to Abū Bakr al-Ṣiddīq in closeness to and approval from the Prophet ﷺ who said: "I have two ministers from the inhabitants of the heaven and two ministers from the inhabitants of the earth. The former are Jibrīl and Mīkā'īl, and the latter are Abū Bakr and 'Umar."[164] He said of the latter: "These two are [my] hearing and eyesight"[165] and instructed the Companions: "Follow those that come after me: Abū Bakr and 'Umar."[166]

[164]Narrated from Abū Sa'īd al-Khudrī by al-Tirmidhī who said it is *ḥasan*, and from Ibn 'Abbās by al-Ḥākim with a chain al-Dhahabī graded *ḥasan* in the *Siyar* (1/2:511).
[165]Narrated *mursal* from the *Tābi'ī* 'Abd Allāh b. Ḥanṭab by al-Tirmidhī, al-Ḥākim (3:69), and others cf. al-Qārī, *al-Mirqāt* (1994 ed. 10:424 §6064).
[166]Narrated from Ḥudhayfa by Aḥmad, al-Tirmidhī, and Ibn Mājah with chains al-Dhahabī said were fair *(ḥasan)* through Zā'ida b. Qudāma.

3
ʿUmar's Inheritance of the Prophetic Knowledge

The Prophet ﷺ said: "I saw [in dream] as if I was presented a vessel of milk, so I drank from it, then I gave the rest of it to ʿUmar b. al-Khaṭṭāb." They said: "What do you say its meaning is, Messenger of Allah?" He replied: "Knowledge."[167]

Another time, the Prophet ﷺ said: "As I was sleeping I saw the people being brought up for trial wearing shirts. Some of those shirts were so short they barely reached down to the breasts while some of them reached further down. I saw ʿUmar b. al-Khaṭṭāb wearing a shirt so long that he was dragging it behind him." They asked, "What is its meaning, Messenger of Allah?" The Prophet ﷺ replied: "[His high rank in] the Faith."[168]

[167]Narrated from Ibn ʿUmar by al-Bukhārī, Muslim, al-Tirmidhī, al-Dārimī, and Aḥmad.
[168]Narrated from Abū Saʿīd al-Khudrī by al-Bukhārī, Muslim, and Aḥmad.

4
'Umar's Gift of Truthful Inspiration

'Umar was given the gift of true inspiration which is the characteristic of the Friends of Allah named *kashf* or "unveiling."[169] The Prophet ﷺ said: "In the nations long before you were people who were communicated to [by the angels] *(muḥaddathūn)* although they were not Prophets. If there is anyone of them in my Community, truly it is 'Umar b. al-Khaṭṭāb."[170] This narration is elucidated by the two narrations, "Allah has engraved truth on the tongue of 'Umar and his heart"[171] and "Had there been a Prophet after me, truly, it would have been 'Umar."[172]

Tirmidhī said Ibn 'Uyayna explained "communicated to" *(muḥaddathūn)* to mean "made to understand" *(mufahhamūn)*, while in his narration Muslim added: "Ibn Wahb explained 'communicated to' as 'inspired' *(mulham)*." This is the majority's opinion according to Ibn Ḥajar who said: "'Communicated to' means 'by the angels'."[173] Following are the definitions given by al-Ḥakīm al-Tirmidhī, al-Nawawī, and Ibn Ḥajar respectively in *Khatm al-Awliyā'*, *Sharḥ Ṣaḥīḥ Muslim* and *Fatḥ al-Bārī*:

> The difference between prophethood *(nubuwwa)* and sainthood *(wilāya)* is that the former consists in speech *(kalām)* proceeding *(yanfaṣil)* from Allah ﷻ by revelation *(waḥyan)* accompanied by a spirit *(rūḥ)* from Allah. The revelation comes to pass and is sealed with the spirit. Thus does revelation come. This phenomenon is the one that obligates its confirmation [by the recipient]. Whoever rejects it has committed disbelief, since he rejected the Speech of Allah. But sainthood is for those upon whom Allah has bestowed His communication *(ḥadīth)* in a different way, connecting him with Him. The recipient thus receives communication which proceeds from Allah ﷻ in the authoritative language of truth *('alā lisān al-ḥaqq)*, accompanied by tranquility *(al-sakīna)*. It is received by the tranquility that lies in the heart of the one communicated to *(al-muḥaddath)* who then accepts it and rests therein. Someone asks: What is the differ-

[169]See the chapter on *kashf* in our *Sunna Notes I.*

[170]Narrated from Abū Hurayra and 'Ā'isha by al-Bukhārī and Muslim, the latter without the words "although they were not Prophets."

[171]Narrated from (i) Ibn 'Umar by Tirmidhī *(ḥasan ṣaḥīḥ gharīb)*; Aḥmad; Ibn Ḥibbān (15:318 §6895); (ii) Abū Dharr by Aḥmad; Abū Dāwūd; al-Ḥākim; (iii) Abū Hurayra by Aḥmad; Ibn Ḥibbān (15:312-313 §6889); Abū Ya'lā; al-Ḥākim; Ibn Abī Shayba (12:21); Ibn Abī 'Āṣim, *al-Sunna* (§1250); al-Bazzār (§2501) with a sound chain as indicated by al-Haythamī (9:66); and (iv) Bilāl and Mu'āwiya by al-Ṭabarānī, *Kabīr*. See al-Baghawī, *Sharḥ al-Sunna* (14:85); Ibn Abī 'Āṣim, *al-Sunna* (p. 567 §1247-1250); Ibn Sa'd (21:99); and Ibn al-Athīr, *Jāmi' al-Uṣūl* (9:444).

[172]Narrated from 'Uqba b. 'Amir by Aḥmad and al-Tirmidhī who graded it *ḥasan*, and by al-Ḥākim (3:85) who graded it *ṣaḥīḥ* as confirmed by al-Dhahabī. Also narrated from 'Iṣma b. Mālik by al-Ṭabarānī with a weak chain in *al-Kabīr* (17:298), as stated by al-Haythamī (9:68) and al-Munāwī.

[173]In *Fatḥ al-Bārī* (7:62:§3689).

ence between "communication" and "speech"? Communication is what emerges from the recipient's knowledge manifesting itself at the time that Allah wills. This is the communication of the inmost self *(ḥadīth al-nafs)*, such as the secret thought *(al-sirr)*. Such communication only takes place because of the love of Allah for that particular servant. It moves on to his heart with truth and the heart accepts it with tranquillity. Whoever rejects this does not commit disbelief but failure. It turns into a calamity for him and his heart becomes dulled *(yubhatu qalbuh)*. This person has rejected, in the face of truth, what the love of Allah brought him inside himself in the form of knowledge from Allah, using him as a recipient for truth and granting his heart support. Whereas the first has rejected, in the face of Allah, the very Speech of Allah, inspiration, and spirit. Furthermore, those being communicated to *(al-muḥaddathūn)* have levels. Some are given a third of prophethood, some half, and some more than that, all the way to the level of the one who receives the most – he who possesses the seal of Sainthood. Someone says: "It shocks me to say that someone other than Prophets may possess any part of prophethood!" Have you not heard the ḥadīth of the Messenger of Allah ﷺ: "Following a middle course *(al-iqtiṣād)*, taking the right way *(al-hadī)*, and keeping good demeanor *(al-samt al-ṣāliḥ)* are one in twenty-four parts of Prophethood"?[174] If *those who follow a middle course* (35:32) possess the aforementioned portions of prophethood, then what about *those foremost in good deeds* (35:32)?"[175]

The Scholars have differed concerning "communicated to." Ibn Wahb said it meant "inspired" *(mulham)*. It was said also: "Those who are right, and when they give an opinion it is as if they were communicated to, and then they give their opinion. It was said also: "The angels speak to them..." Al-Bukhārī said: "Truth comes from their tongues." This ḥadīth contains a confirmation of the miracles of the Saints *(karāmāt al-awliyā)*.[176]

The one among [Muslims] who is communicated to, if his existence is ascertained, what befalls him is not used as basis for a legal judgment,

[174]Narrated with the wording "one in twenty-five parts" from Ibn 'Abbās by Abū Dāwūd, Aḥmad, Bukhārī in *al-Adab al-Mufrad* (p. 276), Ṭabarānī, *Awsaṭ*, and al-Khaṭīb, *al-Jāmi' li Akhlāq al-Rāwī* (1991 ed. 1:230-231 §210=1983 ed. 1:155), all with a fair to weak chain because of Qābūs b. Abī Ṭabyān as indicated by Haythamī, *Majma' al-Zawā'id* (8:90). Also narrated from 'Abd Allāh b. Sarjis al-Muzanī with "gentleness" *(al-ta'uda)* instead of "taking the right way" and the wording "one in twenty-four parts" by Tirmidhī *(ḥasan gharīb)*, al-Maqdisī in *al-Mukhtāra* (9:404-405), 'Abd b. Ḥumayd in his *Musnad* (p. 183), and Khaṭīb in *Tārīkh Baghdād* (3:66) and *al-Jāmi'* (1991 ed. 1:619 §928=1983 ed. 1:394), all with a weak chain because of 'Abd Allāh b. 'Imrān. The narration from b. Sarjis corroborates and strengthens that from Ibn 'Abbās and the ḥadīth is therefore fair as stated by al-Tirmidhī and al-Khaṭīb's editor (our teacher Muḥ. 'Ajāj al-Khaṭīb) in *al-Jāmi'* (1991 ed. 1:231), but not sound as claimed by al-Ḥākim and Aḥmad Shākir in Aḥmad's *Musnad* (3:205 §2698, 2:459 §1946). Also narrated with the wording "one in seventy parts" from Ibn 'Abbās by al-Bukhārī in *al-Adab al-Mufrad* (p. 276) with a chain containing Qābūs and with the wording "one in twenty-seven parts" from Ibn 'Abbās by al-Ṭabarānī with a weak chain as stated by al-Haythamī.

[175]Al-Ḥakīm al-Tirmidhī, *Khatm al-Awliyā'* (p. 346-347), chapter ten titled "Signs of the Saints" *('alāmāt al-awliyā')*.

[176]Al-Nawawī, *Sharḥ Ṣaḥīḥ Muslim* (*Kitāb* 44, *Bab* 2, §2398).

and he is obliged to evaluate it with the Qur'ān; if it conforms to it or to the Sunna, he acts upon it, otherwise he leaves it.[177]

To the minimalist claim that since the ḥadīth states "If there is anyone in my Umma, it is 'Umar," it must follow that the number of such inspired people is at most one, namely 'Umar, Ibn Ḥajar replied with the reminder that it is wrong to think that other Communities had many but this Community only one. Thus what is meant by the ḥadīth is the perfection of the quality of *ilhām* – inspiration – in 'Umar, not its lack in other Muslims. Another proof is that Abū Bakr was even more inspired than 'Umar by the Consensus of *Ahl al-Sunna*. This is shown by Abū Bakr's unique leadership at the time of the Prophet's ﷺ death and, again, when he took up arms to exact the *zakāt* from the rebellious Arab tribes.

A miraculous illustration of the Prophet's ﷺ saying about ʿUmar took place in the latter's rule when, from his pulpit in Medina as he was delivering the Jumuʿa sermon, ʿUmar began to shout at the top of his lungs: "O Sāriya, the mountain! O Sāriya, the mountain!" in reference to Sāriya b. Zunaym al-Du'alī, one of his expeditionary commanders who was besieging Nihāwand or Fasā and Dārābajird in Persia at the time and was about to fall into an ambush, whereupon Sāriya and his troops heard him and took to the mountain, saying: "This is the voice of the Commander of the Believers!" After this they fought with their back protected and were granted victory.[178] The Qāḍī Abū Bakr b. al-ʿArabī al-Mālikī said of this miracle: "It constitutes a tremendous rank and an evident gift from Allah, and **it is present in all of the righteous incessantly until the Day of Resurrection**."[179]

[177]Ibn Ḥajar, *Fatḥ al-Bārī* (7:62-63 §3689).
[178]Narrated by al-Wāqidī in *Futūḥ al-Shām* (2:42), Ibn ʿAsākir in his *Tārīkh* (*Tahdhīb* 6:46), al-Khaṭīb in *Ruwāt Mālik* as cited by al-Suyūṭī in *Tārīkh al-Khulafā'* (p. 125= p. 134), Bayhaqī through the narrators of the *Ṣaḥīḥ* in *Dalā'il al-Nubuwwa* and *al-Iʿtiqād* (p. 314=p. 178), Abū Nuʿaym with four chains in *Dalā'il al-Nubuwwa* (p. 579 §525-528), and others cf. al-Ṭabarī, *Tārīkh* (4:178=2:553-554), Ibn al-Jawzī in *Manāqib 'Umar* (p. 172-173), Nawawī, *Tahdhīb al-Asmā'* (2:10), Ibn al-Athīr, *Usd al-Ghāba* (4:65), Ibn Kathīr, *Bidāya* (7:131-135 *isnād jayyid ḥasan*), Ibn al-Qayyim, *al-Rūḥ* (p. 239=p. 534 "Difference between insight and conjecture, *al-firāsatu wal-ṭann*"), Ibn Ḥajar, *Iṣāba* (2:3=3:6 *isnād ḥasan*), and al-Sakhāwī, *Maqāṣid* (p. 468 *isnād ḥasan*). Al-Suyūṭī in *Ziyādat al-Jāmiʿ al-Ṣaghīr*, the *Durar* (p. 288-289 §483), and the *La'āli' al-Maṣnūʿa* said the ḥadīth Master al-Quṭb al-Ḥalabī wrote a monograph on the soundness of this report.
[179]In *ʿĀriḍat al-Aḥwadhī* (13:150) his commentary on Tirmidhī's *al-Jāmiʿ al-Ṣaḥīḥ*.

5

ʿUmar's Congruities with the Divine Rulings *(Muwāfaqāt ʿUmar)*

Our liege lord ʿUmar also had the unique distinction of having many of his views confirmed verbatim by the divine speech in the Qur'ān, whereby he would say something which was soon confirmed by a subsequent revelation. Ibn Shabba addressed this subject meticulously in his *Tārīkh al-Madīna* while al-Suyūṭī listed no less than twenty such congruities in his 19-line poem entitled *Qaṭf al-Thamar fī Muwāfaqāt Sayyidinā ʿUmar* (The Plucking of Fruit On the Congruities of Our Master ʿUmar) which is part of his two-volume *al-Ḥāwī lil-Fatāwī* and has received several commentaries.[180] Among these congruities are the three mentioned by ʿUmar himself in the following report:

> I concurred with my nurturing Lord in three matters: [1] I said to the Prophet ﷺ: "Messenger of Allah! Why do we not pray behind Ibrāhīm's Station?" Whereupon was revealed the verse: *Take as your place of worship the place where Ibrāhīm stood (to pray)* (2:125); [2] the verse of the veil, I said: "Messenger of Allah! You should order your wives to cover because both the chaste and the wicked go in to see them," whereupon was revealed the verse: *And when you ask of them (the wives of the Prophet ﷺ) anything, ask it of them from behind a curtain* (33:53); [3] then the Prophet's ﷺ wives banded together in their jealousy over him so I said to them: *It may happen that his Lord, if he divorce you, will give him instead wives better than you* (66:5) whereupon that verse was revealed.[181]

The last incident is a reference to the time the Prophet ﷺ stayed away from his wives for a month after some of them played a trick on him out of jealousy. The incident is the background to the revelation of the Sura of al-Taḥrīm (Sura 66).[182]

[180] E.g. the Maghrebine Muḥaddith al-Akbar of Damascus Muḥammad Badr al-Dīn al-Ḥasanī, Fatḥ al-Wahhāb fī Muwāfaqāt Sayyidinā ʿUmar b. al-Khaṭṭāb, ed. Ṭaha Fāris (N.p.: Alukah.net, 1435/2014) = Fayḍ al-Wahhāb fī Muwāfaqāt Sayyidinā ʿUmar b. al-Khaṭṭāb, ed. ʿAbd Allāh Badrān and ʿAbd al-Raḥīm Barmū (Damascus: Dār al-Maktabī, 1423/2002); Muḥ. Aḥmad ʿĀmūwah, Jawharat al-Durar ʿalā Qaṭf al-Thamar fī Muwāfaqāt Sayyidinā ʿUmar (Ḥudayda: Dār al-Ashāʿira, 1438/ 2017); and the twelve online classes by the Egyptian Aḥmad Saʿd al-Khaṭīb posted at www.youtube.com/playlist?list=PLqCA--NpH-L9Mg-VstEu7bwd6763hdkMh as of February 2023.

[181] Narrated from Anas by al-Bukhārī and Aḥmad. Ibn Ḥibbān (15:319 §6896) and al-Ṭaḥāwī in *Mushkil al-Āthār* (4:825) narrate a slightly different version, as do Aḥmad and al-Bukhārī. It is also related from Ibn ʿUmar by Muslim and al-Ṭayālisī but with the consultation over the prisoners of the battle of Badr as the third item. See also Ibn ʿAbd al-Barr, *Istīʿāb* (2:462), Nawawī, *Tahdhīb al-Asmā'* (2:8), and al-Suyūṭī's *Tārīkh al-Khulafā'*.

[182] As detailed in our monograph *ʿĀ'isha al-Ṣiddīqa al-Nabawiyya* رضي الله عنها.

6
His Interpretation of Dreams

Almost as much as Abū Bakr, ʿUmar excelled at the interpretation of dreams, as shown in the following report. During ʿUmar's caliphate a man told him that he had seen in his dream the sun and the moon clashing, each with a large array of stars on its side. ʿUmar said: "With which did you side?" He replied: "With the moon." ʿUmar said: "You sided with the obliterated sign *(al-āyat al-mamḥuwwa)*? Then you shall never work for me!" After this, ʿUmar ostracized him. The man was killed at Ṣiffīn, on Muʿāwiya's side.[183]

[183]Narrated by Ibn Abī Shayba (6:180 §30505, 6:206 §30705) and Ibn ʿAbd al-Barr, *Istīʿāb* (1:279-280) and *Bahjat al-Jālis wa-Uns al-Majālis* cf. Ibn Farḥūn, *Dībāj* (p. 441), Ibn Ḥajar, *Iṣāba* (Ḥābis b. Saʿd), *al-Rawḍ al-Unuf* (2:7), *Sīra Ḥalabiyya* (1:463).

7
His Many Excellent Innovations

'Umar was the first Muslim ruler to establish a Public Treasury; the first to levy a customs duty named *'ushr*; the first to organize a census; the first to strike coins; the first to organize a system of canals for irrigation; and the first to formally organize provinces, cities, and districts. He established the system of guest-houses and rest-houses on major routes to and from major cities. He established schools throughout the land and allocated liberal salaries for teachers. He was the first to place the law of inheritance on a firm basis. He was the first to establish trusts, and the first ruler in history to separate the judiciary from the executive.

One of our Master 'Umar's famous excellent innovations during his caliphate was his gathering the multifarious groups praying *tarāwīḥ* into a single congregation as narrated by 'Abd al-Raḥmān b. 'Abd in the *Muwaṭṭa'* and al-Bukhārī's *Ṣaḥīḥ*:

> I went out with 'Umar b. al-Khaṭṭāb to the Mosque and there were the people, scattered separately, here a man praying by himself, there a group praying behind another man. 'Umar said, "By Allah! I think I shall gather those [worshippers] behind a single reciter as this will certainly be more appropriate." So he gathered them behind Ubay b. Ka'b. I went out with him on another night as the people were all praying according to the prayer of their [single] reciter. 'Umar said, "What a wonderful innovation this is! But the prayer you miss due to sleep is better than the one you are performing." He meant [by the missed prayer] the one prayed at the end of the night, as the people used to perform it in the beginning of the night.
>
> 'Umar gathered the people in Ramaḍān to pray behind Ubay b. Ka'b [the men] and behind Tamīm al-Dārī [the women] for twenty-one *rak'a*s, reciting some 200 verses [per *rak'a*] then leaving before the rising of the dawn[184] while Mālik narrates from Yazīd b. Rūmān that they prayed twenty-three.

Ubay b. Ka'b said: "This was never done before!" *(inna hādhā lam yakun)*. 'Umar replied: "I am fully aware of this but it is good *(qad 'alimtu wa lākin-*

[184]Narrated by 'Abd al-Razzāq (4:260 §7730): 'Abd al-Razzāq from *('an)* Dāwūd b. Qays and also other than him, from Muḥammad b. Yūsuf, from al-Sā'ib b. Yazīd, that 'Umar gathered... This is a good chain and the *matn* is confirmed independently. The claim that 'Abd al-Razzaq transmitted this report wrongly is fantasy. However, a second report has a very weak chain (4:261 §7733): 'Abd al-Razzāq *'an* al-Aslamī *'an* al-Ḥārith b. 'Abd al-Raḥmān b. Abī Dhubāb *'an* al-Sā'ib b. Yazīd : *Qāla kunnā nanṣarif min al-qiyām 'alā 'ahdi 'Umara wa-qad danā furū'u al-fajr. Wa-kāna al-qiyāmu 'alā 'ahdi 'Umara thalāthata wa-'ishrīna rak'atan* – 23 *rak'a*s. Al-Aslamī is Ibrāhīm b. Muḥammad b. Abī Yaḥyā, a principal Shaykh of 'Abd al-Razzāq who is discarded *(matrūk)* cf. *Taqrīb* and *Taḥrīr*. Cf. *Tahdhīb al-Kamāl* (2:185-191).

nahu ḥasan)!"[185] He also said: "And a fine innovation this is!" *(ni'mati al-bid'atu hādhih).*"[186]

'Umar's words about the *tarāwīḥ* or congregational supererogatory night prayers in the month of Ramadan explicitly reflect the twofold understanding of *bid'a* which Imām al-Shāfi'ī enshrined in his famous definition.[187] By the word "innovation," 'Umar meant the general congregational prayer of twenty or more *rak'a*s, which was **not** done in the time of the Prophet ﷺ but was innovated on grounds entirely sanctioned and supported by the Law. This is the essence of *al-bid'atu al-ḥasana* and this is how 'Umar, the Companions and *Tābi'īn*, al-Shāfi'ī, and the Sunni Ulema of this *Umma* understood it as indicated, for example, by al-Suyūṭī in his fatwa on *Tarāwīḥ* – which he opens with the words that the Prophet ﷺ never prayed more than eight *rak'a*s, – al-'Askārī, who stated in *al-Awā'il* or "Book of Firsts" that "the first who innovated *(sanna)* the [congregational 20-*rak'a*] prayer of Ramaḍān is 'Umar in the year 14," and al-Ṣan'ānī in *Subul al-Salām.*[188] All this understanding is confirmed in the report of 'Urwa b. al-Zubayr: "'Umar b. al-Khaṭṭāb was the first to gather the people for the [congregational] night prayer of the month of Ramaḍān; the men behind Ubay b. Ka'b and the women behind Sulaymān b. Abī Khathma."[189]

Thus it is misleading to make a figurative interpretation *(ta'wīl)* of the words of 'Umar as referring merely to "a lexical innovation as opposed to a legal innovation" in order to contrive that 'Umar said *bid'a* but did not mean *bid'a.*[190] Rather, 'Umar, Ubay, Ibn 'Umar, al-Shāfi'ī and others all meant an actual innovation by their words and also meant that it was a praiseworthy innovation sanctioned by Allah ﷻ and His Prophet ﷺ.

Accordingly, the Consensus of the Companions formed, during the last three of the four rightly-guided caliphates, that the number of *rak'a*s in the congregational *tarāwīḥ* is twenty or more even though [1] it is not established that the Prophet ﷺ ever prayed more than eight and [2] it is established that he prayed eight in Ramaḍān and outside it. However, as Shaykh al-Islam al-Taqī al-Subkī, al-Zarkashī, and al-Suyūṭī stated, **nowhere in the *Ṣaḥīḥ* is the number of *rak'at*s prayed by the Prophet ﷺ in the first three nights of Ramaḍān, before he stopped, specified.**[191] Those who, in our time, incorrectly inferred from the above facts that the Sunna in congre-

[185]Cited in Ibn Rajab, *Jāmi' al-'Ulūm wal-Ḥikam* (al-Arnā'ūṭ ed. 2:128=al-Zuḥaylī ed. 2:50), misspelt "I have done it" *('amiltu)* in al-Zuḥaylī's edition.
[186]Narrated from 'Abd al-Raḥmān b. 'Abd by Mālik, *Muwaṭṭa' (ni'mati al-bid'atu hādhih)* and al-Bukhārī in his *Ṣaḥīḥ (ni'ma al-bid'atu hādhih).*
[187]See http://www.livingislam.org/n/sdb_e.html, article titled "The Sunni Definition of Bid'a as either Good or Bad" and the section titled "Al-Shāfi'ī's Division of *Bid'a* into 'Good' and 'Bad'" in our *Sunna Notes II.*
[188]Cf. *al-Maṣābīḥ fī Ṣalāt al-Tarāwīḥ* (p. 12-13), al-'Askarī, *al-Awā'il* (1:225-226), and al-Ṣan'ānī, *Subul al-Salām* (2:10).
[189]Narrated from 'Urwa by al-Bayhaqī in *al-Sunan al-Kubrā* (2:494) cf. al-Suyūṭī, *al-Maṣābīḥ* (p. 17-18).
[190] See *Bid'ah Hasanah* series at https://www.youtube.com/watch?v=OgWq9-3l1yg
[191]Al-Suyūṭī, *al-Maṣābīḥ* (p. 9 and 19).

gational *tarāwīḥ* prayers should necessarily be kept to eight *rak'a*s have therefore spoken without knowledge, violated the Prophetic instruction to adhere to the Sunna of the rightly-guided Caliphs, broken the ranks of *ijmā'*, and committed innovation. Al-Suyūṭī said: "Surely, if the exact number of the *Tarāwīḥ* had been a subject of textual stipulation, it would have been impermissible to the first generations to add anything to it. The people of Medina and the early Muslims were certainly more scrupulous than to commit such an act!"[192]

Similarly, Abū Umāma al-Bāhilī ⬥ said: "Truly Allah ordained for you the fast of Ramaḍān but He did not ordain for you its standing in prayer. Its standing in prayer is only something which you all innovated, therefore, persist in it and do not abandon it, for certain people among the Israelites innovated something in pursuit of the good pleasure of Allah, then Allah reproached them for abandoning it." Then he recited: *But monasticism they invented – We ordained it not for them – only seeking the pleasure of Allah, and they observed it not with right observance* (57:27).[193] This is an explicit text showing that the *Salaf* understood that the innovation of monasticism was not bad in itself but only because it was not observed properly by those who had innovated it.

[192]*Ibid.* (p. 14).
[193]Narrated from Zakariyyā b. Abī Maryam by al-Ṭabarī in his *Tafsīr* (27:240).

8
His Invention of the Hijrī Calendar

One day Abū Mūsā al-Ash'arī, the governor of Baṣra at the time, wrote to 'Umar complaining that the ordinances, instructions, and letters from the Caliph were undated and therefore gave rise to problems linked to the sequence of their implementation. Because of this and other similar problems of undatedness, 'Umar convened an assembly of scholars and advisors to consider the question of calendar reform. The deliberations of this assembly resulted in the combined opinion that Muslims should have a calendar of their own. The point that was next considered was from when should the new Muslim calendar era begin. Some suggested that the era should begin from the birth of the Prophet ﷺ while others suggested that it should begin from the time of his death. 'Alī suggested that the era should begin from the date the Muslims migrated from Mecca to Medina, and this was agreed upon. The next question considered was the month from which the new era should start. Some suggested that it should start from the month of Rabī' al-Awwal, some from Rajab, others from Ramaḍān, others from Dhūl-Ḥijja. 'Uthmān suggested that the new era should start from the month of Muḥarram because that was the first month in the Arabic calendar of that time. This was agreed upon. Since the Migration had taken place in the month of Rabī' al-Awwal, two months and eight days after the first of Muḥarram that year, the date was pushed back by two months and eight days, and the new *Hijrī* calendar began with the first day of Muḥarram in the year of the Migration rather than from the actual date of the Migration.[194]

[194]Thus narrated by Abū Khaythama in his *Tārikh* as cited by Ibn Ḥajar in *Fatḥ al-Bārī* (*Manāqib, min ayn arrakhū al-Tārikh*) cf. al-Sakhāwī, *al-I'lān wal-Tawbīkh* (p. 78-80) citing al-Faḍl b. Dukayn's *Tārikh* and, from him, al-Ḥākim but the latter without mention of the *mawlid.*

9

His Finalizing of the Categorical Prophetic Prohibition of *Mut'a* (Temporary Marriage)

'Umar reiterated the Prophetic prohibition of the Jāhilī practice of *mut'a* or temporary marriage, which the Prophet ﷺ had first made at the time of Khaybar in the year 7/628.[195]

The Prophet ﷺ termed marriage "half the Religion"[196] and said its rescinding was "the most detestable to Allah of all permitted acts."[197] He warned the profligate *(dhawwāqūn)* who practice repetitious divorce and marriage, as well as the man who marries with divorce in view, that they shall never experience even the smell of Paradise. There is no common ground whatsoever between those given to those practices today, and the Companions who were temporarily permitted *mut'a* by a special wartime dispensation of the Prophet ﷺ.

'Umar only banned temporary marriage after the Prophet ﷺ himself did. Ibn 'Umar narrated that 'Umar said from the pulpit: "The Messenger of Allah ﷺ forbade *mut'a* after allowing it on three occasions, so if I see any married person practicing it I shall order his stoning, unless he produces four witnesses saying that the Messenger of Allah ﷺ allowed it."[198] Ibn 'Umar also considered *mut'a* strictly prohibited *ḥarām* (as reported by Ibn Ḥazm and Ibn Qudama) and tantamount to fornication *(sifāḥ)* as narrated by Ibn Abī Shayba and 'Abd al-Razzāq.[199] Asked about *mut'a* at one point, Ibn 'Umar became angry and answered: "In the time of the Messenger of Allah ﷺ we were neither adulterers nor fornicators!"[200]

[195]On the abrogated character of *mut'a* see, for example, *I'lā' al-Sunan* (11:58-59).
[196]A "fair" (al-Ḥākim, al-Dhahabī, al-Haythamī in *al-Ifṣāḥ 'an Aḥādīth al-Nikāḥ* al-Suyūṭī) to "weak" (Ibn Ḥajar, al-'Irāqī, and Ibn al-Jawzī) narration from Anas that the Prophet ﷺ said: "When the servant of Allah marries he has completed one half of the Religion. Thereafter let him fear Allah regarding the remaining half" [al-Bayhaqī, *Shu'ab al-Īmān*]; "Whoever marries has achieved one half of the Religion. Thereafter let him fear Allah regarding the other half" [Ibn al-Jawzī, *al-'Ilal al-Mutanāhya*]; "Whoever marries has achieved one half of belief. Thereafter let him fear Allah regarding the other half" [Ṭabarānī in the three *Mu'jams*]; "Whomever Allah has granted a righteous wife He has supported in upholding one half of his Religion. Thereafter let him fear Allah regarding the other half" [al-Ḥākim, *al-Mustadrak* and al-Bayhaqī, *Shu'ab al-Īmān*].
[197] Narrated from (i) Ibn 'Umar by Abū Dāwūd, Ibn Mājah, Ḥākim (*ṣaḥīḥ al-isnād*) "per the criterion of Muslim" according to al-Dhahabī; (ii) Mu'ādh by al-Dāraquṭnī; and, in *mursal* mode, (iii) Muḥārib b. Dithār by Abū Dāwūd and Bayhaqī, *Sunan*. It is a sound hadith per Ibn al-Mulaqqin, *al-Badr al-Munīr* (8:65). Sakhāwī in *al-Maqāṣid al-Ḥasana* said it is also narrated from 'Alī and Abū Mūsā al-Ash'arī.
[198]Narrated in Ibn Mājah's *Sunan*. There is no other ḥadīth narrated from Ibn 'Umar in the Nine Books with the word *mut'a* in it, and Allah knows best.
[199]Ibn Ḥazm, *al-Muḥallā* (9:520), Ibn Qudāma, *al-Mughnī* (6:644), Ibn Abī Shayba *Muṣannaf* (1:22b), 'Abd al-Razzāq (7:502).
[200]Narrated by Sa'īd b. Manṣūr in his *Sunan* (3/1:210).

Others of the major Companions also categorically banned *mut'a* such as 'Alī who said to Ibn 'Abbās: "The Messenger of Allah ﷺ forbade temporary marriage during Khaybar and the consumption of the meat of the domestic asses."[201]

Sabra b. Ma'bad al-Juhanī said: "The Messenger of Allah ﷺ permitted us *mut'a* the year of the Conquest when we entered Mecca and we did not exit it before we had been prohibited from it."[202] Sabra also narrated that the Prophet ﷺ said at the Farewell Pilgrimage: "People! I had permitted you temporary marriage before; but now, whoever of you has any part in it must part with her. Do not take back anything which you may have given them. Allah ﷻ has forbidden it until the day of Resurrection!"[203] 'Alī's narration places the original timing of this Prophetic prohibition at the time of the campaign of Khaybar (year 7) while Sabra's two narrations tell us the Prophet ﷺ temporarily relaxed it at the time of the conquest of Mecca (year 8) then reinstated it, then finalized it once and for all at the Farewell Pilgrimage. There had been another relaxation of the prohibition as inferred from the narration of 'Umar already mentioned, "The Messenger of Allah ﷺ forbade *mut'a* after allowing it on three occasions...."

The above narrations thus abrogate the narration of Ibn Mas'ūd permitting *mut'a*. The proof to this was adduced by Imām Aḥmad in his narration that Ibn Mas'ūd said, "when we were young men" *(shabāb)* whereas at the time of Khaybar his age was over forty.[204] Imām al-Nawawī said: "The truth of the matter is that it was permitted and prohibited on two occasions. It was permitted before Khaybar, then prohibited, then permitted on the day of Awṭāṣ, then prohibited forever after three days of the event."

Ibn 'Abbās himself reportedly explained *mut'a* thus: "Temporary marriage was at the beginning of Islam. A man comes by a town where he has no acquaintances so he marries for a fixed time depending on his stay in the town, the woman looks after his provisions and prepares his food, until the verse was revealed: *Except to your wives or what your right hands possess* (23:5)" Ibn 'Abbās said: "Thereafter, any relationship beyond these two cases is strictly forbidden."[205] This is also the explanation of the Mother of the believers 'Ā'isha for this verse. The more famous position of Ibn 'Abbās was that he was lenient towards those who practiced *mut'a*, for which 'Alī rebuked him (in the narration cited above), but al-Qāḍī 'Iyāḍ avers that Ibn 'Abbās then changed his mind and adopted the view of the rest of the Companions. Another Qur'anic proof against *mut'a* is the order to seek

[201]Narrated in the Nine Books except Abū Dāwūd.
[202]Narrated by Muslim.
[203]Narrated from Sabra by Abū Dāwūd and Aḥmad.
[204]This was mentioned by al-Bayhaqī in *Ma'rifat al-Sunan* (10:175-176 §14098).
[205]Narrated from Ibn 'Abbās by al-Tirmidhī with a weak chain because of Mūsā b. 'Ubayda.

approval from the wife's relatives before marrying her,[206] a condition ignored by those who practice *mut'a*.

Regarding the verse misconstrued by some in order to support the permissibility of *mut'a, So whatever you enjoy from them, give them their recompense, this is an obligation* (4:24), Ibn Kathīr interpreted the generality of the verse to include temporary marriage, saying: "There is no doubt that it was permitted at the dawn of Islam and became forbidden afterwards." This contradicts the position of the *Jumhūr* and at their vanguard Imām al-Shāfi'ī, that the Sunna never abrogates the Qur'ān but only vice-versa. Ibn al-Jawzī said concerning the same verse: "Some commentators have said that what was meant by this verse is temporary marriage and that it was then superseded with what was reported from the Prophet ﷺ when he forbade temporary marriage. This interpretation has no basis. The Prophet ﷺ permitted it then forbade it with his own words, so his later prohibition supersedes the permissibility. As for the verse, it does not touch on temporary marriage. It only relates to enjoyment through proper marriage."

The view of the Prophetic final abrogation of *mut'a* was also the position of Abū Hurayra and Ibn Ḥazm. Al-Shawkānī said: "The fact that some Companions were not aware of this does not negate the large number of Companions who were aware and who have acted upon the prohibition and proclaimed it." The ruling that *mut'a* is absolutely and unconditionally prohibited upon all until the Day of Judgment is the unanimous position of the Sunni Scholars. The Four Schools consider the *mut'a* contract or arrangement null and void. They held, in the light of the Prophetic prohibition, that the practice of *mut'a* consists in a form of fornication *(zinā)* as cited from Imam Ja'far al-Ṣādiq by al-Bayhaqī and Ibn Rushd in *Bidāyat al-Mujtahid*, contrary to the enormities attributed to him in Shī'ī works such as *Furū' al-Kāfī*, *Tahdhīb al-Aḥkām*, and *Minhāj al-Ṣādiqīn*. And Allah knows best.

[206] Per the mass-transmitted hadith, "There is no *nikāḥ* without a guardian."

10
Statutory Penalty *(Ḥadd)* by Lapidation *(Rajm)*

Imām al-Ḥaramayn said: "It is possible for the writing *(rasm)* to be abrogated while the ruling remains, the ruling to be abrogated and the writing to remain, and for them both to be abrogated."[207] The Qur'anic verse of *rajm* was abrogated in recitation *(lafẓ)* and writing *(rasm)* but not in application *(ḥukm)*. This is known through the *mutawātir* practice of the Prophet ﷺ and his four Caliphs. 'Umar ؓ announced in Minā:

> Allah ﷻ sent Muḥammad ﷺ with the truth. He revealed the Book to him. Among what He revealed to him was the verse of *rajm*. We recited it, learnt it, and the Prophet ﷺ did *rajm* and so did we after him. I reckon that in due time someone will come up and say: "We do not find the verse of *rajm* in the Book of Allah," whereupon they will follow misguidance by leaving a categorical obligation Allah revealed. *Rajm* is incumbent against any man or woman that commits adultery if one is married, if the proof is absolutely established, or if there is pregnancy, or confession. I swear by Allah that were it not that people might claim that 'Umar added something to the Book of Allah, I would write it down![208]

Yet 'Umar always sought a way out from capital punishment and always tried to find a legal excuse for perpetrators so as to let them escape with their lives.[209] This took place many times in his caliphate,[210] notably in times of drought.[211] He said, "For me to cancel the statutory penalties on the basis of the *shubuhāt* (ambiguities, uncertainties) is dearer than to implement them on the strength of the *shubuhāt*;"[212] "Verily for me to err in forgiving is dearer to me than that I should err in punishing."[213]

[207]Ibn al-Juwaynī, *al-Waraqāt*, "Divisions of Abrogations."
[208]Narrated in the Nine Books.
[209] ʿAbd al-Razzāq, *Muṣannaf* (7:402); Ibn Ḥazm, *Muḥallā* (8:253).
[210] ʿAbd al-Razzāq, *Muṣannaf* (7:409, 10:224-225); Ibn Abī Shayba, *Muṣannaf* (9:567, 10:23-25); Bayhaqī, *Sunan* (8:236, 8:276); al-Baghawī, *Sharḥ al-Sunna* (10:292-293).
[211] ʿAbd al-Razzāq, *Muṣannaf* (10:242); Ibn Abī Shayba, *Muṣannaf* (Salafiyya ed. 10:28); Ibn Ḥazm, *Muḥallā* (11:343)
[212] Abū Yūsuf, *al-Kharāj* (Cairo: al-Maṭbaʿat al-Salafiyya, 1927; rept. Beirut: Dār al-Maʿrifa, 1399/1979) p. 153; Ibn Abī Shayba, *Muṣannaf* (2;129).
[213] Also narrated from ʿĀʾisha (with the wording "for the imam to err") by Abū Yūsuf, *al-Kharāj* (p.153); al-Bayhaqī, *Sunan* (8:238). All this was also the position of Ibn Masʿūd, Abū Hurayra and ʿĀʾisha and the Companions' consensus formed over it, followed by that of the jurists per Ibn al-Mundhir in *al-Awsaṭ* (2:669) and *al-Ijmāʿ* (p. 143) and Ibn al-Humām, *Fatḥ al-Qadīr* (5:32) with the sole exception of Ibn Ḥazm. See Ibrāhīm Nāṣir al-Bishr, *Darʾ al-Ḥudūd bil-Shubuhāt fī al-Sharīʿat al-Islāmiyya*, unpubl. diss. (Mecca: Jāmiʿat Umm al-Qurā, 1408/1988) pp. 21-57.

11
The 10% Maximum Customs or Import Duty *('Ushr)*

'Umar was the first Muslim ruler to levy *'ushr*, the Customs or Import Duty. It was levied on the goods of the traders of other countries who chose to trade in the Muslim dominions, at up to 10% of the goods imported and on a reciprocal basis. *'Ushr* was levied in a way to avoid hardships, and only on merchandise meant for sale, not goods imported for consumption or for personal use. Goods valued at two hundred dirhams or less were not subject to *'ushr*. Instructions were issued to the officials that no personal luggage was to be searched, and *'ushr* was applied only to goods that were declared as being for the purpose of trade. The rate varied for Muslim and non-Muslim citizens of the Muslim dominions. If the former imported goods for the purpose of trade, they paid a lower rate of *'ushr*: 2½%, that is, the same rate as for *zakāt*. Hence, this was regarded as part of the *zakāt* and not as a separate tax. *Dhimmīs* or non-Muslim citizens of the Muslim dominions who imported goods for the purpose of trade paid a *'ushr* of 5%. In order to avoid double taxation, it was established that if the *'ushr* had been paid once on imported goods, and then these goods were subsequently taken abroad then brought back into the Muslim dominions within the same year, no additional *'ushr* was to be levied on such re-imported goods.[214]

[214] See Muḥammad Rawwās Qal'ahjī, *Mawsū'at Fiqh 'Umar b. al-Khaṭṭāb*, 3rd ed. (Beirut: Dār al-Nafā'is, 11406/1986) pp. 650-656.

12
Other Firsts

Some of ‘Umar’s innovations mentioned in al-Ṭabarānī and Abū Hilāl al-‘Askarī’s *Awā’il* (“Book of Firsts”) and al-Ṭabarī’s *Tārīkh* among others:

1. Establishment of *Bayt al-Māl* or public treasury.
2. Establishment of courts of justice and appointment of judges.
3. The determination of the Hijra calendar which continues to this day.
4. Assumption of the title of *Amīr al-Mu’minīn.*
5. Organization of the War Department.
6. Putting army reserves on the payroll.
7. Establishment of the Land Revenue Department.
8. Survey and assessment of lands.
9. Census.
10. Building of Canals.
11. Founding of the cities of Kufa, Basra, Fustat and Mosul in Iraq, and the administrative caliphal province of al-Jazīra.
12. Division of conquered countries into provinces.
13. Imposition of customs duties.
14. Taxation of the produce of the sea and appointment of officials for its collection.
15. Permission to traders of foreign lands to trade in the country.
16. Organization of jails.
17. Use of the whip.
18. Making rounds at night to inquire into the condition of the people.
19. Organization of the Police Department.
20. Establishment of military barracks at strategic points.
21. Distinction of pedigree and non-pedigree horses.
22. Employment of secret reports and emissaries.
23. Rest-houses on the way from Mecca to Medina for the comfort of travelers.
24. Provision for the care and bringing up of foundlings.

25. Organization of guest-houses in different cities.
26. The ruling that Arabs, whether Muslims or non-Muslims, could not be made slaves.
27. Stipends for the poor among the Jews and the Christians.
28. Establishment of schools.
29. Stipends for school teachers and public lecturers.
30. Persuading Abū Bakr to collect the Qur'ān and execution of the work under his own care.
31. Formulation of the principle of *qiyās* or judicial analogy.
32. More exact division of inheritance.
33. Insertion of the formula "Prayer is better that sleep" in the call to the dawn prayer. Imām Mālik stated that on 'Umar's suggestion the words "I testify that Muḥammad is the Messenger of Allah" were added to the *adhān*, and likewise the words "Prayer is better than Sleep" to the *adhān* for the dawn prayer. However, the more correct report is that it is Bilāl who first spoke the latter formula in the call to the dawn prayer and the Prophet ﷺ retained it.[215]
34. Ordaining the holding of *tarāwih* prayers in one congregation for men and one for women. Later in 'Umar's time, a single congregation was formed.[216]
35. Three divorces pronounced at one session declared binding.[217]
36. Provision of the punishment for drunkenness with eighty stripes.
37. Levy of *zakāt* on horses of merchandise.

[215]As stated by al-Zuhrī in Ibn Mājah's *Sunan* and Sa'īd b. al-Musayyab in Aḥmad's *Musnad*, and narrated with sound chains from Bilāl by Ibn Mājah and from 'Abd Allāh b. Zayd by Aḥmad. The report that mentions 'Umar is in Mālik's *Muwaṭṭa'*, book of the Call to prayer, without chain.
[216]*Tarāwīh* in congregation is a *sunna kifāya* for which the Prophet ﷺ did not specify the number of *rak'a*s but stipulated that "whoever prays behind its imām will have the reward of praying all night" [Narrated from Abū Dharr in the four *Sunan* – al-Tirmidhī said it is *ḥasan ṣaḥīḥ* – as well as Aḥmad, al-Dārimī, al-Bayhaqī in *al-Sunan al-Kubrā* (1:406 §1289) and al-Nasā'ī in *al-Sunan al-Kubrā* (3:83 §1373)]. Al-Tirmidhī relates from Imām Aḥmad that he said: "Nothing has been formally stipulated about its number." Accordingly, they varied from 8 – in imitation of what is narrated from the Prophet's ﷺ personal practice – to twenty in the time of the rightly-guided Caliphs and as per the Companions' consensus, to forty or thirty-six in Medina at the time of al-Aswad b. Yazīd then Nāfi' and Mālik, all apart from *witr*. See al-Suyūṭī's *al-Miṣbāḥ fī Salāt al-Tarāwīḥ* for the Shāfi'ī position and al-Lacknawī's *Tuḥfat al-Akhyār* (p. 93-138) for the Ḥanafī one.
[217]This is the consensus of the *Umma* except Aḥmad b. Taymiyya.

38. Levy of *zakāt* on the Christians of Banū Taghlib in lieu of the non-Muslim duty *(jizya)*.[218]
39. Method of making trusts.
40. Consensus of opinion on four *takbīr*s in funeral prayers.
41. Organization of sermons in mosques.
42. Giving salaries to imāms and *mu'adhdhin*s.
43. Provision of light in mosques at night.
44. Provision of punishment for writing satires and lampoons.
45. Prohibition of the mention of women's names in lyric poems although the custom was very ancient in Arabia.

[218]It was *zakāt* in name but double the normal amount according to their own request – so as to avoid being on a par with non-Arab Christians – as narrated by al-Bayhaqī in *al-Sunan al-Kubrā* (9:216-218 §18559-18561), but its *raison d'être* remained the *jizya* (*al-Sunan al-Kubrā* 9:187 §18410). ‘Umar also imposed the condition that they must not raise their children as Christians. Cf. Ibn Qutayba, *al-Ma'ārif* (p. 318).

13
His Superlative Administration of Justice

Our Master 'Umar took pains to provide effective and speedy justice for the people. He set up an effective system of judicial administration under which justice was administered according to the principles of Islam. *Qāḍīs* were appointed at all administrative levels for the administration of justice and were chosen for their integrity and learning in Islamic law. High salaries were paid to them and they were appointed from among the wealthy and those of high social standing so as not to be influenced by the social position of any litigants. The qadis were not allowed to engage in trade.

From time to time, 'Umar used to issue *firmans* or edicts laying down the principles for the administration of justice. One of his *firmans* read:

> Glory to Allah! Truly Justice is an important obligation to Allah and to man! You have been charged with this responsibility. Discharge this responsibility so that you may win the approbation of Allah and the good will of the people. Treat the people equally in your presence, and in your decisions, so that the weak despair not of justice, and the high-placed harbor no hope of favoritism. The onus of proof lies on the plaintiff while the party who denies must do so on oath. Compromise is permissible, provided that it does not turn the unlawful into something lawful, and the lawful into something unlawful. Let nothing prevent you from changing your previous decision if after consideration you feel that the previous decision was incorrect. When you are in doubt about a question and find nothing concerning it in the Qur'ān or the Sunna of the Prophet ﷺ, ponder the question over and over again. Ponder over the precedents and analogous cases and then decide by analogy. A term should be fixed for the person who wants to produce witnesses. If he proves his case, discharge for him his right, otherwise the suit should be dismissed. All Muslims are trustworthy except those who have been punished with flogging, those who have borne false witness, or those of doubtful integrity.[219]

Al-Dārimī in the *Muqaddima* of his *Sunan* narrates that when our liege lord 'Umar appointed Abū Mūsā al-Ash'arī governor of Basra, he listed keeping streets clean among his duties.

[219] Al-Ṭanṭāwī, *Akhbār 'Umar* (pp. 172-174) citing al-Jāḥiẓ, *al-Bayān wal-Tabyīn*; Ibn Qutayba, *'Uyūn al-Akhbār*; and others.

14
Little Sleep and Permanent Fasting

Ibn Kathīr said in his *Bidāya*: "'Umar would pray *'ishā* with the people then enter his house and not cease praying until dawn, and he did not die before acquiring the habit of fasting permanently."[220] 'Umar wrote to all his deputies around the Muslim world: "Your most important urgent matter, in my view, is prayer. Whoever guards it well and persistently has guarded his Religion and whoever is careless with it is even more careless *(aḍya')* with everything else."[221]

Al-Ḥākim said he heard Imām Abū Bakr Aḥmad b. Isḥāq al-Ṣibghī say:

> I saw in my sleep as if I was in a house in which there was 'Umar with people around him asking him questions. He motioned to me to answer them. I kept being asked and answering while he would say, every time, "You are right, next!; you are right, next!" *(aṣabta imḍi, aṣabta imḍi)*. I said, "Commander of the faithful, what is the salvation from the world or the safe way out of it?" He said to me with his finger: *"Al-du'ā'."* I asked him the same question a second time. He collected himself as if he were prostrating due to humility and said: *"Al-du'ā'."*[222]

[220]Ibn Kathīr, *Bidāya* (7:135). See our *Sunna Notes II: The Excellent Innovation in the Qur'ān and Hadith* for the documentation of the permanent fasting of many major Companions, Successors and subsequent imams of the *Salaf* and *Khalaf*.
[221]Narrated by Mālik in his *Muwaṭṭa'*.
[222]Cited by al-Dhahabī in the *Siyar* (Fikr ed. 12:126).

15
His Concern for the Welfare of Slaves, the Aged and Women

Our liege lord 'Umar used to go out at night searching for people in need of help.[223] Imām Mālik narrated that 'Umar would go to the villages every seventh day of the week *(sabt)* and, if he found a slave doing work that was too much for him, lightened it for him.[224] It is related he once said to ʿAmr b. al-ʿĀṣ: "ʿAmr, when did you start turning people into slaves whom their mothers gave birth to as free men?"[225]

One time ʿUmar went out with people and he passed by an old woman who hailed him so he stopped to listen to her. Time passed until someone said to him, "Commander of the believers, you have held up the men of the Quraysh for this old woman?" ʿUmar replied, "Woe to you! Do you know who she is? This is a woman whose complaint Allah heard from above seven heavens! This is Khawla bint Tha'laba concerning whom Allah revealed, *The One God has certainly heard the words of her that pleads with you about her husband and complains to the One God while the One God is hearing your exchange* (al-Mujādila 58:1). By Allah! I swear that if I were to stand until night fell I would not part with her except for prayer but then I would come back to her."[226]

One night, 'Umar heard a young woman reciting in her house:

This long night begins and ends with tears,
Keeping me sleepless without bedmate to play with.
Were it not for fear of Allah with Whom nothing compares,
The sides of this bed would have shaken out of joint!

(Taṭāwala hādhā al-laylu wa(i)khḍalla jānibuhu

[223]Ibn al-Jawzī, *Sirat 'Umar* (p. 71); al-Samhūdī, *Tārīkh al-Madīna* (2:759); Ibn Qudāma, *al-Mughnī* (7:301). Cf. Malik's *Muwaṭṭa'* ('Abd al-Bāqī ed. 2:980).
[224]In *al-Muwaṭṭa'* ('Abd al-Bāqī ed. 2:980 toward the end of book 54, *Isti'dhān*).
[225]Narrated by Ibn ʿAbd al-Ḥakam in *Futūḥ Miṣr wa-Akhbāruhā* (p. 114) and Ibn al-Jawzī in *Tārīkh ʿUmar* (p. 120) cf. *Kanz al-ʿUmmāl* (12:660), all with a broken chain through Abū 'Abda Yūsuf b. 'Abdah al-Azdī whose narrations from Thābit (such as this one) are disclaimed *(munkar)*. In addition the content itself is disclaimed such as 'Umar commanding for both 'Abd Allāh b. 'Amr and his father to be lashed and insulting them. Yet modern writers made it famous such as Sayyid Quṭb in *Fī Ẓilāl al-Qur'ān* (3:1364, 6:3969), Maḥmūd 'Aqqād in *'Abqariyyat 'Umar* and Zakariyyā al-Kāndihlawī in *Ḥayāt al-Ṣaḥāba*.
[226] Narrated from Abū Yazīd al-Madanī by Qadi Ismāʿīl al-Jahḍamī al-Mālikī in his *Aḥkām al-Qur'ān* and Ibn Abī Ḥātim in his *Tafsīr*, both under this verse; al-Bayhaqī, *al-Asmā' wal-Ṣifāt* (2:322 §886); Ibn Ḥajar, *Iṣāba* (8:115), entry on Khawla bint Mālik b. Thaʿlaba al-Fihriyya. Her husband was her much older paternal cousin Aws b. al-Ṣāmit as narrated from Khawla by Aḥmad, *Musnad* (45:300-301 §27319). The anthropomorphists pounced on the wording of *from above seven skies* to construe them in the literal sense in defense of their heresy.

wa'arraqanī an lā ḍajī'a ulā'ibuhu
fa-lawlā ḥidhāra Allāhi lā shay'a mithlahu
lazu'zi'a min hādhā al-sarīri jawānibuhu.)

'Umar said: "What is wrong with you?" She said: "I have been without my husband for four months and I miss him fiercely *(ishtaqtu ilayh)*!" He said: "Are you going to do wrong?" She said: "Allah forbid!" He said: "Control yourself the time it takes my mail to reach him!" Then he sent for him. After this he went to see Ḥafṣa and asked her: "I need your help with something that worries me. How long does it take a woman to really miss her husband?" She bowed her head in shame. He insisted: "Truly, Allah is not ashamed of the truth!" She motioned by hand, "Three, four months." After this, 'Umar ordered that no troops should be kept away for more than four months.[227]

[227]Narrated by 'Abd al-Razzāq (7:151) cf. Ibn Qudāma, *al-Mughnī* (7:31 or 7:301), *Ibn al-Jawzī, Sīrat 'Umar* (p. 71), and al-Samhūdī, *Tārīkh al-Madīna* (2:759).

16
His Retraction on the Pulpit after Being Publicly Corrected by a Woman

As he was delivering a *khuṭba* ʿUmar said, "Do not exaggerate in the dowries of women. If it were a generous act in this life or Godfearingness in the presence of Allah, the Prophet of Allah would have been more assiduous in it than you. The Messenger of Allah ﷺ never exceeded twelve ounces. One might spend a lot and then have rancor in his heart about it later."[228] A tall woman stood up and said, "It is not up to you, Ibn al-Khaṭṭāb! Verily Allah says *even if you have given one of them a quintal*[229]—of gold—*then it is illicit for you to take back anything from it* (al-Nisāʾ 4:20 per the reading of Ibn Masʿūd)." He said, "Verily a woman disputed with ʿUmar and she beat him."[230]

In another version he said, "so let it not reach me that any of you remits or receives more than what the Messenger of Allah remitted, or else I shall put the difference in the treasury," after which he came down, whereupon a woman of the Quraysh stood before him and said, "Commander of the believers, is the Book of Allah more deserving to be followed or your statement?" He said, "Nay, the Book of Allah! Why?" She said, "You just forbade people from exaggerating in the dowries of women whereas Allah Most High says in His Book, *and if you have given one of them a quintal, do not take back anything from it*," whereupon ʿUmar said two or three times, "Everyone is more knowledgeable than ʿUmar." Then he went back to the pulpit and said, "I had forbidden you to exaggerate in the dowries of women. Behold! Let every man do as he sees fit with his wealth."[231]

In another version he replied, "A woman said what is correct and a man made a mistake."[232] In another he said to himself audibly, "Everyone

228 "Narrated to here only from Abū al-ʿAjfāʾ Harim b. Musayyab al-Sulamī al-Baṣrī in the four *Sunan* and al-Tirmidhī rated it *ḥasan ṣaḥīḥ*" per al-Zaylaʿī in *Takhrīj Aḥādīth al-Kashshāf* (1:295-296). Also al-Dārimī. This is rigorously authentic per al-Dāraquṭnī, *ʿIlal* (2:233-239 §241).

229 "I.e. 12,000 dirhams [of silver] or 1,000 dinars [of gold]" in al-Wāḥidī, *Basīṭ* (Āl ʿImrān 3:14).

230 Narrated from Abū ʿAbd al-Raḥmān al-Sulamī by ʿAbd al-Razzāq, *Muṣannaf* 6:180 §10420) and Ibn al-Mundhir in his *Tafsīr* under this verse.

231 Narrated from (i) al-Shaʿbī by Saʿīd b. Manṣūr in his *Sunan* (1:195 §598) and al-Ṭaḥāwī, *Mushkil al-Āthār* 13:57-58 §5059); (ii) in short form, Bakr b. ʿAbd Allāh al-Muzanī by Saʿīd b. Manṣūr, *Sunan* (1:195-196 §599)—Bayhaqī rated the latter a strong *mursal* chain, *Sunan* (7:380 §14335); also, with the wording "never exceeded 400 dirhams" and "all people have more understanding than ʿUmar," from al-Shaʿbī, from (iii) Masrūq by Ibn Abī Khaythama, *al-Tārīkh al-Kabīr* (3:116-117 §4064) and by Abū Yaʿlā al-Mawṣilī (see Haythamī, *al-Maqṣad al-ʿAlī fī Zawāʾid Abī Yaʿlā al-Mawṣilī* (2:335 §756), and "its chain is strong" per al-Zaylaʿī, *Takhrīj* (1:296) and Suyūṭī, *Durr*; "good and strong" per Ibn Kathīr in his *Tafsīr* under this verse; also from al-Shaʿbī, from (iv) Shurayḥ in the entry on him by Abū Nuʿaym, *Ḥilya* per Ibn Ḥajar, *al-Kāfī al-Shāf fī Takhrīj Aḥādīth al-Kashshāf* (p. 71).

232 Narrated from ʿAbd Allāh b. Muṣʿab by al-Zubayr b. Bakkar in *al-Akhbār al-*

knows more than you, even women!" In another version he said to his companions, "You hear me say such as this and after that you do not point out my mistake to me? You leave it to a woman who is not of the more knowledgeable ones?"[233]

Muwaffaqiyyāt, ed. Sāmī Makkī al-ʿĀnī, 2nd ed. (Beirut: ʿĀlam al-Kutub, 1416/1996) pp. 507-508 §430 and Ibn ʿAbd al-Barr, *Jāmiʿ* (1:530 §864). See also ʿAlī al-Ṭanṭāwī, *Akhbār 'Umar* (p. 393).

[233] al-Zaylaʿī, *Takhrīj Aḥādīth al-Kashshāf*, ed. ʿAbd Allāh Saʿd, 4 vols. (Riyadh: Dār Ibn Khuzayma, 1414/1994) 1:294-295.

17
His Constant Weeping and Emotional Nature

Ibn al-Mubārak reports in *al-Zuhd* that 'Umar left his home another night to guard the city when, seeing a lamp in a home, he approached it only to find an old woman gathering wool to spin and saying:

Upon Muḥammad the prayers of the righteous!
May the divinely-chosen, elect ones bless you!
I passed the night awake, crying before dawn;
Oh, if I only knew – and death comes by turns;
Shall the [final] abode reunite me with the Beloved?

('alā Muḥammadin ṣalātu al-abrār;
ṣallā 'alayka al-muṣṭafawna al-akhyār.
qad kuntu qawwāman baqiyyat al-asḥār;
ya layta shi'rī wal-manāyā adwār;
hal tajma'unī wa-ḥabība al-dār?)

Hearing this, 'Umar sat and cried then knocked on the door, identifying himself. She said, "What business do I have with 'Umar and what brings 'Umar at this hour?" He said, "Open, may Allah have mercy upon you, and have no fear." She opened the door and he entered, saying "Repeat those words to me that you had said." She repeated them and when she concluded the recitation he said, "I ask you to include me with you two!" She said:

And 'Umar, forgive him, O Granter of forgiveness!
(wa-'Umara faghfir lahu yā ghaffār).[234]

Another time 'Umar was approached by some people who complained, "We have an imām who, after praying the *'aṣr* prayer with us, begins to sing!" 'Umar went with them and asked the man to recite what he sang to them. He said:

My heart, every time I scold it, returns to pleasures
that fatigue me.
I never see it occupied except with empty pastimes
all the time, harming me.
O My evil companion, what childishness is this?
Life has passed and you still play?
My youth has gone and left me
before I ever put it to its right use!
My soul! You and your lusts are nothing.
Fear Allah. Fear Him. Fear Him!

'Umar repeated the last verse over and over, weeping. Then he said, "Whoever of you must sing, let him sing such things."[235]

[234]Ibn al-Mubārak, *al-Zuhd wa al-Raqā'iq* (§1024).

'Abd Allāh b. 'Īsā b. Abī Laylā related: "There were always tracks in 'Umar's face caused by tears." Al-Ḥasan al-Baṣrī and Hishām b. al-Ḥasan narrated that he sometimes lost consciousness after reciting a verse from the Qur'ān, whereupon he would be taken ill and visited for days.[236]

This refutes the claim by Ibn al-Jawzī and Ibn Taymiyya that such emotional reactions never took place among the Companions.[237] The Companion Sa'īd b. 'Āmir b. Ḥidhyam was put in charge of governing Caesarea by 'Umar who asked him why he sometimes fainted in public. Sa'īd replied: "There is nothing wrong with me but I witnessed the slaying of Khubayb and was there at the time of his last supplication [against those who killed him: 'O Allah! Count them and destroy them to the last man' in *Ṣaḥīḥ al-Bukhārī*]. By Allah! I do not remember him – even in a public gathering – except it makes me faint."[238] This increased the esteem of 'Umar for Sa'īd. The latter also said: "The Quraysh had quartered him then they placed him on his trunk and said: 'Would you not love for Muḥammad to be in your place right now [and for you to be safe and sound among your kin]?' He said: 'By Allah! I would not love for myself to be among my kin and children if Muḥammad were to be pricked by a thorn.' **Then he cried out: *Yā Muḥammad!*"**[239]

Imām Aḥmad narrates from Abū Ḥayyān that when Ibn Mas'ūd passed by the furnace of a blacksmith as they were fanning the fire, he fell unconscious.[240] The same is reported from Mālik b. Dīnār, al-Rabī' b. Khuthaym in front of Ibn Mas'ūd, certain *Tābi'īn* of Baṣra, some of whom – such as the qāḍī Zurāra b. Abī Awfā and Abū Juhayr – were reported to die on the spot; Yaḥyā b. Sa'īd al-Qaṭṭān as related from Aḥmad b. Ḥanbal; 'Alī b. al-Fuḍayl b. 'Iyāḍ, and al-Shāfi'ī.[241] Al-Dhahabī relates that a number of people died upon hearing the recitation of Ṣāliḥ al-Murrī the Baṣran admonisher.[242] Abū Sulaymān al-Dārānī said, "I never saw anyone look more fearful than al-Ḥasan [b. Ṣāliḥ b. Ḥayy al-Hamdānī (d. 169)]. He stood one night reciting *Whereof do they question one another?* [Sura 78] and he fainted. He

[235]Narrated by the *ḥāfiẓ* Ibn al-Sam'ānī as cited in *Kanz al-'Ummāl* (§8944).
[236]Narrated by Ibn Abī Shayba (13:269); Abū Nu'aym, *Ḥilya* (1:88 §133) through Abū Bakr b. Abī Shayba; Ibn al-Jawzī, *Manāqib 'Umar* (p. 168); Ibn Qudāma, *al-Riqqa wa al-Bukā'* (p. 166); al-Dhahabī in the *Siyar*.
[237]Cf. Ibn al-Jawzī, *Talbīs Iblīs* (p. 252) and Ibn Taymiyya, *Fatāwā* (11:5-7 *al-Ṣūfiyya wa al-Fuqarā'*).
[238]Narrated by Ibn Hishām (4:127-128) cf. Ibn Kathīr, *Bidāya* (4:66).
[239]Narrated from Khālid b. Ma'dān by Abū Nu'aym in *Ḥilyat al-Awliyā'* (1985 ed. 1:245-246) and Ibn al-Jawzī in *Ṣifat al-Ṣafwa* (1:621-622 and 1:666 chapters on Khubayb b. 'Adī and Sa'īd b. 'Āmir b. Ḥidhyam).
[240]Aḥmad, *al-Zuhd* (p. 248 §880).
[241]Ibn Qudāma, *al-Riqqa wa al-Bukā'* (p. 293 and 331), Abū 'Ubayd in *Faḍā'il al-Qur'ān* (p. 65), Ibn Sa'd (7:150), al-Bayhaqī, *Shu'ab al-Īmān* 5:25), Abū Nu'aym, *Ḥilya* (8:297), al-Nawawī, *al-Tibyān* (p. 81), al-Dhahabī, *Siyar* (Risāla ed. 8:442), al-Mizzī, *Tahdhīb al-Kamāl* (21:960), etc.
[242]In the *Siyar* (Risāla ed. 8:47).

could not complete it until dawn."[243] The immediate cause of the death of 'Abd Allāh b. Wahb was that after he heard the ḥadīths on the afflictions of the hereafter read back to him from his own *Jāmi'* he fainted then was carried to his house where he died shortly after.[244] Al-Ḥākim said he saw his teacher, Imām Abū Bakr al-Ṣibghī, "more than once supplicate right after the *adhān* weeping, at times banging his head on the wall until, one day, I feared lest he bled."[245] As for Imām Sufyān al-Thawrī he urinated blood due to his intense fear of Allah Most High.

The above reports take precedence over the disapproval of those who fainted upon hearing Qur'ān narrated from a handful of the *Salaf* such as Ibn 'Umar, 'Ā'isha, Anas, Asmā', 'Abd Allāh b. al-Zubayr and Qatāda.[246] Al-Nawawī said: "The correct position is not to criticize except in the case of those who merely pretend to have such an emotional state."[247]

[243]Narrated by Ibn Ḥajar in *Tahdhīb al-Tahdhīb* (2:288).
[244]Narrated by Ibn Farḥūn in *al-Dībāj al-Mudhahhab* (p. 216).
[245]Cited by al-Dhahabī in the *Siyar* (Fikr ed. 12:127).
[246]Cf. Abū 'Ubayd in *Faḍa'il al-Qur'ān* (p. 111), al-Bayhaqī in the *Shu'ab* (5:24), Abū Nu'aym in the *Ḥilya* (3:167-168), and 'Abd al-Razzāq in his *Tafsīr* (2:172). Cf. 'Āmir Ṣabrī's notes on al-Malīnī's *al-Arba'īn* (p. 135-138).
[247]Al-Nawawī, *al-Tibyān* (p. 82).

18
His Scrupulous Fear of Allah

When Iraq and Persia were conquered and their treasures were brought, the Muslims saw wealth they had never seen nor imagined before. 'Umar wept. Someone said: "This is a day of thanks and joy, not a day of weeping." He replied: "By Allah, I have not gone where you went, but – by Allah! – such as this [wealth] never became abundant among a people except it caused fighting among them." Then he turned to the Qibla, raised his hands to the heaven, and said: "O Allah! I seek refuge in You from being led unwittingly to perdition, for I heard You say *We shall lead them on from whence they know not* (7:182, 68:44)." Then he ordered Surāqa b. Mālik b. Ju'shum[248] – a tall, emaciated black Bedouin – to wear the gold armlets and bracelets of Chosroes. Surāqa wore them, exclaiming "*Allāhu akbar! Allāhu akbar!*" The Prophet ﷺ had said long before, looking at Surāqa's arm: "I can see you wearing the armlets of Chosroes." Then 'Umar said: "Glory to Allah Who took them away from Kisrā b. Hurmuz and adorned with them Surāqa b. Ju'shum, a bedouin Arab from the Banū Midlaj!" Then 'Umar turned over and over the crown of Chosroes with a stick, saying: "Truly, the one who carried this to us is trustworthy." A man said to him: "You are the trustee of Allah *(anta amīnullāh)*. They shall carry to you whatever you carry to Allah. If you seek after luxury they will seek after luxury." 'Umar said, "Spoken truly."[249]

Ibn 'Abbās narrated:

After every prayer, 'Umar would sit in his place to hear the needs of the people. After he had finished with them, he would retire. One time, he prayed several prayers after which he retired immediately and did not sit to hear the people's needs. I asked his attendant: "Yarfa', is the Commander of the Believers unwell?" He said no. I sat back down next to 'Uthmān b. 'Affān. Yarfa' came and summoned the two of us to go in. We went in to see 'Umar and, lo and behold, in front of him were great heaps of gold and silver, on top of each a cover. He said: "I found that you were those of the Madīnans with the most relatives, so take this and distribute it, and whatever surplus is left, return it." 'Uthmān took some, but I asked: "And if there is still some need, will you give some to us?" He said: "A speck! *(kashkhasha)*." Then he said: "Was this not with Allah when Muḥammad and his friends used to eat strips of leather [in hunger]?" I said: "Yes, by Allah! It was with Allah when Muḥammad was alive, and if it had been granted to him he would have used it differently

[248]The man whose horse got trapped as he was pursuing the Prophet ﷺ and Abū Bakr during their flight to Medina.
[249]Narrated by Ibn Sa'd (5:90), al-Bayhaqī in *al-Sunan al-Kubrā* (6:357) al-Shāfi'ī in *al-Umm* (4:157), and Ibn 'Abd al-Barr in *al-Istī'āb* (2:581) cf. al-Māwardī, *A'lām al-Nubuwwa* (p. 155), al-Nawawī, *Tahdhīb al-Asmā'* (1:205), Ibn Kathīr, *Bidāya* (7:67), Ibn Ḥajar, *Iṣāba* (3:41), al-Suyūṭī, *Khaṣā'iṣ* (2:193).

than you." He became angry and said: "And what would he have done?" I said: "He would have eaten and fed us." At this 'Umar burst into tears until his joints shook. Then he said: "Would that I left it [the Caliphate] acquitted, with nothing against me and nothing for me!"[250]

[250]Narrated by Ya'qūb b. Shayba in *Musnad 'Umar* (p. 99), al-Ḥumaydī in his *Musnad* (1:18 §30), Ibn Sa'd (3:288), and al-Bayhaqī in *al-Sunan al-Kubrā* (6:358).

19
'Umar and Women

Although 'Umar loved his wives tenderly and they treated him with affection and care, particularly Umm 'Āṣim Jamīla bint Thābit al-Awsiyya – who never let him out to the Mosque without walking him to the door and kissing him goodbye[251] – yet his reputation is that of a severe critic of women. "What! He is too rough to live with, and harsh on women!" supposedly exclaimed Umm Kulthūm the daughter of Abū Bakr when 'Ā'isha asked her why she would turn down his proposal for marriage.[252] In reality, he was intensely scrupulous with everyone and not with any group in particular, and he was even stricter with his own household – men and women. He birched one of his sons whom he had seen wearing new clothes and letting his hair down. When his wife asked him why, he said: "I saw him puffed up with self-approval and wished to teach his ego a lesson."[253] He took away his other son's profit from the sale of a camel and poured it into the public treasury with the words: "Tend the camel of the son of the Commander of the believers! Feed the camel of the son of the Commander of the believers! Clean the camel of the son of the Commander of the believers!" He took his wife 'Ātika's prayer rug and struck her on the head with it when she told him it was a gift from Abū Mūsā al-Ash'arī then called the latter and struck him with it too, with the words: "Do not gift anything to my wives, we have no need of your gifts!" He distributed woolen garments to the women of Medina to the last piece, which he then gave to an old woman in preference to his own wife Umm Kulthūm the daughter of 'Alī, with the words: "Umm Sulayṭ deserves it more, she sewed for the people at the battle of Uḥud."[254] He himself gave the reason for this stricter standard at home, when he gathered his entire household and told them:

> I have forbidden the people to do such-and-such. People look to you the way birds look at a piece of meat. When you fall, they fall. When you fear, they fear. By Allah! Let me not see one of you brought to me for falling into what I have forbidden the people to do, or I will double the punishment for him due to his relationship to me! Whoever among you wishes, let him go forward and whoever wishes, let him fall behind.[255]

[251]According to Ibn al-Jawzī in *Manāqib 'Umar* (p. 206).
[252]Narrated through al-Wāqidī by al-Ṭabarī in his *Tārīkh* (2:564), Ibn al-Athīr in *Usd al-Ghāba* (3:27), and Ibn Kathīr in the *Bidāya*. It seems unlikely that the very young Umm Kulthūm expressed such elaborate judgments on 'Umar's personality.
[253]Narrated by 'Abd al-Razzāq (10:416).
[254]Narrated from Tha'laba b. Abī Mālik by al-Bukhārī in two places.
[255]Narrated by Ibn Sa'd (3:289) with a chain per Bukhārī and Muslim's criteria.

20
The Meccans' Roughness with Women

The Prophet ﷺ disliked wife-beaters. He discouraged Fāṭima bint Qays from marrying Abū al-Jahm b. Ḥudhayfa al-Qurashī "because he is a wife-beater" *(ḍarrābun lil-nisā')* while in another version the Prophet ﷺ says "he never puts down his stick."[256] In Medina the Prophet ﷺ said to the men: "Do not hit the maidservants of Allah!" *(lā taḍribū imā' Allah)*. Then 'Umar came to the Prophet ﷺ saying "Now the women are rebelling *(dha'irna)* against their husbands!" The Prophet ﷺ gave a dispensation *(rakhkhaṣa)* to beat them. Women started pouring in to see the wives of the Prophet ﷺ and complain about their husbands. Seeing this, the Prophet ﷺ said: "Many women have poured in to see the family of Muḥammad, complaining of their husbands, and the latter [men] are surely not the best of you!"[257]

In a version cited by al-Rāzī 'Umar states: "We the Quraysh used to have our men holding sway over our women. Then we came to Medina and found that their women held sway over their men. Then our women mixed with their women until they rebelled *(dha'irna)* against their husbands. So I came to the Prophet ﷺ and told him: 'The women are rebelling against their husbands!' So he ﷺ gave permission *(adhina)* to beat them, whereupon women started pouring in."[258] The Prophet ﷺ elsewhere said: "The best of you are the best-mannered towards their wives."[259] It is one of his lofty characteristics that "he never once struck a woman or a slave, nor anyone except in battle" as narrated from those that lived closest to him, 'Ā'isha and Anas.

A narration states that 'Umar once beat his wife while both were guests of al-Ash'ath, after which he supposedly said to the latter that the Prophet ﷺ said: "A man is not asked why he beat his wife."[260] This entire narration is weak – as stated by the Ḥanbalī historian and hadith scholar al-Maqrizī – in his *Mukhtaṣar Kitāb al-Witr* (p. 50) because it comes only through 'Abd al-Raḥmān Muslī who not only is "not known" as stated by al-Dhahabī in *al-Mughnī fil-Ḍu'afā'*, but is not known to narrate anything else whatsoever in all of ḥadīth literature, which makes him "of complete unknown reliability" *(majhūl)* per the criterion of Ibn Ḥajar in *Taqrīb al-Tahdhīb* that one from

256Narrated from Fāṭima bint Qays by Muslim, Mālik, al-Nasā'ī, Abū Dāwūd, Ibn Mājah, and Aḥmad while al-Tirmidhī cites it. Cf. Ibn Ḥajar, *Iṣāba* (7:61 §9703).
257Narrated from Iyās b. 'Abd Allāh b. Abi Dhubāb by al-Shāfi'i in his *Musnad*, Abū Dāwūd, al-Nasā'ī, Ibn Mājah, al-Ṭabarānī in *al-Kabīr*, Abū Nu'aym in *Ma'rifat al-Ṣaḥāba*, and al-Ḥākim. Al-Nawawī and al-Suyūṭī graded it a sound *(saḥīḥ)* narration in *Riyāḍ al-Ṣāliḥīn* and *al-Jāmi' al-Ṣaghīr* respectively.
258Al-Rāzī, *al-Tafsīr al-Kabīr* (3:222).
259Narrated from 'Ā'isha by al-Tirmidhī *(ḥasan gharīb ṣaḥīḥ)*.
260In the sense that he should not disclose something shameful about his wife. Narrated by Abū Dāwūd, Ibn Mājah, and Aḥmad (Arnā'ūṭ ed. 1:275 §122 *isnād ḍa'īf* = Shākir ed. 1:219 §122 *isnād ḍa'īf*).

whom only one person narrated, without declaration of his being trustworthy, is called *majhūl*.[261]

It is also narrated that 'Umar at home was pliant to the point of not replying when his wife yelled at him. When he went out he was asked about it and replied, "I bear with her because I owe her many rights. For she always cooks my food, she always bakes my bread, she always washes my clothes, she breastfeeds my children, and none of that is obligatory for her, and my heart feels at rest with her away from what is forbidden. So I bear with her because of that."[262]

[261]Muḥammad 'Awwāma, introduction to Ibn Ḥajar's *Taqrīb*. The fact that the latter actually graded 'Abd al-Raḥmān Muslī as "passable" *(maqbūl)* is a mistake as pointed out by al-Arnā'ūṭ and Ma'rūf in their *Taḥrīr Taqrīb al-Tahdhīb* since the definition of *maqbūl* is, "Whoever narrated very few ḥadīths which contain nothing on the basis of which they should be discarded: if he is corroborated [by other narrations] then he is called *maqbūl*." Even if we retained the latter rank for Muslī, it is not enough to raise his narration to the rank of "fair" because *maqbūl* means his narration can serve to mutually strengthen another, other-chained but similarly weak narration with an identical or similar content which may then result in the grading of *ḥasan* – and there is no such narration.
[262]Cited by al-Shablanjī (d. >1290) in *Nūr al-Abṣār fī Manāqib Āl Bayt al-Nabī al-Mukhtār* (1317/1899 Egyptian ed. p. 57); Abū al-Yusr 'Ābidīn, *al-Budūr fī Aḥwāl Rabbāt al-Khudūr* (p. 67); and al-Ṭanṭāwī, *Akhbār 'Umar* (p. 298).

21
Women Praying in the Mosque

'Umar was incapable of forbidding his wife 'Ātika bint Zayd – whom he married after she was widowed of 'Abd Allāh b. Abī Bakr al-Ṣiddīq – from leaving the house to pray in the Mosque. 'Ātika would ask 'Umar permission to go to congregational prayer in the mosque and he would remain silent. She would continue, "I swear I will go out unless you forbid me." She used to go out for *Ṣalāt al-'Ishā* and *Ṣalāt al-Fajr*. She was asked once: "Why do you go out like that, knowing how jealous he is?" She replied: "And what prevents him from forbidding us?"[263] 'Umar once said to her: "I swear that you know very well I dislike it." She said: "By Allah! I shall not stop until you forbid me." 'Umar replied: "I truly do not forbid you." The day 'Umar was stabbed to death in the mosque, she was present there.[264] Her next husband, al-Zubayr b. al-'Awwām, was less lenient than 'Umar and reportedly forbade her from going out to the mosque.[265]

'Umar only banned loiterers – both men and women – from the Mosque after the last prayer of the day, not worshippers, as clearly shown by the evidence. Khawla bint Qays said: "We used to be, in the time of the Prophet ﷺ, Abū Bakr, and the beginning of 'Umar's caliphate, in the mosque, women who might intermix *(qad tukhālilna)*. Sometimes we flirted *(ghazalnā)* and at times one of us might even be groped *(wa-rubbamā 'ālaja ba'ḍunā fīhi al-khawṣ)*. 'Umar said: 'I swear I shall make free women of you again.' So he brought us out *(akhrajanā)* of the Mosque unless we attended the prayers punctually."[266] Abū Sa'īd the *Mawlā* of Abū Sa'īd al-Khudrī said:

> 'Umar patrolled the mosque after *'ishā'* and would leave no-one inside except he got them out except lone worshippers standing at prayer. One night, he saw a group of the Companions of the Prophet ﷺ sitting together, among them Ubay b. Ka'b. He said: "Who are you?" Ubay replied: "A group of your relatives, Commander of the Believers." "And what is keeping you now that the *Ṣalāt* is over?" "We sat down to remember Allah ﷻ." 'Umar joined them and said to the man nearest to him: "Go ahead." The man began to supplicate. Then he told each one to supplicate, one by one until he ended up with me, as I was sitting by his side. He said: "Let us hear it." I became paralyzed and began to shake. He no-

[263]Narrated by Ibn Abī Shayba (1:106).
[264]*Al-Muḥalla* of Ibn Hazm (3:139).
[265]Cf. Ibn Ḥajar, *Iṣāba*. As for Ibn 'Abd al-Barr's report in *al-Tamhīd* (23:405-407) that 'Ātika supposedly put three pre-conditions to her marrying 'Umar – "that he not hit her, that he not prevent her from saying the truth, and that he not prevent her from praying in the Prophet's ﷺ Mosque" – its chain contains Muḥammad b. Mujabbar who is completely unknown unless he is Muḥammad b. 'Abd al-Raḥmān b. Mujabbar who is discarded.
[266]Narrated by Ibn Sa'd in his *Ṭabaqāt* (8:295-296) from the Companion Sawda bint Abī Ḍubays, from Khawla bint Qays. Cf. also *Kanz* (8:326 §23131).

ticed this and said: "Just say, 'Allah, our Lord, forgive us!' 'Allah, our Lord, show us mercy!'" Then 'Umar himself supplicated. No-one in that gathering wept more than him. Then he said: "Good. Now, all of you, leave!"[267]

'Umar never prevented nor forbade women from attending the mosque for prayers. This general permission and conditional prohibition is how he understood the meaning of the ḥadīth of the Prophet ﷺ: "Do not forbid the bondswomen of Allah from [going to] the mosques of Allah!"[268] 'Umar also narrated that the Prophet ﷺ said more explicitly, "If your women ask permission to go out to *Ṣalāt*, do not forbid them!"[269] (On condition they come out *tafilāt*, *i.e.* without any perfume on their persons, as per the Prophet's ﷺ ḥadīth related by Zaynab bint Mu'āwiya al-Thaqafiyya the wife of Ibn Mas'ūd in Muslim and the narration of Abū Hurayra in Abū Dāwūd and the *Musnad*s.)

Accordingly, 'Umar permitted women from attending the mosque for the five obligatory prayers and the Sunna prayers of *Tarāwīḥ*. To that end he made sure they had a separate entrance and exit to the Mosque – which he forbade men from using – and separate ablution facilities.[270] He had them pray *Tarāwīḥ* prayers in the Mosque separately from the men and ordered Sulaymān b. Abī Ḥathma to be imām for them at the far end of the Mosque, while Ubay b. Ka'b and Tamīm al-Dārī were imāms for the men. Then 'Uthmān had men and women all pray behind a single imām, but he took measures to prevent women from leaving until the men had left first.[271]

It is 'Ā'isha that absolutely forbade the women from going to the mosques even for the five prescribed prayers. She gave her reason in the famous statement: "If the Messenger of Allah ﷺ had seen what the women of our time do, he would have forbidden them to go to the mosques just as the Israelite women were forbidden!"[272]

[267]Narrated by Ibn Sa'd (3:294) and Ibn al-Jawzī in *Manāqib 'Umar* (p. 76) cf. al-Ṭanṭāwī, *Akhbār 'Umar* (p. 304).
[268]Narrated from Ibn 'Umar by al-Bukhārī, Muslim, and others.
[269]Narrated by Aḥmad.
[270]Ibn Ḥazm, *al-Muḥallā* (3:131 and 4:119).
[271]Narrated by Ibn Sa'd (5:26) and Ibn Ḥazm, *al-Muḥallā* (3:139).
[272]Narrated by al-Bukhārī, Muslim, and in the *Sunan*.

22
Precautionary Pre-Emption *(Sadd al-Dharā'i')*

During his caliphate, 'Umar forbade certain actions out of precautionary pre-emption *(sadd al-dharā'i')*. For example, he forbade Anas from praying towards a grave after seeing him do so;[273] he hit a man for praying while facing another and hit the latter for facing the former through his *ṣalāt*;[274] he forbade Muslims in non-Muslim countries (Azerbaijan at the time) from dressing in the manner of non-Muslims;[275] he would hit the fasters of Rajab on their hands until they helped themselves to food lest it be confused with the Jāhiliyya-time obligatory fasting of that month.[276] He also forbade praying in churches whether or not they contained statues while Ibn 'Abbās prayed in them as long as they did not contain them.[277]

It is narrated that our liege lord 'Umar cut down a tree claimed to be that under which the *bay'a* of the Prophet ﷺ took place lest it be venerated after the fashion of Jāhiliyya.[278] The fact that this tree was not the actual tree of the *bay'a* is illustrated by the following evidence:[279]

- The tree of the *bay'a* was not known to the Companions as narrated from Ibn al-Musayyib in al-Bukhārī and Muslim.

[273] Narrated by Ibn Abī Shayba (1:106) and 'Abd al-Razzāq (1:404).
[274] Narrated by 'Abd al-Razzāq (2:38), al-Nawawī in *al-Majmū'* (2:232), and Ibn Qudāma in *al-Mughnī* (2:242).
[275] Narrated by Aḥmad in his *Musnad* with a sound chain according to al-Arnā'ūṭ (1:252-253 §92). Ibn Taymiyya in his *Iqtiḍā' al-Ṣirāṭ al-Mustaqīm* (1907 ed. p. 60) said: "This is a prohibition on the part of 'Umar directed at Muslims against all that belongs to the manner of dress of non-Muslims *(mushrikūn)*." For some reason, this particular passage was left out of the English translation of the *Iqtiḍā'* entitled *Ibn Taymiyya's Struggle Against Popular Religion* (1976). Like cigarette smoking, unislamic fashion (in dress, hair, hygiene, perfumes, etc.) is among the ways in which present-day Muslims have slavishly followed in the footsteps of non-Muslims. The rulings pertaining to these matters vary between the permissible *(mubāḥ)* and the strictly prohibited *(harām)*.
[276] Narrated by Ibn Abī Shayba, *Muṣannaf* (3:102). It was a preferential prohibition, cf. Ibn 'Abbās's detestation of fasting on that month for the same reason as related from Ibn Abī Zayd by al-Ṭurṭūshī in *al-Ḥawādith wal-Bida'*, and the detestation of its integral fasting by many Companions cf. Ibn Rajab, *Laṭā'if al-Ma'ārif* (*waẓā'if shahri Rajab*). Otherwise it is a praiseworthy fast since it is one of the sacred months as demonstrated by al-Nawawī in *Sharh Ṣaḥīḥ Muslim* (Kitāb 37 Bāb 2 §10) and others. See https://livingislam.org/fmr_e.html
[277] Narrated by al-Bukhārī *ta'līqan*.
[278] Narrated through the narrators of the *Ṣaḥīḥayn* by al-Fākihī, *Akhbār Makka* (5:77-78); Ibn Abī Shayba (1:106=2:150); Ibn Sa'd (1:73) cf. Ibn Ḥajar, *Fatḥ* (7:448).
[279] al-Ḥabīb 'Alī al-Jafrī drew my attention to this aspect of the Companion-*Sīra* in our first blessed face-to-face meeting in Beirut the year 2004.

- He narrated from his father – one of the Companions: “We tried to find it more than once and could not.” Al-Ḥākim cited it after stating that it was said the tree had been taken away by a flood.[280]

- Not even was its exact location known, as narrated from ʿAbd Allāh b. ‘Umar in al-Bukhārī’s *Ṣaḥīḥ*.

- Ibn Saʿd narrated from the centenarian superlative historian Abū al-Ḥasan ʿAlī b. Muḥammad al-Madā’inī,[281] from Juwayriyya b. Asmā’, from Nāfiʿ: “A group of the Companions of the Messenger of Allah ﷺ went out years after that [the *bayʿa*] but none of them was able to pinpoint the tree and they differed over it. Ibn ʿUmar said: ‘It [the tree] was a mercy from Allah.’”[282]

- Ibn ʿUmar even used to water a certain tree under which the Prophet ﷺ had prayed so that it would not die.[283] If the tree-cutting related from his father were true of the actual tree of the *bayʿa*, he would have desisted from such a concern. And Allah Most High knows best.

[280]In his *Maʿrifat ʿUlūm al-Ḥadīth* (p. 162, type 7).
[281]Yaḥyā b. Maʿīn described him as *thiqa thiqa thiqa* cf. *Siyar* (9:127).
[282]Narrated by Ibn Saʿd (2:81=2:105) with a stronger chain for *Sīra* reports than that of the tree-cutting.
[283]Narrated by al-Bayhaqī in his *Sunan* (5:245 §10049).

23
Writing vs. Learning of Hadith; Dislike of Story-Tellers (*Quṣṣāṣ*)

ʿUmar disliked the compilation of ḥadīth in books, however, he commanded people to learn ḥadīth by heart exactly as they had to learn the Qur'an. He did so during his caliphate in writing: "Learn the inheritance laws, the *Sunna*, and grammar the same way as you learn the Qur'ān!"[284]

Al-Ḥārith b. Muʿāwiya asked ʿUmar permission to speak in gatherings to which ʿUmar assented reluctantly: "As you like!" Al-Ḥārith said, "I will only decide what you say!" ʿUmar said: "I fear for you that you will speak in gatherings and begin to feel superior to them. Then you will continue to speak in public until you imagine yourself as high above them as the Pleiades. Then Allāh will lower you accordingly below their feet the Day of Resurrection!"[285]

[284]Narrated through trustworthy narrators by Ibn Abī Shayba (10:459, 11:236), al-Dārimī, Saʿīd b. Manṣūr at the very beginning of his *Sunan*, al-Bayhaqī in his (6:209), and Ibn ʿAbd al-Barr in *Jāmiʿ Bayān al-ʿIlm* (2:1008-1009 §1920-1921).
[285]Narrated by Aḥmad. See on this topic *The Four Imams and Their Schools* (pp. 126-134, "Unreliability of the Righteous") and our introduction to Qārī's *Encyclopedia of Hadith Forgeries* (pp. 29-30, "Semi-shaykhs and storytellers").

24
His Detestation of Worldliness

'Umar was intransigent and severe in separating truth from falsehood and the Prophet ﷺ conferred on him the title of *al-Fārūq*, saying: "Indeed, indeed! the devil parts ways with 'Umar."[286] He ﷺ also said: "This is a man who does not like vanity *(al-bāṭil)*. This is 'Umar b. al-Khaṭṭāb."[287]

Ṭāriq b. Shihāb narrated: "When 'Umar came to Syro-Palestine the army came to him as he was wearing a waist-wrap, two *khuffs*, and a turban *('imāma)*; he took his camel by the reins and waded into the water, whereupon they said to him: 'Commander of the Believers! The army and patriarchs of Shām are meeting you and you are in this state?' 'Umar said: 'We are a nation Allah ennobled and made mighty with Islam. We shall not seek nobility and might with other than it' *(innā qawmun a'azzanā Allāhu bil-Islam, falan naltamisa al-'izzata bighayrih)*."[288]

Another version from Ṭāriq states: "'Umar b. al-Khaṭṭāb went out to al-Shām and with us was 'Ubayda b. al-Jarrāḥ. They arrived at a watering-place. 'Umar was mounted on his camel. He came down, removed his *khuffs*, placed them on his shoulder, then took the reins of his camel and waded into the water with her. Abū 'Ubayda said: 'O Commander of the Believers, you do this? You remove your *khuffs*, place them on your shoulder, take your camel's reins, and wade into the water with her? I do not like the fact that the people of this country are looking at you from above [while you are doing this].' 'Umar replied: 'Woe! Had other than you said that, Abū 'Ubayda, I would have made of him an exemplary punishment before the Umma of Muḥammad ﷺ! Truly we were the lowliest of nations, then **Allah ennobled us and made us mighty with Islam. By whatever means we seek nobility and might other than it, Allah shall abase us**!'"[289]

Another narration states that someone stopped 'Umar on top of his camel as he was on the way to being welcomed by the people of the city: "Commander of the Believers! What if you rode a fine horse for their leaders and potentates to see you when they meet you?" 'Umar replied: "Why do I see you [focused] down here? The whole affair comes only from up there" and he pointed to the sky. "Let go of my camel."[290]

[286]Narrated from Burayda by Aḥmad with a strong chain, al-Tirmidhī as part of a longer ḥadīth with the wording "the devil certainly fears 'Umar," and Ibn Ḥibbān. Al-Tirmidhī said it is *ḥasan ṣaḥīḥ gharīb* and al-Suyūṭī indicated that it is *ṣaḥīḥ* in *al-Jāmi' al-Saghīr*.
[287]Narrated from al-Aswad b. Sarī' by Aḥmad through two weak chains because of 'Alī b. Zayd but see n. 55. This narration describes 'Umar as "swarthy and tall, bald, and left-handed."
[288]Narrated by Ibn Abī Shayba (7:10, 7:93) and Hannād b. al-Sarī, *al-Zuhd* (2:417).
[289]Narrated by al-Ḥākim (1:61-62=1990 ed. 1:130) who declared it *ṣaḥīḥ* as per the criterion of al-Bukhārī and Muslim.
[290]Narrate by Ibn Abī Shayba (7:93) and Abū Nu'aym in the *Ḥilya* (1985 ed. 1:47).

25
'Umar and an Innovator in the Faith

During 'Umar's caliphate a man from Iraq named Ṣabīgh b. 'Isl came to Medina and began to ask repeatedly about the meaning of the ambiguous verses *(mutashābihāt)* of Qur'ān. 'Umar summoned him. When he came he asked him: "Who are you?" He replied: "I am the servant of Allah, Ṣabīgh." 'Umar said: "And I am the servant of Allah, 'Umar." Then he struck him on the head with a birch. He went on until his head bled. Then Ṣabīgh said: "Commander of the believers, stop! No trace remains of what was in my head."[291] In another version, 'Umar said to him: "Uncover your head." He did, revealing two braids. 'Umar said: "By Allah! Had I found you tonsured, I would have cut off your head."[292] Meaning, if you had been a recidivist, because they used to shave the heads of convicts (as took place with 'Umar's own son, 'Abd al-Raḥmān, for drunkenness).[293] In another version, 'Umar lashes Ṣabīgh until his back is a welt, leaves him to recover, then has him lashed again, then leaves him to recover, then summons him a third time, whereupon Ṣabīgh swears to his repentance. Then 'Umar wrote to Abū Mūsā al-Ash'arī, instructing him to see that no Muslim keep company with Ṣabīgh nor speak to him. After that, people would flee him like the plague and Ṣabīgh could not sit in any circle except it disbanded instantly because of him. This became unbearable for him and he begged Abū Mūsā for lenience, whereupon the latter wrote 'Umar who wrote back, lifting the ban.[294]

[291]Narrated from Sulaymān b. Yasār with a sound chain by al-Dārimī and cited by al-Qurṭubī in his commentary on the verse He it is Who has revealed unto you (Muḥammad) the Scripture wherein are clear revelations. They are the substance of the Book; and others (which are) allegorical. But those in whose hearts is doubt pursue that which is allegorical seeking (to cause) dissension by seeking to explain it (3:7). Mālik narrated in his *Muwaṭṭa'* from Ibn Shihāb al-Zuhrī, from al-Qāsim b. Muḥammad who said: "I heard a man asking 'Abd Allāh b. 'Abbās about the spoils of war. The latter answered: 'Horses are part of the spoils of war, and the battle-gear and property carried by the enemy killed in battle.' Then the mean asked the same question again and Ibn 'Abbās gave the same answer. Then the man said: 'The spoils Allah mentioned in His Book, what are they?' and he did not stop asking him until he almost created nuisance for him. Then Ibn 'Abbās said: 'Do you know what this man's similitude is? He is like Ṣabīgh whom 'Umar beat up.'"

[292]Narrated from al-Ḥasan by al-Firyābī cf. al-Suyūṭī, *al-Durr al-Manthūr* (7:614).

[293]Narrated by 'Abd al-Razzāq (9:232-233).

[294]Narrated from Nāfi', Abū 'Uthmān al-Nahdī, and Zur'a by Ibn 'Asākir (6:385) cf. al-Ṭanṭāwī, *Akhbār 'Umar* (p. 178-179).

26
'Umar and the Syrian Plague

When 'Umar departed from Medina and travelled to Syro-Palestine in the year 17/638 or 18/639 until he reached Sargh on the Hijaz-Syro-Palestine border where he met with Abū 'Ubayda b. al-Jarrāḥ and his companions among the commanders of the armies, who informed him that a plague was rife in the lands of Syro-Palestine. Ibn 'Abbās said that 'Umar said, "Tell the first Emigrants to come." When they came he consulted with them and informed them of what he had been told, whereupon they differed in their opinions. Some said, "You came out for a purpose and we do not think you should go back on it." Others said, "With you are the remnant of the people and the Companions of the Messenger of Allah and we do not consider that you should go and expose them to this pestilence." He dismissed them and called the Helpers, who answered in the same way as the Emigrants and differed likewise. Then he summoned the elders of the Quraysh among the post-Conquest Emigrants who were unanimous in going back and not exposing the people to the pestilence. 'Umar then made the announcement among the people, "Verily I am riding back home in the morning so prepare yourselves to ride back." Abū 'Ubayda b. al-Jarrāḥ said, "What! Fleeing from the decree of Allah?" 'Umar replied, "I anyone else than you had said it , O Abū 'Ubayda! Yes. We are fleeing from the decree of Allah unto the decree of Allah. Have you considered if you had camels and you had alighted in a valley that had two parts, one verdant and one arid, would it not be the case, if you graze them in the verdant part, that you have done so by the decree of Allah, and you graze them in the arid part you have done so by the decree of Allah?" Whereupon 'Abd al-Raḥmān b. 'Awf came back from some matter for which he had absented himself and said, "Verily I have some knowledge about this matter. I heard the Messenger of Allah say, 'When you hear news about it—i.e. pestilence and plague—in a certain land then do not venture into that land; and if it befalls in a land in which you find yourselves, then do not exit it to flee from it.'" Hearing this, 'Umar gave praise and thanks to Allah then left.[295]

Al-Ṭabarī narrates a very weak-chained report through Muḥammad b. Ḥumayd al-Rāzī (discarded) and Layth b. Abī Sulaym with a *mursal* chain from 'Amra bint 'Abd al-Raḥmān b. Sa'd b. Zurāra that "'Umar died saying, 'I repent unto Allah of three things: from my flight from the plague; from my declaring [non-alcoholic] grape syrup (*al-ṭilā'*) to be licit;[296] and from my returning when Abū Bakr sent for me, at the time I was in the army of Usāma b. Zayd."[297] The first part is confirmed, however, by Aḥmad

[295] Narrated from Ibn 'Abbās by Mālik (Jāmi', mā jā'a fīl-ṭā'ūn), Bukhārī (Ṭibb, mā yudhkaru fīl-ṭā'ūn) and Muslim (Ṭibb, al-ṭā'ūn wal-ṭiyara wal-kahāna).
[296]A fatwa he gave to the people of Syria per 'Abd al-Razzāq, Mālik, al-Nasā'ī and al-Bayhaqī cf. Qal'ahjī, *Mawsū'at Fiqh 'Umar b. al-Khaṭṭāb* (pp. 115-116).
[297]Al-Ṭabarī, *Tahdhīb al-Āthār: al-Juz' al-Mafqūd*, ed. 'Alī Riḍā b. 'Abd Allāh b. 'Alī Riḍā (Damascus and Beirut: Dār al-Ma'mūn lil-Turāth, 1416/1995) p. 75 §91.

b. Muḥ. b. 'Īsā al-Qāḍī al-Birtī's (d. 280) fair narration in his *Musnad 'Abd al-Raḥmān b. 'Awf* from 'Abd Allāh b. 'Amr b. al-'Āṣ that he heard 'Umar say upon waking up from a nap, "O Allah, forgive me my return from Sargh."[298]

While in Syria, our liege lord 'Umar was brought water for ablution and said afterwards: "I never tasted sweeter water, from where did you get it?" They pointed him to the house of an elderly women. He went and said to her: "Old woman, submit and you shall be safe! Muḥammad came with the truth from Allah." She uncovered her snow-white hair and said: "Now? With one foot of mine in the grave?" Whereupon 'Umar said: "O Allah, bear witness!" *I.e.* bear witness that I tried.[299]

[298]Also narrated by Ibn Abī Shayba, *Muṣannaf* (7:10) as mentioned by Ibn Ḥajar, *Fatḥ* (10:197).

[299]Narrated thus by al-Dāraquṭnī in his *Sunan* (1:32 "*Wuḍū'* with water from *Ahl al-Kitāb*"), al-Bayhaqī in his *Sunan* (1:32 §128), Ibn Ḥazm in *al-Muḥallā* (11:196), the latter with the wording, "O Allah, bear witness! There is no compulsion in the Religion," and Ibn Ḥajar in *Taghlīq al-Ta'līq* (2:131). In Muḥ. Hashim Kamali's *Freedom of Expression in Islam* the report is rendered thus: "Abū Zahra [*Tanẓīm al-Islam lil-Mujtama'*, Cairo, Dār al-Fikr al-'Arabī, n.d., p. 184)] also tells of an incident where an elderly Christian woman came as a supplicant to the Caliph 'Umar b. al-Khaṭṭāb who met her request with favour. Afterwards, he invited her to embrace Islam but she refused. At this the Caliph became anxious, fearing his invitation might have amounted to compulsion, and he expressed his remorse in these words: 'O my Lord, I did not mean to compel her, as I know that there must be no compulsion in religion ...righteousness has been explained and distinguished from misguidance.' Thus, the Caliph 'Umar expressed the point that only God Most High can prevail upon the hearts and minds of people in matters of faiṭh"

27
‘Umar and the Nile

When ‘Amr b. al-‘Āṣ, the governor of Egypt, wrote to ‘Umar that the Nile had ceased to flow and was causing a drought in Egypt and fears of mass migrations, ‘Umar wrote back and said, “Place the note I included with this letter, into the Nile.” The note said:

> From the slave of Allah, ‘Umar the Commander of the Believers to the Nile of the people of Egypt. To proceed: If you flow on your own behalf and command, then do not flow as we are in no need of you; but if you flow upon the command of Allah, the One, the All-Compelling Subduer – and He is the One that causes you to flow – then we ask Allah Most High to cause you to flow!

Ibn al-‘Āṣ threw the note into the Nile and it flowed again the very next day.[300]

[300]Narrated by Ibn Kathīr in *al-Bidāya* (7:100).

28
'Umar and the Friends of Allah (*Awliyā'*)

The Prophet ﷺ called 'Umar one day. He answered: "Twice at your obedient service *(labbayka wa-sa'dayk)*, Messenger of Allah!" 'Umar narrates:

I thought he would send me on some errand for something he needed. He ﷺ said: "'Umar, there will be in my Community, among the least of people *(fī ākhir al-nās)*, a man named Uways al-Qaranī. A certain disease will afflict his body but he will supplicate to Allah ﷻ and He will remove it from him except a small spot on his side. Whenever he sees it, he mentions Allah ﷻ. When you see him, give him my greeting and order him to supplicate for you, for he is dear to his Lord and pious toward his mother. If he were to swear by Allah, He would certainly fulfill his oath. He will intercede for as many people as the entire tribes of Rabī'a and Muḍar." I looked for him in the life of the Messenger of Allah ﷺ to no avail. Then I looked for him during the Caliphate of Abū Bakr, to no avail.[301] Then I looked for him for one half of my leadership. One day I was asking fellow travellers: "Is there any among you from Murād? Is there any among you from Qaran? Is Uways al-Qaranī among you?" An old man among them said: "He is my brother's son. You are asking about a man of very modest condition. Such as you does not ask about him, Commander of the Believers!" I said: "I think that, in comparison to him, you are doomed!" But he repeated the same words. Meantime, I was led to a mangy mount on which rode a disheveled man. In my heart I became convinced it was Uways. I asked him, "Are you Uways al-Qaranī?" He said yes. I said: "Then the Messenger of Allah ﷺ sends his salam to you." He said: "Upon the Messenger of Allah greetings, and upon you, Commander of the Believers!" I continued: "And he orders you to supplicate for me." Thereafter, I would meet him every year or every season, at which time I would tell him what was on my mind and he would tell me what was on his mind.[302]

The unburnable Yemeni Successor Abū Muslim al-Khawlānī ('Abd Allāh b. Thuwab)[303] was another Friend of Allah who was a Qur'ān teacher in Syro-Palestine and whom 'Umar gave thanks to Allah for meeting. The *dajjāl* and pseudo-prophet al-Aswad al-'Ansī had unsuccessfully tried to burn him in a huge furnace in the days of the *ridda* wars, after which Abū Bakr and 'Umar would call Abū Muslim "the Ibrāhīm of this *Umma*."[304]

[301]The story that both Abū Bakr and 'Umar met Uways is a forgery cf. Ibn 'Arrāq, *Tanzīh al-Sharī'a*.

[302]Narrated by al-Khaṭīb who said it is *gharīb jiddan* in his *Riwāyat al-Ṣaḥāba 'an al-Tābi'īn*, Ibn 'Asākir (9:431), al-Khiraqī in his *Fawā'id* cf. *Kanz* (§37827), and Ibn Ḥajar in *Nuzhat al-Sāmi'īn* (p. 26 chain only).

[303] Thus vowelized in the Hyderabad edition of al-Bukhārī's *al-Tārīkh al-Kabīr*.

[304] Ibn Ḥibbān (2:339-340). He is buried in Dārayya, Syria and is one of those Abū Nu'aym and others listed as "the Eight Ascetics": 'Āmir b. 'Abd Qays al-Ḥaḍramī,

Two men looking for him found him praying and one of them counted three hundred *rak'as* before he finished.[305] He is the one who narrated from Mu'ādh, from the Prophet, ﷺ the Divine Hadith, "Those who love one another for the sake of My Majesty shall have pulpits of light, and the Prophets and *shahids* shall yearn to be in their position."[306]

Bayhaqī narrated that during the Caliphate of 'Umar, a fire appeared in al-Ḥarra [near Medina]. 'Umar summoned Tamīm al-Dārī, saying to him, "You control it!" Tamīm replied, "But who am I and what am I, Commander of the Believers?" But 'Umar did not stop insisting until they both went near the area of the fire. There, Tamīm began to goad *(yaḥūsh)* the fire with his hands until the fire went into [a hole in] a mountain gorge *(shi'b)*. 'Umar said, "The one who sees is not like the one who does not see!" He said this three times.[307]

Qurṭubī in his *Tafsīr* on the verse *Allah knows that which every female bears and that which the wombs absorb and that which they grow* (13:8) mentioned that a man came to 'Umar stating he found his wife pregnant after two years of absence. 'Umar held a consultation on her lapidation for adultery. Mu'ādh b. Jabal said to him: "You may have jurisdiction over her but not over the foetus. Leave her until she gives birth." She then gave birth to a boy whose front teeth were coming out. Recognizing the resemblance in him the husband exclaimed, "This is my son, by the Lord of the Ka'ba!" 'Umar then said: "Women can no longer give birth to the like of Mu'ādh. Were it not for Mu'ādh, 'Umar would have perished!" *(lawlā Mu'ādhun lahalaka 'Umar.)*[308]

Abū Muslim al-Khawlānī, Uways al-Qaranī, al-Rabī' b. Khuthaym, al-Aswad b. Yazīd, Masrūq, Sufyān al-Thawrī and al-Ḥasan al-Baṣrī—mostly Yemenis and Iraqis.

305 Cited by al-Dhahabī in his notice on Abū Muslim al-Khawlānī in the *Siyar*.

306 See "The Hadith of the *Awliyā* on Pulpits of Lights" in our *Muḥammadan Light*.

307 Narrated from Mu'āwiya b. Ḥarmal al-Ḥanafī by Bayhaqī and Abū Nu'aym cf. Ibn Kathīr, *Bidāya* (6:153); Dhahabī, *Siyar* (Risāla ed. 2:447) and *Tārīkh* (*Khulafā'* p. 615). The latter commented "this Mu'āwiya is not known" but Ibn Ḥajar in the *Iṣāba* (3:497) identified him as Musaylima al-Kadhdhāb's brother-in-law. He saw the Prophet ﷺ, fought on Musaylima's side and entered Islam in the time of 'Umar.

308 Narrated by Bayhaqī, *Sunan* (7:443 §15335) cf. Dhahabī, *Siyar* (1:452) and Ibn Ḥajar, *Iṣāba* (6:137). This report is the basis of the *majnūna* narration in Abū Dāwūd and Aḥmad but they do not have the words "Were it not…". It was corrupted to read 'Alī instead of Mu'adh in the Shī'ī sources beginning with the *Musnad* attributed to Zayd b. 'Alī and some chainless Sunni sources cf. Ibn Qutayba, *Mukhtalif al-Ḥadīth* (Dār al-Jīl ed. p. 162); Ibn 'Abd al-Barr, *Istī'āb* (3:1103). Ghumārī in *al-Burhān* (p. 71) said it is related by Ibn Abī Khaythama in his *Tārīkh* but I could not find it there.

29
'Umar's *Tawassul* (Using Means to Allah) Through al-'Abbās as Intercessor[309]

Al-Bukhārī narrated in his *Ṣaḥīḥ* that in a time of drought 'Umar accomplished the prayer for rain through the intercession of al-'Abbās b. 'Abd al-Muṭṭalib 🙵, the uncle of the Prophet 🙵, saying: "O Allah! We would use our Prophet as a means to You and You then sent us rain; now we use our Prophet's uncle as a means to You, therefore send us rain!"[310]

Al-Suyūṭī mentions the context of this event in his *Tārīkh al-Khulafā'*:

In the year 17 'Umar enlarged the Prophetic mosque. That year there was a drought in the Ḥijāz. It was named the Year of Cinders *('ām al-ramāda)*. 'Umar prayed for rain for the people by means of al-'Abbās. Ibn Sa'd narrated from [the Ṣaḥābī] Niyār al-Aslamī that when 'Umar came out to pray for rain, he came out wearing the cloak *(burd)* of the Messenger of Allah 🙵. Ibn 'Awn narrated that 'Umar took al-'Abbās's hand and raised it up, saying, "O Allah, we seek a means to You with the uncle of Your Prophet to ask that You drive away from us the drought and water us with rain!"[311]

Al-'Abbās supplicated in the following terms:

O Allah, truly no tribulation descends except because of sins, nor is lifted except upon repentance! **The people have turned to you by means of me because of my position in relation to your Prophet,** and here are our

---

[309]Sources for this section: (i) Yūsuf Aḥmad al-Dajwī (Kawtharī's Shaykh), four articles on *tawassul* originally published in *Majallat al-Azhar* and reprinted at the beginning of Ghawjī's edition of al-Kawtharī's *Maḥq al-Taqawwul*; (ii) Wahbī Ghawjī, Introduction to *Maḥq al-Taqawwul*; (iii) 'Abd Allāh al-Ghumārī, *Irghām al-Mubtadi' al-Ghabī bi-Jawāz al-Tawassul bil-Nabī* (Compelling the Dunderheaded Innovator to Accept the Permissibility of Using the Prophet as a Means), ed. Ḥasan 'Alī Saqqāf, 2nd ed. (Ammān: Dār al-Imām al-Nawawī, 1992); (iv) Kawtharī, *Maḥq al-Taqawwul fī Mas'alat al-Tawassul* (Eradication of Gossip Concerning the Use of Intermediaries) in his *Maqālāt* (Essays), republished as a monograph with introduction and notes by our teacher Wahbī Sulaymān Ghāwjī (1997); [5] Abū al-Ḥasanayn 'Abd Allāh b. 'Abd al-Raḥmān al-Makkī al-Hāshimī, *al-Salafiyya al-Mu'āṣira: Munāqashāt wa-Rudūd* (Contemporary Salafism: Discussions and Rebuttals) p.143-145; [6] Maḥmūd Mamdūḥ, *Raf' al-Mināra bi-Aḥādīth al-Tawassul wal-Ziyāra* (Raising the Beacon with the Hadiths of Seeking Means and Visitation [of the Prophet]) p. 118-121; our teachers [7] Muḥammad b. 'Alawī al-Mālikī, *Mafāhīm Yajib an Tuṣaḥḥaḥ* (Necessary Correction of Certain Misconceptions), 10th ed. (p. 153-156) and [8] Sāmir al-Naṣṣ, *al-Wasīla ilā Fahm Ḥaqīqat al-Tawassul* (The Means to Understand the Reality of Using Means), Beirut: Dar al-Tawfīq, 2003.

[310]Narrated from Anas by Bukhārī in the book of *Istisqā'* of his *Ṣaḥīḥ* as quoted in the 1959 edition of *Fatḥ al-Bārī* (2:494), al-Baghawī in *Sharḥ al-Sunna* (3:409), Ibn Khuzayma in his *Ṣaḥīḥ* (2:337-338 §1421), Ibn Ḥibbān in his (7:110-111 §2861).

[311]*Tārīkh al-Khulafā'* (Beirut, 1992 Aḥmad Fāris ed. p. 140).

hands [raised up] towards you – despite our sins – and our forelocks in repentence, so send down water for us!

"Whereupon," the narrator goes on to say, "the sky let down water as thick as ropes, quenching the earth and reviving the people."[312]

Shaykh Muḥammad 'Alawī al-Mālikī said: "Whoever understands from this that 'Umar only used al-'Abbās as his means and not the Messenger of Allah 🕮, because al-'Abbās is alive and the Messenger of Allah is dead – that person's understanding is dead." Nor do these reports provide any proof for the claim that 'Umar considered it forbidden to seek the intercession of the Prophet 🕮 in the matter. Rather, he only considered it permissible to use that of his uncle, as the scholars pointed out.[313]

The event of the *tawassul* of *Sayyidunā* 'Umar through al-'Abbās shows the following:

[1] Nowhere in the ḥadīth is there any indication that there was no *tawassul* through the Prophet in the time of 'Umar. Such a view is an inference or an extrapolation that is not based on explicit evidence.

[2] On the contrary, 'Umar implicitly made *tawassul* through the Prophet 🕮 at that very time, by wearing his blessed cloaks as he came out for the prayer for rain as mentioned in the report by Ibn Sa'd. In Muslim's *Ṣaḥīḥ* Asmā' says that she inherited the mantle of the Prophet 🕮 from her sister 'Ā'isha and that they used it to seek a cure for people.

[3] The use of the Prophet's uncle illustrates that *tawassul* is essentially through the Prophet 🕮 as the importance of al-'Abbās 🕮 in this respect is only in his relationship to the Prophet as 'Umar 🕮 himself states with the words "the uncle of our Prophet" in al-Bukhārī's version already mentioned; "the status of al-'Abbās in relation to Your Prophet" in al-Lālikā'ī's version; and as al-'Abbās states:

"O Allah, truly no tribulation descends except because of sins, nor is lifted except upon repentance. The people have turned to you by means of me **because of my position in relation to Your Prophet**, and here are our hands [raised up] towards you – despite our sins – and our forelocks in repentance, so send down water for us and preserve Your Prophet in the person of his uncle." Whereupon the sky let down water as thick as ropes and the people came over to al-'Abbās passing their hands over him and saying to him: "Congratulations to you, irrigator of the two Sanctuaries!" Whereupon 'Umar said, "He/This is, by Allah, the means to Allah and the place of nearness to Him!"[314]

[312]Cited from al-Zubayr b. Bakkār's narration in *al-Ansāb* by Ibn Ḥajar in *Fatḥ al-Bārī* (2:497).
[313]See al-Ghumārī's *Irghām al-Mubtadi'*; Muḥammad b. 'Alawī's *Mafāhīm* (10th ed. p. 153-156); Maḥmūd Mamdūḥ's *Raf' al-Mināra* (p. 118-121), etc.
[314]See two notes up (note 312).

So the *tawassul* continues to be solely through the Prophet ﷺ despite appearances to the contrary, for he is the ultimate recourse of human beings seeking nearness to Allah as he himself taught the blind man (“Say, ‘O Muḥammad, I turn with you to Allah…’”) and as several *Saḥāba* explicitly said, such as in the following reports:

(a) Report of the Bedouin who said to the Holy Prophet ﷺ:

We have come to you when even our virgins’ milk is dry,
and the mother worries for her own life over her child’s,
The child lets down his arms sitting still
for hunger, a hunger unstilled and uninterrupted.
We have nothing left from what our people eat
except bitter colocynth and camel-wool mixed with blood.
And we have none but you to flee to,
for where can people flee except to the Messengers?

Then the Prophet ﷺ stood up and he was dragging his garment. He climbed up the pulpit and said: “O Allah, send us water....” whereupon rain fell abundantly. Then the Prophet ﷺ said: “If Abū Ṭālib were alive he would have liked to see this. Who will recite for us what he said?” Hearing this, ‘Alī stood up and said: “Messenger of Allah, I think you mean his saying [about you]:

A fair-skinned one by whose face rainclouds are sought,
A caretaker for the orphans and protector of widows.
With him the clan of Hāshim seek refuge from calamities,
For they possess in him immense favor and grace....”[315]

(b) Report of Sawād b. Qārib al-Sadūsī who declaimed:

Truly, you are the nearest of all Messengers as a means to Allah,
son of the noblest and purest ones! ....
Therefore, be an intercessor for me the Day none but you among them
shall be of the least benefit for Sawād b. Qārib!

Whereupon the Prophet smiled, upon him peace, and said: “You have obtained success, Sawād!”[316]

(c) Report of Ḥassān b. Thābit who declaimed:

[315]Narrated by al-Bayhaqī in *Dalā’il al-Nubuwwa* (6:141) cf. Ibn Kathīr, *al-Bidāya wal-Nihāya* (6:90-91) and Ibn Ḥajar, *Fatḥ al-Bārī* (1989 ed. 2:629) but its basis is in al-Bukhārī’s *Ṣaḥīḥ*. See the extensive documentation on the various narrations of this poetry in our *Muḥammadan Light in the Qur’ān and Sunna*. Sayyid Aḥmad b. Zaynī Daḥlān saw therein, among others, proof of Abū Ṭālib’s belief in the Prophethood of our liege lord Muḥammad ﷺ as discussed in his *Asnā al-Maṭālib fī Islāmi Abī Ṭālib*.

[316]Narrated by Abu Ya‘lā, *Mu‘jam* (p. 265), al-Ṭabarānī in *al-Kabīr* (7:94 §6475), Abu Nu‘aym in *Dalā’il al-Nubuwwa* (p. 114 §63), al-Taymī in the *Dalā’il* (p. 132), al-Ḥākim in the *Mustadrak* (3:705), al-Bayhaqī in the *Dalā’il* (2:251) cf. Ibn ‘Abd al-Barr, *Istī‘āb* (2:675), Ibn Kathīr, *Tafsīr* (4:169) and *Bidāya*, Ibn Ḥajar, *Fatḥ al-Bārī* (7:180) and *Iṣāba* (3:219).

O Pillar of those who rely upon you,
O Immunity of those who seek refuge in you
and Resort of those who seek herbage and rain,
and Neighboring Protector of those in need of shelter!
O you whom the One God has chosen for His creatures
by planting in him perfection and purity of character![317]

[4] The background to 'Umar's prayer for rain shows that there was also an explicit *tawassul* through and dream-vision of the Prophet, upon him peace, by the *Ṣaḥābī* Bilāl b. al-Ḥārith as narrated in two versions:

(a) Version 1 from the *Ṣaḥābī* Mālik al-Dār:

> The people suffered a drought in 'Umar's *khilāfa*, whereupon a man came to the grave of the Prophet ﷺ and said: "Messenger of Allah! Ask for rain for your Community, for verily they have but perished." After this the Prophet ﷺ appeared to him in a dream and told him: "Go to 'Umar and give him my greeting, then tell him that they will be watered. Tell him: Be clever!" The man went and told 'Umar. The latter wept and said: "My Lord! I spare no effort except in what escapes my power."[318]

[317]Narrated by Ibn 'Abd al-Barr in *al-Istī'āb* (1:276) and Ibn Sayyid al-Nās in *Minaḥ al-Madḥ* (p. 73).

[318]Narrated by Ibn Abī Shayba (6:356 §32002=12:31-32) and Bayhaqī, *Dalā'il al-Nubuwwa* (7:47) with a sound chain per Ibn Kathīr, *Jāmi' al-Masānīd* (1:223 *isnāduhu jayyidun qawī*) in *Musnad 'Umar* and *al-Bidāya* (7:91-92=7:105 *isnāduhu ṣaḥīḥ*) and Ibn Ḥajar in *Fatḥ al-Bārī, Istisqā'*, Chapter 3 (1989 ed. 2:629-630=1959 ed. 2:495 *isnād ṣaḥīḥ*) and *Iṣāba* (6:164 §8350=3:484) where he says Ibn Abī Khaythama cited it. It is also thus narrated by al-Khalīlī in *al-Irshād* (1:313- 314). Ibn 'Abd al-Barr cites it in *al-Istī'āb* (2:464=3:1149) and al-Dhahabī in the *Siyar* (Fikr ed. 1/2:524). Ibn Ḥajar identifies Mālik as 'Umar's treasurer and says that the man who visited and saw the Prophet ﷺ in his dream is identified as the Companion Bilāl b. al-Ḥārith. Ibn Ḥajar counts this ḥadīth among the reasons for al-Bukhārī's naming of the chapter "The people's request to their leader for rain if they suffer drought" in the *Ṣaḥīḥ*, although al-Bukhārī does not narrate it there. In his aspersions on *Fatḥ al-Bārī* the Wahhābī Ibn Bāz condemns the act of the Companion who came to the grave, calling it "aberrant" *(munkar)* and "a means to associating partners to Allah" *(wasīla ilāl-shirk)* while Nāṣir Albānī denies the authenticity of the ḥadīth in his booklet *al-Tawassul* (p. 120) on the claim that Mālik al-Dār is "unknown" *(majhūl)* on the sole basis of his brief mention by Ibn Abī Ḥātim al-Rāzī in *al-Jarḥ wa al-Ta'dīl* (8:213 §14252). This is contradicted by the notices of three authorities Albānī did not cite: Ibn Sa'd, al-Khalīlī, and Ibn Ḥajar! Furthermore, Ibn Abī Khaythama and al-Bukhārī narrated from him. "Mālik al-Dār [was] 'Umar b. al-Khaṭṭāb's freedman. He narrated from Abū Bakr and 'Umar. He was known" per Ibn Sa'd (5:12). "Mālik al-Dār is agreed upon and the Successors have approved highly of him," said Abū Ya'lā al-Khalīl b. 'Abd Allāh al-Khalīlī al-Qazwīnī in *Kitāb al-Irshād* (1:313) cf. 'Abd Allāh al-Ghumārī, *Irghām al-Mubtadi'* (p. 9). Ibn Ḥajar said in *al-Iṣāba* (6:164 §8350): "Mālik b. 'Iyāḍ [was] 'Umar's freedman. He is the one named Mālik al-Dār. He saw the Prophet ﷺ and heard narrations from Abū Bakr al-Ṣiddīq. He narrated from Abū Bakr and 'Umar, Mu'ādh, and Abū 'Ubayda. From him narrated Abū Ṣāliḥ al-Samān and his (Mālik's) two sons 'Awn and 'Abd Allāh. Bukhārī narrated from him in *al-Tārīkh al-Kabīr* (7:304 §10633) as well as Ibn Abī Khaythama." Albānī is further refuted in the lengthy analysis given by Mamdūḥ in *Raf' al-Minara* (p. 262-278), which refutes other similar attempts cf. Ibn Bāz's aspersions on *Fatḥ al-Bārī*, Abū Bakr Jazā'irī's tract *Wa-Jā'ū Yarkuḍūn*, Ḥammād al-Anṣārī's typical articles *al-Mafhūm al-Ṣaḥīḥ lil-Tawassul* also titled

(b) Version 2 from al-Ṭabarī's *Tārīkh*:

> In the year of the drought called al-Ramāda during the successorship of 'Umar the Companion Bilāl b. al-Ḥārith, while slaughtering a sheep for his kin, noticed that the sheep's bones had turned red because the drying flesh was clinging to them. **He cried out "Yā Muḥammadāh!!" Then he saw the Prophet ﷺ** in a dream ordering him to go to 'Umar with the tidings of coming rain on condition that 'Umar show wisdom. Hearing this, 'Umar assembled the people and came out to pray for rain with al-'Abbās, the uncle of the Prophet ﷺ.[319]

[5] 'Umar had made *tawassul* through the Prophet ﷺ in the past since he said: "We would use our Prophet as a means to You..." *i.e.* in his and Abū Bakr's rule (and not only during the life of the Prophet ﷺ), as it is improbable that they never once experienced drought in the previous 8.5 years. "But to restrict this sentence to the Prophet's lifetime is a deficiency stemming from idle lust, a manipulation of the text of the report, and figurative interpretation without proof." (Al-Kawtharī)

[6] At any rate the major *Ṣaḥāba* did make *tawassul* through the Prophet ﷺ after his time as established by the report from our Mother 'Ā'isha رضي الله عنها in al-Dārimī's *Sunan*, in the 15th Chapter of the Introduction titled: "The generosity of Allah to His Prophet after his death," related from Aws b. 'Abd Allāh with a good chain:

> The Medinans complained to 'Ā'isha of the severe drought that they were suffering. She said: "Go to the Prophet's grave and open a window towards the sky so that there will be no roof between him and the sky." They did so, after which they were watered with such rain that vegetation grew and the camels got fat. That year was named the Year of Plenty.[320]

[7] 'Umar had made *tawassul* through the Prophet ﷺ in the campaign of Tabūk and had therefore directly experienced the Divine munificence and Prophetic generosity.

> When the travel provision of the people decreased they thought of slaughtering their camels but 'Umar came to the Prophet ﷺ and said, "How will they survive without their camels?" The Prophet ﷺ said, "Call to them to bring every remainder of their travel provisions." A piece of leather was spread and they brought whatever they had. The Messenger of Allah ﷺ stood and supplicated then he blessed over the food and summoned them to bring their bags. The people supplied themselves to the

Tuḥfat al-Qārī fil-Radd 'alā al-Ghumārī and other such literature.

319Narrated by al-Ṭabarī, *Tārīkh* (2:509).

320The reader will find extensive documentation on this report in our teacher Shaykh Hisham Kabbani's *Encyclopedia of Islamic Doctrine* (4:47-52) and it was declared authentic by all the Sunni experts of ḥadīth, last in date Shaykh Nabīl b. Hāshim al-Ghamrī in his 1999 10-volume edition of and commentary on al-Dārimī titled *Fatḥ al-Mannān* (1:564-566) where he rejects the typical objections of al-Albānī and his likes to this ḥadīth.

last one. Then the Messenger of Allah said ﷺ, "I bear witness that there is no god but Allah and that I am the Messenger of Allah!"[321]

[8] 'Umar used al-'Abbās to show people the status of the Prophet's family in the society and teach them to respect and venerate them, as Ibn Ḥajar said in explanation of the report of Anas cited above: "It is desirable to seek the intercession of benevolent righteous people and the Prophet's relatives, and it shows al-'Abbās's great merit and that of 'Umar due to the latter's humbleness before al-'Abbās and his recognition of his due right."[322]

This is confirmed by al-Ājurri's narration in *al-Sharī'a* and Aḥmad in *Faḍā'il al-Ṣaḥāba* that Ka'b al-Aḥbār took al-'Abbās's hand and said, "I shall hide it away [this handshake] for your intercession on my behalf." Al-'Abbas replied: "Why, will I have the power of intercession?" Ka'b said: "Yes, there is none from the Household of the Prophet, upon him and them peace, except they have the power of intercession!"[323] Ka'b al-Aḥbār also said to *Sayyidinā* 'Umar: "Whenever the Israelites had a drought they sought intercession through their Prophet's household."[324]

Indeed, al-'Abbās came out surrounded by al-Ḥasan and al-Ḥusayn.[325]

[9] It is known that 'Umar had a particular veneration for the Prophetic Household *(Ahl al-Bayt)* as illustrated by the following reports:

(a) Ibn Sa'd narrated from al-Sha'bī and al-Ḥasan al-Baṣrī that al-'Abbas had some need of 'Umar one day and said to him: "Commander of the Believers, suppose the uncle of Mūsā came to you as a Muslim; how would you treat him?" He replied, "I swear by Allah that I would treat him well!" Al-'Abbās said, "Well, I am the uncle of Muḥammad the Prophet ﷺ!" 'Umar said, "Abu al-Faḍl, and what do you suppose? By Allah, your father ['Abd al-Muṭṭalib] is certainly dearer to me than my own father!" He said, "By Allah?" 'Umar said, "By Allah, yes! Because I know that he ['Abd al-Muṭṭalib] is dearer to the Messenger of Allah than my own father, therefore I prefer the love of the Messenger of Allah ﷺ to my love."

(b) A man disparaged 'Alī b. Abī Ṭālib in the presence of 'Umar whereupon the latter said: "Do you know the dweller of this grave? He is Muḥammad b. 'Abd Allāh b. 'Abd al-Muṭṭalib. And 'Alī is the son of Abū Ṭālib b. 'Abd al-Muṭṭalib. Therefore, do not mention 'Alī except in a good way for if you dislike him you will harm this one in his grave."[326] In another ver-

[321]Narrated from Salama b. al-Akwa' by al-Bukhārī and Muslim and from Abū Hurayra by Muslim and Aḥmad.
[322]Ibn Ḥajar, *Fatḥ al-Bārī* (1959 ed. 2:497).
[323]*Faḍā'il al-Ṣaḥāba* (2:937 §1802).
[324]Narrated by Ibn 'Abd al- Barr in *al-Istī'āb* (2:814).
[325]Narrated by Ibn 'Asākir as cited by Haytamī in *al-Sawā'iq al-Muh ṣriqa* (p. 176).
[326]Narrated by Aḥmad with a good chain in *Faḍā'il al-Ṣaḥāba* (2:641 §1089).

sion he says, "What is the matter with you, may Allah disgrace you! You have harmed the Messenger of Allah ﷺ in his grave!"[327]

(c) After 'Umar saw al-Ḥusayn b. 'Alī b. Abī Ṭālib waiting at his door he said to him: "You are more deserving of permission to enter than [my son] 'Abd Allāh b. 'Umar! You see the goodness that was placed on our head; [therefore] first Allah; then you [the Prophetic Household]!" and he placed his hand on his head as he spoke.[328]

(d) Jābir ﷺ said he heard 'Umar b. al-Khaṭṭāb say on the pulpit after he married Umm Kulthūm, the daughter of 'Alī and Fāṭima ﷺ:

> Do not disparage me [for marrying a young girl], for I heard the Prophet say, upon him blessings and peace: "On the Judgment Day every means will be cut off and every lineage severed except my lineage."[329]

'Umar desired to place himself in the Prophet's ﷺ lineage through this marriage due to the precedence of *Ahl al-Bayt* in the Prophet's intercession, upon him and them peace.

[10] Nor is this intercession solely by way of the Prophet's ﷺ mere supplication *(du'ā)* and by means of al-'Abbās's mere supplication as innovatively claimed.[330] Rather, it was by means of their person *(dhāt) and du'ā* as literally stated in the following reports among many others:

(a) Intercession through the person of the Prophet ﷺ according to Ibn 'Umar رضي الله عنهما in al-Bukhārī's *Ṣaḥīḥ*:

> 'Abd Allāh b. Dīnār said: "I heard Ibn 'Umar reciting the poetic verses of Abū Ṭālib: "A fair-skinned one by whose face rainclouds are sought, a caretaker for the orphans and protector of widows." 'Umar b. Ḥamza said: Sālim narrated from his father (Ibn 'Umar) that the latter said: "The poet's saying came to my mind as I was looking at the face of the Prophet ﷺ while he was praying for rain – and he did not come down until the rain water flowed profusely from every roof-gutter: "A fair-skinned one by whose face rainclouds are sought, a caretaker for the orphans and protector of widows." A narrator adds: "These were the words of Abū Ṭālib."[331]

(b) Intercession through al-'Abbās's person according to 'Umar:

> People! The Messenger of Allah ﷺ considered al-'Abbās like his father, venerating him and greatly respecting him and his rights. Therefore,

[327]Cited from 'Urwa by al-Qurṭubī in his *Tadhkira* (1:106).
[328]Narrated by al-Khaṭīb (1:141) cf. *Tahdhīb al-Kamāl* (6:404), *Tahdhīb al-Tahdhīb* (2:300), and *Iṣāba* (2:78).
[329]Narrated by Ṭabarānī through the narrators of Bukhārī and Muslim per Haythamī.
[330]This claim was never made before Ibn Taymiyya and it was revived by al-Albānī.
[331]Note that in his translation of al-Bukhārī (2:65), Muḥammad Muḥsin Khān alters the wording of the ḥadīth to read: "A white person who is requested to pray for rain" in place of "by whose face rain is sought." This is *tahrīf* i.e. textual and semantic manipulation of the most important source in Islam after the Qur'ān.

O people! take the lead of the Messenger of Allah ﷺ in the person of his uncle al-'Abbās and take the latter as your means to Allah ﷻ in the context of your tribulation.[332]

[11] 'Umar showed the possibility of *tawassul* through X even though Y – also present – may be better than X. He showed that *tawassul* through the inferior in the presence of the superior is permissible as there is Consensus that the best of all living human beings after Prophets then, namely 'Umar, 'Uthmān, and 'Alī are all three superior to al-'Abbās ﷺ. This was also a mark of humbleness on 'Umar's part as already cited from *Fatḥ al-Bārī.* Another example of this is the *tawassul* of Mu'āwiya for rain through the *Ṣaḥābī* Yazīd b. al-Aswad al-'Āmirī as narrated by Abū Zur'a al-Dimashqī in his *Tārīkh* and his *tawassul* through the *Tābi'ī* Abū Muslim al-Khawlānī as narrated by Aḥmad in *al-Zuhd.*[333]

[12] 'Umar used al-'Abbās also as a precaution lest people's faith in the Prophet ﷺ be shaken in case the prayer were not answered.

[13] Finally, the Sunna prayer for rain formally has to be performed by the outward, political Imām of the Muslims or his deputy. It is in that function that the office of the Messenger of Allah ﷺ had ceased and was taken over, first by Abū Bakr, then by 'Umar. Al-'Abbās's position in this event was that of the deputy of the latter as the Commander of the Believers. And Allah knows best.

As for the claim that "Shāh Walī Allah in his book *al-Balāgh al-Mubīn* ("The Crystal-Clear Conveyance") infers that 'Umar did not consider it allowed to ask those who had left this world or the absent for intercession," this is contrary to the view reported from Shāh Walī Allah in his book *Fuyūḍ al-Ḥaramayn* ("The Outpourings of the Two Sanctuaries). The apparent contradiction is explained by the fact that some books of Shāh Walī Allah may not be free from Wahhabi interpolations.[334]

It is known that the beasts themselves ask for rain as in the Prophetic ḥadīth of the ant narrated from Abū Hurayra by al-Dāraquṭnī, his student al-Ḥākim, and others;[335] and the Sunna requires us to bring the beasts out during the prayer for rain, and the Prophet said ﷺ, "Were it not for the

[332]Narrated from 'Umar with a sound chain by al-Balādhīrī and Ibn 'Abd al-Barr cf. al-Haytamī in *al-Sawā'iq al-Muḥriqa* (p. 176) and with weak chains from Ibn 'Umar by al-Zubayr b. Bakkār in *al-Ansāb* and Ibn 'Asākir (8:932) as cited by Ibn Ḥajar in the *Fatḥ* (1959 ed. 2:497). Shaykh Maḥmūd Mamdūḥ in *Raf' al-Mināra* (p. 120) rejected al-Albānī's claim in his *al-Tawassul* (p. 67-68) that the chain of this ḥadīth is "mixed up" *(muḍṭarib)* as inapplicable here.
[333]Cf. al-Tahānawī, *I'lā' al-Sunan* (8:193).
[334]As mentioned to us by Shaykh Muhammad Abū al-Hudā al-Ya'qūbī (private communication). See also https://www.livingislam.org/n/itsw_e.html.
[335]Cf. Ibn Abī Shayba (6:62, 7:71); Abū al-Shaykh, *al-'Aṭama* (5:1572); Ibn Kathīr, *Tafsīr* (3:360); Ibn Ḥajar, *Talkhīṣ al-Ḥabīr* (2:97 §718); Ibn al-Mulaqqin, *Khulāṣat al-Badr* (1:250); al-Ṣan'ānī, *Subul al-Salām* (2:83); al-Shawkānī, *Nayl al-Awṭār* (4:27); al-Tahānawī, *I'lā' al-Sunan* (8:193).

beasts they [who withhold *zakāt*] would never be granted rain!"[336] and "Were it not for the pasturing beasts punishment would be poured on you literally!"[337] So we may hope for the intercession of beasts, but not for that of the Prophet Muḥammad ?

Furthermore, the *Khalīfa* 'Umar b. al-Khaṭṭāb did not consider the Prophet to be absent nor to have left this world. Otherwise, why did he address the Prophet and Abū Bakr in their graves as narrated by al-Ṭabarānī through trustworthy narrators[338] and why was "nothing more important to him" – as narrated from him by al-Bukhārī in his *Ṣaḥīḥ* – than to be buried near them?

---

[336]Narrated by Ibn Mājah.
[337]Narrated by Abū Yaʿlā, al-Bazzār and others.
[338]See the report of Qays b. Abī Ḥāzim below (section titled "'Umar the *Shahīd*").

30
Tabarruk (Deriving Blessing) with the *Muṣḥaf*

It is mentioned in the books of the latter-day Hanafi masters such as Shaykhī Zādah (Damād Afandī) in *Majma' al-Anhur*, al-Ḥaṣkafī in *al-Durr al-Mukhtār* and Ibn 'Ābidīn in its *Ḥāshiya* entitled *Radd al-Muḥtār* that every morning 'Umar would take the *muṣḥaf* and place it over his face, saying, *Kitābu Rabbī* (the Book of my nurturing Lord) or *Manshūru Rabbī* (the Edict of my nurturing Lord) or *'Ahdu Rabbī* (the Covenant of my nurturing Lord). What is preserved is that that act was done and those words were spoken by the junior Companion 'Ikrima b. Abī Jahl (who embraced Islam on the conquest of Mecca), as narrated from Ibn Abī Mulayka by Abū Bakr Muḥammad b. al-'Abbās b. Najīḥ al-Bazzāz al-Baghdādī (d. 345) in his *Ḥadīth Shu'ba* and Sibṭ Ibn al-Jawzī in *Mir'āt al-Zamān.*

31
Some Sayings of Our Master 'Umar

- "O Allah! Grant me to die a shahid and make my death in the country of Your Prophet."[339] When 'Umar's daughter expressed doubt that both would happen together, he replied: "Allah is able to make it happen."
- "Take account of yourselves before you are brought to account" *(ḥāsibū anfusakum qabla an tuḥāsabū)*.[340]
- "Would that I were raised with a clear balance *(kifāfan)*: with nothing for me and nothing against me."[341]
- "If a stray camel died on the shore of the Euphrates I would fear that Allah would ask me to account for it."[342]
- From 'Abd Allāh b. 'Awn, Muḥammad b. Ghālib b. Ḥarb, and al-Aḥnaf b. Qays: "Learn before you become leaders!"[343] Al-Qārī said in *al-Asrār al-Marfū'a*, "Some said it meant 'before you marry and become the leaders of households and servants'.... Al-Thawrī said, '**Whoever rushes to leadership will massacre knowledge** and whoever does not rush shall study [lit. 'write'] then study then study some more!'"[344] Imām al-Shāfi'ī also said, "Learn *fiqh* before you reach leadership for when this happens, there is no way to study it anymore."[345]
- From al-Aswad b. Hilāl al-Muḥāribī: When 'Umar was made Caliph he stood on the pulpit and said: "People! I am going to invoke Allah, therefore say *āmīn* in witness to it *(hayminū lahā)*! Allah, my Lord! I am rough, so make me gentle! I am stingy so make me generous! I am weak so make me strong!"[346]
- From 'Abd Allāh al-Qurashī: 'Umar looked at a young man who was praying with his head cast down so he said to him: "What is this? Hold your head up! There is no extra humility *(al-khushū')* after what is in the heart. Whoever displays humility to the people be-

[339]Narrated from Aslam by al-Bukhārī.
[340]Abū Nu'aym, *Ḥilya* (1:88 §135); Ibn al-Jawzī, *Ṣifat al-Ṣafwa*, chapter on 'Umar.
[341]Cited by Ibn al-Jawzī in *Ṣayd al-Khāṭir* (p. 241).
[342]Narrated by Ibn Sa'd (3:105).
[343]Narrated by al-Khaṭīb in *Naṣīḥat Ahl al-Ḥadīth* (p. 24).
[344]Sufyān also said – Allah be well-pleased with him: "I never saw rarer *zuhd* than the renouncing of leadership. You might see a man renounce food, money, and dress, but when it comes to leadership, he maneuvers and battles" and "Among the best of people is the Sufi learned in *Fiqh*."
[345]Narrated from Aḥmad b. Ṣāliḥ by al-Khaṭīb in *Naṣīḥat Ahl al-Ḥadīth* (p. 21).
[346]Narrated by Abū Nu'aym in *Ḥilyat al-Awliyā'* (1985 ed. 1:53) and Ibn Sa'd in *al-Ṭabaqāt al-Kubrā* (3:275) cf. *al-Fā'iq* (4:113).

yond what is in his heart only displays hypocrisy on top of hypocrisy."[347]

- Anas said: "I heard 'Umar say as he was alone behind a wall: 'By Allah! You shall certainly fear Allah, O son of al-Khaṭṭāb, or He will punish you!'"[348]

- 'Umar remarked to Ḥudhayfa that he sometimes refrained from praying the funeral prayer over one of the deceased so the latter told him that the Prophet ﷺ had revealed to him the names of twelve of the hypocrites, whereupon 'Umar asked Ḥudhayfa, "I adjure you by Allah! Tell me, am I one of them?" Ḥudhayfa replied, "No, and I will not tell anyone anything further after this."[349]

- "People resemble their times more than their own parents."[350]

- Jābir said he heard 'Umar b. al-Khaṭṭāb say on the pulpit after marrying Umm Kulthūm, the daughter of 'Alī and Fāṭima: "Do not disparage me [for marrying a young girl], for I heard the Prophet ﷺ say: 'On the Judgment Day every means will be cut off and every lineage severed except my lineage.'"[351] He desired to place himself in the his ﷺ lineage through this marriage due to the precedence of *Ahl al-Bayt* in the Prophet's ﷺ intercession. 'Alī gave her away to 'Umar although he was afraid at first that 'Umar might not accept her due to her youth. 'Alī told 'Umar: "I shall send her to you and if you agree, then she is your wife and I have married her to you."[352] The dowry was 40,000 dirhams. She bore him Zayd al-Akbar, known as Ibn al-Khalīfatayn ("Son of the Two Caliphs" *i.e.* 'Umar and 'Alī) who became renowned for his handsomeness, and a daughter, Ruqayya. After 'Umar died she remarried, upon 'Alī's wish, with 'Awn b. Ja'far b. Abī Ṭālib. When 'Awn died 'Alī remarried her with Muḥammad b. Ja'far.[353] Zayd died a young man, childless, from a stone throw in the time of Mu'āwiya. Umm Kulthūm died at the same time and either 'Abd Allāh b. 'Umar or Sa'īd b. al-'Āṣ b. Sa'īd – who had asked for Umm Kulthūm's hand after 'Umar died] prayed over the both of

[347]Narrated by al-Dīnuri as cited in *Kanz al-'Ummāl* (§22527).
[348]Ibn Qudāma, *Mukhtaṣar Minhāj al-Qāṣidīn li-Ibn al-Jawzī* (p. 426); al-Dhahabī.
[349]Narrated by al-Ṭabarī in his *Tafsīr* (11:11), al-Bazzār through trustworthy narrators according to al-Haythamī (3:42), al-Bayhaqī in his *Sunan al-Kubrā* (8:200), al-Azdī in *Musnad al-Rabī'* (p. 361 §929), Ibn Abī Shayba (7:481).
[350]Narrated by Ibn Qutayba in *'Uyūn al-Akhbār* (2:1) cf. Abū Ghudda in al-Qārī's *Maṣnū'* (p. 198) and al-Ṣurayfīnī cf. *Maqāṣid, Ziyādat al-Jāmi' al-Ṣaghīr*, and *Kashf al-Khafā'* as a saying of 'Umar; and by Abū Nu'aym in the *Ḥilya* (2:177) as a saying of 'Urwa.
[351]Narrated by al-Ṭabarānī. Al-Haythamī said its narrators are those of al-Bukhārī and Muslim. See extensive documentation in our *Musnad of Ahl al-Bayt*.
[352]Narrated by 'Abd al-Razzāq (6:163 §10353) and al-Khaṭīb in his *Tārīkh* (6:182) in the entry on Ibrāhīm b. Mihrān b. Rustum al-Marwazī, with a fair chain according to al-Aḥdab in *Zawā'id Tārīkh Baghdād* (5:209-214 §901).
[353]Some reports claim that when Muḥammad b. Ja'far died she remarried with his brother 'Abd Allāh b. Ja'far who survived her, but this third remarriage seems historically unlikely and the series stops at Muḥammad as per Ibn Qutayba.

them.[354] When 'Alī was struck down by Ibn Muljam, Umm Kulthūm reportedly said: "*Mā lī wa-li-ṣalāt al-ṣubḥi, qutila zawjī 'Umaru ṣalāta al-ghadāh, wa-qutila abī ṣalāta al-ghadāh!* – What does the morning prayer want with me? My husband 'Umar was killed at the morning prayer, and my father was killed at the morning prayer!"[355]

- From 'Āmir b. Rabī'a: "I saw 'Umar pick up a straw from the ground and say: 'Would that I were this straw! Would that I was nothing! Would that my mother never bore me!'"[356]
- From 'Ubayd Allah b. 'Umar b. Ḥafṣ: 'Umar was seen carrying a slaughtered animal on his back. He was asked why, and he replied: "I was infatuated with myself and wanted to humble myself."[357] Al-Ḥasan narrated: "'Umar gave a sermon when he was Caliph wearing a waist-wrap patched in twelve places."[358]
- From Mujāhid: "We found that the goodness of our lives was patience."[359]
- From 'Urwa b. al-Zubayr: "Know that greed is poverty and despair sufficiency. When a man despairs of something, he does without it."
- From al-Sha'bī: "By Allah! My heart has softened for the sake of Allah until it became softer than butter, and it has hardened for the sake of Allah until it became harder than stone."
- From 'Awn b. 'Abd Allāh b. 'Utba: "Sit with the Oft-Repentant *(al-tawwābīn)*, for they are the most soft-hearted of people."
- From Aslam, 'Umar's freedman: "Be the vessels of the Book and the well-springs of the Science, and ask Allah for your sustenance day by day."
- From Abū 'Uthmān al-Nahdī: "Winter is the treasure of those devoted to worship." 'Umar memorized Sūrat al-Baqara in twelve years and when he had learned it completely he slaughtered a camel.[360]
- From Dāwūd b. 'Alī: "If a sheep dies on the shore of the Euphrates I fear lest Allah ask me to account for it on the Day of Resurrection."
- From Yaḥyā b. Abī Kathīr: "If it were announced from the heaven: 'O people! You are all entering Paradise except one,' I would fear to be

[354]Ibn Sa'd (8:337-340=8:463-464); *'Uyūn al-Akhbār* (4:71); *al-Siyar wal-Maghāzī* (p. 248); *Tārīkh al-Ya'qūbī* (2:260); *Nasab Quraysh* (p. 352); al-Ṭabarī, *Tārīkh* (4:199 and 5:335); Ibn 'Abd al-Barr, *al-Istī'āb* (4:490-491); al-Nawawī, *Tahdhīb al-Asmā' wa al-Lughāt* (2:267 §1219); al-Dhahabī, *Siyar* (Fikr ed. 5:22-24) and *Tārīkh al-Islam* (4:58-59, 4:137-139, 4:227); Ibn Ḥajar, *Iṣāba* (4:492 §1481); Ibn al-Athīr, *Usd al-Ghāba* (7:387-388) and *al-Kāmil fi al-Tārīkh* (3:54, 4:12); etc.
[355]Narrated from al-Aṣbagh al-Ḥanṭalī by Dhahabī in *Tārīkh al-Islam* (3:648-649).
[356]Ibn 'Asākir, *Tārīkh Dimashq* (44:313) and al-Dhahabī.
[357]Al-Suyūṭī in *Tārīkh al-Khulafā'* and al-Dhahabī.
[358]Abū Nu'aym, *Ḥilya* (1:89 §140).
[359]This and the next nine reports in Abū Nu'aym's *Ḥilya* 1:86-91.
[360]Narrated from Ibn 'Umar by al-Dhahabī.

he; and if it were announced: 'O people! You are all entering the Fire except one,' I would hope to be he."

32
The Prophecy that 'Umar would be a *Shahīd*

The Prophet ﷺ one day saw 'Umar wearing a certain shirt whereupon he asked him, "Is it new or has it been washed already?" 'Umar replied, "It has been washed already." The Prophet ﷺ said, "'Umar, wear new clothes, live a glorious life, and die a shahid!"[361]

Qays b. Abī Ḥāzim narrated that one day, 'Umar addressed the people from the pulpit in Medina and said in his address: "Verily there is in the Gardens of 'Adn a palace which has five hundred doors, each posted with five thousand of the ladies of Paradise, and none but a Prophet shall enter it." At this point he turned to the grave of the Messenger of Allah ﷺ and said: "Congratulations to you, O dweller of this grave!" Then he continued: "And none but a Most-Truthful One *(ṣiddīq)* shall enter it." At this point he turned towards Abu Bakr's grave and said: "Congratulations to you, Abū Bakr!" Then he said: "And none but a shahid shall enter it," and he pointed to himself. He continued, speaking to himself out loud: "And when did you inherit shahada, 'Umar?" Then he said: "Truly, the One who brought me out from Mecca unto the migration to Medina is able to grant me shahada!"[362]

[361]Narrated with a chain of trustworthy narrators through al-Zuhrī per Būṣirī, *Miṣbāḥ al-Zujāja* (4:82), all of them used by Bukhārī and Muslim per Haythamī, *Majma' al-Zawā'id* (9:73-74), from Ibn 'Umar by Aḥmad in his *Musnad* (Arnā'ūṭ ed. 9:440-442 §5620) and *Faḍā'il al-Ṣaḥāba* (1:255 §322-323), Ibn Mājah, Ibn Ḥibbān (Arnā'ūṭs ed. 15:320-322 §6897), al-Bazzār (*Zawā'id* §2504), Abū Ya'lā in his *Musnad* (§5545), Ṭabarānī in *al-Kabīr* (12:283 §13127) and *al-Du'ā'* (p. 143 §399), Ibn al-Sunnī and al-Nasā'ī in their *'Amal al-Yawm wal-Layla* (respectively §269 and 1:275 §311), Abū Nu'aym in *Akhbār Aṣbahān* (1:139), Azdī in his *Jāmi'* (11:223), 'Abd b. Ḥumayd in his *Musnad* (p. 238 §723), Ibn 'Abd al-Barr in *al-Istī'āb* (3:1157), and al-Baghawī in *Sharḥ al-Sunna* (12:50 §3112), all through 'Abd al-Razzāq (§20382) whom some of the Imāms considered mistaken in his narration of this ḥadīth through Zuhrī. Consequently it was rated inauthentic by Bukhārī *("lā shay'")* in Tirmidhī's *'Ilal* (p. 373), Ibn 'Adī *("munkar")* in *al-Kāmil* (5:1948), Nasā'ī in *'Amal al-Yawm wal-Layla* quoting Yaḥyā b. Sa'īd al-Qaṭṭān cf. Bayhaqī in *al-Sunan al-Kubrā* (6:85 §10143), and Ibn Abī Ḥātim (*bāṭil*), *'Ilal* (1:490). Ṭabarānī relates it through another chain through al-Thawrī instead of Zuhrī in *al-Du'ā'* (§400), cf. Haythamī, *Mawārid al-Ṭam'ān* (1:536 §2381) and al-Bazzār also narrates it from Jābir with a weak chain in his *Musnad* (*Zawā'id* §2503). But Ibn Ḥibbān considered it sound and Ibn Ḥajar concluded that the narration is at the very least "fair" *(ḥasan)* in *Natā'ij al-Afkār* (1:136-138) as does Arnā'ūṭ in his edition of Ibn Ḥibbān. Also narrated with a weak *mursal* chain–as Abū al-Ashhab Ja'far b. Ḥayyān al-'Uṭāridī did not meet the *Ṣaḥāba*–by Ibn Abī Shayba (8:453, 10:402), Ibn Sa'd (3:329) and al-Dūlābī, *al-Kunā wal-Asmā'* (1:109).

[362]Ṭabarānī, *al-Awsaṭ* through trustworthy narrators cf. Haythamī (9:54-55).

33
'Umar's Fatal Stabbing ﷺ and His Last Speech

'Amr b. Maymūn said:

> I saw 'Umar b. al-Khaṭṭāb a few days before he was stabbed in Medina. He was standing with Ḥudhayfa b. al-Yamān and 'Uthmān b. Ḥunayf to whom he said, "What have you done? Have you imposed more taxation on the land [*i.e.* Iraq] than it can bear?" They replied, "We have imposed on it what it can bear because of its great yield." 'Umar again said, "Check whether you have imposed on the land what it cannot bear." They said, "We have not." 'Umar added, "If Allah should keep me alive I will let the widows of Iraq need no men to support them after me." But only four days had elapsed when he was stabbed. The day he was stabbed, I was standing and there was nobody between me and him except 'Abd Allāh b. 'Abbas. Whenever 'Umar passed between the two rows, he would say, "Stand in straight lines." Once he saw no defect in the rows he would go forward and start the prayer with the magnification. He would recite the Sura of Yūsuf or al-Naḥl or the like in the first *rak'a* so that the people may have time to join the prayer. As soon as he said the *takbīr* I heard him shout, "The dog has killed me!" or "eaten me!" at the time he stabbed him. A non-Arab unbeliever used a double-bladed dagger and continued stabbing all the persons he passed on his right and left until he had stabbed thirteen people, seven of whom died. Seeing that, one of the Muslims threw a cloak on him. Realizing he had been captured, the non-Arab unbeliever killed himself, 'Umar took the hand of 'Abd al-Raḥmān b. 'Awf and told him to lead the prayer. Those who were standing by 'Umar's side saw what I saw but the people who were in the other parts of the Mosque did not see anything. Not hearing the voice of 'Umar they kept saying, "*Subhān Allāh!*" "*Subḥān Allāh!*" 'Abd al-Raḥmān b. 'Awf led the people in a short prayer. When they finished the prayer 'Umar said, "O Ibn 'Abbās! Find out who attacked me." Ibn 'Abbās investigated briefly and returned, saying, "The slave of al-Mughīra." 'Umar said, "The craftsman?" Ibn 'Abbās said yes. 'Umar said, "May Allah curse him! I did not treat him unjustly. Praise belongs to Allah Who has not caused me to die at the hand of a man who claims himself to be a Muslim. No doubt, you and your father (al-'Abbās) loved to have more non-Arab unbelievers in Medina." Al-'Abbās had the greatest number of slaves. Ibn 'Abbās said to 'Umar. "If you wish, we will do." He meant, "If you wish we will execute them." 'Umar said, "You are mistaken, for you cannot kill them after they have spoken your language, prayed towards your Qibla and performed the same Hajj as you." Then 'Umar was carried to his house and we went along with him, and the people were as if they had never suffered a calamity before. Some said, "Do not worry (he will recover)." Some said, "We are afraid (he will die)." An infusion of dates was brought to him and he drank it but it came out (of the wound) of his

belly. Then milk was brought to him and he drank it, and it also came out of his belly. The people then knew that he was *mayyitun* (about to die). We went to him, and the people came, praising him. A young man[363] came saying, "O chief of the believers! Receive the glad tidings from Allah to you due to your company with Allah's Messenger and your superiority in Islam which you know. Then you became the ruler and you ruled with justice and finally you have been granted shahada." 'Umar said, "Would that all these privileges will counterbalance my shortcomings so that my slate is clean!" When the young man walked away, behold, [the bottom of] his waistcloth was touching the ground. 'Umar said, "Call the young man back to me." Then he said, "My nephew, lift up your garment for this will preserve it longer and it is more pious to your nurturing Lord." Then he said said, "O 'Abd Allāh b. 'Umar, check if I owe any debt." When the debt was checked it amounted to eighty-six thousand [dirhams] or so. 'Umar said, "If the property of 'Umar's family covers the debt then pay it out of that; otherwise request it from the Banū 'Adīy b. Ka'b. If their funds are insufficient, ask among the Quraysh and do not ask any beyond them. So pay this debt on my behalf. Go to ʿĀʾisha the Mother of the believers and say, ''Umar is saluting you,' and do not say: 'The commander of the believers,' because today I am not the commander of the believers. And say: ''Umar b. al-Khaṭṭāb is asking permission to be buried with his two companions (i.e. the Prophet and Abū Bakr).'" 'Abd Allah greeted ʿĀʾisha and asked for the permission for entering, and then entered and found her sitting and weeping. He said to her, "'Umar bin al-Khaṭṭāb is paying his salutations to you, and asks the permission to be buried with his two companions." She said, "I had the idea of having this place for myself, but today I swear I will indeed prefer 'Umar to myself." When he returned it was said, "Here is 'Abd Allah b. 'Umar, he is back." 'Umar said, "Sit me up." Somebody propped him up against himself and 'Umar asked, "What news do you have?" He said, "What you love to hear, Commander of the believers! She has given the permission." 'Umar said, "Praise be to Allah, **there was nothing more important to me than this.**[364] So once I have expired then you all carry me, then you [Ibn ʿUmar] greet 'Āʾisha and say: ''Umar b. al-Khaṭṭāb asks permission!,' and if she gives me permission, bring me in, and if she refuses, then take me to the graveyard of the Muslims." Then the Mother of the believers Ḥafṣa came with women walking with her. When we saw her, we got up so she went in to see him and wept there for some time. Then the men asked for permission to enter so she went further inside for them and we heard her weeping inside. They said, "Give instruction, Commander of the believers, appoint a successor!" 'Umar said, "I do not find anyone more suitable for the job than the following persons or group whom Allah's Messenger was

[363] Namely Ibn ʿAbbās as explicitly narrated from al-Miswar b. Makhrama by al-Bukhārī.
[364]Compare this to the impious saying of certain people that "there is nothing there."

pleased with at the time that he died." Then he named ʻAlī, ʻUthmān, al-Zubayr, Ṭalḥa, Saʻd and ʻAbd al-Raḥmān; and he said, "ʻAbd Allāh b. ʻUmar will be a witness to you, but he will have no share in the rule,"—as if condoling with him—"so if the command befalls Saʻd then that is that. Otherwise, let whoever is given the command use his help, for verily I have not dismissed him because of any inability or dishonesty." He added, "I instruct the successor after me to take special care of the first Emigrants, namely to recognize their due right and protect their sacred honor; and I instruct him to treat the Helpers well—*those who took up the Abode and the faith before them* (al-Ḥashr 59:9), namely to be accepting of those of them who do good and to be forgiving of those of them that do wrong; and I instruct him to treat the people of the cities well for they are the defenders of Islam, the collectors of wealth and the enragement of the enemy, and that nothing be taken from them except their surplus, with their consent; and I instruct him to treat the desert Arabs well, for verily they are the original Arabs and the constituent of Islam, namely that he should take from the peripheries of their wealth and have it spent back on their poor; and I instruct him to see to the covenantees of Allah and the covenantees of the Messenger of Allah, namely that their covenant be fulfilled with them and to fight in their defense and that they should not be overburdened other than to their ability." Then when his soul was seized we carried him out and marched until ʻʻAbd Allāh b. ʻUmar gave the greeting and said, "ʻUmar b. al-Khaṭṭāb is asking permission." ʻĀʼisha said, "Bring him in." He was brought in and was laid there, with his two companions. When his burial was over, this particular group [he had recommended] gathered. ʻAbd al-Raḥmān said, "Put your commandership in the hands of three of you." Al-Zubayr said, "I have given all my right over to ʻAlī." Ṭalḥa said, "I have given all my right over to ʻUthmān." Saʻd said, "I have given all my right over to ʻAbd al-Raḥmān b. ʻAwf." ʻAbd al-Raḥmān then said, "Which of you two [=ʻUthmān and ʻAlī] has relinquished this matter so that we shall entrust it to him, with Allah as his witness, and Islam?" Whereupon both shaykhs were silenced. ʻAbd al-Raḥmān said, "Will you both leave this matter to me, and I take Allah as my Witness that I will not choose but the better of you?" They said, "Yes." So ʻAbd al-Raḥmān took the hand of one of them[365] and said, "You [=ʻAlī] are related to Allah's Messenger and one of the earliest Muslims as you know well. So I ask you by Allah to promise that if I select you as a ruler you shall indeed do justice, and if I select ʻUthmān as a ruler you shall indeed listen and indeed obey." Then he took the other aside and said the same to him. Then, once he had taken the solemn promise, he said, "Raise your hand, O ʻUthman!" Then he [=ʻAbd al-Raḥmān] pledged his loyalty to him, after which ʻAlī pledged his loyalty to him, and the people of the Abode [=Medina] entered and gave him the pledge of allegiance.[366]

[365] I.e. he took him aside and spoke to him in private as next mentioned explicitly.
[366] Narrated from ʻAmr b. Maymūn by al-Bukhārī (Aṣḥāb al-Nabī ṣallā Allāhu ʻalayhi wa-sallam, qiṣṣat al-bayʻa wal-ittifāq ʻalā ʻUthmān b. ʻAffān). See also Abū

As 'Umar's head lay in Ibn 'Umar's lap after his stabbing he said to him: "Lay my cheek on the ground." Then he said: "Woe to me! My mother's woe to me if my Lord does not grant me mercy!"[367] The next morning al-Miswar woke him for the dawn prayer. 'Umar rose saying: "Yes, and there is no part in Islam for whoever leaves prayer." He prayed bleeding from his wounds.[368] To the visitors who told him *Jazāka Allāhu khayran* (Allah recompense you with goodness!) he would reply: "I am hopeful and fearful" *(rāghib wa rāhib)*.[369]

When 'Umar was stabbed, Ka'b al-Aḥbār said: "If 'Umar swore to Allah [supplicating], He would delay his death." The people said: "*Subḥān Allah!* [How can that be when] Allah says *and when their term comes they cannot put it off an hour nor advance it* (16:61 cf. 7:34, 10:49)?" Ka'b said: "Did He not say *And no one grows old who grows old, nor is aught lessened of his life, but it is recorded in a Book* (35:11)?"[370]

Nu'aym, *Ḥilyat al-Awliyā'* (1:73-92); al-Dhahabī, *Siyar A'lām al-Nubalā'* (1/2:509-565 §3); and Shiblī Nu'māni, 'Umar the Great (2:336-338).
[367]Ibn Sa'd (3:344), Abū Nu'aym, *Ḥilya* (1:89 §137), and al-Dhahabī.
[368]Narrated from al-Miswar b. Makhrama by Mālik in his *Muwaṭṭa'*, Ibn Sa'd (3:350-351), and Ibn al-Jawzī in *Manāqib 'Umar* (p. 222).
[369]Narrated from Ibn 'Umar by al-Bukhārī and Muslim.
[370]Narrated from Ibn al-Musayyib by 'Abd al-Razzāq (11:224) with a sound chain cf. his *Tafsīr* (2:137).

34
'Alī's Eulogy of 'Umar –Allah be Well-Pleased with Them

Ibn 'Abbās narrated:

When 'Umar was placed on his deathbed, the people gathered around him, invoked Allah, and prayed for him before the body was taken away, and I was among them. I felt somebody placing his elbow on my shoulder and heard him invoking Allah's Mercy for 'Umar and saying: "O 'Umar! You have not left behind you a person whose deeds I would like to imitate more than yours, nor would I more prefer to meet Allah with other than your deeds. By Allah! I always thought that Allah would keep you with your two companions, for very often I used to hear the Prophet saying: I, Abū Bakr and 'Umar went somewhere; I, Abū Bakr and 'Umar entered someplace; and I, Abū Bakr and 'Umar went out." I turned around and saw that it was 'Alī b. Abī Ṭālib.[371]

I narrated it as part of my reading of Ibn al-Jazarī's *Asnā al-Maṭālib fī Manāqib Sayyidinā 'Alī b. Abī Ṭālib* with al-Sayyid Muḥammad Abū al-Hudā al-Ya'qūbī. Ibn al-Jazarī said it is agreed upon by al-Bukhārī and Muslim as well as narrated by al-Nasā'ī and Ibn Mājah.

[371] "Muslim narrated it with his chain while Mālik narrates it from Ja'far al-Ṣādiq, from his father." Ibn Rushd, *al-Bayān wal-Taḥṣīl* (18:519).

35
After ʿUmar's Burial in 'Ā'isha's House

'Ā'isha said: "I used to enter my house – where the Messenger of Allah ﷺ and my father (Abū Bakr) were buried – and loosen my garment thinking it is only my husband and my father. But when 'Umar b. al-Khaṭṭāb was later buried [there], I did not enter the room except that I wore my garment close to me, out of shyness before 'Umar."[372]

[372]Narrated by Aḥmad with a sound chain as stated by al-Haythamī, by al-Ḥākim (4:7=1990 ed. 4:8 and 3:61=1990 ed. 3:63) who said it is sound by the criteria of al-Bukhārī and Muslim, and by Muḥibb al-Dīn al-Ṭabarī in *al-Samt al-Thamīn* (p. 90). Compare this also to the impious saying of those that say "there is nothing there."

36
ʿUmar's Posterity

Our liege lord ʿUmar had nine sons and four daughters: the great Imām ʿAbd Allāh Abū ʿAbd al-Raḥmān (from Zaynab bint Maẓʿūn); ʿAbd al-Raḥmān the Elder (from Zaynab also); Zayd the Elder (from Umm Kulthūm bint ʿAlī b. Abī Ṭālib min Fāṭimat al-Zahrā' *raḍīya Allāhu ʿanhum*); ʿĀṣim (from Umm Kulthūm Jamīla bint ʿĀṣim b. Thābit; Zayd the Younger (from Mulayka bint Jarwal al-Khuzāʿiyya); ʿUbayd Allah (from Mulayka also); ʿAbd al-Raḥmān the Middle, known as Abū Shaḥmat al-Majlūd (from Lahiyya, a slave woman); ʿAbd al-Raḥmān the Younger, known as Abū al-Mujabbar (from a slave woman); ʿIyāḍ (from ʿĀtika bint Zayd); Ḥafṣa (from Zaynab also); Ruqayya (from Umm Kulthūm bint ʿAlī also); Fāṭima (from Umm Ḥakīm bint al-Ḥārith); and Zaynab (from Fukayha, a slave woman).

Among his descendants in the Middle East are the following families: Abū Bakr, Abū al-Hudā, al-Baysār, al-Tājī al-Fārūqī, al-Ḥāmidī, al-Khaṭṭābiyya, al-Khayrī (family of the famous Ḥanafī authority Khayr al-Dīn al-Ramlī d. 1081), al-Rāfiʿī, al-Zuwaytīnī, ʿAbd al-Hādī, al-ʿAbsī, ʿUthmān, al-ʿArāqīb, al-ʿAqqād, al-ʿUqaylī, al-ʿAlabī, al-ʿUmarī, al-ʿAnānī, Fūflayya (tree of ʿAbd al-Ghanī al-Nābulusī and the Banū Qudāma and Jammāʿilī Ḥanbalīs), al-Lādiqī, al-Masādīn, al-Nābulusī (cf. above), al-Nuṣūlī, and al-Nuʿmān.

37
ʿAbd Allāh b. ʿUmar's Dream of His Father

From ʿAbd Allāh b. ʿUmar: "[Long after ʿUmar's death] I saw a palace in my sleep, and was told it belonged to ʿUmar b. al-Khaṭṭāb. Then I saw him come out of it, wearing a cover as if he had just bathed. I said: 'How did you fare?' He said: 'Well! But I would have fallen headlong if I had not found a forgiving Lord.' Then he asked: 'How long is it since I left you?' I said: 'Twelve years.' He said: 'I only just finished rendering account.'"[373]

[373]Narrated by Abū Nuʿaym in the *Ḥilya* (1:54) with a weak chain.

38
'Umar, the Barrier Between the *Umma* and *Fitna*

'Umar was the barrier between the Prophet's ﷺ Community and the onset of dissension. His death is one of the earliest signs of the Final Hour. One day he asked Ḥudhayfa about the "dissension that shall surge like the waves of the sea" mentioned by the Prophet ﷺ. Ḥudhayfa answered: "You need not worry about it, Commander of the Believers, for between you and it there is a gate closed shut!" 'Umar said: "Will the gate be opened or broken?" Ḥudhayfa said: "Broken!" 'Umar replied: "That is more appropriate than that it be let open." The narrator [Abū Wā'il] said: "We feared to ask Ḥudhayfa who was that gate, so we sent Masrūq to ask him and he said: 'That gate was 'Umar.'" They asked him, "Did 'Umar know that?" He replied, "Yes, as surely as night precedes tomorrow, and I was speaking to him unambiguously!"[374]

'Uthmān b. Maẓ'ūn, Abū Dharr, Ibn 'Abbās, and Khālid b. al-Walīd similarly narrated that the Prophet ﷺ said of 'Umar: "This is the bolt of dissension *(hādhā ghalqu al-fitna)*. There shall not cease to stand between you and dissension a strongly shut gate as long as this man lives among you." [375] Al-Ṭabarānī also narrated from Abū Dharr that the Prophet ﷺ said: "No dissension can reach you as long as this man is among you," meaning 'Umar.[376] Khālid b. al-Walīd ؓ addressed the people in al-Shām one day and a man said to him: "The dissensions have appeared!" Khālid replied: "Not as long as Ibn al-Khaṭṭāb is alive! That shall only happen after his time."[377] Khālid would not say such a thing of his own opinion, so it appears he heard it from the Prophet ﷺ or from whoever heard it from him.

---

[374]Narrated from Abū Wā'il Shaqīq b. Salama by al-Bukhārī and Muslim.
[375]Narrated by al-Ṭabarānī in *al-Kabīr* (9:38 §8321), al-Bazzār, al-Wāsiṭī in *Tārīkh Wāsiṭ* (p. 244-245), and Ibn Qāni' in *Mu'jam al-Ṣaḥāba* (2:258 §774) with a weak chain, cf. al-Haythamī (9:72), but the report is confirmed by the next narration. The same is also narrated from Ibn 'Abbās by al-Daylamī in *al-Firdaws* (1:438 §1785).
[376]Narrated by al-Ṭabarānī in *al-Awsaṭ* (2:267-268 §1945) with a chain of trustworthy narrators according to Ibn Ḥajar in *Fatḥ al-Bārī* (1959 ed. 6:606) except that al-Haythamī (9:73) suspects a missing link between al-Ḥasan al-Baṣrī and Abū Dharr. The full narration states that Abū Dharr called 'Umar "the padlock of dissension" *(qufl al-fitna)*.
[377]Narrated by Aḥmad, al-Ṭabarānī in *al-Kabīr* (4:116 §3841), Nu'aym b. Ḥammād in *al-Fitan* (1:45, 1:281 §819), all with a chain containing an unknown narrator – Qays b. Khālid al-Bajalī – but the undiscredited *Tābi'ī* is an acceptable narrator, hence Ibn Ḥajar in *Fatḥ al-Bārī* (1959 ed. 13:15) declared the chain "fair" *(ḥasan)*. Cf. al-Haythamī (7:307-308) and al-Mubārakfūrī in *Tuḥfat al-Aḥwadhī* (6:368).

39
ʿUmar's Narrations from the Prophet ﷺ

The arch-master of Hadith Yaʿqūb b. Shayba b. al-Ṣalt al-Sadūsī (182-262) authored a monumental *Musnad* of which al-Dāraquṭnī said, "Even if Yaʿqūb's *Musnad* were written on the door of a hammam it would be obligatory to copy it" and al-Dhahabī said, "There is no *Musnad* better than it." The part of it containing *Musnad Abī Hurayra* alone was said to consist in 200 parts. Alas most of it is lost but a fraction of the *Musnad ʿUmar* survived and was published, containing but 44 reports.[378]

The ascetic Ḥanbalī hadith scholar Abū Bakr al-Najjād gathered eighty-five reports in his *Musnad ʿUmar*. Imam Aḥmad himself gathered about 400 in his, while the hadith scholar and exegete Ibn Kathīr compiled no less than 1,022 Prophetic and non-Prophetic reports narrated with their chains from ʿUmar b. al-Khaṭṭāb–may Allah be well-pleased with him–in his *Musnad al-Fārūq*.[379]

[378] *al-Juzʾ al-ʿĀshir min Musnad Amīr al-Muʾminīn ʿUmar b. al-Khaṭṭāb Riḍwān Allāh ʿalayh*, ed. ʿAlī b. ʿAbd Allāh al-Ṣayyāḥ (Riyadh: Dār al-Ghurabāʾ, 1423/2002). This edition is the definitive one and is superior to the two earlier editions brought out in Lebanon by Sāmī Ḥaddād (1940) and Kamāl al-Ḥūt (1985).
[379] Abū Bakr Aḥmad b. Salmān b. al-Ḥasan al-Najjād, *Musnad ʿUmar b. al-Khaṭṭāb*, ed. Maḥfūẓ al-Raḥmān Zaynullāh (Medina: Maktabat al-ʿUlūm wal-Ḥikam, 1415/1994); ʿImād al-Dīn Abū al-Fidāʾ Ismāʿīl b. ʿUmar b. Kathīr, *Musnad al-Fārūq Amīr al-Muʾminīn Abī Ḥafṣ ʿUmar b. al-Khaṭṭāb*, ed. Imām b. ʿAlī b. Imām, 3 vols. (Fayyūm: Dār al-Falāḥ, 1430/2010).

'Uthmān b. 'Affān

رضی الله تعالی عنه

'Uthmān b. 'Affān b. Abī al-'Āṣ b. Umayya
b. 'Abd Shams, Abū 'Amr, Abū 'Abd Allāh,
Abū Layla al-Qurashī al-Umawī, the
Prophet's ﷺ Friend, *Amīr al-Mu'minīn*, third
of the Rightly-Guided Caliphs of the Prophet ﷺ,
third of the Ten promised Paradise,
most truthful of the Companions in his virtue,
who recited the entire Qur'ān in a single *rak'a*,
named *Dhul-Nūrayn* or "Possessing Two Lights"
in reference to his successive marriage with Ruqayya
then Umm Kulthūm the Prophet's ﷺ daughters,
one of those who emigrated twice:
first to Abyssinia and then to Medina,
who died a shahid as the Prophet ﷺ had predicted.
He gathered together the volume of the Qur'ān
which he had read entirely before the Prophet ﷺ,
and none in Islam opens the *Muṣḥaf* or recites
or reads from the Qur'ān except
our Master 'Uthmān receives a share of their reward
–Allah Most High grant him the greatest reward,
shower him with His mercy,
and be well-pleased with him!

ʿUthmān b. ʿAffān b. Abī al-ʿĀṣ b. Umayya b. ʿAbd Shams, Abū ʿAmr, Abū ʿAbd Allāh, Abū Layla al-Qurashī al-Umawī ﷺ (47BH-d. Dhūl-Ḥijja 35/577-June 656) the Prophet's Friend, *Amīr al-Mu'minīn*, the third of the four Rightly-Guided Caliphs of the Prophet ﷺ and third of the Ten promised Paradise. He is named *Dhū al-Nūrayn* or "Possessing Two Lights," a reference to his successive marriage with two daughters of the Prophet ﷺ, Ruqayya then Umm Kulthūm. He is among those who emigrated twice: once to Abyssinia, and again to Medina. He gathered together the Qur'ān which he had read in its entirety before the Prophet ﷺ. During his tenure as Caliph, Armenia, Caucasia, Khurāsān, Kirman, Sijistān, Cyprus, and much of North Africa were added to the dominions of Islam. "The possessions of Islam extended to the far Eastern ends of the earth and the far West [Spain] as well. The territories of the Maghreb were conquered to their farthest tip – al-Andalus, Qayrawān, Sibta, and the lands bordering the ocean. On the Eastern side, lands were conquered to the farthest end of China. Chosroes was killed, his empire collapsed entirely, and the cities of Iraq, Kurāsān, and al-Ahwāz were conquered. Land tax was brought from East and West to the Commander of the Believers, ʿUthmān b. ʿAffān."[380] He was murdered in his house at 82 years of age. Aḥmad b. Ḥanbal narrated through ʿUthmān b. ʿAffān 162 ḥadīths from the Prophet ﷺ in his *Musnad*. Among the Companions who narrated from him in the Nine Books are Anas, Abū Hurayra, Jundub, ʿAbd Allāh b. al-Zubayr, ʿAbd Allāh b. ʿAbbās, ʿAbd Allāh b. ʿUmar. A host of prominent Successors narrated from him, among them al-Zuhrī, Ibn al-Musayyib, al-Daḥḥāk, and ʿAlqama.

[380]al-Qasṭallānī, *al-Mawāhib al-Lādunniyya*.

1
ʿUthmān's Islam, his Marriage to the Prophet's daughter and their emigration to Abyssinia

Our liege lord ʿUthmān b. ʿAffān was one of the very first to enter Islam at the invitation of Abū Bakr as already mentioned.[381] There is a second account to the effect that he became Muslim at the invitation of the Prophet ﷺ, to whom ʿUthmān was related through his maternal aunt the eloquent pre-Islamic seer and poetess Saʿdā bint Kurayz b. Rabīʿa b. Ḥabīb b. ʿAbd Shams, the full sister of ʿUthmān's mother Arwā bint Kurayz. Arwā and Saʿdā's mother was Umm Ḥakam al-Bayḍā' bint ʿAbd al-Muṭṭalib the Prophet's paternal aunt and thus they were also the Prophet's cross-cousins,[382] and Saʿdā had been the first to encourage ʿUthmān to follow the Prophet, then Abū Bakr encouraged him and took him to the Prophet ﷺ who said to him, "ʿUthmān, answer Allah Who is inviting you to His garden, for verily I am the Messenger of Allah to you and to all His creatures."[383]

After that the Prophet gave ʿUthmān his daughter Ruqayya in marriage and later asked his adopted son Usāma b. Zayd, "Have you seen a *zawj* (pair) more handsome than the two of them?"[384] ʿUthmān was extremely happy with the marriage but was worried about the vicious persecution led against the Prophet ﷺ by ʿUthmān's relatives—his paternal uncle al-Ḥakam b. al-ʿĀṣ, his mother's husband ʿUqba b. Abī Muʿayṭ and the latter's sons, his two uterine brothers al-Walīd b. ʿUqba and ʿUmāra b. ʿUqba. The Prophet told them to emigrate to Abyssinia for their safety. There were two distinct waves starting in the fifth year of the Prophethood with barely over a dozen people—among them ʿUthmān and Ruqayya—and, after the group came back the same year erroneously thinking the polytheists had become Muslim, a second wave of over 100 new Muslims including some second-timers from the first group. Their names are listed in the books of *Sīra*.[385]

[381] See the section on Abū Bakr, chapter 6.
[382] A cross-cousin is one of two cousins who are the children of a brother and a sister respectively.
[383] Ibn Ḥajar, *Iṣāba* (8:176-178 §11296, Saʿdā bint Kurayz) citing Abū Saʿd al-Naysābūrī's *Sharaf al-Muṣṭafā*. The account also mentions ʿUthmān was anxious to marry Ruqayya the daughter of the Prophet lest the latter marry her off to her cousin ʿUtba b. Abī Lahab.
[384] Abū al-Qāsim al-Baghawī, *Muʿjam al-Ṣaḥāba*; al-Ṭabarānī, *Kabīr* (1:76 §97). "This was before the Verse of the Veil was revealed" per Haythamī, *Majmaʿ* (9:80).
[385] E.g. Ibn Hishām (Saqqā ed. 1:327-330).

2
'Uthmān's Generosity, Piety, Virtue and Humbleness

'Uthmān was extremely wealthy and generous. When he heard the Prophet ﷺ say: "Whoever equips the army of al-'Usra,[386] Paradise is for him," he brought the Prophet ﷺ a thousand gold dinars which he poured into his lap. The Prophet ﷺ picked them up with his hand and said repeatedly: "Nothing shall harm 'Uthmān after what he did today."[387] It is also narrated that equipped the army of al-'Usra with seven hundred ounces of gold,[388] or seven hundred and fifty camels and fifty horses.[389]

From the time that he became Muslim ʿUthmān would buy and free a slave every single Jumuʿa. If he did not find one he would free two on the following Jumuʿa.[390]

The Prophet ﷺ said: "The most compassionate of my Community towards my Community is Abū Bakr; the staunchest in the Religion of Allah is 'Umar; and the most truthful in his virtue is 'Uthmān."[391] The "seven or nine" pebbles were heard by Abū Dharr glorifying Allah "like the buzzing of bees" in the hands of the Prophet ﷺ, Abū Bakr, 'Umar, and 'Uthmān successively.[392] He ﷺ then said, "This is the succession of Prophethood."[393]

The Prophet ﷺ particularly praised 'Uthmān for his sense of virtue and said: "Shall I not feel shy before a man when even the angels feel shy before him?"[394] Imām al-Qushayrī said: "The Prophet ﷺ pointed to the fact that even though he held the self-respect *(ḥishma)* of 'Uthmān in the high-

[386]For the campaign of Tabūk on the border of al-Shām.

[387]Narrated from ʿAbd al-Raḥmān b. Samura by Aḥmad and al-Tirmidhī who graded it *ḥasan gharīb*. Also narrated from 'Uthmān by al-Bukhārī with a different wording.

[388]Narrated from 'Abd al-Raḥmān b. 'Awf by Abū Ya'lā in his *Musnad* and Ibn 'Asākir in *Tārīkh Dimashq* (39:69).

[389]Narrated from al-Ḥasan al-Baṣrī by Ibn 'Asākir in *Tārīkh Dimashq* (39:70).

[390] Narrated by al-Dārimī and cited by Daḥlān, *al-Fatḥ al-Mubīn* (p. 197).

[391]Part of a longer ḥadīth narrated with sound chains from Anas by al-Tirmidhī who graded it *ḥasan ṣaḥīḥ*, Ibn Mājah, and Aḥmad.

[392]Narrated from (i) Abū Dharr by Bukhārī, *Tārīkh al-Kabīr* (8:442-443 §3635); Ibn Abī ʿĀṣim, *Sunna* (2:543 §1146); Bazzār (9:431-434 §4040, §4044); Ṭabarānī, *al-Awsaṭ* (2:59 §1244) with a sound chain as stated by Haythamī, *Majmaʿ al-Zawāʾid* (6:191, 8:298-299); Khaythama, *Juzʾ* (p. 105-106, *faḍāʾil al-Ṣaḥāba*); Abū Nuʿaym, *Dalāʾil al-Nubuwwa* (§338, §538); and (ii) Anas by Khaythama, *Juzʾ* (p. 106); al-Thaʿlabī, *Tafsīr* (Isrāʾ 17:44). Ibn Ḥajar only remembered the first chain in his discussion of the report in *Fatḥ al-Bārī* (6:592), probably because the chains from Anas were deemed disclaimed cf. Dhahabī, *Tārīkh al-Islām* (Tadmurī ed. 1:353).

[393] Narrated from Abū Dharr by al-Bayhaqī, *Dalāʾil al-Nubuwwa* (6:64-65). Others related the statement only as a saying of al-Zuhrī.

[394]Narrated from 'Ā'isha by Muslim and Aḥmad and from Ḥafṣa by the latter.

est esteem, yet the position or situation between himself and Abū Bakr and 'Umar was more transparent (*al-ḥālatu al-latī baynahu wa-bayna Abī Bakrin wa-'Umara kānat aṣfā*).[395]

Al-Sakhāwī said:

> I was asked about the context in which the angels of the Merciful were bashful before our liege lord 'Uthmān and replied that I did not find it in any truly reliable report. However, our teacher, al-Badr the genealogist[396] informed us in one of his works, as related from al-Jamāl al-Kāzarūnī, that when the Prophet ﷺ linked the Emigrants and *Anṣār* in brotherhood in Medina while Anas b. Mālik was absent, 'Uthmān stepped forward to fill in, his chest bared, so the angels stayed back out of modesty. The Prophet ﷺ then ordered him to cover his chest and they went back to their places. He ﷺ asked them the reason and they said, "Pudeur (*ḥayā'an*) before 'Uthmān." This needs to be researched further.[397]

Our liege lord 'Uthmān b. 'Affān was humble and was seen in the time of his caliphate sleeping alone in the mosque, wrapped in a blanket with no one around him and, another time, riding on a mule with his son Nā'il behind him. He was seen delivering a *khuṭba* wearing a four-dirham robe. Shuraḥbīl b. Muslim said, "'Uthmān would feed people the food of princes but he himself would eat [bread with] vinegar and olive oil."[398]

[395] *Risāla Qushayriyya*, ed. 'Abd al-Ḥalīm Maḥmūd and Maḥmūd al-Sharīf (Cairo: Mu'assasat Dār al-Sha'b, 1409/1989) p. 475.
[396] The Ḥasanī Sayyid and Jurist Badr al-Dīn Ḥasan b. Muḥammad b. Ayyūb al-Qāhirī al-Shāfi'ī (767-866) who authored *Sharḥ al-Tanqīḥ lil-Walī al-'Irāqī.*
[397] Al-Sakhāwī, *al-Ajwibat al-Marḍiyya* (1:353 §94 and 3:1085 §309).
[398] Daḥlān, *al-Fatḥ al-Mubīn* (p. 199), citing Ibn al-Jawzī's *Ṣifat al-Ṣafwa.*

3
His Night Worship, Perpetual Fasting, and Some of His Exclusive Special Merits

It is related through several sound chains that 'Uthmān recited the Qur'ān in a single *rak'a*.[399] Ibrāhīm b. Rustum al-Marwazī said: "Four are the Imāms that recited the entire Qur'ān in a single *rak'a*: 'Uthmān b. 'Affān, Tamīm al-Dārī, Sa'īd b. Jubayr, and Abū Ḥanīfa."[400] 'Uthmān's wife said to his killers when they breached his house, "Know, if you are going to kill him, that he would stand in prayer all night and recite a full reading of the Qur'ān in a single *rak'a*!"[401] "Many people might criticize that but the fact is that it is not disapproved for a memorizer of the Qur'ān who continually recites it day and night, so that when he recites it all it does not take more than a few hours.... The Qur'ān was his intimate friend in his seclusion."[402]

Al-Dānī said 'Uthmān had recited the entire Qur'ān to the Prophet ﷺ, after which the students who in turn took it from him were Abū 'Abd al-Raḥmān al-Sulamī, al-Mughīra b. Abī Shihāb, Abū al-Aswad al-Du'alī and Zirr b. Ḥubaysh.[403]

Ruḥayma—al-Zubayr b. 'Abd Allāh's grandmother—related that 'Uthmān fasted the whole year and used to spend the night in prayer except for a rest in its first part.[404] Ibn al-Mubārak also narrated that 'Uthmān used to fast all year round.

'Alī ؓ said: "'Uthmān was one of those who were *mindful of their duty and did good works, and again were mindful of their duty, and believed, and once again were mindful of their duty and did right. Allah loves those who do good* (5:93)."[405] Ibn 'Umar said 'Uthmān was meant by the verse *is he who pays adoration in the watches of the night, prostrate and standing, fearing the Hereafter and hoping for the mercy of his Lord—?* (39:9).[406]

399 'Abd al-Razzāq, *Muṣannaf* (3:354); Ibn Abī Shayba, *Muṣannaf* (1:99); Bayhaqī, *Sunan* (2:396, 3:25); Ibn Ḥazm, *Muḥallā* (3:53); Abū Nu'aym, *Ḥilya* (1:56) cf. al-Lacknawī, *Iqāmat al-Ḥujja* (p. 59-60).
400 Cited by al-Khaṭīb in *Tārīkh Baghdād* (13:356), Dhahabī in *Manāqib Abī Ḥanīfa* (p. 22), and al-Suyūṭī in *Tabyīḍ al-Ṣaḥīfa* (p. 94-95).
401 Ibn Abī Shayba (1:56, 1:98); Abū Nu'aym, *Ḥilya* (1:56) cf. al-Lacknawī, *Iqāmat al-Ḥujja* (pp. 59-60).
402 Muḥammad Sharīf 'Adnān al-Ṣawwāf, *'Uthmān b. 'Affān Dhū al-Nūrayn wa-Aṣdaq al-Nāsi Ḥayā'an* (Riyadh: Maktabat al-'Ubaykān, 1421/2000) pp. 61-62.
403 al-Dhahabī, *Siyar* (Risāla ed. *al-Khulafā' al-Rāshidūn* p. 149).
404 Ibn Abī Shayba (1:128); Abū Nu'aym, *Ḥilya* (1:56) cf. al-Lacknawī, *Iqāmat al-Ḥujja* (p. 59-60).
405 Narrated from Ḥasan by Abū Nu'aym, *Ḥilya* (1:93 §155) with a sound chain.
406 Narrated from Yaḥyā al-Bakkā' by Abū Nu'aym with a weak chain.

Anas narrated that at the time the Prophet ﷺ received the oath of allegiance at *Bay'at al-Riḍwān*, he had sent 'Uthmān as an emissary to the Meccans so he was absent whereupon the Prophet ﷺ said: "O Allah! Truly 'Uthmān is catering to Allah's need and to His Messenger's need *(inna 'Uthmāna fī ḥājat Allah wa-fī ḥājati Rasūlih)*," whereupon he struck his own hand on top of the other, so the hand of the Messenger of Allah ﷺ for 'Uthmān was better than their own hands for themselves.[407] Abū Nu'aym cited it in his *Faḍā'il al-Khulafā' al-Rāshidīn* as a merit which no one else shared with 'Uthmān.

Another such exclusive merit is the fact that Allah and His Prophet put 'Uthmān among the Companions of Badr although he was not physically there, because the Prophet had ordered him to remain in Medina to be at the bedside of his sick daughter Ruqayya, 'Uthmān's wife, who died after their return from Badr. Thereafter the Prophet made no difference between him and the rest of the Companions of Badr in the equal allocation of spoils and he added that Allah had guaranteed his *ajr* (reward) also.[408] This is why 'Uthmān is included in Shaykh Khālid al-Baghdādī's *Jāliyat al-Akdār wal-Sayf al-Battār* (The Removal of Hardships and the Trenchant Sword) and other intercessory supplications containing lists of the veterans of Badr.

[407]Narrated by al-Tirmidhī *(ḥasan ṣaḥīḥ gharīb)* and others.
[408]Narrated from Ibn 'Umar by Bukhārī, Tirmidhī, and Aḥmad.

4.1
Some of ʿUthmān's Excellent Innovations: His Codex of the Qur'ān

Anas narrated: When Ḥudhayfa campaigned with the people of Iraq and al-Shām in Armenia, the Muslims contended with regard to the Qur'ān in a reprehensible manner. Ḥudhayfa came to 'Uthmān and told him: "Commander of the Believers, rescue this Community before they differ in the Qur'ān the way Christians and Jews differed in the Books!" 'Uthmān was alarmed at this and sent word to Ḥafṣa the Mother of the Believers: "Send me all the volumes in which the Qur'ān has been written down." When she did, 'Uthmān ordered Zayd b. Thābit, Sa'īd b. al-'Āṣ, 'Abd Allāh b. Zubayr and 'Abd Al-Raḥmān b. al-Ḥārith b. Hishām to copy them into volumes. He said, "If you all differ with Zayd concerning the Arabic then write it in the dialect of Quraysh for truly the Qur'ān was only revealed in their dialect."[409] There is Consensus around the integral contents of 'Uthmān's volume[410] and that one who denies or questions it in whole or in part has left Islam.[411]

The Prophet ﷺ predicted the promulgation of the ʿUthmanic Quranic volumes and gave glad tidings to those of his Umma whose bodies and souls would be engrossed in the reading of the *muṣḥaf* and its belief and practice in the following hadith narrated from ʿUmar:

> "Do you know which of the people of belief are the best in belief?" They said, "The angels." The Prophet said, "So they are and it is right for them, and what would prevent them when Allah gave them the level that He gave them? Rather, other than them." We said, "Messenger of Allah, the Prophets." He said, "So they are and it is right for them. Rather, other than them." We said, "Messenger of Allah, then who are they?" He said, "A people that shall come later—they are still in the loins of men—whereupon they shall believe in me although they have not seen me, and they shall find *al-waraq al-muʿallaq* (the suspended leaves) whereupon they shall put its contents into practice. These ones are the best of the people of belief in their belief."[412]

[409]Narrated from Anas by al-Bukhārī and al-Tirmidhī who graded it *ḥasan ṣaḥīḥ*.
[410]As stipulated by Ibn Ḥazm, *Marātib al-Ijmāʿ*; al-Qāḍī 'Iyāḍ in al-Nawawī's *Sharḥ Ṣaḥīḥ Muslim* (4:109); and Ibn Ḥajar in *Fatḥ al-Bārī* (Cairo ed. 12:131).
[411] Ibn al-Qaṭṭān al-Fāsī, al-Iqnāʿ fī Masāʾil al-Ijmāʿ (al-Ijmāʿ fīl-Īmān, al-Qurʾān).
[412] Narrated from (i) Aslam the *mawlā* of ʿUmar by Bazzār (1:412-413 §288-289), one of them a *ḥasan* chain per al-Haythamī, *Majmaʿ al-Zawāʾid* (10:65); Abū Yaʿlā (1:147 §160); Abū al-Qāsim al-Baghawī, *Ḥadīth Muṣʿab al-Zubayrī* (p. 97 §127); Ḥākim (4:85-86, *ṣaḥīḥ*; Dhahabī: *bal ḍaʿīf*); al-Thaʿlabī (al-Baqara 2:3); al-Khaṭīb, *Sharaf Aṣḥāb al-Ḥadīth* (pp. 33-34 §62); Ibn ʿAsākir (58:255); (ii) ʿAbd Allāh b. ʿAmr by Ibn ʿArafa, *Juzʾ Ḥasan b. ʿArafat al-ʿAbdī*, ed. ʿAbd al-Raḥmān Faryawāʾī (Kuwait: Dār al-Aqṣā, 1406/1985) p. 52 §19; Bayhaqī, *Dalāʾil* (6:538); al-Khaṭīb, *Sharaf Aṣḥāb al-Ḥadīth* (pp. 32-33 §61); (iii) Anas by al-Bazzār (13:487 §7294) in

When 'Uthmān finished copying the Qur'ān-volumes *(maṣāḥif)*, Abū Hurayra said to him: "You have done right and been given success! I bear witness that I certainly heard the Messenger of Allah ﷺ say: 'Truly, those that love me most in my *Umma* are a people that shall come after me, believing in me without having seen me, that shall practice what is in the suspended leaves *(ya'malūna bimā fīl-waraq al-mu'allaq)*.' I said, 'What leaves?' until I saw the *maṣāḥif*!" This pleased 'Uthmān who ordered that ten thousand [dirhams] be disbursed to Abū Hurayra and said to him: "By Allah, I did not know you were keeping our Prophet's ḥadīth from us!"[413]

the wording "they shall find a Book" per al-Haythamī, *Kashf al-Astār* (3:318-319 §2840) and *Majma' al-Zawā'id* (10:65); (iv) Abū Hurayra by Abū Nu'aym, *Tārīkh Aṣbahān* (1:363); al-Sahmī, *Tārīkh Jurjān*, ed. Muḥ. 'Abd al-Mu'īd Khān, 2nd ed. (Hyderabad: Dā'irat al-Ma'ārif al-'Uthmāniyya, 1387/1967; rept. Beirut: 'Ālam al-Kutub, 1407/1987) p. 404 §687; Bayhaqī, *Dalā'il* (6:538); and (v) Abū Jumu'a al-Anṣārī by al-Ṭabarānī, *Kabīr* (4:27-28 §3540). It has a sound witness-report per Ibn Ḥajar in *al-Amālī al-Muṭlaqa* (pp. 37-40 §81) and is an overall fair or rather sound hadith per the editors of Ibn al-Mulaqqin's *Mukhtaṣar Istidrāk al-Dhahabī 'alā Mustadrak al-Ḥākim*, ed. Sa'd b. 'Abd Allāh Āl Ḥumayd, 'Abd Allāh al-Luḥaydān, 8 vols. (Riyadh: Dār al-'Āṣima, 1411-1415/1991-1994) 5:2456-2462 §840; Ibn Ḥajar, *al-Maṭālib al-'Āliya bi-Zawā'id al-Masānīd al-Thamāniya*, ed. Sa'd Nāṣir 'Abd al-'Azīz al-Shathrī et al., 19 vols. (Riyadh: Dār al-'Āṣima and Dār al-Ghayth, 1419/1998) 12:394-397 §2922) respectively.

[413]Narrated through al-Wāqidī by Ibn 'Asākir (39:244 §7972); Ibn Kathīr, *Bidāya* (Iḥyā' al-Turāth ed. 7:243); and—with a forged chain—from Nubayṭ al-Ashja'ī by Ibn 'Asākir (39:243-244) per al-Suyūṭī, *Khaṣā'iṣ* (2:220).

4.2
He Did Not Shorten the Prayer While Travelling

In the latter part of his Caliphate, 'Uthmān did not shorten the prayer while travelling.[414] The non-shortening of prayer during travel is also reported from 'Ā'isha, Salmān al-Fārisī, and fourteen other Companions according to Abū Bakr Muḥammad b. Yaḥyā al-Ash'arī al-Mālikī (674-741) in his book *al-Tamhīd wa al-Bayān fī Maqtal al-Shahīd 'Uthmān.*[415]

'Ā'isha as a rule did not shorten prayers in travel and gave as her reason the fact she found no hardship in travel, whereas *qaṣr* was stipulated to alleviate hardship. The same is true of Sa'd b. Abī Waqqāṣ. She even fasted while travelling and considered shortening to two a dispensation *(rukhṣa).* This is the Shāfi'ī and Ḥanbalī position. It is also reported from Ibn 'Abbās that he left the choice open for the traveler to pray two or four.[416] The report that Ibn 'Abbās said, "Whoever prays four cycles while travelling it is as if he prayed two while not travelling" has a weak, broken chain as Ḥumayd b. 'Alī al-'Uqaylī is rejected by al-Dāraquṭnī and al-Daḥḥāk b. Muzāḥim never met Ibn 'Abbās.

[414]Narrated from 'Urwa b. al-Zubayr by al-Bukhārī and Muslim as well as Abū Dāwūd and Aḥmad. This is also the choice of 'Ā'isha.
[415]Cf. Muḥibb al-Dīn al-Khaṭīb's notes on Ibn al-'Arabī's *al-'Awāṣim* (p. 80).
[416]Cf. al-Jaṣṣāṣ, *Aḥkām al-Qur'ān* (2:252), al-Nawawī in *al-Majmū'* (4:223), and Ibn Qudāma in *al-Kāfī* (1:200) and *al-Mughnī* (2:55).

4.3
His Additions to the Two Holy Sanctuaries

Our liegelord ʿUthmān added land to the Sacred Sanctuary in Mecca by buying out several people. Others refused to sell so he placed the value of their houses and lands to the Treasury, demolished them and remitted the values to them. In Medina he bought a land which he then donated to the Prophetic Mosque in the time of the Prophet ﷺ for which he got "a house in Paradise,"[417] and during his caliphate in the year 29 he enlarged the mosque and built it up.[418] Thus ʿUthmān shares in the huge rewards not only of reading the *Muṣḥaf* but also of every act of worship in the two Sanctuaries.

Imām al-Nawawī said:

> It was narrated in *Ṣaḥīḥ al-Bukhārī* from Ibn 'Umar that he said: "In the time of the Messenger of Allah ﷺ the mosque was built with sun-dried clay bricks, its roof was made of palm branches, the pillars were of palm wood. Abū Bakr did not add to it anything; 'Umar added to it and built it the way that it used to be during the time of the Prophet ﷺ with bricks and palm branches and palm-wood pillars. 'Uthmān, in turn, changed it, adding considerably to it, and he built up its walls with engraved stone and freestone, put up pillars of engraved stone, and a roof of teak [Indian oak]." It is required to keep *Ṣalāt* in the *masjid* that used to exist during the time of the Messenger of Allah ﷺ. For the previously-mentioned sound ḥadīth: "A prayer in this, my mosque, is better than a thousand prayers in any other mosque" applies only to what was in place in his own time.[419] If one prays in congregation, stepping forward to the first row, and those rows immediately behind it, is best. Let him pay attention to what I have warned about. In the two *Ṣaḥīḥ* books on the authority of Abū Hurayra the Prophet ﷺ said: "My Pulpit overlooks my Pond." Al-Khaṭṭābī said that the meaning of this narration is that he who keeps the prayers at my *minbar* shall be given water from the Prophet's Pond on the Day of Judgment. The other ḥadīth in the *Ṣaḥīḥ* was mentioned before: "Between my grave and the *minbar*, lies one of the Gardens of Paradise."[420]

[417] Tirmidhī (Manāqib ʿUthmān, ḥasan); Nasāʾī (Aḥbās, waqf al-masājid); etc.
[418] al-Dhahabī, Siyar (al-Khulafāʾ al-Rāshidīn, ʿUthmān b. ʿAffān).
[419] Al-Haytamī said: "There is divergence among the scholars concerning this but there is no sound ḥadīth from the Prophet ﷺ differing from what al-Nawawī said."
[420] Nawawī, *Īḍāḥ fī Manāsik al-Ḥajj* (Damascus: Dār Ibn Khaldūn, n.d.) pp. 140-150.

4.4
His adding a supplication to the last *rak'a* of *Tarāwīḥ*

Our liege lord ʿUthmān would add a standing supplication of *qunūt* to the last *rakʿa* of *tarāwīḥ*, which he would read after bowing and before prostrating.[421] He recited *qunūt* in the last *rakʿa* of the dawn prayer in the same manner, then switched to reciting it before bowing—in the dawn prayer only—so as to give people more time to join the prayer.[422]

421 al-Nawawī, *al-Majmūʿ* (3:520).
422 Ibn Qudāma, Mughnī (Ṣalāt, masāʾil ṣalāt al-jamāʿa).

5
Did he collect the Zakat in the Month of Rajab?

Imām Mālik narrated in the *Muwaṭṭa'* (per its western narrations as well as Muḥammad b. al-Ḥasan's) that 'Uthmān would say[423] on the pulpit: "Truly this is the month of your zakat, therefore, whoever owes a debt, let him repay his debt and purify the rest by remitting zakat." ʿAbd al-Razzāq, Ibn Abī Shayba and others narrated the same report as did al-Qāsim b. Sallām in *al-Amwāl* and others,[424] all without mention of any specific month but al-Qāsim added the comment of Ibrāhīm b. Saʿd (one of the narrators in his chain) "I think it is the month of Ramadan." The latter is based on al-Zuhrī's report that "ʿUthmān would give that sermon in the month of Ramadan."[425]

Shaykh ʿAbd al-Qādir al-Jīlānī in the chapter on the merits of Rajab in his *Ghunya* asserted ʿUthmān gave that sermon in the month of Rajab and said, "Behold, this is the muted month of Allah and it is the month of your zakat." The Damascene Ḥanbalī scholar Ibn Rajab in the chapter on Rajab in *Laṭāʾif al-Maʿārif* stated "the people of these lands [i.e. Syro-Palestine] customarily bring out the sakat in the month of Rajab." He followed it up with the claim that there is nothing in the Sunna to that effect "but it is related that ʿUthmān said," and he proceeded to cite the report of the *Muwaṭṭaʾ*.[426] The uncertainty is stated in al-Athram and Ibrāhīm b. al-Ḥārith's report of Imam Aḥmad's comment about ʿUthmān's statement that "he did not explain (or it was not explained) in what sense he [=ʿUthmān] meant it (or in what sense it is meant)."[427] Al-Bājī in *al-Muntaqā* and Ibn al-ʿArabī in *al-Masālik*—their respective commentaries on the *Muwaṭṭaʾ*—only mentioned among its possible meanings the sense that "it could have been the custom of their majority to bring out the zakat at that time"[428] whether it was Muḥarram, Rajab, Shaʿbān or Ramadan.

[423] *Kāna yaqūlu*, "i.e. explicitly in the sense of repeatedly every year" per Ibn ʿĀshūr, *Jamharat Maqālāt wa-Rasāʾil al-Ṭāhir b. ʿĀshūr*, ed.Muḥ. al-Ṭāhir al-Maysāwī, 4 vols. (Amman: Dār al-Nafāʾis, 1436/2015) 2:951.

[424] ʿAbd al-Razzāq, *Muṣannaf* (4:92); Ibn Abī Shayba, *Muṣannaf* (2:414 §10555, *Zakāt, mā qālū fīl-rajul yakūn ʿalayhi al-dayn man qāla lā yuzakkīh*); al-Qāsim b. Sallām, *al-Amwāl* (Ḥuwaynī ed. 2:94 §1167).

[425] Cited by al-Qanāziʿī (d. 413) in *Tafsīr al-Muwaṭṭaʾ*, ed. ʿĀmir Ḥasan Ṣabrī, 2 vols. (Qatar: Dār al-Nawādir, 1429/2008) 1:254.

[426] Ibn Rajab, *Laṭāʾif al-Maʿārif*, (al-Sawwās ed. p. 231).

[427] In Ibn Rajab, *Majmūʿ Rasāʾil Ibni Rajab*, ed.Ṭalʿat al-Ḥulwānī, 2nd ed., 4 vols. (Cairo: al-Fārūq al-Ḥadītha, 1424-1425/2003-2004) 2:614.

[428] See also Ibn ʿĀshūr's view in his Kashf al-Mughaṭṭā min al-Maʿānī wal-Alfāẓ al-Wāqiʿati fīl-Muwaṭṭā.

6
His Physical Description

'Uthmān was neither tall nor short, extremely handsome, brunet, large-jointed, wide-shouldered, with a large beard which he dyed yellow, dark to sand-colored hair which reached to his shoulders and gold-braced teeth. 'Abd Allāh b. Ḥazm said: "I saw 'Uthmān, and I never saw man nor woman with a more beautiful face than him."[429]

As illustrated elsewhere in this volume 'Uthmān often wore a turban face-veil in public in avoidance of *fitna*, similar to Ḥanẓala al-Asadī who "was of the handsomest of people and used to veil his face lest men harbor jealousy towards him" among a handful of Meccans who did the same for the same reasons such as the famous Zayd b. Muhalhal al-Ṭā'ī known as Zayd al-Khayl, 'Amr b. Ḥamamat al-Dawsī, al-Zabarqān Ḥuṣayn b. Badr al-Bahdalī, Subay' al-Ṭahawī and others.[430] 'Uthmān would cover his face even while in *iḥrām* (consecrated state) performing his Hajj: "It is allowed for a man in *iḥrām* to cover his face according to the people of learning. It is related from 'Uthmān that he covered his face while in the state of *iḥrām*, and it is the position of al-Shāfi'ī."[431]

[429] Narrated by al-Ṭabarānī, *al-Mu'jam al-Kabīr* (1:75 §94); Abū Nu'aym, *Ma'rifat al-Ṣaḥāba* (1:60 §228); Ibn 'Asākir, *Tārīkh Dimashq* (39:17)..
[430] Abū Ja'far Muḥ. b. Ḥabīb b. Umayya al-Hāshimī al-Baghdādī, *al-Muḥabbar*, ed. Ilse Lichtenstädter (Hyderabad: Dā'irat al-Ma'ārif al-'Uthmāniyya, 1361/1942) p. 201, 232-233.
[431] al-Baghawī, *Sharḥ al-Sunna* (7:240).

7
"He of the Two Lights" and Ibn Masʿūd's praise

Our liege lord 'Uthmān got his nickname of "Dhūl-Nūrayn" because he married two of the Prophet's daughters in succession – first Ruqayya then Umm Kulthūm – and the Prophet ﷺ said: "Is there not a widow's father, is there not a widow's brother that would marry off [his daughter or sister to] 'Uthmān? Truly, I gave him my daughter in marriage, and if I had a third one I would have married her off to him, and I did not do this except through revelation."[432]

They would say, "We know of no one who married two of the daughters of a Prophet other than him;"[433] whereas others shared with him the merits of having prayed to the two *qiblas* and having taken part in the two *hjiras*.

Abū Nuʿaym al-Aṣbahānī narrated in his *Faḍāʾil al-Khulafāʾ al-Arbaʿa* that after ʿUmar's demise and the succession of ʿUthmān, Ibn Masʿūd took the news to Kufa and travelled there in eight days, climbed the pulpit, glorified Allah then said, "O people, verily the Commander of the believers has died and no day was seen in which there was more sobbing than on that day. We the Companions of Muḥammad gathered and left no stone unturned to choose the best of us and the possessor of the *fuwaq* (arrow-nocks) [= special gifts], so we gave him our pledge," meaning ʿUthmān.[434]

[432]Narrated with a strong but *mursal* chain from the Successor 'Ubayd Allah b. al-Ḥurr by al-Nasawī in *al-Ma'rifa wal-Tārīkh* (3:159-160), Ibn al-A'rābī in *al-Mu'jam* (2:562-563 §1102-1103) and, through him, Ibn 'Asākir (39:45), the strongest chain in this chapter.
[433] Al-Ājurrī, *al-Sharīʿa* (*Idhikr khilāfat Amīr al-Muʾminīn ʿUthmān*); Ibn Shāhīn, *Sharḥ Madhāhib Ahl al-Sunna* (Qurṭuba ed. p. 118 §90); Abū Nuʿaym, *Maʿrifat al-Ṣaḥāba* (1:62 §238-239); al-Bayhaqī, *al-Sunan al-Kubrā* (7:115 §13427).
[434]Narrated by Ibn Saʿd, *Ṭabaqāt* (3:46); Aḥmad, *Faḍāʾil al-Ṣaḥāba* (1:467); Fasawī, *al-Maʿrifa wal-Tārīkh* (2:761); Ṭabarānī, *Kabīr* (9:168-169); Abū Nuʿaym, *Faḍāʾil al-Khulafāʾ al-Arbaʿa wa-Ghayrihim*, ed. Ṣāliḥ b. Muḥammad al-ʿAqīl (Medina: Dār al-Bukhārī, 1417/1997) p. 165 §211. The nocks signify great merits.

8
The Prophet's Prediction of 'Uthmān's Death as a *Shahīd*

Anas ﷺ said: "The delegation of Banū al-Muṣṭaliq instructed me to ask the Messenger of Allah ﷺ, 'If we come next year and do not find you, to whom should we remit our [obligatory] *ṣadaqāt*?' I conveyed to him the question and he replied: 'Remit them to Abū Bakr.' I told them his answer but they said, 'What if we do not find Abū Bakr?' I conveyed to him the question and he replied: 'Remit them to 'Umar.' They asked again, 'What if we do not find 'Umar?' He said, 'Tell them, Remit them to 'Uthmān – and may you perish the day 'Uthmān is killed!'"[435]

The Prophet ﷺ spoke of 'Uthmān's eventual trial on numerous occasions:

- ... "'Then 'Uthmān came and I [Abū Mūsā] said, this is 'Uthmān asking permission to enter.' He replied, 'Give him permission and give him the glad tidings of Paradise after a trial that shall befall him.' He entered but found no room to sit on the edge of the well, so he sat opposite them on the other side of the well and dangled his legs," repeating – in one version – "*Allāhumma ṣabran!*" all the while.[436] A version has, "he entered with eyes brimming with tears."[437]
- The Prophet ﷺ said: "A dissension shall surge like so many bull's horns. At that time, he [pointing to a man wearing a veil] and whoever is with him are on the side of right." Ka'b b. Murra al-Bahzī ran up to the man, lifted his veil and turned him towards the Prophet ﷺ saying: "Him, Messenger of Allah?" The Prophet ﷺ said yes. It was 'Uthmān b. 'Affān.[438]
- Abū Hurayra said at the time 'Uthmān was besieged: "I heard the Messenger of Allah ﷺ say: 'There shall be a dissension and strife.' We said, 'Messenger of Allah! What do you order us to

[435]Narrated from Anas by Abū Nu'aym, *Ḥilya* (1985 ed. 8:358), Ibn 'Asākir (39:177), and Nu'aym in the *Fitan* (1:107-108 §260, 1:125 §295) cf. *Kanz* (§36333). This ḥadīth is among the proofs of Prophethood.
[436]Hadith of Abū Mūsā al-Ash'arī already mentioned in the section on Abū Bakr al-Ṣiddīq (2nd chapter).
[437] Muṣ'ab al-Zubayrī, *Nasab Quraysh* (p. 102); *Min Ḥadīthi Khaythama* (p. 102, *isti'dhān aṣḥāb Rasūl Allāh*); Ibn 'Asākir (39:134-135)
[438]Narrated from Ka'b b. Murra al-Bahzī by al-Tirmidhī *(ḥasan ṣaḥīḥ)*, Ibn Mājah with a weak chain, Aḥmad with several fair chains in his *Musnad* and *Faḍā'il al-Ṣaḥāba* (1:450), al-Ḥākim (1990 ed. 3:109, 4:479 *ṣaḥīḥ*), Ibn Abī Shayba (6:360 §32025-32026, 7:442 §37090) with three chains, al-Ṭabarānī in *al-Kabīr* (19:161-162 §359, §362, 20:315 §750), and Nu'aym b. Ḥammād in *al-Fitan* (1:174 §461).

do then?' He replied, 'Stay with the leader and his friends,' pointing to 'Uthmān."[439]

- 'Ā'isha رضي الله عنها said: "The Messenger of Allah ﷺ on his deathbed summoned 'Uthmān and spoke to him confidentially at length, whereupon the face of the latter changed. The Day of the House [= when 'Uthmān was besieged] we told him, 'Will you not put up a fight?' He said, 'No! The Messenger of Allah ﷺ took a covenant from me [not to fight at the time of my *shahada*] and I will fulfill it.'"[440]

- "'Uthmān! It may be that Allah shall vest you with a shirt. If the hypocrites demand that you remove it, do not remove it!" He repeated it thrice.[441]

The above reports are mentioned among the 179 reports compiled by ʿAbd Allah the son of Imam Aḥmad in his book on the merits of ʿUthmān as well as in Aḥmad Zaynī Daḥlān's book on the Rightly-Guided Caliphs.[442]

[439]Narrated from Abū Hurayra by al-Ḥākim (3:99=1990 ed. 3:105; 4:434=4:480) and al-Dhahabī confirmed it as sound; Ibn Abī Shayba (10:363 §32049); al-Ṭabarānī in *al-Awsaṭs* (9:175 §9457); Ibn Abī 'Āṣim in *al-Sunna* (2:587 §1278); and al-Bayhaqī in *al-I'tiqād* (p. 368).

[440]Narrated from Abū Sahla, 'Uthmān's freedman, by al-Tirmidhī *(ḥasan ṣaḥīḥ gharīb)*, Aḥmad in the *Musnad* and *Faḍā'il al-Ṣaḥāba* (1:494), Ibn Mājah, Ibn Ḥibbān, al-Ḥākim (1990 ed. 3:106), Ibn Sa'd (3:66), Abū Ya'lā in his *Musnad* (8:234), and al-Bazzār (2:60) with sound chains.

[441]Narrated from 'Ā'isha with sound chains by al-Tirmidhī *(ḥasan gharīb)*, Ibn Ḥibbān, Aḥmad, Ibn Mājah, and al-Ḥākim.

[442] ʿAbd Allah b. Aḥmad b. Ḥanbal, *Faḍāʾil ʿUthmān b. ʿAffān*, ed. Ṭalʿat Fuʾād al-Ḥulwānī (Jeddah: Dār Mājid ʿAsīrī, 1421/2000); Aḥmad Zaynī Daḥlān, *al-Fatḥ al-Mubīn* (pp. 190-192).

9
His Killing Marks the Onset of Dissension (*Fitna*)

The plot to kill our liege lord 'Uthmān marked the onset of dissension *(fitna)* in the Community. It is in because of this plot that Abū Dharr departed from Medina and not, as is commonly believed, because 'Uthmān expelled him. Ibn 'Asākir said in his history of Damascus: "'Uthmān did not expel Abū Dharr but the latter exited of his own will to al-Rabadha – in the desert 100 kms. East of Medina – out of fear of the *fitna* against which the Prophet ﷺ had warned. But because he exited shortly after an incident that took place between him and the Commander of the believers, it was thought that he had expelled him." Then he cited the narration from Umm Dharr رضي الله عنها who said: "I swear by Allah that it is not 'Uthmān that banished Abū Dharr. Rather, the Messenger of Allah ﷺ said: 'When buildings reach Sal', exit from here.' When buildings reached Sal' and beyond Abū Dharr left for Syro-Palestine."[443] Abū Dharr would forbid anyone to speak ill of 'Uthmān and would recall to them what he had seen of 'Uthmān's miraculous gift when he heard the pebbles glorifying Allah in his palm.[444]

[443]Narrated by Ibn 'Asākir in *Tārīkh Dimashq* (66:202) and al-Ḥākim (1990 ed. 3:387 *ṣaḥīḥ* per the criteria of al-Bukhārī and Muslim), cf. Ibn Sa'd (4:226), al-Khallāl in *al-Sunna* (1:107), Ibn 'Asākir (1:91, 66:191-192, 66:198), *Fatḥ* (3:274), *Iṣāba* (7:16) and *Siyar* (Fikr ed. 3:389=Risala 2:63). Sal' is a mountain in Medina.
[444] Ibn 'Asākir (39:118-120). See the first chapter.

10
The Great Innovation of "Verifiable Sourcing of Transmission" (*Isnād*) and Ancillary Disciplines

Together with deadly division, the great sign of this dissension was the spread of falsehood. The timeline for the spread of falsehood was foretold by the Prophet ﷺ in the ḥadīth: "I recommend to you my Companions, then those that come after them, then those that come after them. Afterwards, falsehood will spread."[445] In anticipation of this the sciences of hadith and hadith criticism were innovated within the half-century that followed the death of 'Uthmān so as to sift true Prophetic and Companion-reports from false ones. This process was done through verification of the authenticity of transmission chains *(isnāds)* in respect of the honesty and competence of transmitters and examination of the conditions and contents of transmission in their minutest historical, linguistic, and doctrinal details. Muḥammad b. Sīrīn (d. 110) said: "We used to accept as true what we heard, then lies spread and we began to say, 'Name your transmitters.' If they belonged to *Ahl al-Sunna* their ḥadīth would be accepted while *ahl al-bida'* were identified and their ḥadīth was rejected."[446] Confirming this is al-Ḥasan al-Baṣrī's (d. 110) reaction to someone who requested his *isnād*: "O man! I neither lie nor was ever called a liar!"[447] Sufyān al-Thawrī (d. 161) said: "When certain narrators used lies, we used history against them"[448] and Ibn al-Mubārak (d. 181) declared: "The *isnād* is an integral part of the Religion, otherwise anyone can say anything."[449] All this is based on the saying of the Companions and Successors: **"Truly this knowledge is our Religion, therefore let each of you look carefully from whom he takes his Religion.**"[450]

[445]Narrated from 'Umar by Tirmidhī who graded it *ḥasan ṣaḥīḥ gharīb*, Aḥmad with a sound chain and Ibn Mājah, as part of a longer ḥadīth. See al-Tirmidhī's *al-'Ilal al-Kabīr* (p. 323 §596) and al-Dāraquṭnī's *'Ilal* (2:65-68).
[446]Narrated by Muslim in the introduction to his *Ṣaḥīḥ* and by al-Tirmidhī in his *Sunan* and *'Ilal*.
[447]Narrated by al-Mizzī in *Tahdhīb al-Kamāl* (1:259).
[448]Cited by al-Sakhāwī in *al-I'lān wal-Tawbīkh* (p. 9).
[449]Narrated by Muslim in the introduction to his *Ṣaḥīḥ* and al-Khaṭīb in his *Tārīkh* (6:166). Ibn al-Subkī in *Ṭabaqāt al-Shāfi'iyya al-Kubrā* (1:314) mentions this and other similar statements of the *Salaf*: "The *isnād* is the believer's weapon" (Sufyān al-Thawrī); "Religion does not disappear except with the disappearance of the *isnād*" (Awzā'ī); "Every religion has its knights, and the knights of this Religion are the bearers of *isnāds*" (Yazīd b. Zuray'); "Pursuing the highest *isnād* [*i.e.* the shortest chain with the least narrator-links] is part of the Religion" (Aḥmad b. Ḥanbal).
[450]Narrated *mawqūf* from Abū Hurayra by al-Khaṭīb in *al-Jāmi' li-Akhlāq al-Rāwī* (1991 ed. 1:195 §137, §140) and Ibn 'Abd al-Barr in *al-Tamhīd* (1:45); from Anas by Ibn 'Abd al-Barr in *al-Tamhīd* (1:45-46) and al-Mizzī in his *Tahdhīb* (26:438); *maqṭū'* from Ibn Sīrīn by Muslim in the introduction to his *Ṣaḥīḥ*, al-Tirmidhī at the very end of the *Shamā'il*, Dārimī in the introduction to his *Sunan*, Khaythama in his *Juz'* (p. 167), Ibn Abī Shayba (5:334 §26636), Ibn Sa'd (7:194), Ibn Shāhīn in *al-Ma'rifa wal-Tārīkh* (3:154), Jūzjānī in *Aḥwāl al-Rijāl* (p. 36, 211), Rāmahurmuzī in *al-Muḥaddith al-Fāṣil* (p. 414), Ibn 'Adī (4:174), Ibn 'Asākir (28:298), al-Mizzī

The principle of authentication was founded by the Prophet ﷺ himself and inaugurated by Abū Bakr the Most Truthful after him. Thereafter, it was put into use by the rest of the major Companions and their successors, including the great above-named Imāms of superlative religion and science. This is proven *in nuce* by the Prophet's ﷺ questioning of the man who said he had seen the new moon of Ramaḍān: "Do you bear witness that there is no God except Allah and that Muḥammad is the Messenger of Allah?" When he replied in the affirmative, the Prophet ﷺ accepted his news.[451] Subsequent practice illustrates and builds on the same principle of ḥadīth verification.[452]

in his *Tahdhīb* (25:352), al-Sam'ānī in *Adab al-Imlā' wal-Istimlā'* (p. 55), Ibn 'Abd al-Barr in *al-Tamhīd* (1:46), al-Bājī in *al-Ta'dīl wal-Tajrīḥ* (2:677), al-Khaṭīb in *al-Faqīh wal-Mutafaqqih* (2:378§1133-1134), and Dhahabī in *Mu'jam al-Muḥaddithīn* (p. 228) and the *Siyar* (Risāla ed. 4:611); also from Ibn Sīrīn and al-Ḍaḥḥāk by Ibn Abī Ḥātim in *al-Jarḥ wal-Ta'dīl* (2:15) and Khaṭīb in the *Kifāya* (p. 121), and from Zā'ida b. Qudāma by al-Rāmahurmuzī in *al-Muḥaddith al-Fāṣil*. Also narrated *marfū'* from Anas by Ibn 'Adī (1:155, 236), al-Khaṭīb in *al-Jāmi' li-Akhlāq al-Rāwī* (1991 ed. 1:194 §136, §139), Tammām in his *Fawā'id* (1:135 §312), and al-Jurjānī in *Tārīkh Jurjān* (p. 473), and Abū Hurayra by al-Sajzī in *al-Ibāna* and others, both with weak chains cf. Ibn al-Jawzī in *al-'Ilal al-Mutanāhiya* (1:131), al-Sakhāwī in *Fatḥ al-Mughīth* (1:327=Sunna ed. 2:59), and Ibn Rajab in *Sharḥ 'Ilal al-Tirmidhī* ('Itr ed. 1:61=1:362). The latter adds it is also related as a saying of Zayd b. Aslam, al-Ḥasan al-Baṣrī, and Ibrāhīm al-Nakha'ī by Ibn Ḥibbān in *al-Majrūḥīn* (1:15-16). This great precept is also narrated as a saying of al-Awzā'ī by Ibn 'Asākir (6:361) and Mālik by al-Khaṭīb in the *Kifāya* (p. 159), Ibn 'Asākir (55:361 and 352), Ibn 'Abd al-Barr, *Tamhīd* (1:47, 1:67), and al-Nawawī, *Tibyān*, last third of the chapter on the etiquette of the teacher cf. al-Dhahabī, *Siyar* (Risāla ed. 5:342).

[451] Narrated with a fair chain from Ibn 'Abbās by Tirmidhī, Abū Dāwūd and Dārimī.

[452] See "Isnād-Criticism of the First Four Caliphs" in *Sunna Notes I* (pp. 120-131).

11
Tawassul (Using the Prophet ﷺ as a Means) at the Core of the *Isnād*

A further benefit of *isnād* is its importance in *tawassul* or seeking support from Allah ﷻ through the persons of the Prophet ﷺ, the Companions, the Successors, and those who transmitted from the latter in uninterrupted fashion down to our times. This is established by the following ḥadīth:

> Abū Sa'īd al-Khudrī related that the Messenger of Allah ﷺ said: "A time will dawn upon the people when swarms *(fi'āmun)* of them will be sent out on an expedition and they will say: 'See if there is any of the Companions of the Prophet ﷺ among you.' One man will be found and they shall be granted victory through him. Then a second group will be sent out on an expedition and they will ask whether there is any among them who saw one or more of the Companions of the Prophet ﷺ, and they will be granted victory through him. Then a third group will be sent out on an expedition and they will say: 'See if there is any among them who saw one or more of those who saw one or more of the Companions of the Prophet ﷺ.' Then a fourth group will be sent out and they will say: 'See if you can find among them someone who saw someone who saw someone who saw the Companions of the Prophet ﷺ.' One man will be found, and they will be granted victory through him."[453]

[453]Narrated by Muslim (Faḍā'il al-Ṣaḥāba); Bukhārī (al-Jihād wal-Sayr); Aḥmad.

12
The Killing of Our Master 'Uthmān ﷺ

Ibn 'Umar said: "As 'Uthmān was delivering a sermon, Jahjāh al-Ghifarī walked up to him, snatched his staff, and broke it on his knee. A shard of wood entered his thigh and it got gangrened and was amputated. He died that year.[454] Al-Qāḍī 'Iyāḍ relates in his book *al-Shifā'*, chapter entitled "Esteem for the things and places connected with the Prophet ﷺ," that this staff had belonged to the Prophet ﷺ.

'Abd Allāh b. Salām said to the Egyptians at the time they were besieging the Commander of the Believers 'Uthmān b. 'Affān: "Never did the sword of Allah not remain sheathed from harming you since the Prophet ﷺ came to it until this very day."[455] Yazīd b. Abī Ḥabīb said: "I have heard that most of those that rode to kill 'Uthmān were later seized by demonic possession." Al-Dhahabī mentioned that 'Alī had pronounced a curse on 'Uthmān's killers. Abū Bakrah said: "I would prefer to be hurled down from the sky to having anything to do with the blood of 'Uthmān."[456]

One of the pretexts for the climate of hatred stirred up against the Caliph was the grievance of some parties from Egypt and Iraq that 'Uthmān was favoring his relatives among the Banū Umayya with public offices and their demand that he remove them.

Ibn al-Musayyib related that a group of seven hundred Egyptians came to complain to 'Uthmān about their governor Ibn Abī Sarḥ's tyranny, so 'Uthmān said: "Chose someone to govern you." They chose Muḥammad b. Abī Bakr, so 'Uthmān wrote credentials for him and they returned. On their way back, at three days' distance from Medina, a black slave caught up with them with the news that he carried orders from 'Uthmān to the governor of Egypt. They searched him and found a message from 'Uthmān to Ibn Abī Sarḥ ordering the death of Muḥammad b. Abī Bakr and some of his friends. They returned to Medina and besieged 'Uthmān. The latter acknowledged that the camel, the slave, and the seal on the letter belonged to him, but he swore that he had never written nor ordered the letter to be written. It was discovered that the letter had been hand-written by Marwān b. al-Ḥakam. 'Uthmān was besieged for twenty-two days during which he refused both to give up Marwān and to resign. He was killed on the last day of Dhul-Ḥijja, on the day of *Jumu'a*, by several men who had crept into his house

[454]Narrated by al-Ṭabarī in his *Tārīkh* (4:366) and al-Dhahabī.
[455]Part of a longer ḥadīth narrated by al-Ṭabarānī with a sound chain as stated by al-Haythamī in *Majma' al-Zawā'id*.
[456]Narrated by al-Ṭabarānī in *al-Kabīr* (1:88) with a chain of narrators all used in the *Ṣaḥīḥ* books as per al-Haythamī (9:110).

led by Muḥammad b. Abī Bakr (13-38) who later repented and was murdered in Egypt.

During the siege of his house some people asked 'Uthmān, "Verily you are the Imam of all and what you can see is happening to you now; and the imam of the dissension [=Marwān b. al-Ḥakam] is now leading us in prayer, and we feel it is criminal of us to pray [behind him]!" 'Uthmān answered, "Prayer is the most excellent thing people can do. So if people do what is most excellent then do what is most excellent together with them; and if they do evil then stay away from their evildoing."[457]

Ibn 'Umar related from 'Uthmān that the night before the latter's murder he had seen the Prophet ﷺ in his dream telling him: "Take heart! Verily you shall break your fast with us tomorrow night."[458]

When his assailants came in they found him reading the Qur'ān. 'Uthmān was first stabbed in the head with an arrow-head, then a man placed the point of his sword against his belly, whereupon his wife Nā'ila tried to prevent him with her hand, losing fingers. Then 'Uthmān and Nā'ila's servant were killed as the latter fought back. She ran out of the house screaming for help and the killers dispersed. It is narrated that 'Uthmān was killed as he was reading the verse *And Allah will suffice you for defense against them. He is the Hearer, the Knower* (2:137). Several reports state that at the time of 'Uthmān's siege and death Zayd b. Thābit had marshalled three hundred *Anṣār* in his defense together with Abū Hurayra, Ibn 'Umar, al-Ḥasan, al-Ḥusayn and 'Abd Allāh b. al-Zubayr, but 'Uthmān forbade all of them to fight.[459]

[457] Narrated from 'Ubayd Allāh b. 'Adī b. Khiyār by al-Bukhārī.
[458] Narrated from Ibn 'Umar by al-Ḥākim who declared it sound (3:110).
[459] See the chapter on 'Uthmān in al-Dhahabī's *Siyar A'lām al-Nubalā'*.

13
ʿUthmān's Posterity

Our liege lord ʿUthmān had nine sons and seven daughters:

1. ʿAbd Allāh the Younger (from Ruqayya the daughter of the Messenger of Allah ﷺ) who died on the fourth year of the Hijra at age six;
2. ʿAbd Allāh the Elder (from Fākhita bint Ghazwān);
3. ʿAmr, the oldest and noblest in descendants (from Umm ʿAmr bint Jundub al-Azdiyya);
4. Abān (d. 105) (from Umm ʿAmr) who also had much offspring, the famed jurist, Qur'an transmitter, hadith authority, governor of Medina for seven years under the Caliph 'Abd al-Malik b. Marwān and historian who authored the earliest known compilation on the Prophetic *Sīra*[460] and whose *Sīra* folios were lost;
5. Khālid (from Umm ʿAmr);
6. ʿUmar (from Umm ʿAmr);
7. Saʿīd (from Fāṭima bint al-Walīd);
8. al-Walīd (from Fāṭima);
9. ʿAbd al-Malik (from Umm al-Banīn bint ʿUyayna b. Ḥiṣn) who died in his childhood;
10. Maryam (from Umm ʿAmr);
11. ʿĀ'isha (from Ramla bint Shayba b. Rabīʿa);
12. Umm Abān (from Ramla);
13. Umm ʿAmr (from Ramla);
14. Maryam (from Nā'ila bint al-Qarāfiṣa);
15. Umm al-Banīn (from a slavewoman); and
16. Umm Saʿīd (from Fāṭima bint al-Walīd).

Among his descendants in the Middle East are the following families: al-Jābī, Ḥarb, al-Zakī the *qāḍīs* of Damascus, Ṭahbūb (the latter are Umawīs, possibly descending from ʿUthmān), al-ʿAdawī and al-Manīnī. Mawlānā Khālid al-Naqshbandī (1190 or 1193-1242) was our liege lord ʿUthmān's descendant and is buried in Mount Qasyūn in Damascus.

[460]Cf. Muḥammad Abū Shahba, *al-Sīra al-Nabawiyya* (1:28).

14
Some of 'Uthmān's Sayings

Among our liege lord 'Uthmān's sayings:

- "If I were between Paradise and the Fire, unsure where I will be sent, I would choose to be turned into ash before finding out where I was bound."

- "I swear by Allah that I never committed fornication in the Time of Ignorance nor in Islam. Islam only increased me in virtue."

- His servant Hāni' narrated: "Whenever 'Uthmān stood before a grave he wept until his beard was wet. He was asked: 'You have seen battle and death without a tear, yet you cry for this?' He said: 'The grave is the first abode of the hereafter. Whoever is saved from it, what follows is easier; whoever is not saved from it, what follows is harder. The Prophet ﷺ said: "I have not seen anything more frightful than the punishment in the grave."'"[461] 'Uthmān also related from the Prophet ﷺ that whenever the latter finished burying someone, he would stand by the grave and say: "All of you, ask Allah to forgive your brother and make him steadfast, for he is now being questioned."[462]

- 'Uthmān was seen performing ablution then smiling. He said: "Will you not ask me what caused me to smile?" They said: "What caused you to smile, Commander of the Believers?" He replied: "I saw the Messenger of Allah ﷺ perform ablution as I just did then smile and say: 'Will you not ask me what made me smile?' and they said: 'What made you smile, Messenger of Allah?' He replied: 'Truly, when a worshipper asks for ablution then washes his face, Allah sheds from him every sin that he committed with his face; likewise, when he washes his two arms; likewise, when he washes his two feet.'"[463]

- To some of his companions who came in to see him after having looked at a woman on their way 'Uthmān said: "Each of you comes in with fornicating eyes." They said: "What! Is there revelation after the Prophet?" He replied: "Not revelation, but truthful insight" *(lā wa-lākin firāsa ṣādiqa)*.[464]

[461]Narrated from 'Abd Allāh b. Abī al-Jad'a' by al-Tirmidhī *(ḥasan ṣaḥīḥ gharīb)*, Ibn Mājah, al-Ḥākim *(ṣaḥīḥ)*, Aḥmad, and al-Dārimī.
[462]Narrated by Abū Dāwūd, al-Bayhaqī in *al-Sunan al-Kubrā* (4:56), and al-Ḥākim (1:370).
[463]Narrated from Ḥimrān b. Abbān by Aḥmad, Abū Ya'lā, and al-Bazzār with chains of sound narrators according to al-Haythamī.
[464]Cited by al-Qurṭubī in his *Tafsīr* (10:44) and al-Qārī in *Sharḥ Musnad Abī Ḥanīfa*, ḥadīth *ittaqū firāsat al-mu'min.*

- His Mawlā al-Ḥārith narrated that ʿUthmān was asked what the *bāqiyāt al-ṣāliḥāt* (enduring good deeds, e.g. al-Kahf 18:46, Maryam 19:76) were. He replied: "They are *lā ilāha illallāh, subḥān Allāh, al-ḥamdu lillāh, Allāhu akbar* and *lā ḥawla wa-lā quwwata illā bi-l-Lāh.*"[465]

- From Mujāhid: ʿUthmān said in a *khuṭba*, "Son of Ādam, know that the angel of death who was put in charge of you has been without cease passing you over and going to someone else since you first came to this world, and the time has almost come he has passed over someone else and come to you. So take utmost care, be ready! Care for your own soul and do not entrust it to another. *Wa-s-salām.*"[466]

- From al-Ḥasan: ʿUthmān said in a *khuṭba*, "Whoever Allah is with fears nothing; and whoever Allah is against, then in whom can he place his hope after that?"[467]

- From Badr b. ʿUthmān from his paternal uncle: In the last *khuṭba* he gave ʿUthmān said, "Verily Allah only gave you the life of this world so that you would pursue the hereafter with it. He did not give it to you so that you would dedicate yourself to it. Verily the life of this world passes away and the hereafter abides forever. So never let the one that passes away make you arrogant and preoccupy you away from the one that abides forever. Give priority to what abides over what passes!"[468]

[465]Narrated from 'Uthmān by Imām Aḥmad with a sound chain per Aḥmad Shākir in his edition (*Musnad* 1:383 §513) and al-Haythamī, *Majmaʿ al-Zawāʾid* (1:297).
[466]Dīnawarī, *al-Mujālasa wa-Jawāhir al-ʿIlm* (2:73-74 §207); Ibn ʿAsākir (39:238); Badr al-Dīn Ibn Jamāʿa, *Mashyakha* (Dār al-Gharb ed. 2:594-595); Ibn Kathīr, *Bidāya* in the latter part of the biographical entry on our Liege lord ʿUthmān.
[467]Ibn ʿAsākir (39:238).
[468]Sayf b. ʿUmar, *al-Fitna wa-Waqʿat al-Jamal*, ed. Aḥmad Rātib ʿArmūsh, 7th ed. (Beirut: Dār al-Nafāʾis, 1413/1993) p. 64; and, through him, Ibn Abī al-Dunya in *al-Zuhd* and *Dhamm al-Dunyā*l al-Ṭabarī, *Tārīkh* (4:384, 4:422); al-Bayhaqī, *Shuʿab* (Branch 71: *al-Zuhd wa-qaṣr al-amal, mā balaghanā ʿan al-Ṣaḥāba*); Ibn ʿAsākir (39:238); and Ibn Kathīr (ditto).

15
His Excellence in this World and His Arch-Intercessorship in the Next

The doctrine and consensus of *Ahl al-Sunna wal-Jamāʿa* has formed over the position phrased by Ibn Khafīf (276-371) in his *ʿAqīda* as, "The best of human beings after the Messenger of Allāh ﷺ is Abū Bakr, then ʿUmar, then ʿUthmān, then ʿAlī ؓ."[469]

The Prophet ﷺ said: "More men will enter Paradise through the intercession of a certain man than there are people in the tribes of Rabīʿa and Muḍar." The elders considered that this was ʿUthmān b. ʿAffān ؓ.[470]

A thief was brought before ʿUthmān one day. He said to the thief: "I see that you are handsome. One such as you does not steal!" Then he asked him: "Do you memorize any of the Qur'ān?" The man said, "Yes, I memorize Sūrat al-Baqara." ʿUthmān said: "Go! Your hand was spared because of Sūrat al-Baqara."[471]

[469]Cf. Abū Ḥanīfa, *alFiqh al-Akbar* and al-Ṭaḥāwī, *ʿAqīda*. Ibn Ḥajar said in *Fatḥ al-Bārī* (1959 ed. 7:58 §3494): "*Ahl al-Sunna* without exception agree that ʿAlī is given precedence after ʿUthmān, then come the rest of the Ten promised Paradise [Abū Bakr, ʿUmar, ʿUthmān, ʿAlī, al-Zubayr b. al-ʿAwwām, Ṭalḥa, ʿAbd al-Raḥmān b. ʿAwf, Abū ʿUbayda b. al-Jarrāḥ, Saʿd b. Abī Waqqāṣ and Saʿīd b. Zayd b. ʿAmr] then those who fought in the battle of Badr." Ibn Mājah and Aḥmad narrated from Rāfiʿ ibn Khadīj that Jibrīl said to the Prophet ﷺ: "Also among us, those who witnessed Badr are the best of the angels." Al-Khaṭīb in *al-Jāmiʿ* (2:445-448) gives the following order of precedence in Islam among the Companions: (i) first the Ten Promised Paradise; (ii) then the senior Companions among those who fought at Badr (all those who fought at Badr having been promised Paradise); (iii) then those who gave *bayʿat al-riḍwān* under the Tree <and those *Anṣār* distinguished for the two pacts preceding Emigration *(al-ʿaqabatayn)* according to Abū Manṣūr al-Baghdādī as reported by Ibn Jamāʿa in *al-Manhal al-Rawī* (p. 112)>; (iv) then those who entered Islam the year of the conquest of Makka; (v) then the younger Companions who saw the Prophet ﷺ as children. See also Shāh Walī Allāh's two treatises on the *tafḍīl* of Abū Bakr and ¢Umar over all other human beings besides Prophets; al-Nābulusī's book *Lamaʿān al-Anwār* already cited; al-Haytamī's *Fatāwā Ḥadīthiyya* (p. 155); and Muḥammad Abū Zahra's monograph *Abū Ḥanīfa* (p. 96).

[470]Narrated from Abū Umāma by al-Tirmidhī *(ḥasan)*, Ibn Mājah, and al-Ḥākim.

[471]Narrated from ʿImrān b. Abān by al-Zubayr b. Bakkār al-Asadī (d. 256) in *al-Muwaffaqiyyāt* cf. al-Suyūṭī, *al-Durr al-Manthūr* (1:54) cf. *Kanz* (§13953). See also Abū Nuʿaym, *Ḥilya* (1:92-100 §3); al-Dhahabī, *Siyar* (1/2: 566-614 §4).

16
Quranic Verses that Allude to ʿUthmān b. ʿAffān

The following verses are listed among the Quranic references to the immense merit of our liege lord ʿUthmān:[472]

- *Those that spend their wealth in the way of the One God then do not follow up what they spent with reminders of past favors and with harm: theirs are their wages with their nurturing Lord, and they have nothing to fear, and they shall not grieve* (al-Baqara 2:262).

- *Or he that is constantly devoted in the watches of the night, prostrating and standing, apprehending the hereafter and urgently hoping the mercy of his nurturing Lord—? Say, "Are they equal, those who know and those who do not know?" Only they heed admonishment who possess minds and hearts!* (al-Zumar 39:9).

- *Verily those for whom was foreordained the best goodness from Us—those ones are kept far from it* (al-Anbiyāʾ 21:101).

- *... are they equal, he and the one who enjoins justice and is himself on a straight path?* (al-Naḥl 16:76).

- *Of the believers are men who are true to what they covenanted with the One God. Of them is he that has fulfilled his solemn pledge, and of them is he that awaits. And they never altered with any alteration* (al-Aḥzāb 33:23).

[472] Sayyid Aḥmad Zaynī Daḥlān, *al-Faḍl al-Mubīn* (p. 181).

17
Hadiths Narrated by our Liegelord ʿUthmān

Imam Aḥmad in his *Musnad ʿUthmān b. ʿAffān* narrates 161 reports from ʿUthmān while al-Suyūṭī relates no less than 422 reports in his,[473] the last of which being ʿUthmān b. Ziyād's narration of the supplication of *qunūt* (standing in prayer) which ʿUmar and ʿUthmān used to recite in the dawn prayer when leading:

> O Allah! Verily we seek help from You, and we ask forgiveness from You, and we praise You for every goodness, and we are not ungrateful to You, and we repudiate and leave all that openly disobey You. O Allah! Verily You do we worship, and to You do we pray and prostrate, and unto You do we make haste and are prompt, and we hope for Your mercy and we fear Your punishment. Verily Your punishment of the disbelievers is befalling!

473 al-Suyūṭī, *Musnad ʿUthmān b. ʿAffān*, ed. al-Ḥāfiẓ ʿAzīz (Hyderabad Deccan: al-Dār al-Salafiyya, 1403/1983.

'Alī b. Abī Ṭālib

رضي الله تعالى عنه

'Alī b. Abī Ṭālib 'Abd Manāf b. 'Abd al-Muṭṭalib
b. Hāshim b. 'Abd Manāf,
Abū al-Ḥasan al-Qurashī al-Hāshimī,
Amīr al-Mu'minīn, the first male believer in Islam,
the Prophet's ﷺ standard-bearer in battles,
the Invincible Lion of Allah,
the heir of the Prophetic Household *('itra)*
and head of the 'Alawī lineage,
the Patron *(mawlā)* of the Muslims,
the Gate of the City of Knowledge,
wisest of the Companions after the Two Shaykhs,
"Possessor of a wise heart and enquiring tongue."
He was killed by a Khārijī assassin at age fifty-eight.
Imām Aḥmad said: "There is no Companion about
whom are reported as many merits as 'Alī."
– Allah Most High be well-pleased with him!

ʿAlī b. Abī Ṭālib b. ʿAbd al-Muṭṭalib b. Hāshim b. ʿAbd Manāf, Abū al-Ḥasan al-Qurashī al-Hāshimī ؓ (16BH-Ramadan 40/606-January 661), *Amīr al-Mu'minīn*, the first male believer in Islam,[474] the Prophet's ﷺ standard-bearer in battle, the Gate of the City of Knowledge, the most judicious of the Companions, the "Possessor of a wise heart and enquiring tongue." The Prophet ﷺ raised him and nicknamed him *Abū Turāb* or "Sandy."[475] He was named Ḥaydar by his mother Fāṭima bint Asad. He accepted Islam when he was six years old, or seven, or eight, or nine or fourteen depending on the narrations, but it is established from Ibn ʿAbbās that he was the first male Muslim after the Prophet ﷺ, Khadīja being the first Muslim and Abū Bakr the first man – Allah ﷻ be well-pleased with them. He was killed at age fifty-eight. Aḥmad b. Ḥanbal narrated 828 Prophetic hadiths through ʿAlī b. Abī Ṭālib in his *Musnad*. From him narrated Abū Bakr, ʿUmar, his sons al-Ḥasan and al-Ḥusayn, Ibn ʿAbbās, ʿAbd Allāh b. al-Zubayr, and others.

[474]At the age of 7 or 8 according to ʿUrwa, or less as established by al-Ḥākim's (3:111) sound narration per the criteria of the Two Shaykhs from Ibn ʿAbbās, "The Prophet ﷺ gave ʿAlī the flag to carry on the day of Badr (Ramadan 2/March 624) and he was twenty years old."

[475]Sahl b. Saʿd said that ʿAlī liked to be called by that patronym. Its story is related in al-Bukhārī and Muslim: After a quarrel with Fāṭima ʿAlī went to the Mosque, where the Prophet ﷺ found him asleep with sand sticking to his back which he proceeded to wipe away, saying, "Get up, Abū Turāb!" The shaykhs of *taṣawwuf* interpreted this name to refer to the people who declare Allah's Oneness and to the state of self-extinction *(fanā')* whose fountainhead, after the Prophet ﷺ, is ʿAlī ؓ cf. Muḥammad al-Bāqī Billāh, *al-Mathwā*; ʿAbd al-Ḥaqq al-Dihlawī, *Sharḥ Sifr al-Saʿāda*; Ibrāhīm b. ʿArab Shāh, *Sharḥ Shamā'il al-Tirmidhī*; ʿAbd al-Raḥmān Jāmī, *Dīwān* and *Shawāhid al-Nubuwwa*, all as cited by al-Ghumārī, *al-Burhān* (p. 69).

1
'Alī's Surname of "Lion" (Ḥaydar)

When the Prophet ﷺ gave 'Alī the flag at Khaybar, Marḥab [a fighter from Khaybar] came out and declaimed:

Khaybar knows my name is Marḥab!
In full armor a tried champion!
Wars come to me and blaze!

'Alī replied:

I'm he whose mother called Ḥaydarah!
Like the beast of jungles, awesome to see!
I pay my enemies in full – an ample scope!

He struck Marḥab's head, killing him. Victory followed at his hands."[476]

'Alī was surnamed Ḥaydar by his mother Fāṭima bint Asad,[477] whom the Prophet ﷺ is related to have named his second mother and at whose grave he made a remarkable intercession in the ḥadīth which reads: "O Allah who lives and never dies, who quickens and puts to death! Forgive the sins of my mother Fāṭima bint Asad, make wide the place wherein she enters through the right of Your Prophet *(bi-ḥaqqi nabiyyik)* and the Prophets who came before me. For You are the most merciful of those who show mercy."[478] Al-Kawtharī said of this ḥadīth: "It provides textual evidence that

[476]Narrated from Salama b. al-Akwa' by Muslim.
[477]As narrated by al-Ḥākim (3:108).
[478]Narrated from Anas by Ṭabarānī, *Kabīr* (24:351), *Awsaṭ* (1:152); Abū Nu'aym in his *Ḥilya* (1985 ed. 3:121) with a chain containing Rawḥ b. Ṣalāḥ concerning whom there is difference of opinion among the authorities. He is unknown according to Ibn al-Jawzī in *al-'Ilal al-Mutanāhiya* (1:260-270), Ibn 'Adī in *al-Kāmil* (3:146 §667) and Dāraquṭnī in *al-Mu'talif wal-Mukhtalif* (3:1377); Ibn Mākūlā in *al-Ikmāl* (5:15) declared him weak while Ḥākim asserted he was trustworthy and highly dependable *(thiqa ma'mūn)* as cited by Ibn Ḥajar, *Lisān* (2:465 §1876). Ibn Ḥibbān included him in *al-Thiqāt* (8:244, cf. Muḥ. b. 'Alawī, *Mafāhīm Yajib an Tuṣaḥḥaḥ*, 10th ed. p. 145 note 1 citing him as "Abū Ḥātim") and Fasawī considered him trustworthy one time and another time weak (cf. Maḥmūd Mamdūḥ, *Raf' al-Mināra* p. 148). Haythamī (9:257) said: "Ṭabarānī narrated it in *al-Kabīr* and *al-Awsaṭ* and its chain contains Rawḥ b. Ṣalāḥ whom Ibn Ḥibbān and al-Ḥākim declared trustworthy although there is some weakness in him, and the rest of its sub-narrators are the men of sound ḥadīth." Mamdūḥ in his discussion of this ḥadīth in *Raf' al-Mināra* (pp. 147-155) considers Rawḥ truthful *(ṣadūq)* and not weak *(da'īf)*, according to the rules of ḥadīth science when no reason is given with regard to a narrator's purported discreditation *(jarḥ mubham ghayr mufassar)*. He noted (pp. 149-150) that although Albānī in his *Silsila Ḍa'īfa* (1:32-33) claims it is a case of explicated discreditation *(jarḥ mufassar)* yet the latter himself declares identically-formulated discreditation cases as unexplicated and therefore unacceptable in two different contexts. Ibn 'Alawī adds that the ḥadīth is also narrated from Ibn 'Abbās by Ibn 'Abd al-Barr and from Jābir by Ibn Abī Shayba, but without the *du'ā*.

there is no difference between the living and the dead in the context of using a means *(tawassul)*, and this is explicit *tawassul* through the Prophets, while the ḥadīth of the Prophet ﷺ from Abū Sa'īd al-Khudrī 'O Allah, I ask You by the right of [the promise made to] those who ask You *(biḥaqqi al-sā'ilīna 'alayk)*'[479] constitutes *tawassul* through the generality of Muslims, both the living and the dead."[480]

[479]A fair *(ḥasan)* ḥadīth of the Prophet ﷺ according to Maḥmūd Mamdūḥ in his monograph *Mubāḥathat al-Sā'irīn bi Ḥadīth Allāhumma Innī As'aluka bi-Ḥaqqi al-Sā'ilīn*, narrated from Abū Sa'īd al-Khudrī by Aḥmad in his *Musnad* with a fair chain according to Ḥamza al-Zayn (10:68 §11099) – a weak chain according to al-Arnā'ūṭ (17:247-248 §11156) who considers it, like Abū Ḥātim in *al-'Ilal* (2:184), more likely a *mawqūf* saying of Abū Sa'īd himself; Ibn Mājah with a chain he declared weak, Ibn al-Sunnī in *'Amal al-Yawm wal-Layla* (p. 40 §83-84), Bayhaqī in *al-Da'awāt al-Kabīr* (p. 47=1:47 §65), Ibn Khuzayma in *al-Tawḥīd* (p. 17-18) [and his *Ṣaḥīḥ* (2:458?) as indicated by Būṣīrī in his *Zawā'id* (1:98-99)], al-Ṭabarānī in *al-Du'a* (p. 149=2:990), Ibn Ja'd in his *Musnad* (p. 299), al-Baghawī in *al-Ja'diyyat* (§2118-2119) and – *mawqūf* – by Ibn Abī Shayba (6:25=10:211-212) and Ibn Abī Ḥātim in *'Ilal al-Ḥadīth* (2:184). Al-'Irāqī in *Takhrīj Aḥādīth al-Iḥyā'* (1:291) graded it *ḥasan* as a *marfū'* Prophetic ḥadīth, as did the ḥadīth Masters al-Dimyāṭī in *al-Muttajir al-Rābiḥ fī Thawāb al-'Amal al-Ṣāliḥ* (p. 471-472), Ibn Ḥajar in *Amālī al-Adhkār* (1:272) and Mundhirī's shaykh the ḥadīth Master Abū al-Ḥasan al-Maqdisī in *al-Targhīb* (1994 ed. 2:367 §2422=1997 ed. 2:304-305) and as indicated by Ibn Qudāma in *al-Mughnī* (1985 Dār al-Fikr ed. 1:271).

[480]Al-Kawtharī, *Maqālāt* (p. 410).

2
'Alī's Learning, Wisdom and Humbleness

Our Master 'Alī was the repository of Prophetic wisdom among the Companions. The latter, when asked about difficult legal rulings, deferred to others the responsibility of answering, while 'Alī, alone among them, used to say: "Ask me!"[481] 'Umar said: "I seek refuge in Allah from a problem which Abū al-Ḥasan cannot solve." Similarly 'Ā'isha رضي الله عنها said: "He is the most knowledgeable about the Sunna among those who remain," and Ibn 'Abbās: "If a trustworthy source tells us of a *fatwā* by 'Alī, we do not look any further concerning it."[482]

Sulaymān al-Ahmusī narrated from his father that 'Alī said: "By Allah! No verse was ever revealed except I knew the reason for which it was revealed and in what place and concerning whom. Truly my Lord has bestowed upon me a wise heart and a speaking tongue!"[483]

At the same time 'Alī humbly declared: "What cools my liver most, if I am asked something I know not, is to say: 'Allah knows best'."[484]

[481]Narrated from Sa'īd b. al-Musayyab by Ibn 'Abd al-Barr in *al-Istī'āb* (3:40-41), Ibn 'Asākir in *Tārīkh Dimashq* (42:399), and al-Suyūṭī in *Tārīkh al-Khulafā'*.
[482]All three reports are narrated by Ibn Sa'd (2:339), Ibn 'Abd al-Barr in *al-Istī'āb* (3:39-40), and al-Suyūṭī in *Tārīkh al-Khulafā'*.
[483]Narrated by Ibn Sa'd (2:338), Ibn 'Abd al-Barr in *al-Istī'āb* (3:36-37), and Abū Nu'aym in the *Ḥilya* with the wording: "And an enquiring tongue."
[484]Narrated from Abū al-Bakhtari by al-Dhahabī in the *Siyar* (1/2:633).

3
His Revilement of Pre-Islamic Idols

It is narrated that Abū Ṭālib would give ʿAlī milk to pour on top of al-Lāt but he would drink the milk and urinate on al-Lāt.[485]

ʿAlī narrated: "I went out with the Prophet ﷺ until we reached the Kaʿba whereupon he said to me: 'Sit.' He then climbed on my shoulders and I tried to stand but he noticed some weakness in me. He climbed down and sat for me telling me, 'Climb on my shoulders.' I climbed on his shoulders then he stood and I felt as if I could touch the top of the sky if I wanted. Then I climbed on top of the House and there was a yellow copper statue which I began to budge right and left, front and back until I dislodged it. The Messenger of Allah ﷺ then said to me: 'Throw it down.' I threw it down and it broke into pieces exactly like a glass vessel. I climbed down then I and the Messenger of Allah ﷺ ran away as fast as we could in between the houses lest anyone see us."[486]

[485] Narrated from Nāfiʿ by Abū Nuʿaym cf. *al-Mustaṭraf* (1:387).

[486] Narrated with a chain of trustworthy narrators cf. al-Haythamī (6:23) except that Nuʿaym b. Ḥakīm al-Madāʾinī's narrations are only fair (*ṣadūq ḥasan al-ḥadīth* in *Taḥrīr al-Taqrīb*): by Aḥmad and his son in the *Musnad* (Arnāʾūṭ ed. 2:73-74 §644 and 2:430 §1302, Shākir ed. 1:443-444 §644 and 2:138 §1301); Ṭabarī in *Tahdhīb al-Āthār* (1:236-238 §31-33=*Musnad ʿAlī*); Ibn Abī Shayba (Salafiyya ed. 14:488-489= Awwāma ed. 20:470-471 §38062); Bazzār (3:21-22 §769); Abū Ya'lā in his *Musnad* (§292); al-Ḥākim through two chains (2:366-367); al-Nasāʾī in *Khaṣāʾiṣ ʿAlī* (p. 22); al-Muḥibb al-Ṭabarī, *al-Riyāḍ al-Naḍira*. Arnāʾūṭ declared its chain "weak," Shākir "sound," and al-Dhahabī "impeccable" but its content "rejected" *(munkar)*. I asked my teacher Dr. Nūr al-Dīn ʿItr of the reason for al-Dhahabī's rating and he attributed it to the facts that (1) the Prophet ﷺ is not related to have destroyed any idol before the conquest of Mecca; (2) the Kaʿba was hardly ever deserted; (3) its structure is taller than the added height of two men, all of which justifies al-Dhahabī's verdict. And Allah knows best.

4

His Betrothal and Marriage to Fāṭima

'Alī ⬥ said: "Fāṭima's hand was asked in marriage from the Messenger of Allah ﷺ [but he refused], so a freedwoman that belonged to me at the time said to me: 'Did you hear that Fāṭima's hand was asked in marriage? Then what prevents you from going to see the Messenger of Allah ﷺ about it?' I went to see him. We held the Messenger of Allah ﷺ in great awe and reverence, so when I stood before him I became tongue-tied. I could not say a word. The Messenger of Allah ﷺ said: 'What brings you?' I stayed silent. He said: 'Perhaps you came to ask Fāṭima's hand?' I said yes! The Prophet ﷺ said, 'Do you have anything with which to make your union licit?' I said, 'No, by Allah, Messenger of Allah!' He said: 'Then what did you do with the shield I equipped you with?' I said, 'It is a Ḥaṭīm-made shield, it hardly costs four hundred dirhams!' The Prophet ﷺ said: 'Go! I have given you her hand in marriage. Send it to her and make it licit with that dowry.'"[487]

[487]Narrated broken-chained from 'Alī by al-Bayhaqī, *Sunan* (7:2̶̶̶̶̶̶̶̶ ̶̶̶̶̶̶̶̶̶and ̶̶̶ Dūlābī, *al-Dhurriyya al-Ṭāhira* (p. 64) while the dowry segme̶̶̶̶̶̶̶̶̶̶̶̶̶̶̶̶̶ ̶̶̶from 'Alī by Abū Ya'lā (1:388 §503), al-Bayhaqī (7:234 §14128), a̶̶̶̶̶̶̶̶̶̶̶̶̶̶̶al-Ḍyā al-Maqdisī, *Mukhtāra* (2:339 §716).

5
His Courage and Sense of Justice

'Alī was a skilled and fearless fighter . He once said: "I never duelled with anyone except I overcame him."[488] The Prophet ﷺ gave him his standard to carry on the day of Badr and in subsequent battles.

When 'Alī lost his coat of mail during his caliphate and later found it in the possession of a Christian, he took the matter to the judge Shurayḥ. 'Alī said, "This is my coat of mail which I neither sold nor gave away." Shurayḥ turned to the Christian and asked what he contended. The Christian replied, "This coat of mail belongs to me but I do not call the Commander of the believers a liar." Shurayḥ asked 'Alī: "Commander of the believers, do you have any proof?" 'Alī smiled and said, "No, I have no proof." Then Shurayḥ ruled in favor of the Christian who went on his way but then returned, saying, "I bear witness that these are indeed the laws of the Prophets! The Commander of the believers took me before his own judge who ruled against him! And I bear witness that there is no god but Allah and that Muḥammad is His servant and Messenger. By Allah, this coat of mail belongs to you, Commander of the believers. I was following the army as you were going to Ṣiffīn when your coat of mail fell from your camel." 'Alī said, "Since you have embraced Islam, the coat of mail is yours!" and he mounted him on a horse.[489]

[488]Narrated from 'Alī by al-Bazzār (3:15) with a chain of trustworthy narrators cf. al-Haythamī (9:46-47) and al-Muḥibb al-Ṭabarī, *al-Riyāḍ al-Naḍira* (2:32 §448).
[489]Narrated by Ibn Kathīr in *al-Bidāya wal-Nihāya* (8:4-5).

6
The Conquest of Khaybar

Al-Bukhārī and Muslim narrated that Salama b. ʻAmr b. al-Akwaʻ ؓ said: "'Alī stayed behind because of ophthalmia when the Messenger of Allah ﷺ was in Khaybar. He said: 'How can I stay behind and not go with the Messenger of Allah ﷺ?' So he went out and caught up with him. On the eve of the victory granted by Allah the Messenger of Allah ﷺ said: 'I swear that tomorrow I shall give the flag to a man whom both Allah and His Messenger love, through whom Allah woll grant victory.' Then, lo and behold! There was ʻAlī among us unexpectedly. They said, 'Here is ʻAlī!' so he gave him the flag and Allah granted victory through him."[490]

A different wording from Salama b. al-Akwaʻ adds to the above: "Then he spat into his eyes and he was cured. He gave him the flag... victory followed at his hands."[491]

Another wording from Salama adds: "Then ʻAlī took it [the flag] and planted it right under their fort, whereupon one of the Jews looked down at him from the top of the fort and said: 'Who are you?' He replied: ''Alī' The Jew said: 'You will overcome *(ʻalawtum)*, by the [Book] revealed to Mūsā!' ʻAlī did not return until Allah granted victory at his hands."[492] Abū Nuʻaym said in his *Dalā'il al-Nubuwwa*: "There is in it a sign of the advanced knowledge of the Jews, thanks to their books, as to who is sent to fight against them and shall be granted victory." The account was also narrated from Ibn ʻUmar, Ibn ʻAbbās, Saʻd b. Abī Waqqāṣ, Abū Hurayra, Abū Saʻīd al-Khudrī, ʻImrān b. Ḥuṣayn, Jābir, and Abū Laylā al-Anṣārī. Abū Nuʻaym narrated all of them, and they all contain the account of the spitting into the eyes and their healing.

Burayda ؓ narrated that the Messenger of Allah ﷺ said: "Tomorrow I will give the flag to a man <whom Allah and His Messenger love and> who loves Allah and His Messenger, and who will take it by force" at a time ʻAlī was not there yet. The Quraysh competed for it then ʻAlī arrived on his camel, eyes inflamed with ophthalmia. The Prophet ﷺ said: "Come near" then he spat into his eyes – they were never sore again until he died – and gave him the flag.[493]

Shaykh Muḥammad Abū al-Hudā al-Yaʻqūbī related to me as part of my reading with him of Ibn al-Jazarī's *Asnā al-Maṭālib fī Manāqib Sayyidinā*

[490]Narrated from Salama b. al-Akwaʻ by al-Bukhārī, Muslim, and Aḥmad. The incident is also related from Sahl b. Saʻd, Burayda, Abū Hurayra, and others.
[491]Narrated from Salama b. al-Akwaʻ by Muslim.
[492]Narrated from Salama by Ibn Hishām, *Sīra* (4:305-306), al-Ṭabarānī in *al-Kabīr* (7:35 §6303), and Ibn Ḥibbān in *al-Thiqāt* (2:13) cf. *Rawḍ* (4:76), *Zād* (3:285).
[493]Narrated from Burayda by al-Nasā'ī in *al-Sunan al-Kubrā* (5:179 §8601), al-Ṭabarī in his *Tārīkh* (2:137).

Alī b. Abī Ṭālib (The Purest Pursuits Concerning the Virtues of Our Liege Lord 'Alī b. Abī Ṭālib) in his house in the Ṣabbūra suburb of Damascus in the latter days of Rabīʿ al-Awwal 1425/in mid-May 2004 that 'Umar b. al-Khaṭṭāb said, "'Alī b. Abī Ṭālib was given three traits, to have only one of which would be dearer to me than possessing many red camels: his marrying Fāṭima the daughter of the Messenger of Allah ﷺ; his living in the Mosque with the Messenger of Allah, sharing with him whatever was licit therein to him; and carrying the standard on the Day of Khaybar."

'Alī ؓ said: "My eyes were never sore nor inflamed again after the Messenger of Allah spat into my eyes on the day of Khaybar."[494]

Another version states that Abū Laylā asked 'Alī why he wore summer clothes in winter and winter clothes in summer to which he replied: "The day of Khaybar the Prophet ﷺ summoned me when my eyes were sore. I said to him: 'Messenger of Allah! I have ophthalmia.' He blew on my eyes and said: 'O Allah! remove from him hot and cold.' I never felt hot nor cold after that day."[495]

---

[494]Narrated by Aḥmad, Abū Yaʿlā (1:445 §593), and al-Ṭayālisī (p. 26 §189) with strong narrators cf. al-Haythamī (9:122), *Mukhtāra* (2:422-423 §810-811).
[495]Narrated from 'Abd Allāh b. Abī Laylā by Aḥmad and Ibn Mājah with weak chains.

7

The Non-Sunni View of the Preferability of Our Liege lord 'Alī Over the Three Caliphs

In his book written in affirmation of the superiority of our liege lord 'Alī entitled *al-Burhān al-Jalī*, the Moroccan Shaykh Aḥmad al-Ghumārī saw in the ḥadīths of Khaybar proofs for the preferability of 'Alī ☙ over Abū Bakr and 'Umar. His brother 'Abd Allāh's student, Maḥmūd Saʿīd Mamdūḥ, did the same in his 300-page *Ghāyat al-Tabjīl fī Tark al-Tafḍīl* and one of our teachers told me during a road trip from Damascus to Rankūs that he held a similar view to the effect that "the superiority of Abū Bakr is probabilistic *(ẓannī)* rather than decisive *(qaṭʿī)*." Such views violate the consensus of *Ahl al-Sunna* and fly in the face of mass-transmitted evidence.

Those who uphold such views build on four errors:

1. They confuse the "consensus vs. majority" *(ijmāʿī/jumhūrī)* issue on another *afḍaliyya* – that of our liege lords 'Uthmān and 'Alī – and shift the latter debate to misapply it to Abū Bakr and 'Alī where preference was not an issue among *Ahl al-Sunna*. "The only divergence among those [of the Companions and Successors] who differed," Imām al-Shāfiʿī said, "was about 'Alī and 'Uthmān."[496]

2. They confuse the licitness of *loving 'Alī more* than Abū Bakr and 'Umar with the illicitness of *preferring him* to Abū Bakr and 'Umar. "Among the sayings of Zayn al-'Ābidīn the son of Muḥammad al-Bakrī (d. 991) the son of Shaykh Abū al-Ḥasan al-Bakrī al-Mis}rī al-Shāfiʿī: 'Abū Bakr is better than 'Alī, however, love and attraction are a different matter.'"[497] Abū al-Bakhtarī al-Ṭā'ī (d. 82) said: "I do not claim that 'Alī is better than Abū Bakr and 'Umar! However, I find in him an attraction *(lawṭ)* I do not find in them."[498]

3. They are unaware of the mass-transmitted, decisive weight of the evidence that the Two Shaykhs are preferable in the many Prophetic and Companion-reports to that effect.

4. They are trying to include our liege lord 'Alī into the *afḍaliyya muṭlaqa* of Sayyida Fāṭima, whereas the scholars have specified that it is exclusive: "Know that the *faḍīla* of the Four Caliphs is restricted to being over other than the children of Fāṭima, may Allah be well-pleased with her," accord-

---

[496]Narrated by al-Bayhaqī in *Manāqib al-Shāfiʿī* (1:432-434) with his chains and *al-Iʿtiqād* ('Abd al-Razzāq 'Afīfī 1999 ed. p. 522) without chains cf. Muḥammad b. 'Alawī al-Mālikī, *al-Manhal al-Laṭīf* (p. 179-180, *Afḍal al-Ṣaḥāba*).
[497]Cited by al-Qinnawjī in *Abjad al-'Ulūm* (3:163).
[498]Ibn al-Athīr, *Nihāya* (article *l-w-ṭ*).

ing to 'Abd al-Ḥaqq al-Dihlawī in *Takmīl al-Īmān*. "Fāṭima and her brother Ibrāhīm are better than the Four Caliphs by agreement" according to 'Alam al-Dīn al-'Irāqī (d. 704); and Imām Mālik said: "I do not prefer anyone at all to the offspring of the Messenger of Allah."[499] Even so, this is a "filial preferability" *(tafḍīl bid'iyya)* rather than an absolute one.

The explicit preferability *(tafḍīl)* given by the Prophet ﷺ to our liege lord Abū Bakr al-Ṣiddīq over all other Companions including our liege lord 'Alī b. Abī Ṭālib is narrated not only from Ibn 'Umar in al-Bukhārī and the *Sunan* and *Musnad*, his father 'Umar, Abū Mūsā al-Ash'arī, and others but from the members of *Ahl al-Bayt* themselves:

- 'Alī b. Abī Ṭālib as narrated from him by Muḥammad b. al-Ḥanafiyya in al-Bukhārī and Abū Dāwūd ("Who is the best of human beings after the Messenger of Allah?" "Abū Bakr;" "then who?" "'Umar"); this was reiterated by 'Alī from the pulpit in al-Kūfa[500] and is actually a mass-narrated *(mutawātir)* saying of his – from more than eighty narrators according to al-Dhahabī – also narrated from Wahb al-Suwā'ī, 'Alqama b. Qays, Shurayḥ, and 'Abd Khayr by Aḥmad in his *Musnad*, each through several chains; from 'Abd Allāh b. Salama by Ibn Mājah with a fair chain and Ibn Abī Shayba; from Shurayḥ by Ibn Shādhān, al-Khaṭīb, Ibn Abī Shayba, al-Lālikā'ī, Ibn Mandah, Ibn 'Asākir, and others; and *mursal* from Ḥabīb b. Abī Thābit by al-Taymī.[501]

- Muḥammad al-Bāqir b. 'Alī b. al-Ḥusayn as narrated by Abū Nu'aym in the *Ḥilya*, Ibn al-Jawzī in *Manāqib 'Umar,* al-Taymī in *al-Ḥujja fī Bayān al-Maḥajja*, and al-Maqdisī in *al-Nahī 'an Sabb al-Ṣaḥāba* ("Whoever does not know the preference of Abū Bakr and 'Umar is ignorant of the Sunna");

- Zayn al-'Ābidīn 'Alī b. al-Ḥusayn as narrated by 'Abd Allāh b. Aḥmad in *Zawā'id al-Zuhd*, Ibn al-Jawzī in *Manāqib 'Umar*, and al-Taymī in *al-Ḥujja fī Bayān al-Maḥajja* ("Their level then is the same as now and they lie right next to the Prophet!");

- 'Abd Allāh b. al-Ḥasan b. 'Alī swore between the Grave and the Pulpit in Medina that "'Umar is better than me and all humanity" as narrated by Ibn 'Asākir and al-Ḍiyā' al-Maqdisī in *al-Nahī 'an Sabb al-Ṣaḥāba*.

Imām al-Shāfi'ī said: "The best of human beings *(afḍal al-nās)* after the Messenger of Allah are Abū Bakr, then *(thumma)*'Umar, then 'Uthmān, then 'Alī." This is related from him by both his students Ibn 'Abd al-

[499]All of which as cited in *Jāmi' al-'Ulūm fī Iṣṭilāḥāt al-Funūn*, known as *Dastūr al-'Ulamā'*, article *Āl*, by Qadi 'Abd al-Nabī Aḥmadnagrī (12th c.). See also the third part of our *Musnad Ahl al-Bayt*.

[500]Narrated by Ibn Abī 'Ās}im, *al-Sunna* (2:480); 'Abd Allāh b. Aḥmad in his additions to the *Musnad* and *Faḍā'il al-Ṣaḥāba* (1:336); Ibn Shāhīn, *al-Sunna* (p. 316).

[501]See al-Taymī's *al-Ḥujja fī Bayān al-Maḥajja* (Dār al-Rāya ed. 2:345-348 §325-332) and Abū Nu'aym's *Faḍā'il al-Khulafā' al-Arba'a* (p. 135-141 §156-168) and *al-Imāma wal-Radd 'alā al-Rāfiḍa* (p. 270-271 §58-61).

Ḥakam and al-Rabī' b. Sulaymān, while his student Imām Abū Thawr related from al-Shāfi'ī the statement: "None of the Companions and Successors differed over the preferential superiority *(tafḍīl)* of Abū Bakr and 'Umar and their being given precedence *(taqdīm)* over all Companions; the only divergence, among those of them who differed, was about 'Alī and 'Uthmān. As for us we do not find fault with any of the Prophetic Companions whomsoever oever what they did."[502] Imām al-Nawawī said: "Know that each of Abū Bakr and 'Umar is better than 'Alī according to the Consensus *(ijmā')* of *Ahl al-Sunna*. The proofs for this in well-known sound ḥadīths are too famous and countless to be listed."[503] Similarly al-Haytamī: "The preferability of Abū Bakr over the other three [of the first four Caliphs] and that of 'Umar over the other two is agreed upon by Consensus *(mujma' 'alayh)* of *Ahl al-Sunna* and there is no disagreement among them concerning this."[504] Similarly al-Qārī: "It is patent that to prefer 'Alī to the Two Shaykhs contravenes the doctrine of *Ahl al-Sunna wa al-Jamā'a* according to what the totality of the *Salaf* follow."[505]

Muḥammad Abū Zahra in his book *Abū Ḥanīfa* cites, without comment, a Shī'ī claim – from Ibn Abī al-Ḥadīd's *Sharḥ Nahj al-Balāgha* – that the following Companions and Successors held 'Alī to be preferable to all other Companions:

al-'Abbās b. 'Abd al-Muṭṭalib and his children
Abū Ayyūb al-Anṣārī
Abū Dharr al-Ghifārī
Abū al-Haytham
Abū al-Ṭufayl 'Āmir b. Wā'ila
'Ammār b. Yāsir
the Banū Hāshim in their entirety
Burayda
Ḥudhayfa b. al-Yamān
Jābir b. 'Abd Allāh
Khālid b. Sa'īd b. al-'Āṣ among the Banū Umayya
Khuzayma b. Thābit
al-Miqdād b. Aswad
Sahl b. Ḥunayf
Salmān al-Fārisī
Ubay b. Ka'b
'Umar b. 'Abd al-'Azīz among the Banū Umayya
'Uthmān b. Ḥunayf, and
al-Zubayr in the beginning.

502 Narrated by al-Bayhaqī in *Manāqib al-Shāfi'ī* (1:432-434) with his chains and *al-I'tiqād* ('Abd al-Razzāq 'Afīfī 1999 ed. p. 522) without chains.
503 Al-Nawawī, *Fatāwā* (p. 264).
504 Al-Haytamī, *Fatāwā Ḥadīthiyya* (p. 155).
505 Al-Qārī, Sharḥ al-Fiqh al-Akbar (p. 140).

Shaykh Aḥmad al-Ghumārī also attributes this view to "a number of the Companions, Successors and the pious *Salaf*" – and is likewise untroubled by lack of any proof beyond Ibn Ḥazm's citations from various Companions and Successors in his *Fiṣal* to the effect that some put 'Alī first, then al-Zubayr b. al-'Awwām; some Ja'far b. Abī Ṭālib then Ḥamza; some Sa'd b. Mu'ādh then Usayd b. Ḥuḍayr al-Anṣārī then 'Abbād b. Bishr; some Abū Salama; some 'Abd Allāh b. Mas'ūd; some 'Umar; and some, such as Dāwūd al-Ẓāhirī, refrained from naming any individual Companions but preferred all of them to the rest of humanity apart from Prophets. Ibn Ḥazm then declared his view – as he also did in his *al-Mufāḍala bayn al-Ṣaḥāba* – that the best of human beings after the Prophets is Abū Bakr, followed by the Prophet's ﷺ wives.[506]

The above is arguably a mix of the four confusions already mentioned for the most part, as well as largely based on opinion rather than Divine or Prophetic ordainment such as the Qur'ān, the Sunna and Consensus. Nor are the views attributed to the *Salaf* accurate as shown by the reports from al-Shāfi'ī. Similarly Abū Ḥanīfa gave one of the pithiest definitions of Islamic orthodoxy: "The doctrine of *Ahl al-Sunna wal-Jamā'a* consists in preferring the Two Shaykhs *(tafḍīl al-shaykhayn)* [Abū Bakr and 'Umar], loving the Two Sons-in-law *(ḥubb al-khatanayn)* ['Alī and 'Uthmān], and [deeming lawful the] wiping on leather socks [in ablution] *(al-masḥ 'alāl-khuffayn)*."[507] The middle part of his statement is elucidated by al-Awzā'ī's saying: "Love of 'Alī and 'Uthmān together – Allah be well-pleased with them! – is not found except in the heart of a Believer."[508]

The Māturīdī School considers that (1) Abū Bakr al-Ṣiddīq is the best of this *Umma* after the Prophet ﷺ as stated in *Tabṣirat al-Adilla* by Abū al-Mu'īn Maymūn b. Muḥammad al-Nasafī (d. 508) and that (2) the status of preferability of each of the Four Rightly-Guided Caliphs to be on a par with the actual order of their Caliphate *(wa-faḍluhum 'alā tartībi khilāfatihim)* as stated explicitly in *al-Fiqh al-Akbar* and its commentaries as well as in *Lubāb al-Kalām* by 'Alā' al-Dīn Muḥammad b. 'Abd al-Ḥamīd al-Asmandī (d. 552), *al-Bidāya fī Uṣūl al-Dīn* by Nūr al-Dīn Aḥmad b. Maḥmūd al-S}ābūnī (d. 580), the *'Aqīda al-Rukniyya* by Rukn al-Dīn 'Ubayd Allah b. Muḥammad al-Samarqandī (d. 701).

The Ash'arī School holds the same position as is clear from *Jawharat al-Tawḥīd* 76: "Their status in preferability is as [their order] in caliphate"

[506]Muḥammad Abū Zahra, *Abū Ḥanīfa* (p. 96); Aḥmad al-Ghumārī, *al-Burhān al-Jalī* (p. 77-78, 85-86); Ibn Ḥazm, *al-Fiṣal* (4:90-91, 111). See also al-Ash'arī, *Maqālāt al-Islāmiyyīn* (2:147=458-459) and al-Baghdādī, *Uṣūl al-Dīn* (p. 293).

[507]Narrated by Ibn 'Abd al-Barr in *al-Intiqā'* through several different chains. Cf. Abū Ḥanīfa in *Lisān al-Aḥkām*. Also related from Sufyān al-Thawrī by al-Lālikā'ī in *I'tiqād Ahl al-Sunna* (1:152) despite al-Ghumārī in *al-Burhān* (p. 82) who cites from Ibn Abī Khaythama through 'Abd al-Razzāq a report that Sufyān al-Thawrī preferred 'Alī to Abū Bakr and 'Umar. In actuality it is well-established that Sufyān's position hinged over 'Alī and 'Uthmān.

[508]Cited by al-Dhahabī in *Siyar A'lām al-Nubalā'* (1997 ed. 7:95).

and al-Dardīr's *Sharḥ al-Kharīdat al-Bahiyya*: "It is obligatory to believe that Muḥammad is the best of all Messengers and Prophets, upon him and all of them blessings and peace, and that he is the last of them, and following him in preferability are the major Messengers, then the rest of the Messengers, then the Prophets, then the Companions of the Messenger of Allah ﷺ, and the best of them is Abū Bakr, then 'Umar, then 'Uthmān, then 'Alī." One of its commentators said: "Abū Mans}ūr al-Māturīdī said, 'Our Companions all concur that the best of them are the Four Caliphs according to the order given'... and this preference is decisive both outwardly and inwardly *(wa-hādhā al-tafḍīlu qaṭ'iyyun fil-ẓāhir wal-bāṭin)*, as al-Ash'arī said." Al-Ghazālī stipulates the same as the obligatory belief of every Muslim in his *Qawā'id al-'Aqā'id* while al-Zabīdī commented that there is consensus over it[509] as does Ibn Abī Sharīf in his commentary on Ibn al-Humām's *Musāyara*. Al-Baghdādī said in his "Exposition of the Principles Over which Sunnis Have Concurred" at the conclusion of *al-Farq bayn al-Firaq*: "They held that Abū Bakr and 'Umar were preferable over all those after them and they only differed over the preference between 'Alī and 'Uthmān, may Allah be well-pleased with all of them." Finally, Shaykh Muḥyī al-Dīn Ibn 'Arabī in Chapter 93 of his *Futūḥāt* states that "There is no one in the entire *Umma* preferable to Abū Bakr except 'Īsā Ibn Maryam."

Al-Haytamī in his *Ṣawā'iq al-Muḥriqa* mentions that Ibn al-Bāqillānī, Imām al-Ḥaramayn in *al-Irshād*, and al-Māzarī in his commentary on *Ṣaḥīḥ Muslim* all considered the superiority of Abū Bakr probabilistic, contravening in this Imām al-Ash'arī who considered Abū Bakr's superiority to be decisively established and did not deem it permissible for the second-best to be caliph (as stated by al-Baghdādī). Ibn Mujāhid in the Forty-Sixth Consensus of his *Risāla ilā Ahl al-Thughar* (which Mamdūḥ misattributes to al-Ash'arī himself) narrates from al-Ash'arī: "They held by consensus that the best of the Ten Promised Paradise were the Four Imāms: Abū Bakr, then 'Umar, then 'Uthmān, then 'Alī." The same order of preference is also mass-transmitted from Imām Aḥmad and the *Mudawwana* narrates that when Imām Mālik heard a questioner ask about the order of preferability of the Four Imāms, "First Abū Bakr, the 'Umar," he interrupted him saying: "Is there any doubt about this?" Yaḥyā b. Sa'īd al-Qaṭṭān similarly said: "Glory to Allah! I never saw anyone doubt the preferability of Abū Bakr and 'Umar over 'Alī. Any divergence was only between 'Alī and 'Uthmān."[510]

In light of the agreement of those named above among the Companions and *Ahl al-Bayt* in addition to the *Salaf*, the Four Imāms of Law, al-Ash'arī, and the Māturīdī School, Imām al-Haytamī correctly rejects as unreliable, "strange... anomalous" the claim by Ibn 'Abd al-Barr (on which relied Abū Zahra and al-Ghumārī) that there was disagreement over the preference of Abū Bakr over 'Alī. Nevertheless, he agreed with the legal theorists such as

[509]Cf. al-Zabīdī, *Itḥāf al-Sādat al-Muttaqīn* (2:41-42).
[510]*Siyar*, chapter on Yaḥyā b. Sa'īd.

al-Āmidī and al-Rāzī, as opposed to al-Ash'arī, that the second-best could indeed be caliph and therefore that the Consensus over the preferability of Abū Bakr bore probabilistic rather than decisive force:

> The firm establishment of imamate, even if decisive, does not denote decisive preferability; rather, at most, probable preferability. How could it be otherwise when there is no decisive proof over the invalidity of the imamate of the second-best *(al-mafḍūl)* when the best *(al-fāḍil)* exists? However, we found that the *Salaf* gave them preference thus, and our best opinion of them dictates that if they had not seen some indication concerning this, they would not have all concurred over it. We are therefore duty-bound to follow them in this matter and resign the truth of the matter to Allah Most High.... Consensus over the most deserving to hold imamate does not dictate consensus over who is preferable, since *Ahl al-Sunna* reached consensus that 'Uthmān was more deserving of caliphate than 'Alī while differing who was more preferable than the other.[511]

The status of the view of preferability *(tafḍīl)* of 'Alī ﷺ over Abū Bakr and 'Umar at best is a "light innovation" *(bid'a khafīfa)* in the terms of al-Dusūqī[512] and at worst brings one out of the fold of *Ahl al-Sunna* and constitutes Shī'īsm – if not decisively then most probably. Al-Dāraquṭnī was once asked to arbitrate between two groups in Baghdād who differed whether 'Uthmān was preferable to 'Alī or vice-versa. He relates: "At first I withheld from taking any position and considered reserve best. But then I reached the conclusion that Religion dictated other than silence. So I said: 'Uthmān is better than 'Alī with the agreement of the assembly of the Companions. This is the position of *Ahl al-Sunna*, and it is the first knot of the *Rāfiḍa* one cuts loose." Al-Dhahabī comments:

> To prefer 'Alī [to 'Uthmān] is neither *Rafḍ* nor a *bid'a*, for several of the Companions and Successors did.[513] Both 'Uthmān and 'Alī possess great merits and precedence and are among the foremost shahids. However, the vast majority of the Community agree to give precedence to 'Uthmān,[514] and this is our position also; and better than both of them without doubt are Abū Bakr and 'Umar. Whoever differs with this is a dyed-in-the-wool Shī'ī. Whoever disrespects the Two Shaykhs [Abū Bakr and 'Umar] while accepting the validity of their imāmate is a disgusting *Rāfiḍī*.[515] As for those who both insult them and reject the validity

[511]Al-Haytamī, *Ṣawā'iq* (p. 56-58) cf. Ibn 'Abd al-Barr, *Istī'āb* (chapter on 'Alī ﷺ).
[512]In his Ḥāshiya 'ala al-Sharḥ al-Kabīr lil-Dardīr (1:329).
[513]See Haytamī, *Fatāwā Ḥadīthiyya* (p. 155) and Ibn Ḥazm's *Fiṣal* and *Muḥallā* as quoted in Ghumārī's *al-Burhān al-Jalī* (p. 85-88). Ibn Jamā'a in *al-Manhal al-Rawī* said (p. 112): "Al-Khaṭṭābī said that some of *Ahl al-Sunna* in Kūfa gave precedence to 'Alī over 'Uthmān, and this is Ibn Khuzayma's position." Al-Shāfi'ī alluded to this position when he said in his *Dīwān*: "I call upon my Lord to witness that 'Uthmān is of high merit / and that 'Alī's high merit is shared by none."
[514]As in the texts of al-Shāfi'ī and Abū Ḥanīfa already cited as well as the latter's *Fiqh al-Akbar* and al-Ṭaḥāwī's *'Aqīda*.
[515]Imām Aḥmad is related to define the *Rāfiḍī* as "He who insults Abū Bakr and

of their imāmate, they are extremist *Rāfiḍīs* – may Allah lead them to perdition![516]

Even so, Imām Aḥmad relatedly said: "There was no disagreement among the Companions of the Messenger of Allah ﷺ that 'Uthmān is better than 'Alī."[517] And also: "Whoever prefers 'Alī to Abū Bakr maligns the Prophet ﷺ; whoever gives 'Alī preference over 'Umar maligns the Prophet ﷺ and Abū Bakr; and whoever gives 'Alī preference over 'Uthmān maligns the Prophet ﷺ, Abū Bakr, 'Umar, and the Emigrants. Nor do I believe that the deeds of such a person are accepted."[518]

In the opening of his four-volume *Kashf Mushkil Ḥadīth al-Ṣaḥīḥayn* Ibn al-Jawzī mentioned the anecdote that a Rāfiḍī asked a Sunni: "Who is nobler than five under a cloak, the sixth of whom is Jibrīl?" whereupon the Sunni replied: "Two in the cave, the third of whom is Allah."[519]

It is strange that Shaykh Maḥmūd Mamdūh's *Ghāyat al-Tabjīl* displays commendations by three Shaykhs of the Bā 'Alawīs although the book contravenes the Bā 'Alawī position as given by the *Quṭb* 'Abd Allāh al-Ḥaddād in his *'Aqīda* which states: "A Muslim must firmly believe in the immense merit *(faḍl)* of the Companions of the Messenger of Allah and their order of precedence *(wa-tartībihim)*,"[520] and in his book of fatwas entitled *al-Nafā'is al-'Ulwiyya* he states that there is no rank between Ṣiddīq and Nabī. In his collected sayings entitled *Tathbīt al-Fu'ād*, we read: "When the Zaydis came and asked us: 'Why did you put others before your forefather 'Alī b. Abī Ṭālib?' We replied: 'He himself is the one who put other than himself before himself and preferred other than himself to himself, and so we did the same.' When they said: 'He only did this out of *taqiyya*,' we

'Umar" in al-Khallāl, *al-Sunna* (3:493).

[516]Al-Dhahabī, *Siyar A'lām al-Nubalā'*, chapter on 'Alī æ. Al-Qārī said in *Sharḥ al-Shifā'* (2:92): "Al-Nawawī said that cursing the Companions is one of the most depraved acts *(min akbar al-fawāḥish)*, while the author ['Iyāḍ] counts it among the major sins *(kabā'ir)*. Such offense is punished with corporeal punishment according to the vast majority, while according to some of the Mālikīs and Ḥanafīs the offender is executed. In some of the books of the latter, it is stated that to insult the two Shaykhs (Abū Bakr and 'Umar) constitutes disbelief *(kufr)*." Al-Nawawī said in *Sharḥ Ṣaḥīḥ Muslim*: "Know that to insult the Companions is prohibited and constitutes one of the major grave indecencies *(al-fawāhish al-muharramāt)* whether with regard to those of them involved in a dissension or other than them, because they entered those conflicts on the conviction of their *ijtihād* and interpretation."

[517]In al-Khallāl's *al-Sunna* (2:392).

[518]In Ibn al-Jawzī's *Manāqib Aḥmad* (p. 162).

[519]I was unable to consult Shāh Walī Allah's two treatises in print, *Izālat al-Khafā' 'an Khilāfat al-Khulafā'* in two volumes (Karachi, 1286H), a work on the early Caliphal model whose contents have also been included in *Anfās al-'Ārifīn*; and especially the 336-page *Qurrat al-'Aynayn fī Tafḍīl al-Shaykhayn* (Delhi: 1320H), both of them in Persian.

[520] The latter phrase became, under the pen of Mostafa Badawi's English and French translations, "that their status was of various ranks." However, the author did not say *rutab*, the plural of *rutba* (rank), but *tartīb* (sequential order), purposely echoing the standard Ash'arī and Māturīdī doctrinal texts which state the necessity of putting our liege lords Abū Bakr and 'Umar first.

said: ‘We are not nearly as brave, strong and courageous as he, therefore the *taqiyya* that was good enough for him is good enough for us also.’” Then he continued explaining the process of caliphate giving primacy to the two Shaykhs in which our liege lord ‘Alī was actively and willingly involved.[521] More to the point than all of the above is ‘Abd al-Qādir al-‘Aydarūs’s quotation in *al-Nūr al-Sāfir ‘an Akhbār al-Qarn al-‘Āshir* (Year 914) from *al-shaykh al-kabīr wal-‘alam al-shahīr al-quṭb al-rabbānī, shams al-shumūs* Abū Bakr b. ‘Abd Allāh al-‘Aydarūs Bā ‘Alawī (851-914) who often said when *tafḍīl* was discussed: “I swear it by Allah Most High! If Allah raised my father Shaykh ‘Abd Allāh and my teacher Shaykh Sa‘d from the dead, and it was said to me that our liege lord ‘Alī is better in the presence of Allah than our liege lord Abū Bakr – may Allah be well-pleased with both of them – I would not retract the belief of *Ahl al-Sunna wal-Jamā‘a* that Abū Bakr and ‘Umar and ‘Uthmān are better than ‘Alī – Allah be well-pleased with them!”

[521]Aḥmad b. ‘Abd al-Karīm al-Ḥasāwī al-Shajjār, *Tathbīt al-Fu’ād bi-Dhikr Majālis al-Quṭb al-Imām ‘Abd Allāh b. ‘Alawī b. Muḥammad al-Ḥaddād*, ed. Aḥmad b. al-Ḥasan b. ‘Abd Allāh al-Ḥaddād, 2 vols. (Tarīm: al-Ḥāwī, n.d.) 2:226-227.

8
Hadiths on the Immense Merits of Our Master 'Alī

Imām Aḥmad said: "There is no Companion about whom are reported as many merits as 'Alī b. Abī Ṭālib."[522] Following are some more of the ḥadīths to that effect.

- The Prophet ﷺ said to 'Alī – as part of a long ḥadīth in which he also praised: "You are part of me and I am part of you."[523]
- The Prophet ﷺ left 'Alī behind in the campaign of Tabūk. The latter said: "Messenger of Allah, are you leaving me behind with the women and children?" The Prophet ﷺ replied, "Are you not happy to be, next to me, like Hārūn was next to Mūsā save that there is no Prophet after me?"[524] Shaykh Muḥammad Abū al-Hudā al-Yaʿqūbī said of this hadith, "It is a Prophetic glad tiding for ʿAlī that he would outlive the Prophet and a historical report that Mūsā died before Hārūn."
- The Prophet ﷺ said: "I am the city of knowledge and 'Alī is its gate." Another version states: "I am the house of wisdom and 'Alī is its gate."[525]

[522]Narrated by al-Ḥākim in *al-Mustadrak* (3:107).
[523]Narrated from al-Barā' b. 'Azib by al-Bukhārī as part of the ḥadīth of the treaty written with the Quraysh for the Prophet's Minor Pilgrimage, al-Tirmidhī *(ḥasan ṣaḥīḥ)*, and Aḥmad with four chains.
[524]Narrated from Sa'd b. Abī Waqqāṣ in the *Ṣaḥīḥayn*, Tirmidhī, Ibn Mājah, Aḥmad.
[525]Narrated from 'Alī and Ibn 'Abbās by Tirmidhī *(gharīb munkar)*; Ṭabarānī, *Kabīr* (11:66); Khaṭīb, *Tārīkh* (11:48-51), Abū Nu'aym, *Ḥilya* (1:103 §193=1985 ed. 1:64), Baghawī, *Maṣābīḥ al-Sunna* (Qalam ed. 2:517 §2679), and Ḥākim (3:126=1990 ed. 3:137-138). Al-Tirmidhī termed it "single-chained and rejected" as did his teacher al-Bukhārī while Ibn Ma'īn in *Su'ālāt Ibn al-Junayd* (p. 285 §51) declared it a baseless lie as did Abū Zur'a al-Rāzī in *Su'ālāt al-Bardha'ī* (2:519-520), Ibn al-Jawzī in his *Mawḍū'āt* (1:353) citing Ibn 'Adī's *Kāmil* (3:1247-1248), Ibn Ḥibbān in *al-Majrūḥīn* (2:94), Ibn Ṭāhir al-Maqdisī (known as Ibn al-Qaysarānī) in his *Dhakhīrat al-Ḥuffāẓ* (§754, 5992) and *Ma'rifat al-Tadhkira* (p. 127 §308) cf. 'Irāqī in *Takhrīj Aḥādīth al-Iḥyā'*; Qazwīnī in his epistle on Baghawī's *Maṣābīḥ*, Ibn 'Arrāq in *Tanzīh al-Sharī'a* (1:377-378), Dhahabī in *Talkhīṣ al-Mustadrak*, *Tartīb al-Mawḍū'āt* (p. 102-104 §282-293) and the *Mīzān* (1:415, 3:668), Aḥmad b. Taymiyya in *Aḥādīth al-Quṣṣāṣ* (p. 62) and *Majmū' al-Fatāwā* (4:410-413, 18:123-124), and Mu'allamī al-Yamānī in his edition of Shawkānī's *Fawā'id* (p. 308-310). Aḥmad termed it "unheard of" in his *'Ilal* (p. 127-129 §303), Dāraquṭnī in his *'Ilal* (3:248) "inconsistent and uncorroborated" *(muḍṭarib ghayr thābit)*, al-Qurṭubī in his *Tafsīr* (al-Ra'd 13:43) "spurious" *(bāṭil)*. Ibn Daqīq al-'Īd as reported by al-Sakhāwī in *al-Maqāṣid* (p. 67), said: "This ḥadīth is not confirmed by scholars and is held by some to be spurious." Baghawī termed it "single-chained and inconsistently transmitted." Ṭabarī indicated its weakness in *Tahdhīb al-Āthār* (1:105 §174 *Musnad 'Alī*). Ibn Ḥajar in *al-Ajwiba 'alā al-Qazwīnī* at the end of al-Baghawī's *Maṣābīḥ al-Sunna* (Ma'rifa ed. 3:1791) and at the beginning of al-Qārī's *Mirqāt* (Fikr ed. 1:548-549) said it was weak *(ḍa'īf)* and possibly "fair" *(ḥasan)* while Suyūṭī in the *La'āli'* (1:306) reports from him the latter grading. Al-'Alā'ī in his

- After the Prophet ﷺ came to Medina, 'Alī came to him in tears, saying, "You have paired all your Companions as brothers and you have not paired me with anyone as a brother!" The Prophet ﷺ replied, "You are my brother in this world and the next."[526]

- The Prophet ﷺ said: "Anyone whose patron *(mawlā)* I am, 'Alī is his patron!"[527] 'Umar said: "Congratulations, 'Alī! You have become the patron of every single believer."[528] "It is mass-transmitted from both the Commander of the Believers and the Prophet" per Ibn al-Jazarī in *Asnā al-Maṭālib*. It is also narrated with the addition: "O Allah!

Risālat al-Mawḍū'āt (p. 26)=*al-Naqd al-Ṣaḥīḥ limā U'turiḍa 'alayh min Aḥādīth al-Maṣābīḥ* (p. 55) concluded: "The truth is that the ḥadīth is fair *(ḥasan)* in view of its multiple means of transmission, being neither sound *(ṣaḥīḥ)* [as claimed by Ḥākim] nor weak *(ḍa'īf)*, much less a forgery." Among those who also declared it *ḥasan* are Sakhāwī in the *Maqāṣid* (p. 98), Zarkashī in *al-Tadhkira* (p. 163-165), al-Shawkānī in *al-Fawā'id al-Majmū'a* (p. 349=p.373), Haytamī in his *Fatāwā Ḥadīthiyya* (p. 269) and Fattanī in *Tadhkirat al-Mawḍū'āt*. Suyūṭī in the *Durar al-Muntathira* (p. 115-117 §133), *La'āli'* (1:334), *Ta'aqqubāt* (p. 56) and *Ḥāwī* (2:117) also settles on Ibn Ḥajar and 'Alā'ī's grading of *ḥasan*. Aḥmad al-Ghumārī in *al-Burhān* (p. 75-76) declared it *ṣaḥīḥ* while Aḥdab in *Zawā'id Tārīkh Baghdād* (4:128-138 §612) declared it very weak cf. also Ibn al-Mubārak's *al-Zuhd* (p. 314), Zabīdī, *Itḥāf* (6:244), Haythamī (9:114), Samhūdī, *al-Ghammāz* (p. 43), and al-Ghumārī's *Subul al-Sa'āda wa Abwābuhā bi Siḥḥati Ḥadīth Anā Madīnatu al-'Ilmi wa 'Aliyyun Bābuhā* and *Fatḥ al-Malik al-'Alī bi Taṣḥīḥ Ḥadīth Bāb Madīnat al-'Ilmi 'Alī*. Ibn Qudāma in *Ithbāt Sifat al-'Uluw* (p. 42) cited the report of 'Alī's courage *(shajā'a)* and knowledge *('ilm)* together with 'Umar's justice *('adl)* as mass-transmitted *(mutawātir)* truths that necessitate categorical assent.

[526]Narrated from Ibn 'Umar by al-Tirmidhī *(ḥasan gharīb)*, Ibn Hishām (2:150), and Ibn 'Abd al-Barr in *al-Istī'āb* (3:1089).

[527]A sound ḥadīth narrated from Zayd b. Arqam or Abū Sarīḥat al-Ghifārī from al-Tirmidhī *(ḥasan gharīb)* with a sound chain, from Sa'd b. Abī Waqqāṣ by Ibn Mājah, from Ibn 'Abbās by al-Ḥākim (3:134, *ṣaḥīḥ*), and from 'Alī, al-Barā', Zayd b. Arqam (cf. our *Sunna Notes III: The Binding Proof of the Sunna*, Section on the ḥadīth "I have left among you two matters…"), and Burayda al-Aslamī by Aḥmad both in his *Musnad* and in *Faḍā'il al-Ṣaḥāba* (§947) through various chains both fair and sound as well as al-Ṭabarānī in *al-Kabīr*, Ibn Abī 'Āṣim (§1354), Ibn Abī Shayba (12:57), Ibn Ḥibbān with two chains, one sound by Muslim's criterion, one fair (15:374-376 §6930-6931), Ḥākim (2:130 *ṣaḥīḥ* as per al-Bukhārī and Muslim's criteria; 3:109-110, 371), al-Bazzār (§2535) and Abū Ya'lā in their *Musnads*, and – from 'Alī with two fair chains and one weak chain – al-Ṭaḥāwī in *Sharḥ Mushkil al-Āthār* (2:307f.=5:13-15 §1760-1762). Ṭaḥāwī also narrated it with a sound chain from Jābir b. 'Abd Allāh from 'Alī (5:16 §1763) and three weak chains from Sa'd b. Abī Waqqāṣ (5:20-22 §1766-1768), cf. al-Nasā'ī in *Khaṣā'iṣ 'Alī* (94-96). Al-Nawawī in his *Fatāwā* (p. 262) and Dhahabī in the *Siyar* (1/2:621) declared the ḥadīth sound while Suyūṭī declared it *mutawātir* and al-Kattānī confirmed him in *Naṭm al-Mutanāthir* (p. 194) where he names twenty-five narrators of this ḥadīth among the Companions. The ḥadīth master Ibn 'Uqda gathered all its chains in a large monograph. Zayla'ī's questioning of its authenticity in *Naṣb al-Rāya* (1:189) is meaningless and Allah knows best. Aḥmad b. Taymiyya in his *Minhāj al-Sunna* disputes its authenticity and goes on to declare "categorically false" the addition (which is also *ṣaḥīḥ*): "O Allah! Be the patron of whoever takes him as a patron" etc. On the latter's aberrations in Hadith rulings see Ibn Ḥajar, *Lisān* (6:319), al-Lacknawī, *al-Raf' wal-Takmīl* (p. 330), *al-Ajwibat al-'Ashara* (p. 174-176), *Tuḥfat al-Kamala* in the *Raf'* (p. 198-199 n.), and Kawtharī's still-manuscript *al-Ta'aqqub al-Ḥathīth limā Yanfīhi Ibnu Taymiyyata min al-Ḥadīth* among others.

[528]Narrated from al-Barā' by 'Abd al-Razzāq and Ibn Abī Shayba.

Be the patron of whoever takes him as a patron, and the enemy of whoever takes him as an enemy."[529] Nawawī specifies twenty different meanings for *mawlā* in Arabic and cites al-Shāfi'ī's explanation of this ḥadīth as referring to the pact of Islam among all the believers on the basis of the verse *That is because Allah is patron of those who believe, and because the disbelievers have no patron* (47:11).[530] 'Abd Allāh al-Talīdī said in commentary of this ḥadīth: "What is meant by patronage *(muwālāt)* here is the patronage of love *(maḥabba)*, Islam, and support *(al-nuṣra)*. It is not the imāmate that is meant. For the latter sense differs from fact whereas the Prophet ﷺ does not inform us of other than fact. Also, the latter sense would lead to declaring as misguided the first three caliphs as well as the Emigrants and Helpers who reached consensus in pledging their allegiance to them."[531]

- 'Alī narrated: "On the day of Badr the Prophet ﷺ said to me and to Abū Bakr: 'On the right of one of you is Jibrīl and on the right of the other Mīkā'īl, while Isrāfīl – a huge angel – takes part in combat and is in the battle-ranks.'"[532]
- The Prophet ﷺ said: "'Alī is part of me and I am part of 'Alī! No one conveys something on my behalf except I or he."[533] The context of this ḥadīth was the conveyance of Sūrat *Barā'a* to the Quraysh and the rescinding of the Prophet's ﷺ pact with them.[534] The scholars stated that the Prophet's ﷺ phrase "X is part of me and I am part of X" is a hyperbole signifying oneness of path and agreement in obeying Allah. The Prophet ﷺ said that phrase also about the following: the Companion Julaybib who was found dead after a battle next to seven

[529]Narrated from (i-ii) 'Alī and Zayd b. Arqam by al-Ṭaḥāwī, *Mushkil* (5:18 §1765, *ṣaḥīḥ* per Arnā'ūṭ), al-Nasā'ī, *Khaṣā'iṣ 'Alī* (§79) and *Faḍā'il al-Ṣaḥāba* (§45), Ḥākim (3:109, *ṣaḥīḥ*) and Ṭabarānī, *Kabīr* (§4969); (iii) Zayd or Abū Sarīḥa by al-Tirmidhī *(ḥasan gharīb)*; (iv) Abū al-Ṭufayl by Aḥmad, *Musnad* (Arnā'ūṭ ed. 2:262-263 §950-952 *ṣaḥīḥ li-ghayrih)*, al-Bazzār (§2541), al-Nasā'ī, *Kubrā* (5:132-134), *Khaṣā'iṣ 'Alī* (p. 107-108) and *Musnad 'Alī* as well as al-Ḥākim (3:371) both with weak chains because of 'Imrān b. Abbān who is weak, Iyās b. Nadhīr al-Ḍabbī, who is unknown, and al-Ḥasan b. al-Ḥusayn al-Ashqar al-'Uranī who is weak. Cf. al-Dhahabī's marginalia and Ibn Ḥajar, *Tahdhīb al-Tahdhīb* (1:342). Note that the latter and al-Mizzī, *Tahdhīb al-Kamāl* (3:441, 9:199) identify 'Uranī as "Ḥusayn b. Ḥasan al-Ashqar." Also narrated from Sa'd b. Mālik (Abū Sa'īd al-Khudrī) by Ḥākim (3:126) with a chain containing Muslim b. Kaysān al-Mulā'ī al-A'war whom some weakened and some discarded.
[530]Cf. al-Bayhaqī, *Manāqib al-Shāfi'ī* (1:337).
[531]Marginalia on 'Iyāḍ's *al-Shifā* entitled *Itḥāf Ahl al-Wafā* (p. 353).
[532]Narrated with an impeccable chain by al-Ḥākim (3:134) from his Shaykh al-Ḥasan b. Ya'qūb al-'Adl, from the *ḥāfiẓ* Muḥammad b. 'Abd al-Wahhāb al-Farrā', from Ja'far b. 'Awn al-Makhzūmī, from Mis'ar b. Kidam, from Abū 'Awn al-Thaqafī [Muḥammad b. 'Ubayd Allah], from Abū Ṣāliḥ al-Ḥanafī al-Kūfī ['Abd al-Raḥmān b. Qays] from 'Alī ﷺ per Muslim's criterion according to al-Dhahabī.
[533]Narrated from Ḥubshī b. Janāda with a fair chain by al-Tirmidhī *(ḥasan ṣaḥīḥ gharīb)*, Aḥmad, al-Nasā'ī in *al-Sunan al-Kubrā*, and Ibn Mājah.
[534]Al-Mubārakfūrī, *Tuḥfat al-Aḥwadhī* (10:152).

enemies killed by him;[535] the Ash'arīs of Yemen;[536] the *Anṣār*;[537] and the Banū Nājya.[538]

- Some people complained to the Prophet ﷺ about 'Alī whereupon he stood and said: "Do not accuse 'Alī of anything! I swear to you by Allah that he is truly a little rough for the sake of Allah (or: in the path of Allah)."[539]
- When the Prophet ﷺ sent 'Alī to Yemen the latter said: "Messenger of Allah! You are sending me to people who are older than me so that I judge between them!" The Prophet ﷺ said: "Go, for verily Allah shall empower your tongue and guide your heart." 'Alī said: "After that I never felt doubt as to what judgment I should pass between two parties."[540]
- The Prophet ﷺ said: "The most compassionate of my Umma to my Umma is Abū Bakr; the staunchest in the command of Allah is 'Umar; the most truthful in his modesty is 'Uthmān and the most judicious is 'Alī."[541] 'Umar said: "'Alī is the best in judgment among us and Ubay the most proficient in the Qur'ānic readings."[542] Ibn Mas'ūd said: "We used to say that the best in judgment among the people of Medina was 'Alī."[543] It is a measure of al-Ḥasan al-Baṣrī's greatness that 'Alī reportedly followed his recommendation in a judicial case if the report is authentic.[544] Imām al-Nawawī excluded Abū Bakr and 'Umar from the meaning of the Prophet's ﷺ statement: "the best in judgment is 'Alī," further adding that the phrase did not necessitate precedence in knowledge nor in absolute merit.[545]

[535]Narrated by Nadla b. 'Ubayd by Muslim.
[536]Narrated from Abū Mūsā al-Ash'arī by al-Bukhārī and Muslim.
[537]Narrated from 'Uthmān by al-Rāmahurmuzī in *al-Amthāl* (p. 236-237) with a weak chain because of Khufāf b. 'Arāba [or 'Arāna] al-'Absī [or 'Ansī] and Wahb b. Tamīm who are both unknown. The ḥadīth is also narrated without the phrase by al-Bazzār in his *Musnad* (2:67-68 §410) with a fair chain according to al-Haythamī (10:41), a weak one according to Ibn Ḥajar in his *Mukhtaṣar* (2:375-376 §2044) because of Mujāhid b. Sa'īd al-Hamdānī; al-Khaṭīb in his *Tārīkh* (13:291) with a chain similar to al-Bazzār's, cf. al-Aḥdab in *Zawā'id Tārīkh Baghdād* (9:227-228 §2036); and Ibn Abī 'Āṣim in *al-Āḥād wal-Mathānī* (3:323) with the same weak chain.
[538]Narrated from Sa'd b. Abī Waqqāṣ by Aḥmad with a weak chain.
[539]Narrated from Abū Sa'īd al-Khudrī by Aḥmad (18:337 §1187) through trustworthy narrators (Haythamī, *Majma'*, 9:129); and Ḥākim (3:134, *ṣaḥīḥ al-isnād*).
[540]Narrated by Aḥmad with two sound chains – one version lacks 'Alī's final words – and Abū Dāwūd cf. 'Abd al-Ḥaqq, *al-Aḥkām al-Wusṭā* (3:342-343).
[541]Part of a longer ḥadīth narrated with two sound chains from Anas by al-Tirmidhī (*ḥasan ṣaḥīḥ*), Ibn Mājah, and Aḥmad.
[542]Narrated from Ibn 'Abbās by Aḥmad, al-Bukhārī, Ibn Sa'd (2:339), Ibn 'Abd al-Barr, *al-Istī'āb* (3:39-41), Ibn 'Asākir (42:404), and Abū Nu'aym in the *Ḥilya*.
[543]Narrated by al-Ḥākim (3:135), Ibn Sa'd (2:338), and Ibn 'Asākir (42:404).
[544]As narrated by 'Abd al-Razzāq (7:412). Cf. Muḥammad R. al-Qal'ajī, *Mawsū'at Fiqh al-Ḥasan al-Baṣrī* (1:21).
[545]Al-Nawawī, *Fatāwā* (p. 264).

- 'Amr b. Sha's al-Aslamī complained about 'Alī upon returning from Yemen where he had accompanied him. News of it reached the Prophet ﷺ who said: "'Amr! By Allah, you have done me harm." 'Amr said: "I seek refuge in Allah from harming you, Messenger of Allah!" He said: "But you did. Whoever harms 'Alī harms me."[546] The Prophet ﷺ also used the terms "Whoever harms X has harmed me" about his uncle 'Abbās[547] as related in our *Musnad Ahl al-Bayt.*

- Umm Salama said to Abū 'Abd Allāh al-Jadali:[548] "Is the Messenger of Allah ﷺ being insulted among you?!"[549] He said: "Allah forbid!" She said: "I heard the Messenger of Allah ﷺ say, 'Whoever insults 'Alī insults me.'"[550]

- 'Alī said: "In truth the Prophet ﷺ made a covenant with me saying: 'None loves you except a believer, and none hates you except a hypocrite."[551] Abū Sa'īd al-Khudrī subsequently said: "In truth we recognized the hypocrites by their hatred for 'Alī."[552] Jābir said: "We did not know the hypocrites of this Community except by their hatred for 'Alī."[553]

- Ṣuhayb, the freedman of al-'Abbās ﷺ said: "I saw 'Alī kiss the hand of al-'Abbās and his foot, saying: 'Uncle! Be pleased with me.'"[554]

- The Prophet ﷺ is related to say: "I am the Master of humankind and 'Alī is the Master of the Arabs."[555]

- Also related from the Prophet ﷺ: "To gaze at 'Alī's face is worship."[556] There are five things gazing at which amounts to worship: the Ka'ba, the Qur'ān, one's parents, the sea, and one's brothers in Is-

[546]Narrated from 'Amr b. Sha's by Aḥmad, Ibn Abī Shayba (12:75), and al-Ḥākim (3:122) with a sound chain as confirmed by al-Dhahabī and al-Haythamī.
[547]Narrated from 'Abd al-Muṭṭalib b. Rabī'a by Aḥmad and Tirmidhī *(ḥasan ṣaḥīḥ).*
[548]Abū 'Abd Allāh al-Jadali is 'Abd b. 'Abd, a *Tābi'i* from Kūfa.
[549]I.e. in Kūfa.
[550]Narrated by Aḥmad and al-Ḥākim (3:121) with a sound chain per the latter, al-Haythamī, and al-Suyūṭī.
[551]Narrated by Muslim, al-Nasā'ī, and Aḥmad.
[552]Narrated by al-Tirmidhī with two chains, one of them sound to al-A'mash.
[553]Cited by Ibn 'Abd al-Barr, *Istī'āb* (3:46-47) and Dhahabī in the *Siyar* (1/2:625).
[554]Bukhārī narrated it in *al-Adab al-Mufrad* and Dhahabī declared its chain fair in the *Siyar* (3:410).
[555]Narrated from Anas by Ṭabarānī, *al-Awsaṭ* with a weak chain because of Khāqān b. 'Abd Allāh b. al-Ahtam and another very weak chain because of Isḥāq b. Ibrāhīm al-Ḍabbī who is discarded *(matrūk)* as stated by al-Haythamī (9:116, 9:132). Also narrated from Sa'īd b. Jubayr, from 'Ā'isha by Ḥākim (1990 ed. 3:133-134=3:124). The latter said it is *ṣaḥīḥ al-isnād* but al-Dhahabī declared it forged by al-Ḥusayn b. 'Alwān and 'Umar b. Mūsā al-Wajīhī.
[556]Narrated from eleven Companions according to al-Suyūṭī in *al-La'āli'* (1:342-346), hence Ibn 'Arrāq considered it authentic in *Tanzīh al-Sharī'a* (1:382-383) while al-Shawkānī in *al-Fawā'id* (1986 ed. p. 380) said: "It is evident that this narration is fair *(ḥasan)* because of its other chains *(ḥasan li-ghayrih)*, not sound as al-Ḥākim (3:141-142) said, nor forged as Ibn al-Jawzī (*al-Mawḍū'āt* 1:359) said." See also al-Ghumārī's *al-Burhān* (p. 222). Al-Dhahabī also considers it forged in his marginalia on the *Mustadrak.*

lam.[557] Sayyid Aḥmad b. 'Alī al-Rifā'ī al-Kabīr–the *Quṭb* of 'Alawī descent–said, "To look at the face of presidents hardens the heart."[558]

- Also narrated from the Prophet ⚘: "Lo! Truly, the people of my House are, among you, similar to Nūḥ's ark. Whoever boards it is saved, and whoever remains away from it perishes."[559] Another version states: "and whoever remains away from it drowns."[560] Another version adds to the latter: "And whoever fights against us at the end of time is like those who shall fight on the side of the Antichrist."[561] Another version adds instead: "And like the gate of Repentance *(bāb ḥiṭṭa)* for the Israelites."[562] Another version adds: "Whoever enters it is forgiven."[563] Imām Mālik spoke of the Sunna in similar terms.[564]

---

[557]Ibn Mas'ūd ⚘ said: "Gazing at one's parents is worship; gazing at the Ka'ba is worship; gazing at the volume of Qur'ān is worship; and gazing at your brethren out of love for Allah's sake is worship." Narrated by Bayhaqī. The statement "Gazing at the Ka'ba is worship" is narrated from 'Ā'isha by al-Daylamī, Ibn Abī Dāwūd in *al-Maṣāḥif*, and Abū al-Shaykh in *al-Thawāb* with weak chains as stated in al-Munāwī's *Fayḍ al-Qadīr* and *Kanz al-'Ummāl*; from Mujāhid by Ibn Abī Shayba and al-Jandī; from Mujāhid and 'Aṭā' as stated by al-Qurṭubī in his *Tafsīr* for the verse *We have seen the turning of your face to heaven* (2:144); from 'Aṭā' as narrated by Ibn Abī Shayba, al-Azraqī, al-Jundī, and Bayhaqī in *Shu'ab al-Īmān*; from Ṭāwūs by Ibn Abī Shayba and al-Jundī with the wording: "Looking at this House is better than the worship of one who fasts, prays at night, and strives in jihād uninterruptedly"; from Ibrāhīm al-Nakha'ī by al-Azraqī with the wording: "One gazing at the Ka'ba is like one who strives in worship in other countries." Gazing at the sea is also counted as worship in some reports, cf. *Kashf al-Khafā'*. Also narrated from Ibn 'Abbās by Azraqī and al-Jundī as cited by al-Suyūṭī in *al-Durr al-Manthūr* with the wording: "Gazing at the Ka'ba is faith itself."
[558]In al-Dhahabī, *Siyar* (15:319).
[559]Narrated from Abū Dharr by al-Ḥākim with a weak chain according to Suyūṭī in *al-Jāmi' al-Saghīr* and by Ṭabarānī in *al-Awsaṭ* (5:306) and Ṭabarī. Al-Ghumārī in *al-Burhān* (p. 69) claimed Ibn Abī Shayba narrated it from 'Alī with a sound chain.
[560]Narrated from 'Abd Allāh b. al-Zubayr by Bazzār with a fair chain cf. Suyūṭī in *al-Jāmi' al-Ṣaghīr* because of Ibn Lahī'a [cf. Ibn Ḥajar, *Mukhtaṣar* (2:333 §1965)]; from Ibn 'Abbās by al-Quḍā'ī in *Musnad al-Shihāb* (2:273), Abū Nu'aym in the *Ḥilya* (1985 ed. 4:306), al-Bazzār and al-Ṭabarānī with a very weak chain as indicated by al-Haythamī (9:168) and Ibn Ḥajar in his *Mukhtaṣar* (2:334 §1967); and from Abū Dharr by Aḥmad in *Faḍā'il al-Ṣaḥāba* (2:785), al-Ḥākim (3:151=1990 ed. 2:373, 3:163), al-Quḍā'ī in *Musnad al-Shihāb* (2:274), all with a similar weak chain according to al-Dhahabī, also by al-Ṭabarānī, Abū Nu'aym in the *Ḥilya* (1985 ed. 4:306), and others.
[561]Narrated from Abū Dharr by al-Bazzār and al-Ṭabarānī, both with very weak chains as stated by al-Haythamī (9:168) and Ibn Ḥajar in his *Mukhtaṣar* (2:333-334 §1966). Al-Quḍā'ī in *Musnad al-Shihāb* (2:273) narrates it with a similar chain.
[562]Narrated from Abū Dharr by al-Ṭabarānī in *al-Kabīr*. Al-Suyūṭī cites it in *Iḥyā' al-Mayt* (p. 74 §26).
[563]Narrated from Abū Sa'īd by al-Ṭabarānī in *al-Ṣaghīr* and *Awsaṭ* with weak chains containing several unknown narrators as stated by al-Haythamī (9:168). Al-Suyūṭī cites it in *Iḥyā' al-Mayt* (p. 76 §27).
[564]"The Sunna is the ark of Nūḥ ⚘: whoever boards it is saved and whoever shuns it perishes."Narrated from Ibn Wahb by al-Khaṭīb in *Tārīkh Baghdād* (7:336) and al-Suyūṭī in *Miftāḥ al-Janna* (p. 162 §391).

- 'Alī said: "Our similitude (*i.e.* the Family of the Prophet ﷺ) in this Community is none other than that of Nūḥ's Ark and the Gate of Repentance for the Israelites."[565]

[565]Narrated from 'Abd Allāh b. al-Ḥārith by Ibn Abī Shayba (6:372) with a sound chain according to al-Ghumārī in *al-Burhān* (p. 69). Also narrated from Abū Dharr by al-Ṭabarānī in *al-Kabīr* and al-Bazzār in his *Musnad* with a very weak chain as indicated by al-Haythamī (9:168).

9

'Alī's Words on the Succession to the Prophet ﷺ

The innovations of those who bore excessive love and admiration for 'Alī appeared in his own lifetime and he himself fought them in word and deed. Time and again, **he himself rejected the claim of those that said the Prophet ﷺ had appointed him as successor after him or claimed that he deserved the Caliphate better than Abū Bakr and 'Umar:**

- 'Alī ؏ said: "The best of this Community after its Prophet are Abū Bakr and 'Umar."[566]

- 'Alī ؏ said: "Truly the Messenger of Allah ﷺ did not appoint any successor."[567]

- 'Alī ؏ said (on the day of the battle of the Camel): "Truly the Messenger of Allah ﷺ did not give us a covenant concerning leadership [after him], but we did see something on our own [concerning his preference]. Then Abū Bakr was made to follow him, and he kept to a righteous path, then 'Umar, and he kept to a righteous path, then the Faith was stabbed in the throat [with the killing of 'Uthmān]."[568]

- 'Alī ؏ said: "The Prophet ﷺ was taken from us, then Abū Bakr was made the successor, so he did as the Prophet ﷺ had done and according to his path until Allah took him from us; then 'Umar was made the successor, so he did as the Prophet ﷺ had done and according to his path until Allah took him from us."[569]

- 'Alī ؏ said: "By Allah! Truly I was the first to confirm his truthfulness ﷺ and so I would never be one who belies him! If I had had a covenant from the Prophet ﷺ in the matter [of the Caliphate], I would never have left the brother of the Banū Taym b. Murra [*i.e.* Abū Bakr] and 'Umar b. al-Khaṭṭāb rise on his [the Prophet's ﷺ] pulpit but I would have fought them with my own hand, even if I had nothing to fight them with other than the mantle I am wearing! However, the Messenger of Allah ﷺ was not killed, nor did he die suddenly. He tarried in his last sickness for several days and nights. The *mu'adhdhin* would come to him and inform him of the prayer, and he would order Abū Bakr to pray as imām although he saw me near him. Then the *mu'adhdhin* would come again to inform him of the prayer, and he would order Abū Bakr to pray as imām although he saw me near

---

[566]See above (p. 244); and *Kashf al-Khafā'* under "I am the city of knowledge."
[567]Cited by al-Bukhārī in *al-Ḍu'afā' al-Ṣaghīr* (p. 11-12), where he relates it as authentic from both 'Umar and 'Alī.
[568]Narrated from Sa'īd b. 'Amr from 'Alī with a weak chain by Aḥmad, al-Lālikā'ī, and others, but it is strengthened by the following narration in Aḥmad.
[569]Narrated from 'Abd Khayr from 'Alī by Aḥmad with two sound chains (as stated by Aḥmad Shākir) in his *Musnad* (2:54-55 §1055, 2:56 §1059), and by his son 'Abd Allāh in *al-Sunna* (p. 231 §1255, p. 233 §1261-1262, cf. p. 229-230 §1245-1246).

him. One of his wives even asked him not to choose Abū Bakr but he refused, became angry and said: 'You are the very women of [the Prophet] Yūsuf! Order Abū Bakr to pray as imām!'

"So when the soul of the Prophet was taken back we investigated our matters and sought for our worldly affairs the one with whom the Messenger of Allah ﷺ had been well-pleased for our Religion, since prayer was ever the backbone of Islam and the pillar of the Religion. Then we pledged our loyalty to Abū Bakr and he was qualified for it. No two people among us differed concerning it."[570]

- 'Alī ؓ said: "Truly your Prophet, the Prophet of Mercy ﷺ was not killed nor did he die suddenly. He tarried in his last sickness for several nights and days. Bilāl would come to him and inform him of the prayer while he saw me around him, but he would say: 'Go to Abū Bakr and let him pray as imam for the people.' <When the soul of the Messenger of Allah ﷺ was taken back I investigated my case and saw that prayer is the backbone of Islam and the pillar of the Faith. So we were well-pleased, for our worldly affairs, with the one with whom the Messenger of Allah ﷺ had been well-pleased for our Religion.>[571] Thus we pledged the oath of allegiance to Abū Bakr."[572]
- Even when the people went to give their pledge to 'Alī after the murder of 'Uthmān, he said: "Not until the veterans of Badr decide."

[570]Part of a long ḥadīth narrated from al-Ḥasan al-Baṣrī, from 'Abd Allāh b. Abī Awfa al-Yashkarī and Qays b. 'Ubād, from 'Alī by Muḥibb al-Dīn al-Ṭabarī in *al-Riyāḍ al-Naḍira* (1:291-293 §136) and al-Suyūṭī in *Musnad 'Alī* (p. 219) from Ibn Rāhūyah's narration with a sound chain as stated in the ḥadīth Master Abū al-Ḥasan 'Abd al-Ghāfir al-Fārisī's *al-Muntakhab min al-Siyāq li-Tārīkh Naysabūr* (5:441) according to Shaykh 'Īsā b. Māni' al-Ḥimyarī in his edition of al-Ṭabarī.

[571]This segment is also narrated *mursal* (without the phrase "and I saw that prayer is the backbone of Islam and the pillar of the Religion") from al-Ḥasan by Ibn Sa'd (3:183) and al-Khallāl in *al-Sunna* (1:274), both with a very weak chain because of Abū Bakr al-Hudhalī who is discarded as a narrator *(matrūk)*. Also cited by Ibn 'Abd al-Barr in *al-Istī'āb* (3:971), Ibn al-Jawzī in *Ṣifat al-Ṣafwa* (1:257), chapter on the Abū Bakr's caliphate and Muḥibb al-Ṭabarī, *al-Riyāḍ al-Naḍira* (2:177 §650).

[572]Narrated from al-Ḥasan al-Baṣrī, from Qays b. 'Ubad, from 'Alī by Ibn 'Abd al-Barr in *al-Tamhīd* (22:129) with the following chain: *akhbaranā* 'Abd Allāh b. Muḥammad [b. Muḥammad al-Qazwīnī] [*ḥāfiz faqīh*]: *(qāla) ḥaddathanā* Muḥammad b. Bakr b. Dāsa [*thiqa*]: *(qāla) ḥaddathanā* Ḥasan b. al-Ḥusayn al-Imām [Ibn Abī Hurayra, *faqīh*]: *(qāla) haddathanā* Ḥajjāj b. Minhāl [*thiqa*]: *(qāla) ḥaddathanā* Ḥammād b. Salama [*thiqa*]: *(qāla) 'an* Ḥumayd [b. Abī Ḥumayd] [*thiqa*] *wa* Thābit [b. Aslam] [*thiqa*]: *(qāla) 'an* al-Ḥasan [al-Baṣrī] [*thiqa*]: *(qāla) 'an* Qays b. 'Ubād [*thiqa*] *(annahu) qāl*: "*Qāla lī 'Aliyyun ibnu Abī Ṭālib….*" This is a chain of trustworthy narrators and al-Dāraquṭnī, Abū 'Alī al-Ṭabarī, and others narrated from Ibn Abī Hurayra as stated by al-Dhahabī in his *Siyar* (12:91 §3088).

10
The Prophet's ﷺ Predicted Timeline for the Rightly-Guided Succession

The Prophet ﷺ gave the greatest proof of the Divinely-ordained sequence of the rightly-guided Successorship in his hadith narrated by Safīna: "Successorship *(al-khilāfa)* in my *Umma* shall last for thirty years. After that, there shall be kingship."[573] Safīna commented: "Mark: Abū Bakr's caliphate, two years; 'Umar's caliphate, 10 years; 'Uthmān's caliphate, 12 years; and 'Alīs caliphate, six years."[574]

This narration is among the *dalā'il al-nubuwwa* (proofs of Prophethood) as the precise sum of the first five caliphates is exactly thirty years: two years and three months for Abū Bakr (Rabi' al-Awwal 11-Jumādā II 13), ten years and a half for 'Umar (Jumādā II 13-Dhū al-Ḥijja 23), twelve years for 'Uthmān (Dhū al-Ḥijja 23-Dhū al-Ḥijja 35), four years and nine months for 'Alī (Dhū al-Ḥijja 35-Ramadan 40) and six months for al-Ḥasan (Ramadan 40-Rabī' al-Awwal 41).[575] Imām Aḥmad adduced the narration of the thirty years as proof for the caliphate of 'Alī in fourth place.[576]

[573]Narrated from Safīna by al-Tirmidhī *(hasan)* and Abū Dāwūd with sound chains; Aḥmad in his *Musnad* with two chains; al-Ḥākim; Ibn Ḥibbān with two fair chains as stated by Arnā'ūṭ (15:34 §6657, 15:392 §6943); Ṭayālisī (p. 151, 479); Ṭabarānī in *al-Kabīr* with several chains. Ibn al-'Arabī weakened the ḥadīth in his controverted work *al-'Awāṣim* (p. 201) to pre-empt the claim that the thirty year-span includes Ḥasan's successorship after 'Alī but al-Ḥasan, after 'Alī's murder, pledged fealty *(bay'a)* to Mu'āwiya in the year 41 as stated by Suyūṭī in *Tārīkh al-Khulafā'* (p. 199). Al-Ḥasan's pledge was foretold by the Prophet ﷺ in his ḥadīth from the pulpit with Ḥasan by his side: "Verily, this son of mine–al-Ḥasan–is a *sayyid* (leader of men), and Allah may well put him in a position to reconcile two great factions of the Muslims." Narrated from Abū Bakrah by Bukhārī with four chains, al-Tirmidhī *(hasan sahīh)*, Nasā'ī, Abū Dāwūd, and Aḥmad with four chains. Ibn al-'Arabī *(ibid.* p. 210) further rejects the authenticity of the thirty-year ḥadīth on the basis of Allah's praise of kingship and its synonymity with prophethood in the verse *And Allah gave him* [Dāwūd ﷺ] *the kingdom and wisdom* (2:251). Another proof adduced against the authenticity of the thirty-year ḥadīth is the much stronger ḥadīth: "Verily, this matter shall not be terminated until there come to pass among them twelve Caliphs, all of them from Quraysh." Narrated from Jābir b. Samura by Bukhārī and Muslim. However, none of these three proofs actually contradicts the thirty-year ḥadīth The twelve caliphs according to Ibn Ḥajar as cited by al-Suyūṭī in *Tārīkh al-Khulafā'* (p. 24) – after Qāḍī 'Iyāḍ – are the Four Rightly-Guided Caliphs, then Mu'āwiya after al-Ḥasan's pledge to him, then his son Yazīd, then 'Abd al-Mālik b. Marwān, then the latter's four sons al-Walīd, Sulaymān, Yazīd, and Hishām, then al-Walīd b. Yazīd b. 'Abd al-Mālik. Al-Walīd ruled for nearly four years and was killed. Then dissension began to spread and they have not agreed on a ruler since.

[574] Aḥmad (36:248 §21919).

[575]Al-Suyūṭī, *Tārīkh al-Khulafā'* (p. 22, 198-199).

[576]In 'Abd Allāh b. Aḥmad b. Ḥanbal, *al-Sunna* (p. 235-236 §1276-1277); Ibn Rajab, *Jami' al-'Ulūm* (2:45), and Ibn Ḥajar, *Fatḥ al-Bārī* (1959 ed. 7:58 §3494).

The above narration is similar to the ḥadīth: "Successorship of Prophethood"[577] as indicated by Ibn Ḥajar who said:

> By "successorship after me," he meant successorship of Prophethood; as for Mu'āwiya and those who followed him, most of them were after the pattern of kings, even if they are still called "successors" *(khulafā')*, and Allah knows best.[578]

[577]See chapter 9 in the section on Abū Bakr al-Ṣiddīq.
[578]In *Fatḥ al-Bārī* (1959 ed. 12:392 §6600).

11
The Meaning of *Ahl al-Bayt* (The People of the Prophet's House)[579]

Jābir b. 'Abd Allāh said: "I saw the Messenger of Allah ﷺ in his Pilgrimage on the Day of 'Arafa mounted on his camel al-Qaṣwā', addressing the people, and I heard him say: 'People! I have left among you that which if you hold to it you will never go astray: the Book of Allah and my mantle *('itra)* – the People of my House.'"[580]

Other versions state: "I am leaving among you that which if you hold to it, you will never go astray, one of them greater than the other: the Book of Allah – a rope extended down from heaven to earth – and my mantle *('itra)*, the People of my House. These two shall never part ways until they come to me at the Pond. Look well to how you act with them after me!"[581]

When the verse of *mubāhala* (mutual imprecation) was revealed: *Come! We will summon our sons and your sons, and our women and your women, and ourselves and yourselves, then we will pray humbly and invoke the curse of Allah upon those who lie* (3:61), the Prophet ﷺ summoned 'Alī, Fāṭima, al-Ḥasan, and al-Ḥusayn, and said: "O Allah, my Lord! These are my Family" *(Allāhumma hā'ulā'u ahlī)*.[582] He repeated this act when the verse of the cleansing of the People of the House was revealed (33:33).[583]

Allah ﷻ said in the Sura of al-Aḥzāb (33:28-34):

28. *O Prophet! Say unto thy wives: If you* [F] *desire the world's life and its adornment, come! I will content you* [F] *and will release you* [F] *with a fair release;*

[579] See our *Musnad of Ahl al-Bayt* on this topic.
[580] Narrated by al-Tirmidhī *(ḥasan gharīb)* with a weak chain because of Zayd b. al-Ḥasan al-Qurashī.
[581] Narrated from Zayd b. Arqam by Tirmidhī *(ḥasan gharīb)* and al-Ḥākim (3:148), the latter with a sound chain as confirmed by Dhahabī, but without the last sentence and the words "my mantle"; from Abū Sa'īd al-Khudrī by Tirmidhī *(ḥasan gharīb)* and Aḥmad with weak chains because of 'Atiyya b. Sa'd al-'Awfī; and from Zayd b. Thābit by Aḥmad and Ṭabarānī, *Kabīr* (5:153) with chains containing al-Qāsim b. Ḥassān who is passable *(maqbūl)* and not trustworthy, contrary to al-Haythamī's claim in *Majma' al-Zawā'id* (1:170). The latter version states: "I am leaving among you two successors *(khalīfatayn)*…" Also narrated from Zayd b. Arqam by Nasā'ī in *al-Sunan al-Kubrā* (5:45, 5:130) with the wording: "I am leaving among you the two weighty matters…"
[582] Narrated from Sa'd b. Abī Waqqāṣ by Muslim, Aḥmad, al-Tirmidhī *(ḥasan ṣaḥīḥ gharīb)*, and al-Ḥākim.
[583] Narrated from Umm Salama by Aḥmad with six chains, al-Tirmidhī with several chains *(ḥasan ṣaḥīḥ)*, al-Ḥākim, al-Ṭabarānī, and others.

29. *But if you* [F] *desire Allah and His messenger and the abode of the Hereafter, then lo! Allah has prepared for the good among you* [F] *an immense reward.*

30. *O you wives of the Prophet! Whosoever of you* [F] *commits manifest lewdness, the punishment for her will be doubled, and that is easy for Allah,*

31. *And whosoever of you* [F] *is submissive unto Allah and His messenger and does right, We shall give her reward twice over, and We have prepared for her a rich provision.*

32. *O you wives of the prophet! You are not* [F] *like any other women. If you* [F] *keep your duty (to Allah), then be not [F] soft of speech, lest he in whose heart is a disease aspire (to you), but utter customary speech.*

33. *And stay in your* [F] *houses. Bedizen not yourselves* [F] *with the bedizenment of the Time of ignorance. Be regular* [F] *in prayer, and pay* [F] *the poor due, and obey* [F] *Allah and His messenger. The wish of Allah is but to remove uncleanness far from you* [M/F], *O Folk of the Household, and cleanse you* [M/F] *with a thorough cleansing.*

34. *And bear in mind that which is recited in your* [F] *houses of the revelations of Allah and wisdom. Lo! Allah is Subtle, Aware.*

The Ulema of Qur'ānic commentary agree one and all that the meaning of *ahl al-bayt* in these verses, similarly to its recurrence in the address of the angels to the family of Ibrāhīm in Sūrat Hūd (11:73), includes both the wives of the Prophet ﷺ and his grandchildren together with 'Alī ؓ:

- Rāzī said: "Allah ﷻ quit using the feminine pronoun in his address and turned to the masculine by saying *li-yudhhiba 'ankum al-rijsa = to remove uncleanness far from you* [masculine plural], so as to include both the women of his ﷺ house and the men [beginning with the Prophet ﷺ]. Explanations have differed concerning the *'Ahl al-Bayt'* but the most appropriate and correct is to say they are his children and wives; al-Ḥasan and al-Ḥusayn being among them and 'Alī being among them... due to his cohabitation with the Prophet's ﷺ daughter and his close companionship with the Prophet ﷺ."[584]

- Al-Baghawī said: "In this verse [Hūd 73] there is a proof that wives are part of *Ahl al-Bayt*. ... He means by *Ahl al-Bayt* [in 33:33] the wives of the Prophet ﷺ because they are in his house. This is the narration of Sa'īd b. Jubayr from Ibn 'Abbās."[585]

[584] Al-Tafsīr al-Kabīr (6:615).
[585] *Ma'ālim al-Tanzīl* (2:393, 3:428).

- Al-Bayḍāwī said: "The Shī'a's claim that verse 33:33 is specific to Fāṭima, 'Alī, and their two sons... and their adducing it as proof of their immunity from sin *('iṣma)* and of the probative character of their consensus, is weak, because restricting the meaning to them is not consistent with what precedes the verse and what follows it. The thread of speech means that they are part of the *Ahl al-Bayt*, not that others are not part of it also."[586]

- Al-Khāzin said: "They [*Ahl al-Bayt*] are the wives of the Prophet ﷺ because they are in his house." Then he mentions the other two explanations, namely, that they are the *'Itra* or that they are the families of 'Alī, 'Aqīl, Ja'far, and al-'Abbās.[587]

- Al-Nasāfī said: "There is in it [verse 33:33] a proof that his wives are part of the Folk of his Household *(min ahli baytihi)*. He said 'from you [M] *('ankum)'* because what is meant are both the men and women of his family *(Āl)* as indicated by *wa yuṭah-hirakum taṭhīran*: 'and cleanse you [M/F] with a thorough cleansing' from the filth of sins."[588]

- Al-Ṭabarī [after citing reports explaining *Ahl al-Bayt* to mean the *'Itra*] and al-Wāḥidī said: "From 'Ikrima [concerning 33:33]: 'It is not as they claim, but the verse was revealed concerning the wives of the Prophet ﷺ.'"[589]

- Al-Zamakhsharī said: "In this [33:33] there is an explicit proof that the wives of the Prophet ﷺ are among the People of his House *(min Ahli Baytihi)*."[590]

- Al-Shawkānī and al-Mubarakfūrī said: "Ibn 'Abbās, 'Ikrima, 'Aṭā', al-Kalbī, Muqātil, and Sa'īd b. Jubayr said the wives of the Prophet ﷺ are specifically meant [in 33:33], and by house are meant the houses of his wives as mentioned before in the verses. While Abū Sa'īd al-Khudrī, Mujāhid, and Qatāda – it is also related from al-Kalbī – said that those meant are specifically 'Alī, Fāṭima, al-Ḥasan, and al-Ḥusayn. They adduced the fact that the pronouns are in the masculine, but this was refuted by the fact that the noun *Ahl* is masculine and therefore necessitates a masculine gender as in the verse [Hūd 73].... A third group stands midway between the two and includes both [the wives and the *'Itra*]... A number of the verifying authorities consider this the most

[586]*Anwār al-Tanzīl* (4:374).
[587]*Lubāb al-Ta'wīl fī Ma'ānī al-Tanzīl* (3:490).
[588]*Madārik al-Tanzīl wa-Ḥaqā'iq al-Ta'wīl* (3:490).
[589]*Jāmi' al-Bayān* (22:7) and *Asbāb al-Nuzūl* (p. 299 §734).
[590]*Al-Kashshāf* (2:212).

correct explanation, among them al-Qurṭubī, Ibn Kathīr, and others."[591]

- *Al-Jalālayn*: "*Ahl al-Bayt* [33:33] i.e. the wives of the Prophet ﷺ."

- Al-Ṣāwī said in *Ḥāshiyat al-Jalālayn*: "It is said the verse [33:33] is comprehensive *('āmma)* to mean the People of his House in the sense of his dwelling and these are his wives, and the People of his House in the sense of his lineage and these are his offspring."

- Al-Suyūṭī said [after citing the narrations of the *'Itra*] that Ibn Sa'd narrated from 'Urwa that he said: "*Ahl al-Bayt* [33:33] means the Prophet's ﷺ wives, and it was revealed in the house of 'A'isha."[592]

- Ibn al-Jawzī said: "Then He showed their superiority over all women when He said: *You* [feminine] *are not like anyone* [masculine] *of the women* (33:32). Al-Zajjāj [the philologian] said that He did not say, 'like any other woman' in the feminine, because the masculine form denotes a general exclusion of both male and female [human beings], one and all."[593]

- Ibn Juzay said: "The *Ahl al-Bayt* of the Prophet ﷺ are his wives, his offspring, and his near relatives such as al-'Abbās, 'Alī, and all for whom receiving *ṣadaqa* is unlawful."[594]

- Al-Bukhārī in his *Ṣaḥīḥ* narrated from Anas that the Prophet ﷺ visited 'Ā'isha and, upon entering her house, said: "*As-Salāmu 'alaykum Ahl al-Bayt! wa raḥmatullah*" Whereupon she responded: "*Wa 'alayka as-Salām wa raḥmatullāh*, how did you find your wives *(ahl)*? May Allah bless you." Then he went around to see all of his wives and said to them exactly what he had said to 'Ā'isha.

- Al-Wāḥidī said:: "*Ahl al-Bayt* [33:33] i.e. the wives of the Prophet ﷺ and the men [and women] of the People of his House."[595]

- Al-Tha'ālibī said: "This verse [11:73] shows that the wife of a man is part of the People of his House *(min Ahli Baytihi)*... and 'the House' in Sūrat al-Aḥzab [33:33] refers to the dwelling quarters [i.e. of the wives]."[596]

[591] *Fatḥ al-Qadīr* (4:278-280) and *Tuḥfat al-Aḥwadhī* (9:48-49).
[592] *Al-Durr al-Manthūr* (6:603).
[593] *Zād al-Masīr* (6:378).
[594] *Tafsīr Ibn Juzay* (p. 561).
[595] *Al-Wajīz* (2:865).
[596] *Al-Jawāhir al-Ḥisān* (2:212).

- Ibn Kathīr and al-Wāḥidī said: "From Ibn 'Abbās: 'This verse [33:33] was revealed concerning the wives of the Prophet ﷺ.'"[597]

- Ibn Jamā'a and al-Suyūṭī said: "*Ahl al-Bayt* in verse 33 are the Prophet ﷺ and his wives. It was also said they are 'Alī, Fāṭima, al-Ḥasan, and al-Ḥusayn, and it was also said they are those for whom *ṣadaqa* is unlawful [i.e. Āl 'Aqīl, Āl 'Alī, Āl Ja'far, and Āl al-'Abbās]."[598]

- Al-Zarkashī said: "The phrasing of the Qur'ān [in Surat al-Aḥzāb] shows that the wives are meant, that the verses were revealed concerning them, and that it is impossible to exclude them from the meaning of the verse. However, since others were to be included with them it was said with the masculine gender: *Allah desires to remove uncleanness far from you* [masculine plural], *O Folk of the Household.* It is then known that this desire comprises all the Folk of the Household – both male and female – as opposed to His saying, 'O wives of the Prophet' and it shows that 'Alī and Fāṭima are more [specifically] deserving of this description [*'Ahl al-Bayt'*] than the wives."[599]

- Al-Jaṣṣāṣ said: "It [11:73] shows that the wives of the Prophet ﷺ are part of the People of his House because the angels name Ibrahim's wife as being of the People of his House, and so has Allah Most High said when addressing the wives of the Prophet ﷺ when He said: *Allah desires to remove uncleanness far from you, O Folk of the Household* (33:33). His wives are part of those meant because the beginning of the address concerns them."[600]

- Abū al-Su'ūd said: "This [33:33], as you see, is an explicit verse and a radiant proof that the wives of the Prophet ﷺ are among the People of his House *(min Ahli Baytihi)*, ruling once and for all the invalidity of the opinion of the Shī'īs who narrow it to mean only Fāṭima, 'Alī, and their two sons, Allah be well-pleased with them. As for what they claim as their proof [ḥadīth of the Mantle], it only shows that they [the Four] are part of *Ahl al-Bayt*, not that other than them are excluded."[601]

The term *ahlu baytī* in the ḥadīth was further defined among the pious *Salaf* as follows:

Ḥusayn b. Ṣabra said to Zayd: "Who are the People of his House, O Zayd? Are not his wives among the People of his House?" Zayd replied:

[597] *Tafsīr Ibn Kathīr* (3:532) and *Asbāb al-Nuzūl* (p. 299 §733).
[598] *Ghurar al-Tibyān* (p. 421 §1201) and *Mufḥimāt al-Aqrān.*
[599] *Al-Burhān fī 'Ulūm al-Qur'ān* (2:197).
[600] *Aḥkām al-Qur'ān* (4:378-379).
[601] *Irshād al-'Aql al-Salīm* (7:103).

"His wives ﷺ are among the People of his House, but the People of his House are [primarily] those for whom *ṣadaqa* is unlawful after him ﷺ." Ḥusayn said: "And who are they?" He replied: "The family of 'Alī, the family of 'Aqīl, the family of Ja'far [all sons of Abū Ṭālib], and the family of 'Abbās [b. 'Abd al-Muṭṭalib]." Ḥusayn said: "Is *ṣadaqa* unlawful for all of these?" Zayd replied yes.[602]

Lexically, the term *'itra* – literally "mantle" – was defined as "A man's relatives such as his children, grandchildren, and paternal cousins"[603] while in the context of the ḥadīths it was explained to mean "Those of the Prophet's Family who follow his Religion and cling to his commands."[604] What emerges from these meanings together with the two wordings of the ḥadīth "I have left among you two matters" is firm evidence that **there is an inseparable connection, until the Last Day, between the Qur'ān, the Sunna, and the Family of the Prophet ﷺ.**

One of the meanings of the Family version is the Prophet's ﷺ specific recommendation of 'Alī b. Abī Ṭālib ﷺ to the Muslims as explicited by the following two narrations:

At the tree of Khumm the Prophet ﷺ took 'Alī by the hand and said: "People! Do you not bear witness that Allah ﷻ is your Lord?" They said yes. He said: "Do you not bear witness that Allah is nearer and His Prophet is nearer to you all *(awlā bikum)* than your own selves [cf. Qur'ān 33:6], and that Allah ﷻ and His Prophet are your two protecting friends *(mawlayākum)* [cf. Qur'ān 3:150, 8:40, 22:78, 66:2]?" They said yes. He said: "Anyone whose patron *(mawlā)* I am, this is his patron!" Or he said – Ibn Marzūq, one of the narrators, was unsure – "'Alī is his patron.[605] Truly I have left among you that which if you hold to it, you shall never go astray: the book of Allah – which is His rope in your very hands – and the people of my House."[606]

On his way back from his Farewell Pilgrimage when the Prophet ﷺ alighted at the brook of Khumm *(ghadīr Khumm)*, he ordered a stop under the large trees then he said: "I seem to be called back [by my Lord], therefore I am responding [to Him]. Truly have left among you the two weighty matters, one of them greater than the other: the Book of Allah and my mantle *('itra)*, the People of my House. Look well to how you treat them after me! For these two shall never part ways until they show up at the Pond." Then he said: "Truly Allah ﷻ is my Patron and I am the patron of every believer." Then he took 'Alī ﷺ by the hand and said, "Anyone whose patron *(mawlā)* I am, this is his patron. O Allah! Be the Patron of whoever takes

[602]Narrated by Aḥmad in his *Musnad* with a sound chain.
[603]*Mu'jam Maqāyīs al-Lugha* (4:217).
[604]Al-Ṭaḥāwī, *Sharḥ Mushkil al-Āthār* (9:88).
[605]See note 527.
[606]Narrated from 'Alī by al-Ṭaḥāwī with a fair chain as stated by al-Arnā'ūṭ in his edition of *Sharḥ Mushkil al-Āthār* (5:13 §1760), while Ibn Ḥajar declared the chain sound *(ṣaḥīḥ)* in *al-Maṭālib al-'Āliya* (§3972).

him as patron, and be the enemy of whoever takes him as enemy." The Companion Abū al-Ṭufayl said to Zayd b. Arqam: "You heard this from the Messenger of Allah?" He replied: "There was no one under those large trees except he saw it with his two eyes and heard it with his two ears."[607]

[607]A sound ḥadīth narrated from Zayd b. Arqam by al-Ṭaḥāwī in *Mushkil al-Āthār* (5:18 §1765) as stated by Arnā'ūṭ, also by al-Nasā'ī in his *Khaṣā'iṣ 'Alī* (§79) and *Faḍā'il al-Ṣaḥāba* (§45), al-Ḥākim (3:109) who declared it sound, and al-Ṭabarānī (§4969). See note 527 for further documentation of this narration and its explanation. The stand-alone ḥadīth "I am leaving among you the two weighty matters: the book of Allah and the People of my House" is also narrated from Zayd b. Arqam with a sound chain – as stated by al-Arnā'ūṭ – by Aḥmad, al-Ṭaḥāwī in *Mushkil al-Āthar* (9:88 §3463), and al-Ṭabarānī (§5040); from Abū Sa'īd al-Khudrī by Aḥmad with a weak chain because of 'Atiyya b. Sa'd al-'Awfi; and from 'Alī by al-Bazzār with a weak chain as indicated by al-Haythamī (9:163).

12

The First Shī‘īs

‘Alī ⚔ said: "The Messenger of Allah ﷺ told me: 'There is in you a similarity to ‘Īsā ﷺ: the Jews hated him to the point that they defamed his mother, and the Christians loved him to the point that they gave him the rank which is not his!'"[608] Then ‘Alī said: "Two types of people shall perish concerning me: a hater who forges lies about me, and a lover who overpraises me."[609] Another version adds: "Truly, I am not a Prophet nor do I receive revelation! But I put into practice the Book of Allah and the Sunna of His Prophet ﷺ as much as I can. Therefore, as long as I order you to obey Allah, it is incumbent upon you to obey me whether you like it or not!"[610]

To those that claimed that he or his family had in their possession other than the Qur'ān which all Muslims had ‘Alī said: "Whoever claims that we have something which we read other than the Qur'ān has lied!"[611] The rest of the ḥadīth states: "Except for this notebook which contains information about the ages of camels [in the payment of *zakāt*] and requitals for crimes." ‘Alī indicated a notebook *(ṣaḥīfa)* which contained ḥadīths and *fiqh* notes. Al-Bukhārī deduced from this ḥadīth, among others, that some of the Companions kept a written record of some of the Prophet's ﷺ hadiths and their explanations.

Finally, when a group of people inspired by the Yemeni Ṣan‘ānī Jew ‘Abd Allāh b. Saba' came to him adamantly saying: "You are He! You are our Lord! *(anta Hū anta Rabbunā)*" he had them executed and ordered the bodies burnt.[612] ‘Abd Allāh b. Saba' was known as Ibn al-Sawdā'. Ibn

---

[608]Narrated to here from Abū Maryam and either Abū al-Bakhtarī or ‘Abd Allāh b. Salama by Ibn Aḥmad in *al-Sunna* (p. 233-234 §1266-1268), al-Ḥārith b. ‘Abd Allāh by Ibn ‘Abd al-Barr in *al-Istī‘āb*, al-Nuwayrī in *Nihāyat al-Arab* (20:5) and in Ibn Abī al-Ḥadīd's *Sharḥ Nahj al-Balāgha* (1:372).

[609]A weak report narrated from ‘Alī by Abū Ya‘la (1:406 §534) and Aḥmad (Shākir ed. 2:167-168 §1377-1378); al-Ḥākim (3:123) declared its chain *ṣaḥīḥ* but al-Dhahabī indicated its weakness due to al-Ḥakam b. ‘Abd al-Mālik as did Ibn al-Jawzī in *al-‘Ilal* (1:227 §357) cf. al-Haythamī (9:133). Also narrated by al-Bayhaqī in *al-Sunan al-Kubrā* (5:137 §8488) and Aḥmad in *Faḍā'il al-Ṣaḥāba* (2:639 §1087, 2:713 §1221, 2:713 §1222).

[610]Narrated by Aḥmad with the same weak chain as the preceding version.

[611]Narrated from Yazīd b. Sharīk by Muslim. Al-Bukhārī narrates something similar from Abū Juḥayfa.

[612]Narrated from ‘Uthmān or ‘Īsā b. Abī ‘Uthmān by Ibn ‘Asākir (39:300-301, 39:317, 42:476, 44:367-368); Abū al-Shaykh in *Ṭabaqāt al-Muḥaddithīn bi-Aṣbahān* (2:342-343); Ibn ‘Abd al-Barr in *al-Tamhīd* (5:317), and others cf. *Fatḥ* (12:270), *Lisān* (3:290), and al-Dhahabī in the *Siyar* (1/2:631). Cf. Ibn Qutayba, *Ta'wīl Mukhtalif al-Ḥadīth* (p. 73), Ibn Ṭāhir's *al-Bid' wal-Tārīkh* (5:129), Sayf b. ‘Umar's *al-Fitna wa-Waq‘at al-Jamal* (p. 48), al-Māliqī's *Maqtal al-Shahīd ‘Uthmān* (p. 67), Abū al-Muṭaffar al-Isfarāyīnī, *al-Tabṣīr fīl-Dīn* (p. 123-124), al-Ījī, *al-Mawāqif* (p. 419) and the heresiographies of al-Ash‘arī, al-Baghdādī, Ibn Ḥazm, and al-Shahrastānī as well as Ibn Taymiyya's anti-Shī‘ī works.

'Asākir narrates with his chains through al-Sha'bī, Shu'ba, and others that 'Alī nicknamed him "The Black Blister" *(al-ḥamīt al-aswad)*, loathed him for his disrespect of Abū Bakr and 'Umar, and considered him one of the thirty Anti-Christs that precede the final Hour.[613]

[613]Cf. al-Dāraquṭnī, *Juz' Abī Ṭāhir al-Dhuhlī* (p. 52 §157), Ibn Abī 'Āṣim, *al-Sunna* (2:565-566 §1325), and Ibn 'Asākir, *Tārīkh Dimashq* (29:6-10). The revisionist Shī'ī claim that 'Abd Allāh b. Saba' is a figment of Sayf b. 'Umar's imagination is put to rest by these reports. For a Shī'ī source on Ibn Saba' see al-Majlisī's *Biḥār al-Anwār* (25:286-287).

13
The Great *Fitna*

When ʿAlī ﷺ was given allegiance as Caliph he moved from Medina to Kūfa in Iraq and made it his capital. His tenure as Caliph lasted five years (35-40) marred by three great dissensions which tore apart the fabric of the Muslim Community: the battle of the Camel (year 36) against the party of ʿĀ'isha رضي الله عنها the Mother of the Believers out of Medina; the three-month battle of Ṣiffīn (Rabīʿ al-Awwal 37) against the party of Muʿāwiya b. Abī Sufyān out of Damascus; and the campaign against the *Khawārij* in the following two years, until he was assassinated by one of them in Kūfa one morning as he came out for the dawn prayer.

ʿAlī said: "When I put my foot in the stirrup, intending for Iraq, ʿAbd Allāh b. Salām came to me and said: 'Do not go to the people of Iraq! If you do, the sword blades shall fall on you there.' ʿAlī replied: 'I swear by Allah that the Messenger of Allah ﷺ told me the same before you did!'"[614]

[614]Narrated from Abu al-Aswad, from ʿAlī by al-Ḥumaydī in his *Musnad* (1:30 §53), Bazzār (2:295-296 §718), Abū Yaʿlā (1:381 §491), Ibn Abī ʿĀṣim in *al-Āḥād* (1:144 §172), Ibn Ḥibbān (15:127 §6733) and Ḥākim (3:140=1990 ed. 3:151) all with chains containing the Shīʿī ʿAbd al-Malik b. Aʿyan and thus weakened by Dhahabī although considered strong by Haythamī (9:138) and fair by Arnā'ūṭ while al-Ḍyā' al-Maqdisī retains it among the sound ḥadīths in *al-Mukhtāra* (2:128-129 §498).

14
Battle of the Camel and Battle of Ṣiffīn

The ostensible motive behind the meeting of the armies on the day of the Camel and the day of Ṣiffīn was the demand for 'Uthmān's killers put to 'Alī on the part of 'Ā'isha and Mu'āwiya's camps, but the winds of war were undoubtedly fanned by sowers of discord from inside all three camps until events completely escaped the control of the Companions. For example, it is related that 'Alī often expressed astonishment at the dissension and opposition that surrounded him in Kūfa itself.

The Prophet ﷺ had predicted these events, notably the battle of the Camel with the narrations: "One of you women[615] shall come out riding a heavy-maned *(adbab)* red camel, and the dogs of Ḥaw'ab [a water-point in a valley between Mecca and Baṣra] shall bark at her. Many will be killed to her right and her left, and she shall escape after near death"[616] "Something shall befall between you and 'Ā'isha." 'Alī said: "Me, Messenger of Allah?" The Prophet ﷺ said yes. He replied, "Then I am the worst of them, Messenger of Allah!" The Prophet ﷺ said, "No, but when this happens, send her back to her safe haven."[617]

A narration states that 'Alī said: "The Prophet ﷺ took my pledge that I must fight traitors, outlaws, and renegades *(al-nākithīn wal-qāsiṭīn wal-māriqīn)*."[618] Another narration states that 'Alī said before the battle of

[615]"Salmā bint Mālik b. Ḥudhayfa b. Badr al-Fazāriyya, Umm Qarafa al-Ṣughrā, the paternal cousin of 'Uyayna b. Ḥiṣn... after she had been captured and enslaved, 'Ā'isha freed her, and the Prophet ﷺ visited the latter while Salmā was with her then he said, 'One of you shall be barked upon by the dogs of Ḥaw'ab.' They said that there were fifty swords hanging in Umm Qarafa's house, belonging to fifty men that were all her unmarriageable kin." Ibn Ḥajar, *al-Iṣāba* (7:708).
[616]A sound ḥadīth as per Ibn Ḥajar in *Fatḥ al-Bārī* (13:55) and al-Dhahabī in the *Siyar* (Risala ed. 11:53) narrated from 'Ā'isha by Ibn Abī Shayba (7:536 §37771= 15:259-260), Abū Ya'lā (8:282 §4868), al-Bazzār (§3275), Aḥmad with two chains of *Ṣaḥīḥ* narrators as per al-Haythamī (7:234), Ibn Rāhūyah in his *Musnad* (3:891 §1569), Ibn Ḥibbān (15:126-127 §6732 *ṣaḥīḥ al-isnād*), al-Ḥākim (3:120=1990 ed. 3:129), Bayhaqī in the *Dalā'il* (6:410), from Ibn 'Abbās by al-Bazzār with a chain of trustworthy narrators, cf. al-Haythamī (7:234) and with a sound *mursal* chain by al-Azdī in his *Jāmi'* (11:365). Cf. also al-Ṭabarī's *Tārīkh* (3:11, 3:18) and Muḥibb al-Dīn al-Ṭabarī's *al-Samṭ al-Thamīn* (p. 93).
[617]Narrated from Abū Rāfi' by Aḥmad, al-Bazzār (9:326 §3881), al-Ṭabarānī in *al-Kabīr* (1:332 §995), all with a fair (cf. *Fatḥ* 13:55, al-Zayn 18:468 §27076) to weak chain (cf. Ibn al-Jawzī, *al-'Ilal* 2:848-849 §1419), contrary to al-Haythamī's (7:234) claim that "all its narrators are trustworthy."
[618]Narrated from (i) Ibn Mas'ūd by Shāshī, *Musnad* (1:342 §322), Ṭarabānī, *Awsaṭ* (9:165) and *Kabīr* (10:91 §10053-10054) cf. Haythamī (6:235); (ii) 'Alqama from 'Alī by Ibn Abī 'Āṣim, *Sunna* (2:439) cf. Dāraquṭnī, *'Ilal* (5:148 §780); (iii) Khulayd al-'Aṣarī by Khaṭīb, *Tārīkh Baghdād* (8:340, "overall a *ṣaḥīḥ* hadith" per Aḥdab, *Zawā'id* 6:401 §1261); (iv) 'Alī b. Rabī'a from 'Alī by al-Bazzār (2:215 §604, 3:27 §774), Abū Ya'lā (1:397 §519), Ṭabarānī in *al-Awsaṭ* (8:213) cf. al-Haythamī (5:186, 7:238), and Zubayr b. Bakkār in *al-Muwaffaqiyyāt* cf. *Khaṣā'iṣ* (2:203-204)

Ṣiffīn: "The traitors are those with whom we just finished fighting (the people of the Camel because they betrayed their pledge to him), the outlaws are those we are about to fight (the people of Syro-Palestine because they ran away from truth and right), and the heretics we have not met yet (the *Khawārij*)."[619]

with a chain containing al-Rabī' b. Sahl who is weak cf. Ibn Ḥajar in *Lisān al-Mīzān* (2:446 §1827) but the latter deems the meaning true; (v) Abū Ayyūb al-Anṣārī by Ḥākim (3:150) with a "thoroughly obscure chain" according to al-Dhahabī, *Mīzān* ('Attāb b. Tha'laba) who said *al-matnu munkar* cf. 'Uqaylī (3:480 *lā yathbutu fī hādhā al-bābi shay'*). Also related as a saying of (vi) 'Ammār b. Yāsir by Abū Ya'lā (3:194 §1623); (vii) Abū Ayyūb by Ṭabarānī, *Kabīr* (4:172 §4049) cf. al-Haythamī (6:235, 7:238), Khaṭīb, *Tārīkh Baghdād* (13:186), Ibn al-Jawzī, *'Ilal* (1:247), and al-Dhahabī, *Siyar* (Risāla ed. 2:410 *khabar wāhin*) and *Mīzān* (Aṣbagh b. Nabāta).

[619]Narrated by al-Khaṭīb in *Muwaḍḍiḥ Awhām al-Jam' wal-Tafrīq* (1:393) cf. Ibn al-Athīr, *Nihāya* and Ibn Ḥajar, *Talkhīṣ al-Ḥabīr* 4:44).

15
ʿAlī's Impartial Respect of His Opponents

Even after the Battle of the Camel, 'Alī never ceased to call 'Ā'isha "the Beloved of the Messenger of Allah ﷺ" *(khalīlat rasūlillah)*.[620]

At Ṣiffīn he said: "People! Do not loathe Mu'āwiya's leadership. If you were to lose him, you would see heads parting with their necks like colocynths *(kal-ḥanẓal)*!"[621]

Asked if the *Khawārij* were unbelievers he said: "It is precisely unbelief they fled." Asked if they were hypocrites, he said: "The hypocrites do not mention Allah except little." Asked what they were then, he said: "They are our brothers who rebelled against us so we fought them for rebelling" *(ikhwānunā baghaw 'alaynā)*, yet the *Khārijī* 'Abd Allāh b. Wahb al-Rāsibī – whose forehead and knees were worn out with frequent prostration – would not call 'Alī ﷺ other than "the atheist" *(al-jāḥid)*![622]

[620]Narrated by al-Dhahabī in the *Siyar* (Risala ed. 2:177) with a chain he graded fair.
[621]Narrated from al-Ḥārith al-A'war by Ibn Abī Shayba (7:548 §37854).
[622]Narrated by al-Ṭabarī in his *Tārīkh* cf. Ibn Kathīr, *Bidāya* (7:290).

16
On the *Awliyā* of Syro-Palestine *(Shām)*

Shurayḥ b. 'Ubayd said that the people of Syro-Palestine were mentioned in front of 'Alī b. Abī Ṭālib ⁂ while he was in Iraq, and some people said to him: "Curse them, Commander of the Believers!" He replied: "No, I heard the Messenger of Allah ﷺ say: 'The Substitutes *(al-Abdāl)* are in Syro-Palestine – forty men, every time one of them dies, Allah substitutes another in his place. By means of them Allah brings down the rain, gives us victory over our enemies and averts punishment from the people of Syro-Palestine.'"[623]

See also the chapter to that effect in our bilingual compilation, *Forty Hadiths on the Excellence of Syro-Palestine (al-Shām) and Its People.*

---

[623]Narrated by Aḥmad, *Musnad* and *Faḍā'il al-Ṣaḥāba* (2:906) and, through him, Ibn 'Asākir 1:289) with a sound chain as indicated by al-Sakhāwī, *Maqāṣid*, Haythamī in *Majma' al-Zawā'id*, al-Munāwī, al-Suyūṭī in *al-Khabar al-Dāll 'alā Wujūd al-Quṭb wa al-Abdāl*, and al-Ghumārī in his notes on the latter who all declared its narrators trustworthy. Al-Suyūṭī similarly declared it sound in *al-Jāmi' al-Ṣaghīr*. Al-Maqdisī in *al-Mukhtāra* (2:110) and Muḥammad b. 'Abd al-Hādī in *Faḍā'il al-Shām* (p. 43 §15) cite the same chain while Ibn 'Asākir (1:296) narrates it through Ismā'īl b. 'Ayyāsh from Ṣafwān b. 'Amr al-Saksakī from Shurayḥ from 'Alī from the Prophet ﷺ cf. al-Sam'ānī in *Faḍā'il al-Shām* (p. 49) through Ṣafwān, from an unnamed Shaykh and al-Suyūṭī's *al-Khabar al-Dāll* (p. 4). To the correct objection that Aḥmad's chain is *munqaṭi'* because Shurayḥ never met 'Alī, al-Haythamī (10:62) replied: "Shurayḥ narrated from al-Miqdād [b. al-Aswad] who is older than 'Alī." Suyūṭī in *al-Khabar al-Dāll* (p. 4-5) cites Ibn 'Asākir's narration of corroborant chains of the same ḥadīth from 'Abd Allāh b. Zurayr al-Ghāfilī from 'Alī from the Prophet ﷺ with weak or very weak chains. Al-Sakhāwī mentions Shurayḥ's narration in his *Maqāṣid* (p. 33 §8) and states that it is more likely a saying of 'Alī himself. This is confirmed by: (1) the *mawqūf* narration of the same ḥadīth from 'Abd Allāh b. Zurayr from 'Alī in Ibn Yūnus's *Tārīkh Miṣr* as cited by Suyūṭī in *al-Khabar al-Dāll* (p. 5-6); (2) The sound *mawqūf* narration of the same ḥadīth from 'Abd Allāh b. Zurayr from 'Alī with a similar chain through 'Uthmān b. Sa'īd al-Dārimī by al-Ḥākim (1990 ed. 4:596) who said it is *ṣaḥīḥ*; (3) The sound *mawqūf* narration of the same ḥadīth from al-Zuhrī from 'Abd Allāh b. Ṣafwān from 'Alī in Imām Aḥmad's *Faḍā'il al-Ṣaḥāba* (2:905), al-Azdī's *al-Jāmi'* (11:249), Ibn Abī al-Dunyā's *al-Awliyā'* (p. 30), al-Bayhaqī, al-Khallāl's *al-Awliyā'*, al-Maqdisī in two places in *al-Mukhtāra* (2:111-112), and Ibn 'Asākir. The same *mawqūf* report is also narrated from al-Zuhrī from Ṣafwān b. 'Abd Allāh b. Ṣafwān from Shurayḥ from 'Alī by Ibn Rāhūyah, al-Dhahabī in *'Ilal Ḥadīth al-Zuhrī*, and al-Bayhaqī in *Dalā'il al-Nubuwwa*, while al-Suyūṭī cited many other chains. Even if the report were established as sound only from 'Alī, it would still have the force of a Prophetic narration as it contains information about the unseen which is not subject to opinion, and is confirmed by other narrations.

17
Keeping Custody of One's Tongue in regard to the Companions

The right view of these terrible events follows the guideline given by the one whom Imām al-Shāfi'ī called "the fifth well-guided Caliph, 'Umar b. 'Abd al-'Azīz ﷺ:"[624] "Those of whose blood Allah ﷻ has kept our hands innocent, we shall not smear our tongues with it."[625]

Sharīk said, "I asked Ibrāhīm b. Ad-ham about what had happened between 'Alī and Mu'āwiya and he wept. I felt remorse that I asked. Then he raised his head and said, 'Truly, whoever knows himself remains occupied with himself and whoever knows his Lord remains occupied with his Lord away from anything and anyone else.'"[626]

[624] Narrated from Abū Ḥātim al-Rāzī, from Ḥarmala by Ibn Abī Ḥātim al-Rāzī, *Ādāb al-Shāfi'ī wa-Manāqibuh*, ed. 'Abd al-Ghanī 'Abd al-Khāliq, 2nd ed. (Cairo: Maktabat al-Khānjī, 1413/1993) p. 189.
[625] Narrated by Ibn Sa'd (5:394) and Abū Nu'aym, *Ḥilyat al-Awliyā'* (9:114). A famous but historically controverted book on the divergences of the Companions is Abū Bakr b. al-'Arabī's (d. 543) *al-'Awāṣim min al-Qawāṣim*, translated as *Defense Against Disaster* (Madinah Press, 1995).
[626] Narrated by Abū Nu'aym in the *Ḥilya* (8:15).

18
The Khawārij

The Prophet ﷺ predicted that 'Alī would fight the *Khawārij*. Abū Sa'īd al-Khudrī ؓ said: "We were with the Messenger of Allah ﷺ one time when his sandal-strings broke, so 'Alī stayed behind, mending them, after which the Prophet ﷺ walked a little and said: 'In truth there shall be, among you, one who shall fight over the interpretation of the Qur'ān just as I fought over its revelation.' Abū Bakr asked, 'Am I he?' The Prophet ﷺ said no. 'Umar asked: 'Am I he?' He ﷺ said: 'No, it is the mender of his sandal.'"[627]

The *Khawārij* or "Seceders" – also known as *Ḥurūriyya* after the village of Ḥurūr, near Kūfa, where they set up military quarters – pre-dated the *Rawāfiḍ* in their revilement of Abū Bakr and 'Umar.[628] They began with a group of up to twenty thousand pious worshippers and memorizers of the Qur'ān *('ubbād wa qurrā')* – without a single Companion of the Prophet ﷺ among them – who were part of 'Alī's army but walked out on him after he accepted arbitration in the crises with Mu'āwiya b. Abī Sufyān and 'Ā'isha. Their ostensibly strict position was on the basis of the verses *The decision rests with Allah only* (6:57, 12:40, 12:67) and *Whoso judges not by that which Allah has revealed: such are disbelievers* (5:44). 'Alī said: "A word of truth spoken in the way of falsehood!" *(kalimatu ḥaqq yurādu bihā bāṭil)*.[629]

[627]Narrated from Abū Sa'īd al-Khudrī by Imām Aḥmad with a sound chain as stated by al-Haythamī (9:133), Ibn Ḥibbān with a sound chain as per al-Arnā'ūṭ (15:385 §6937), al-Ḥākim (3:122) who declared it *ṣaḥīḥ* while al-Dhahabī said in *Talkhīṣ al-'Ilal al-Mutanāhiya* (f° 18): "This ḥadīth has a good chain." Also narrated by al-Baghawī in *Sharḥ al-Sunna* (10:233), Abū Ya'lā in his *Musnad* (§1086), Sa'īd b. Manṣūr in his *Sunan*, Ibn Abī Shayba (12:64), Abū Nu'aym in *al-Ḥilya*, and al-Bayhaqī in *Dalā'il al-Nubuwwa* (6:435) and *Shu'ab al-Īmān*.

[628]As shown by the following ḥadīth: Abū Isḥāq narrated that 'Abd Khayr said that he heard 'Alī say on the pulpit: "The best of this Community after its Prophet are Abū Bakr and 'Umar, and I could name the third if I wished." A man said to Abū Isḥāq: "They claim that you are saying: 'best in evil'!" Abū Isḥāq replied: "Are you a *Ḥurūrī*?" Narrated by Aḥmad (Shākir ed. 2:56 §1060) with a sound chain.

[629]Narrated from 'Ubayd Allah b. Abī Rāfi' by Muslim, al-Nasā'ī in *al-Sunan al-Kubrā* (5:160 §8562), Ibn Ḥibbān (15:387 §6939), and al-Bayhaqī in his *Sunan* (8:171); from Kathīr b. Nimr by al-Ṭabarānī in *al-Awsaṭ* (7:376 §7771); from Kathīr b. Nimr and 'Āṣim b. Ḍamra by al-Bayhaqī in his *Sunan* (8:184); from Kathīr b. Nimr and Abū al-Bakhtarī by Ibn Abī Shayba (7:562 §37930-37931); from one of 'Alī's scribes, 'Abd Allāh b. Ḥunayn, by al-Maḥāmilī (d. 330) in his *Amālī* (p. 173 §144); from 'Awn b. Abī Juḥayfa by al-Ṭabarī in his *Tārīkh* (3:113); and from Qatāda by 'Abd al-Razzāq (10:150). Cited by al-Shāfi'ī in *al-Umm* (4:217), Ibn Ḥibbān in *al-Thiqāt* (2:295), al-Nawawī in *Sharḥ Ṣaḥīḥ Muslim* (7:173), Ibn Ḥajar in the *Fatḥ* (12:284-288) and *Talkhīṣ al-Ḥabīr* (4:45), and Ibn Kathīr in the *Bidāya* (Year 37).

19
Debates of Ibn 'Abbās With the Khawārij

'Alī sent the expert interpreter of the Qur'ān among the Companions, Ibn 'Abbās, to debate the Khawārij. He rejected their adducing of the above verses and explained: "Concerning the verse *Whoso judges not by that which Allah has revealed: such are disbelievers* (5:44): this is not a disbelief *(kufr)* that brings one out of the Religious Community; it is a *kufr* that falls short of *kufr*."[630] That is: abandonment of the rule of Allah does not legally constitute disbelief unless accompanied by a declared or patent denial of its obligatory nature. In elucidation of the verse *The decision rests with Allah only* Ibn 'Abbās recited to them the verses *The judge is to be two men among you known for justice* (5:95) and *Appoint an arbiter from his folk and an arbiter from her folk* (4:35) then said: "Allah ﷻ has thereby entrusted arbitration to men, although if He had wished to decide He would have decided. And is the sanctity of Muḥammad's Community not greater than that of a man and a woman?" Hearing this, four thousand of the *Khawārij* came back with him while the rest either left the field or persisted in their enmity and were killed in the battles of Nahrawān (year 38) – among them Dhūl-Thadiyya whose death the Prophet ﷺ had predicted – and al-Nukhayla (year 39).

The scribe of the Prophet ﷺ at the truce of al-Ḥudaybiya was 'Alī, at which time the Prophet ﷺ told him: "Write: 'These are the terms of the truce between Muḥammad b. 'Abd Allāh and Suhayl b. 'Amr.'" 'Alī stalled and would not write anything less than "Muḥammad the Messenger of Allaḥ" Whereupon the Prophet ﷺ said: "Write it in their terms. Truly you will suffer something similar and be forced!"[631] This is what took place after the battle of Ṣiffīn when the pact of arbitration was drawn between him and Mu'āwiya – Allah be well-pleased with both of them and with the rest of the Companions of the Messenger of Allah ﷺ. Ibn 'Abbās recounted the above incident to the Khawārij and said: "By Allah! Surely, the Messenger of Allah is better than 'Alī and yet he erased himself, but this erasure never erased him from Prophethood!"[632]

[630]*Innahu kufrun dūna kufr*. Narrated from Ibn 'Abbās by al-Ḥākim (2:342 *isnād ṣaḥīḥ*), al-Bayhaqī in *al-Sunan al-Kubrā* (8:20, 10:207), and al-Jaṣṣāṣ in *Aḥkām al-Qur'ān* (2:439). Also narrated from Ibn 'Abbās, 'Aṭā', and Ṭāwūs by al-Tirmidhī cf. Ibn Ḥajar in *Taghlīq al-Ta'līq* (2:43-44); from 'Aṭā' by al-Ṭabarī in his *Tafsīr* (6:256), Muḥammad b. Naṣr al-Marwazī in *Ta'ẓīm Qadr al-Ṣalāt* (2:522); from 'Aṭā' and Ṭāwūs by Ibn Kathīr in his (2:62-65).
[631]Narrated from Muḥammad b. Ka'b, from 'Alqama b. Qays by Nasā'ī in *al-Sunan al-Kubrā* (5:167 §8756) cf. *Fatḥ* (7:503) and *mursal* from Ibn Ka'b by al-Bayhaqī in the *Dalā'il*, both through Ibn Isḥāq cf. al-Suyūṭī, *Khaṣā'iṣ* (1:409), *Sīra Ḥalabiyya* (2:707), and al-Khuzā'ī, *Takhrīj al-Dilālāt* (1995 ed. p. 178= 1985 ed. p. 188).
[632]Narrated by Aḥmad with a sound chain.

After hearing that they had killed the Companion Khabbāb b. al-Arathth and his wife for praising the four Caliphs,[633] 'Alī said: "By Allah! I shall certainly fight them even if my shin be lost"[634] and he declared it licit to fight them. They were the first doctrinal innovators in Islam and considered all sinners apostates as well as all those who differed with them. By this *takfīr* they justified to themselves the killing and spoliation of Muslims including women and children. Muslims who joined them were forced to first declare themselves disbelievers then shave their heads and enter Islam again. Yet they deemed themselves scrupulously pious and the only true Muslims on earth – even in the presence of those the Prophet ﷺ had schooled at his own blessed hands.

[633]Narrated by al-Ṭabarī in his *Tārīkh* (5:2) and al-Dhahabī.
[634]Cited by al-Karmi al-Ḥanbalī in *Aqāwīl al-Thiqāt* (p. 176).

20
The Prophetic Foretelling of the Khawārij and Their Status[635]

The Prophet ﷺ had predicted the appearance of the Khawārij in many ḥadīths. Among them:

- 'Alī sent the Prophet ﷺ a treasure which the latter proceeded to distribute. The Quraysh became angry and said: "He is giving to the nobility of Najd and leaving us out!" The Prophet ﷺ said: "I am only trying to win their hearts over to us." Then a man came with sunken eyes, protruding cheeks, big forehead, thick beard, and shaven head. He said: "Fear Allah, O Muḥammad!" The Prophet ﷺ replied: "And who shall obey Allah if I disobey him? Does Allah trust me with the people of the earth, so that you should not trust me?" One of the Companions–Khālid b. Walīd–asked permission to kill the man but the Prophet ﷺ did not give it. He said: "Out of that man's seed shall come a people who will recite the Qur'ān but it will not go past their throats. They will pass through religion the way an arrow goes through its quarry. They shall kill the Muslims and leave the idolaters alone. If I live to see them, verily I shall kill them the way the tribe of 'Ad was killed."[636]
- "The Khawārij are the dogs of Hell-fire."[637]

[635]See also the mentions of the Khawārij in *The Four Imams and Their Schools* and our translation of 'Alawī b. Aḥmad b. Ḥasan al-Ḥaddād's Introduction to his *Miṣbāḥ al-Anām wa-Jalā' al-Ẓalām fī Radd Shubah al-Bid'ī al-Najdī al-Latī Aḍalla bihā al-'Awāmm* (The Lamp of Humankind and the Illumination of Darkness: Refutation of the Fallacies of the Najdī Innovator by which He Has Led Astray the Common People), one of the earliest rebuttals of the Wahhabi sect written in 1216/1801 by a Shāfi'ī scholar of Tarim (Yemen) who was a contemporary of Muḥammad b. 'Abd al-Wahhāb of Najd (1703-1792), its founder. See also six notes down.
[636]Narrated from Abū Sa'īd al-Khudrī by al-Bukhārī and Muslim.
[637]Narrated from 'Abd Allāh b. Abī Awfa with sound chains by Ibn Mājah and Aḥmad.

21
Timeless Traits of the Khawārij and Their Modern-Day Versions

The characteristics of the Khawārij can be detected, in part or in totality, in the parties that have been spreading chaos in the world in the name of Islam, especially in the past two hundred years down to our time: refashioned religiosity, misapplication of the Qur'ān and Sunna, anathema and murder of Muslims, hatred of the House of the Prophet ﷺ and/or the first three Caliphs as well as subsequent leaders down to the Ottoman caliphate, alienation and hatred of the elite of the *awliyā'* past and present, and a marked lust for political empowerment and self-promotion at any cost. Imām Aḥmad said, as narrated by his close student 'Abdūs b. Mālik:

> Whoever takes up arms against any of the leaders of the Muslims – whom the people generally follow and consider their caliph whether willingly or by force – such a rebel *(hādhā al-khārij)* has split the unity of the Muslims and violated the reports narrated from the Messenger of Allah ﷺ. Such a rebel dies the death of Jāhiliyya. It is not permissible for anyone at all to fight the sultan, nor to take up arms against him. Anyone that does such a thing is an innovator who acts against the Sunna and the path.[638]

Muḥammad b. 'Ābidīn said in the "Chapter on Rebels" *(bāb al-bughāt)* of his magnum opus, *Radd al-Muḥtār*:

> The name of *Khawārij* is applied to those who part ways with Muslims and declare them disbelievers, as took place in our time with the followers of Ibn 'Abd al-Wahhāb (1111-1207) who came out of Najd and attacked the Two Noble Sanctuaries. They claimed to follow the Ḥanbalī school, but their belief was such that, in their view, they alone are Muslims and everyone else is a *mushrik*. Under this guise, they said that killing *Ahl al-Sunna* and their scholars was permissible, until Allah the Exalted destroyed them in the year 1233/1818 at the hands of the Muslim army.[639]

Similarly al-Ṣāwī (d. 1241/1825) states in his supercommentary on *Tafsīr al-Jalālayn* for the verse *Lo! the devil is an enemy to you, so treat him as an enemy. He only summons his faction to be owners of the flaming Fire* (35:6):

> It is said this verse was revealed about the Khawārij, who altered the interpretation of the Qur'ān and Sunna, on the basis of which they declared it lawful to kill Muslims and take their property, as may now be seen in their modern counterparts, namely a sect *(firqa)* in the Hijaz called "Wahhābīs," who *will fancy that they have some standing. Behold, is it not they who are the liars? The devil has engrossed them and so has caused them to forget the remembrance of*

[638]Narrated by Ibn Abī Ya'lā in *Ṭabaqāt al-Ḥanābila* (1:244).
[639]Ibn 'Ābidīn, *Ḥāshiya* (3:309, *Kitāb al-Īmān*).

Allah. They are the devil's party. Behold! Is it not the devil's party who will be the losers? (58:18-19). May Allah the Most Generous extirpate them completely![640]

A number of the scholars of *Ahl al-Sunna* in the Ḥijāz and its surroundings at the time of those events wrote book-length refutations along the same lines, most notably Muḥammad b. 'Abd al-Wahhāb's brother Sulaymān; the Yemeni scholar al-Sayyid 'Alawī b. al-Ḥabīb Aḥmad al-Ḥaddād Bā 'Alawī; the Ḥijāzī scholar Sayyid 'Abd Allāh b. Ḥasan Bāshā Bā 'Alawī; the Mufti of Mecca, Shaykh al-Islam Sayyid Aḥmad Zaynī Daḥlān; Shaykh Ibrāhīm al-Samnūdī al-Manṣūrī (d. 1314), the late erudite scholar Shaykh Salāmat al-'Azzāmī (d. 1376) and others.[641]

[640]Al-Ṣāwī, *Ḥashiya 'alā Tafsīr al-Jalālayn* (v. 58:18-19). "This passage is quoted from the 'Īsā al-Bābī al-Ḥalabī edition published in Cairo around the 1930s. It was also printed in its entirety in the Maktabat al-Mashhad al-Ḥusayni edition (3:307-8) published in Cairo in 1939, which was reproduced by offset by Dār Iḥyā' al-Turāth al-'Arabī (3:307-8) in Beirut in the 1970s. By the early 1980s, the Salafī movement, or oil money, or some combination of the two, had generated enough of a market to tempt Dār al-Fikr [Dār al-Jīl in the nineties] in Beirut to offset the same old printing but with a surreptitious change. In the third volume, part of the bottom line of p. 307 and the top line of 308 have been whited out, eliminating the words 'namely a sect in the Hijaz called *Wahhābīs*' [cf. Dār al-Jil ed. 3:288 line 7 from the top, whiting out the words 'called *Wahhābīs*'], venally bowdlerizing the whole point of what the author is trying to say about the modern counterparts of the Khārijītes in order to sell it to them. The deletion was virtually indistinguishable from an ordinary spacing mistake, coming as it does at the ends of the two pages, though Dār al-Fikr made up for any technical shortcomings in this respect in 1993 with a newly typeset four-volume version of *Ḥashiya al-Ṣāwī 'alā al-Jalālayn*, which its title page declares to be 'a new and corrected *(munaqqaḥa)* printing.' The above passage appears on p. 379 of the third volume with the same wording as the previous coverup, but this time in a continuous text so no one would ever guess that Ṣāwī's words had been removed." Nūḥ Ḥā Mīm Keller at http://masud.co.uk/re-forming-classical-texts/.

[641]Cf. Sulaymān b. 'Abd al-Wahhāb (d. 1210/1795), Faṣl al-Khiṭāb fī Madhhab Ibn 'Abd al-Wahhāb, known as al-Ṣawā'iq al-Ilāhiyya fīl-Radd 'alā al-Wahhābiyya; Sayyid Yūsuf al-Rifā'ī's Advice to Our Brothers the Scholars of Najd (1420/1999); Sayyid 'Abd Allāh b. Ḥasan Bāshā Bā 'Alawī, Ṣidq al-Khabar fī Khawārij al-Qarn al-Thānī 'Ashar (The Truthful News Concerning the Khawārij of the Twelve Century) (al-Lādhiqiyya, 1346/1928); Aḥmad Zaynī Daḥlān (d. 1304/1886), al-Durar al-Saniyya fīl-Radd alā al-Wahhābiyya (The Pure Pearls in Refuting the Wahhābīs) (Cairo, 1319 and 1347), Fitnat al-Wahhābiyya (The Strife of the Wahhābī Sect) and Khulāṣat al-Kalām fī Bayān Umara' al-Balad al-Ḥarām (The Summation Concerning the Leaders of the Holy Land, whose evidence is quoted in full by Yūsuf al-Nabhānī in Shawāhid al-Ḥaqq pp. 151-177), the last two a history of the Wahhābī sect in Najd and Hijaz; al-Sammanūdī, Sa'ādat al-Dārayn fīl-Radd 'alāl-Firqatayn al-Wahhābiyya wal-Ẓāhiriyya (The Bliss of the Two Abodes in the Refutation of the Two Sects: Wahhābīs and Ẓāhirīs); Salāmat al-'Azzāmī, al-Barāhīn al-Sāṭi'a fi Radd Ba'ḍ al-Bida' al-Shā'i'a (The Radiant Proofs in Refuting Some Widespread Innovations) among many other available published works.

22
Mukhdaj Dhūl-Thadiyya the Khārijī from Najd

Ṭāriq b. Zyad narrated that after the battle of Nahrawān our liege lord 'Alī said: "Search [among the bodies], for the Prophet ﷺ said: 'A certain people shall emerge, speaking the word of truth [i.e. the Qur'ān] but it will not go beyond their throats. They will deviate from Islam just as the arrow deviates from its target. Among them will be a black man with a deformed hand *(mukhdaj al-yad)*. In his hand will be black hairs. If he is among them, you will have killed the worst of people. If not, you will have killed the best of people." Ṭāriq said: "We finally found al-Mukhdaj. We fell prostrate and 'Alī prostrated with us."[642] When the body of the Khārijī rebel Mukhdaj Dhūl-Thadiyya ("Breasted") al-'Uranī al-Ḥabashī was finally found by 'Alī after the people had searched for him at length without finding him, he prostrated for a long time in thanksgiving at his death and said: "My beloved told me that the leader of those folk would be a man with a deformed hand *(mukhdaj al-yad)* or a hand misshapen like an Abyssinian woman's breast <on whose teat were hairs like those found on a gerbil's tail>."[643]

'Alī also revealed that this Mukhdaj was one of three brothers, all jinns.[644] This is strengthened by the fact that the Prophet ﷺ also nicknamed Dhūl-Thadiyya "the creek-snake" *(shayṭān al-rad-ha)*.[645] The heresiographers identified him as the Najdī Ḥarqūṣ b. Zuhayr al-Bajalī al-'Uranī.[646]

Someone said: "Praise belongs to Allah Who has exterminated them and relieved us from them forever!" 'Alī said: "Not at all! By the One in Whose hand lies my soul, there are many of them left in the loins of men and the women have not yet given birth to them. **The last of them shall come out with the Dajjāl.**"[647] This is a reference to the words spoken by the Prophet ﷺ at the time he was brought some goods which he distributed, giving to those that were on his right and those that were on his left but not those that were to his back. Then a man stood up behind him and said: "Muḥammad! You did not distribute equitably." He was a black man with shaven hair wearing two white garments. At this the Prophet ﷺ became angry and said:

[642]Narrated by Aḥmad with a sound chain.
[643]Narrated by Muslim, Ibn Mājah, and Aḥmad, the bracketed segment only in Abū Dāwūd and Aḥmad.
[644]Narrated by Aḥmad with a strong chain.
[645]Narrated from Sa'd b. Abī Waqqāṣ by Aḥmad, Abū Ya'lā, and al-Bazzār (4:60-61 §1227) through trustworthy narrators cf. al-Haythamī (6:234 and 10:73), Ibn Abī Shayba (7:560 §37921), al-Ḥumaydī in his *Musnad* (1:40 §74), 'Abd al-Razzāq in *al-Amālī fī Āthār al-Ṣaḥāba* (p. 88 §127), Ibn Abī 'Āṣim in *al-Sunna*, al-Ḥākim (1990 ed. 4:566 *ṣaḥīḥ* but Dhahabī said "far from it, *munkar*"). Ibn Kathīr cites it in *al-Bidāya* (6:217, 7:298) while al-Suyūṭī in *al-Jāmi' al-Ṣaghīr* (§4920) indicated it is *ṣaḥīḥ* and al-Ḍiyā' included it in *al-Mukhtāra* (3:142-143).
[646]'Abd al-Qāhir al-Baghdādī, *al-Farq bayn al-Firaq* (p. 57) and al-Shahrastānī, *al-Milal wal-Niḥal* (p. 115).
[647]Narrated from Ḥibbat al-'Uranī by al-Haytham b. 'Adī in *Akhbār al-Khawārij* as cited by Ibn Kathīr in *al-Bidāya wal-Nihāya* (7:290).

"By Allah! You will never find, after me, a man as equitable as I." Later he said: "There will come forth at the end of time a nation–it seems this man belongs to them–who shall recite the Qur'ān without it going past their throats. They shall deviate from Islam just as the arrow swerves from its target. Their distinguishing mark is shaving.[648] **They shall not cease to rebel until their last one rebels with the Anti-Christ.** If you meet them in battle, kill them! They are the most evil of all people and of all creatures."[649] Some versions mention that Dhūl-Thadiyya bore the traces of frequent prostration between his two eyes – a hallmark of the Khawārij – as with the murderer of 'Alī.

[648]On the basis of the Prophet's ﷺ order to the man who newly entered Islam [Wāthila b. al-Asqa']: "Wash yourself with water and lotus, and shave from yourself the hair of disbelief." Narrated from Wāthila by Ṭabarānī, *Kabīr* (22:82) and *Ṣaghīr* (2:117), and Ḥākim (1990 ed. 3:659) and – with the added order to circumcise – from Kulayb al-Juhanī by 'Abd al-Razzāq (6:10), Aḥmad, Abū Dāwūd and Bayhaqī, *Sunan* (1:172 and 8:323), both versions through weak or very weak chains, but it is confirmed by the report from the Companion Hāshim b. Qatāda al-Rihāwī by al-Ṭabarānī in *al-Kabīr* (19:14) through trustworthy narrators cf. al-Haythamī (1:283) although Ibn al-Mundhir said that there is nothing authentic in this chapter cf. *Fatḥ al-Bārī* (10:341).

[649]Narrated by al-Nasā'ī and Aḥmad with fair chains, al-Ṭabarī in his *Tafsir* (10:156), al-Ṭabarānī in *al-Kabīr*, Ibn Abī Shayba (7:559), al-Ḥākim (1990 ed. 2:160, 2:167 *ṣaḥīḥ* per Muslim's criterion), al-Bayhaqī in *al-Sunan al-Kubrā* (2:312 §3538), and al-Maqdisī included it in the sound narrations of his *Mukhtāra* (8:230-231) as it is closely confirmed by the above-cited narration of Dhūl-Khuwayṣira in the two *Ṣaḥīḥs*; while al-Haythamī (6:229-230) indicated that Aḥmad's chain was good and al-Ṭabarānī's sound. Aḥmad's two versions add: the man "bore the trace of prostration between his eyes."

23
The Murder of Our Master 'Alī and the Execution of his Murderer

The Prophet ﷺ had predicted 'Alī's death as a shahid with the words, "*This* shall be dyed red from *this*," as he pointed to 'Alī's beard and head respectively.[650]

Al-Ḥasan b. 'Alī narrated that the morning of his murder 'Alī said: "Last night I woke up my family [to pray] because it was the night before *Jumu'a* and the morning of Badr – the seventeenth of Ramadan – then I dozed off and the Prophet ﷺ came before me. I said: 'Messenger of Allah! What crookedness and contention have I found coming from your Community!' He said: 'Supplicate against them.' I said: 'O Allah! Substitute them with something that will be better for me, and substitute me with something that will be worse for them.'"

Then 'Alī went out to pray preceded by the *mu'adhdhin* Ibn al-Nabbāḥ and followed by al-Ḥasan. 'Alī came out of the *sudda* (low gateway) calling the people to prayer and was faced by 'Abd al-Raḥmān b. Muljam al-Murādī and another man, both armed with poisoned swords. Ibn Muljam struck him on the head and was caught, while the other only hit the arch of the gate then fled. 'Alī said: "Feed the prisoner and give him water, if I live I shall decide about him, and if I die, kill him as I was killed without further enmity. *Lo! Allah loves not aggressors* (2:190, 5:87, 7:55)." However, Ibn Muljam was subjected to torture. As he was dismembered and blinded he remained impassive, reciting the Sūra *Recite! In the Name of your Lord* (96:1) in its entirety. When they moved to pull out his tongue he resisted. Asked for the reason he said, "I hate to spend a single moment on earth not mentioning

[650]Narrated from **(1)** 'Ammār b. Yāsir with a fair to sound chain cf. Suyūṭī in *Tārīkh al-Khulafā'* (p. 173) by Aḥmad (30:256-267 §18321, §18326 *ḥasan lighayrih*) and in *Faḍā'il al-Ṣaḥāba* (2:687), al-Nasā'ī in *al-Sunan al-Kubrā* (5:153 §8538), al-Bazzār (4:254 §1417, §1424), Abū Nu'aym in the *Dalā'il* (p. 552-553 §490), *Ḥilya* (1:141), and *Ma'rifat al-Ṣaḥāba* (§675), al-Ḥākim (3:151 *ṣaḥīḥ* per Muslim's criterion, incorrectly), Ibn Hishām (3:144), al-Bukhārī in *al-Tārīkh al-Ṣaghīr* (1:71), al-Ṭaḥāwī in *Sharḥ Mushkil al-Āthār* (§811), al-Dūlābī in *al-Asmā' wa al-Kunā* (2:163), Ṭabarī in his *Tārīkh* (2:14), al-Bayhaqī in the *Dalā'il* (3:12-13) and others cf. al-Haythamī (9:136), and *mursal* from 'Ubayd Allah b. Abī Bakr b. Anas b. Mālik by Ibn Sa'd (3:35); **(2)** Jābir b. Samura by Abū Nu'aym in the *Dalā'il* (p. 553 §491), cf. *Khaṣā'iṣ* (2:420); **(3)** the Shī'ī Tha'laba b. Yazīd al-Ḥimmānī, from 'Alī by Ibn Sa'd (3:34), Ibn Abī Ḥātim, Abū Nu'aym in the *Dalā'il* (p. 552 §489), Ibn 'Abd al-Barr in *al-Istī'āb*, and al-Nuwayrī in *Nihāyat al-Arab* (20:211); **(4)** Ṣuhayb, from 'Alī by al-Ṭabarānī in *al-Kabīr* (8:38-39 §7311), Ibn 'Abd al-Barr, *Istī'āb* (3:1125), Ibn 'Asākir, al-Rūyānī, Ibn Mardūyah, and Abū Ya'lā (1:377 §485) cf. *Kanz* (§36563, §36577-8, §36587), Ibn al-Jawzī's *Ṣifat al-Ṣafwa* (1:332), and al-Haythamī (9:136); **(5)** Ḥayyān al-Asadī, from 'Alī by al-Ḥākim (3:142-143 *ṣaḥīḥ*); and **(6)** Zayd b. Wahb, *mawqūf* from 'Alī by al-Ḥākim (3:143) and Ibn Abī Aṣim in *al-Zuhd* (p. 132). Al-Talīdī incorrectly dropped this authentic narration in his *Tahdhīb al-Khaṣā'iṣ*.

Allah.” He was then executed and burnt. His forehead bore the trace of frequent prostration.[651]

[651]Narrated by Ibn Sa‘d (3:39) and Ibn Qutayba in *al-Akhbār al-Ṭiwāl* (p. 215).

24
Our Liege Lord ʿAlī's Grave Site is Unknown

It was decided to make 'Alī's grave a secret lest the *Khawārij* dig it up.[652] Wāqidī said, "He was buried at night and all trace of his grave was obliterated."[653] Ibn Saʿd narrated from al-Shaʿbī that "al-Ḥasan b. ʿAlī prayed over ʿAlī b. Abī Ṭālib, raising four magnifications, and ʿAlī was buried in Kufa near the Masjid al-Jamāʿa [Great Mosque] in the *raḥaba* (patio, empty plot) beyond the Gates of Kinda, before people were done with the dawn prayer."[654] Then all trace of the grave was effaced.[655] This location is the one identified as *ẓahr al-Kūfa* in the very first of Ibn Abī al-Dunyā's six reports on the location of the burial.[656] *Ẓahr al-Kūfa*, "Kufa's outer limit," hosted the then-new cemetery just outside the Kufa city gate—in the direction of the road to Ṣiffīn—where our liege lord ʿAlī, having returned from that battle, had first noticed graves. When he asked whose they were, they named Khabbāb b. al-Aratt (36BH-37/586-657)—one of the Outstrippers who died at 73 years of age and the first Companion to ask to be buried there—and some others. Our liege lord ʿAlī dismounted, prayed over Khabbāb's grave and eulogized him.[657] The report explicitly states "We were at the gate of Kufa with seven graves to our right," whereby that city gate corresponds to the Kinda gate of the Great Mosque and the *raḥaba* is the *ẓahr*.

Balādhurī said, "It is also said he was buried in al-Gharī [i.e. Najaf], and it is also said in al-Kunāsa [a locality in Kufa], and it is also said at the Sudda [i.e. the Mosque gateway where he was struck down]."[658] The 4th-century Buwayhī claim that our liege lord ʿAlī was buried in Najaf was developed by the seventh-century Muʿtazilī Ibn Abī al-Ḥadīd in *Sharḥ Nahj al-Balāgha* and became the dogma of Shīʿīs, who then glossed *ẓahr al-Kūfa* as Najaf.[659] It was also said al-Ḥasan conveyed the body to Medina and that on the way the camel which carried the bier got lost by night and was found by Ṭayyi' tribesmen who buried the body and slaughtered the camel.[660]

[652] al-Balādhurī, *Ansāb al-Ashrāf* (Suhayl Zakkār ed. 2:497).
[653] Ibn Qutayba, *Maʿārif* (p. 209).
[654] Ibn Saʿd, *Ṭabaqāt* (6:12) and Ibn ʿAbd al-Barr, *Istīʿāb* (3:1122); Balādhurī (ditto) through al-Kalbī from Abū Ṣāliḥ; also Ibn ʿAbd Rabbih, *al-ʿIqd al-Farīd* (4:286) in short form while al-Ṭabarī, *Tārīkh* (5:151-152) adds, "at the governorate palace."
[655] Ibn Abī al-Dunyā, *Maqtal Amīr al-Muʾminīn ʿAlī b. Abī Ṭālib*, ed. Ibrāhīm Ṣāliḥ (Damascus: Dār al-Bashāʾir, 1422/2001) p. 73 §82.
[656] Ibn Abī al-Dunyā, *Maqtal ʿAlī b. Abī Ṭālib* (pp. 72-75 §80-85).
[657] Narrated from ʿIkrima b. Qays by Ibn Saʿd (3:167) and Zayd b. Wahb by Abū Nuʿaym, *Maʿrifat al-Ṣaḥāba* (2:908 §2342-2343). See also Ibn Saʿd (6:14).
[658] See p. 293.
[659] As per the sumptuous oversize 324-page tome by Ṣalāḥ Mahdī al-Farṭūsī, *Qabr al-Imām ʿAlī wa-Ḍarīḥuh* (Beirut: Dār al-Muʾarrikh al-ʿArabī, 1429/2008) pp. 49-77.
[660] Narrated from al-Ḥasan b. Shu'ayb al-Farawī by al-Suyūṭī in *Tārīkh al-Khulafā'* and Ibn 'Asākir in *Tārīkh Dimashq* (42:567).

25
The Caliph ʿAlī's Appearance and Character

'Alī was described as having a receding hairline, white hair which he parted in the middle, a thick white beard "like cotton" (al-Shaʿbī) and big, heavy eyes with traces of kohl. He did not use henna. "He dyed [his hair] with henna once then never used it again" per Muḥammad b. al-Ḥanafiyya. Qudāma b. ʿAttāb said, "He was heavyset, broad-shouldered with muscular arms and legs and his height was medium to short. I saw him delivering a *khuṭba* one winter day wearing a shirt of *qahz* (damask) with two striped waist-wraps, with a turban of muslin cotton of the type woven in your countryside." Abū al-Waḍīʾ al-Qaysī said he wore a waist wrap and an untied shawl so that the hair of his chest and stomach could be seen. Rizām b. Saʿīd al-Ḍabbī said, "He was above average in size, big-shouldered with a long beard. You might say, looking at him, that he was swarthy, or rather brown up close." It was said to him in the marketplace in the high season, "You are big-bellied." He replied, "Its top part is knowledge, its bottom part food."

He was staunch in his renunciation of the world even in his own dress. When one of the *Khawārij* criticized him for what he was wearing, he said: "What do you want with my clothing? This is farther from arrogance and more suitable for me as I am imitated by the Muslims."[661] They complained that his waist wrap had patches sewn all over. He said, "It keeps the heart humble and the believer follows its example." Jurmuz said: "I saw 'Alī coming out of his palace wearing a waist-cloth that reached to the middle of his shank and an outer garment tucked up at the sleeves, walking in the marketplace while hitting a small drum *(dirra)* and enjoining upon people Godwariness and honesty in transactions. He would say: 'Observe good measure and do not plump up the meat.'"[662]

When Ibn al-Tayyāḥ came to him with the news that the treasury-house was filled with gold and silver 'Alī summoned the people of Kūfa and distributed everything to them with the words: "Go, Yellow, go, White! – seduce someone else!" Then he ordered the treasury-house swept and prayed two *rak'as* in it.

[661]Narrated from Zayd b. Wahb by Aḥmad in *al-Zuhd* (p. 165), al-Ḥākim (3:143), Ibn al-Jawzī's *Ṣifat al-Ṣafwa* (1:332), and Abū Nu'aym's *Ḥilya*.
[662]Narrated by Ibn Sa'd (3:28); Ibn 'Abd al-Barr, *Istī'āb*; Nuwayrī, *Nihāyat al-Arab* (20:220-221); Ibn 'Asākir, *Tārīkh Dimashq* (42:484). I.e. do not feed the livestock a lot of salt before slaughter so that they will drink much water and plump up the meat.

26
ʿAlī's Posterity in Muslim lands, Especially Syro-Palestine[663]

Our liege lord ʿAlī had many sons and daughters besides 1. al-Ḥasan, 2. al-Ḥusayn, 3. Muḥsin,[664] 4. Zaynab the Elder and 5. Umm Kulthūm whom Fāṭimat al-Zahrā, Allah be well-pleased with them, bore him. Among them:

6. Muḥammad the Elder (from Khawla al-Ḥanafiyya);
7. ʿUmar al-Aṭraf (from Umm Ḥabīb al-Ṣahbā' al-Taghlibiyya);
8. ʿAbd Allāh the Younger (from Laylā bt. Muʿawwadh al-Nahshalī);
9-10. ʿAwn and Yaḥyā (from Asmā' bint ʿUmays);
11. ʿUmar the Younger (from Umm al-Banīn bint Ḥizām b. Khālid al-Waḥīdiyya *thumma* al-Kilābiyya);
12. ʿUthmān the Younger;
13-14. Jaʿfar the Younger and ʿAbd al-Raḥmān (from Umāma bint Abū al-ʿĀṣ b. al-Rabīʿ);
15. Ḥamza;
16. Zaynab the Younger;
17. Umm Kulthūm the Younger;
18. Ruqayya the Elder;
19. Ruqayya the Younger;
20. Fāṭima the Elder;
21. Fāṭima the Younger;
22. Fākhita;
23. Amat Allāh;
24. Jumāna;
25. Ramla (from Umm Saʿīd bint ʿUrwa b. Masʿūd al-Thaqafī);
26. Umm al-Ḥasan (from Umm Saʿīd);
27. Umm Salama;
28. Umm al-Kirām Nafīsa;
29. Maymūna;
30. Khadīja; and
31. Umāma

Among our master ʿAlī's children who died in al-Ṭaff (Karbalā') alongside our liege lord al-Ḥusayn were Abū al-Faḍl al-ʿAbbās the Elder (from Umm al-Banīn); ʿUthmān the Elder (from Umm al-Banīn); Jaʿfar the Elder (from Umm al-Banīn); ʿAbd Allāh the Elder (from Umm al-Banīn); Muḥammad the Younger (from a slavewoman); Abū Bakr ʿAtīq (from Laylā); al-ʿAbbās the Younger (from a slavewoman); and ʿUbayd Allah.

Among our liege lord al-Ḥasan b. ʿAlī's children: Zayd and al-Ḥasan al-Muthannā who were the only two with progeny, ʿUmar, al-Ḥusayn al-Athram, Ṭalḥa, al-Qāsim, Abū Bakr, ʿAbd al-Raḥmān, Jaʿfar, Muḥammad, ʿAbd Allāh and Ḥamza. It is said he also had two more children named Yaʿqūb and Ismāʿīl.

[663] Material for this chapter is taken from Kamāl al-Ḥūt, *Jāmiʿ al-Durar al-Bahiyya li-Ansāb al-Qurashiyyīn fil-Bilād al-Shāmiyya* (Beirut: Dār al-Mashārīʿ, 1424/2003). Also Musāʿid Sālim al-ʿAbd al-Jādir, *Maʿālī al-Rutab li-man Jamaʿa bayna Sharafay al-Ṣuḥbati wal-Nasab* (Kuwait: Maktabat Musāʿid al-ʿAbd al-Jādir, 1425/2004).
[664] He died in childhood cf. Ibn al-Muṭahhar al-Maqdisī, *al-Bad' wal-Tārīkh* (5:75), al-Sakhāwī, *al-Tuḥfat al-Laṭīfa fī Tārīkh al-Madīnat al-Sharīfa* (2:402); and Ibn Ḥajar, *Fatḥ al-Bārī* (3:156).

Among our liege lord al-Ḥusayn b. ʿAlī's children was ʿAlī Zayn al-ʿĀbidīn. All of al-Ḥusayn's line comes through him.[665]

Among the families of Shām said to descend from the Prophet ﷺ:

I. From al-Ḥasan the Godfearing, the Pure Elect Grandson:[666]

ʿAbd al-Razzāq in Damascus, through Shaykh ʿAbd al-Qādir al-Gīlānī.
Abū Jāsim = al-Ḥayālī
al-Āmidī in Damascus.
al-Ankadār = Munaymina
ʿArār in Damascus through the Emir of Ḥijāz Idrīs b. Muṭāʿin
al-Asʿad = al-Azʿar
al-Aṣīl in Aleppo and Damascus through Qaḍīb al-Bān al-Mawṣilī.
ʿAṭāyā in Damascus and ʿAkka, Moroccan Idrīsīs.
al-ʿAṭṭār in Damascus, a famous scholarly family through Qaḍīb al-Bān.
al-Azʿar between Dayr ʿAṭiyya and Ḥimṣ through Qaḍīb al-Bān al-Mawṣilī.
al-Azʿaṭ = al-Azʿar
al-Azhar = al-Azʿar
al-ʿAzzūzī in Beirut, Moroccan Idrīsīs.
Bākīr originally in Aleppo through Qaḍīb al-Bān al-Mawṣilī.
Bakr in Dayr ʿAṭiyya through Shaykh ʿAbd al-Qādir al-Gīlānī.
al-Bānī in Damascus, Aleppo, and Ḥamā through Qaḍīb al-Bān al-Mawṣilī.
al-Baraka in Tripoli and Sidon through Qaḍīb al-Bān al-Mawṣilī.
Barbar in Tripoli through Shaykh ʿAbd al-Salām b. Mashīsh cf. al-ʿIlmī.
Barbīr in Beirut through Qaḍīb al-Bān al-Mawṣilī.
Bayhum in Beirut, branching from the ʿItānīs.
Bayrūtī in Tripoli
al-Bū Ghannām = al-Ḥayālī
al-Bū Ghunayma = al-Ḥayālī
al-Bū Ḥamd al-Bakr = al-Ḥayālī
al-Bū Ḥusayn al-Bakr = al-Ḥayālī
al-Bū Nāṣir = al-Ḥayālī
al-Dabbāgh in the coastal cities from Jaffa to Tripoli, famous Fes Idrīsīs.
al-Dabbūsī = al-Baraka
Darkal in Damascus, merge with the ʿArārs, both Ḥijāzī Ḥasanīs.
Dibs wa-Zayt in Damascus, known today as al-Ḥāfiẓ, said to be Qādirīs.
Diyya in Damascus and Beirut, said to be Moroccan Idrīsīs.
al-Duhaybī in Tripoli and ʿAkkār (North Lebanon) through the Zuʿbīs.
al-Fuqayyāt in Palestine, Qādirīs.
al-Fātik = al-Fātikī
al-Fātikī in Beirut, Moroccans said to be Idrīsīs.
al-Furfūr in Damascus, Qādirīs cf. al-Qāwuqjī.
al-Ghalāyīnī in Aleppo, Damascus and Lebanon, Qādirīs.
Ghandūr in Beirut, a branch of the ʿĪtānīs and/or Fatḥ Allah and al-Shaykh
al-Gīlānī, widespread in Baghdād, Shām, Maghreb and elsewhere.
al-Ḥāfiẓ in and around Ḥamā, originally from Mosul through Qaḍīb al-Bān.
Ḥajjāl = Munaymina
al-Ḥakīm in Damascus, a family of doctors said to branch off the ʿAṭṭārs.
al-Ḥallāq in Sidon and Syria, said to go back to Shaykh ʿAbd al-Qādir.
Ḥamūd in Beirut and Sidon, Moroccan Idrīsites.
al-Ḥasanī in Damascus through Shaykh Badr al-Dīn, Idrīsites.
al-Hashshāsh in Beirut, a branch of the ʿItānīs.
al-Ḥayālī in and around al-Raqqa in Syria, through Shaykh ʿAbd al-Qādir.
al-Hibrī of Beirut, Idrīsīs originating from Morocco.
al-Ḥijāzī in Aleppo through Qaḍīb al-Bān al-Mawṣilī. Also Ḥusaynīs.
al-Ḥuṣṣ in Beirut, a branch of the ʿItānīs.
Idrīs in Lebanon and Ḥimṣ, originally from Morocco.

[665] See two notes down.
[666] Al-Taqī, al-Zakī, al-Sibṭ, al-Mujtabā.

al-'Ilmī in Tripoli and al-Qudus, qāḍīs who descend from Ibn Mashīsḥ
'Īsā in Aleppo, through Shaykh 'Abd al-Qādir al-Gīlānī.
al-'Ishārāt = al-Ḥayālī
'Ītānī in Beirut, Moroccans cf. Bayhum.
Jallūl in Beirut, a branch of the 'Itānīs, originally from Morocco.
Jannūn in Beirut, originally from Fes, not genuine descendents.
al-Jazā'irī al-Ḥasanī in Damascus through the Emir 'Abd al-Qādir.
al-Jibāwī = al-Sa'dī
al-Junaydāt around al-Raqqa in Syria, through Shaykh 'Abd al-Qādir.
al-Kaylānī in Damascus, descendants of Shaykh 'Abd al-Qādir al-Gīlānī.
Kibbī in Beirut and Sidon.
Khalīfa in Qār (Iraq), said to descend through Qaḍīb al-Bān al-Mawṣilī.
al-Khaṭīb in Syria, especially Damascus, through Shaykh 'Abd al-Qādir.
al-Khayyāṭ in Sidon and Beirut, originally Moroccans, some Ḥusaynīs.
Kittānī in Damascus, originating from Morocco.
Kuzbarī in Damascus originating from Ṣafad, also known as Ṣafadī.
al-Layyāt ("tallows") in Dayr al-Layyāt (anciently known as Dayr Yāliā) near al-Mi'rāḍ in Jordan.
Madanī in Kafr Zayd, Palestine and Amman, from Shaykh 'Abd al-Qādir.
Māḍī in Sha'bā, south Lebanon and Beyrouth, originally Meccan.
Maghribī of Tripoli, Idrīsīs and Mashīshīs from Tunisia and Morocco.
Mahāyinī of Damascus, descendants of the Qaḍīb al-Bān of Mosul.
Majdhūb in the Bekaa Valley, lineage of Shaykh 'Abd al-Qādir al-Gīlānī
Mālik of Tripoli, lineage of Muḥammad al-Bāqir b. 'Alī Zayn al-'Ābidīn.
Marandiyya in al-Raqqa and Aleppo, kins of the Zu'bīs, Qādirīs.
Maṭālqa = al-Ḥayālī
Mawṣilī in the cities of Syria, descendants of the Qaḍīb al-Bān of Mosul.
Mdaqqa in Sidon and Beirut, Idrisīs originating from Morocco, lineage of Abū Madyan al-Ghawtḥ
Milkāwī in Malkā and 'Ajlūn, Palestine, lineage of Shaykh 'Abd al-Qādir.
Minqāra of Tripoli. It is said they descend from the 'Aṭṭar of Damascus.
Mugharbil = Munaymnih
Mūmnah in Beirut, said to be a branch of the Munaymniḥ
Munaymnih in Beirut, originating from Morocco and Grenada, Spain. From them branch off the Beiruti families of Inkidār, Ḥajjāl, Sinnū, Shāhīn, Mugharbil and Yamūt.
Muqaddam of Tripoli
Naḥlāwī of Damascus with a small presence in Beirut, of the Kaylānī line.
al-Naqīb of Aleppo and Hama, said to be of the Qaḍīb al-Bān of Mosul.
Nashshāba of Tripoli = al-'Ilmī
Qaḍīb al-Bān in Syria, especially Aleppo.
Qaraq = al-'Ilmī
Qarqāsh = al-Ḥayālī
Qaṣṣār in Syria and Lebanon, originally from Morocco.
Qāwuqjī = al-'Ilmī
al-Qudsī in Aleppo.
al-Rabābi'a in al-Kūra (Jordan), claim to be Qādirīs.
Quṣaybāṭī in Tripoli and Qalamūn, kins of the 'Ilmī, Nashshāba, Qaraq, Qāwuqjī, Riḍā, Sab' and Shalhab per their shared ancestor Sharaf al-Dīn Muḥammad al-'Ilmī al-Quṣaybātī
Riḍā in Qalamūn near Tripoli, through Ibn Mashīsh cf. al-'Ilmī.
al-Rimāl in Damascus through Qaḍīb al-Bān al-Mawṣilī.
Rūmiyya = al-Malkāwī
al-Sab' in Lebanon and al-Quds, Idrīsīs through Ibn Mashīsh cf. al-'Ilmī.
al-Sab' A'yun in Sidon and Beirut, an offshoot of the Sab'.
Sa'd al-Dīn in the Levant, Egypt, and Turkey through Sa'd al-Dīn al-Jibāwī.
al-Sa'dī = Sa'd al-Dīn
Ṣafadī, see Kuzbarī.
al-Ṣalāḥī in Damascus.
Salhab = Shalhab
al-Sanūsī in Damascus and Sidon, from Jaghbūb in Maghreb, Idrīsīs.
al-Ṣawwāf in Damascus through Qaḍīb al-Bān al-Mawṣilī.
Shāhīn in Beirut, see Munaymina.
Shākir in Beirut, Ashtarī Moroccans.

Shalhab in Tripoli, through Sharaf al-Dīn al-Quṣaybātī and Ibn Mashīsh
Shams al-Dīn in Urfah al-Ruha and Damascus, through Qaḍīb al-Bān.
al-Sharābī in Ḥimṣ, Jinānī Idrīsīs from Morocco.
al-Sharābiya al-Bū Muḥammad in al-Ḥasaka, Syria, Zu'bī Qādirīs.
Sha'shā'a in Ghazza, a family of judges through 'Abd al-Salām b. Mashīsh.
al-Shaykh = Fatḥ Allah.
al-Sibā'ī in Ḥimṣ then the Levant, Idrīsīs through Abū al-Sibā' al-Sūsī.
Sinno = Munaymina
Sulaymān al-Khaṭīb in Ma'arrat al-Nu'mān (Syria),said to be Qādirīs.
al-Taghlubī in Damascus through Hilāl al-Jibāwī, Moroccan Idrīsīs.
al-Ṭarābīshī in Aleppo through Qaḍīb al-Bān al-Mawṣilī.
Wazzān of Beirut and Sidon of the famed Idrīsī Wazzān of Morocco.
Yamūt = Mnaymneh
Ya'qūbī of Damascus, Idrīsīs originally from Algeria and Morocco.
Yashruṭī of 'Akka.
Yūnus = Ḥayālī
Zakariyyā in North Lebanon, said to be Qādirīs.
Zayd in Palestine and Jordan, through Shaykh 'Abd al-Qādir al-Gīlānī.
Zaydān = al-Ḥayālī
al-Zu'bī in North Lebanon, Qādirīs.

II. From al-Ḥusayn the Pure, the Blessed, the Grandson:[667]

'Abd Allāh = Qarājah
'Abd al-'Aẓīm
'Abd al-Ḥasīb = Kayyālī
'Abd al-Ḥay
'Abd al-Ṣamad
Abī 'Aysha
Abī Bakr = Qarājah and Ktakhdā
Abī al-Ḍab'āt
Abī Durra
Abī Ghalyūm = Abī Ghalyūn
Abī Ghalyūn
Abī Ḥamra
Abī Kaff
Abī al-Khayr
Abī Lubāda
Abī Markhiya
Abī al-Nūr
Abī Qurṭūma
Abī Sariyya
Abī Sha'r
Abī Ṭāsa
Abī 'Umar
al-'Ābid
'Ābidīn
Abrash
al-'Absa
Ad-hamī
al-'Adhrāwī
Aḥādī
Aḥdab
al-Ahdal
al-Aḥmad al-Ṭfayḥī
al-'Ajlān of Damascus, a famously authentic Ḥusaynī lineage.
al-'Ajlānī = al-'Ajlān
'Alā' al-Dīn
'Alī in Mardīn and Beirut also known as Ḥalīm.
al-'Alī in Ḥarrān.
al-'Ālim = al-Kayyālī
al-Alūsī
'Alwān
al-'Ānī
al-'Aqqāb
'Arabī Kātibī of Damascus and other Syrian cities, also Jordan.
'Arafāt
al-A'raj
al-'Arfī
al-'Ārī
al-'Ārif = al-Kayyālī
al-'Arīs
Arshīd
As'ad
al-'Asāfāt = Bū Jamīl
al-Ashraf
al-'Ashshī in Tripoli, Beirut and Damascus.
'Āshūr in Aleppo
al-Asīr
al-'Aṭā'ita = al-Bū Jamīl
al-'Awīwī
al-'Awsaj
Ayyūb al-Maḥāmīd
Badr = al-Badrī
Badrān
al-Badrī
al-B'āj
al-Bakkāra
al-Balkhī
al-Bandar
Barakāt
al-Barqāwī
al-Bārūdī
al-Bāshā
al-Battī
Baṭṭūsh = al-Kayālī
al-Bay
al-Bayk = al-Mahdī
al-Birkāwī
Birrī, from Shaykh Aḥmad Badawī and 'Alī al-Riḍā

[667] He had four sons of whom three were killed in youth and infancy: his eldest 'Alī al-Akbar, 'Abd Allāh and Ja'far. Al-Ḥusayn's line is entirely through 'Alī Zayn al-'Ābidīn al-Sajjād who had eleven sons, seven of whom had offspring: 'Abd Allāh al-Bāhir, Zayd al-Shahīd, 'Umar al-Ashraf, al-Ḥusayn al-Aṣghar, 'Alī al-Aṣghar, Muḥammad al-Bāqir and – it was said – 'Abd al-Raḥmān. The other four were al-Ḥasan and al-Ḥusayn who both died young, Muḥammad al-Awsaṭ and al-Qāsim.

Bsīsū
Bruways = al-Bū Jamīl
al-Bū ʿĀbid = al-Jamīl
al-Bū ʿAzzām = al-Jamīl
al-Budaywī (Rifāʿīs)
al-Bū Dhyāb = Dyāb
al-Buḥayr
al-Bū Hyāz
al-Bū Jamīl
al-Bū Suhayl = Jamīl
al-Dajjānī
Dakk al-Bāb
al-Damālikha
Daqqāq al-Dūda
al-Daqr, "through the lineage of Muḥ. al-Ḥujjat al-Mahdī" but the latter disappeared at an early age and left no progeny.
Darwīsh
al-Darwīsh
al-Darwīshiyya
al-Dasūqī
Dhākir = al-Sabsabī
al-Dinā
Dyāb
al-Fāʿil
Fakhr al-Dīn
Fakhrī = Fakhr al-Dīn
al-Faqīh al-Khaṭīb = al-Khaṭīb
al-Faqīr
Fatḥ Allāh in Beirut, of Moroccan origin
al-Ghazāl
al-Ḥabbāb
al-Ḥabbāl
al-Ḥadīdī
Ḥājj ʿAlī
al-Ḥājj Ḥusayn
al-Ḥājj Mūsā
al-Ḥajjār
al-Ḥajjī = Qarājah
Ḥajjū al-Rifāʿī
al-Ḥakīm
Ḥākimī
Ḥalāḥila
Ḥalbūṣ
Ḥalīm = ʿAlī
al-Hallūsh in al-Ḥasaka, Rifāʿīs.
al-Ḥalwānī
al-Ḥamawī
al-Ḥāmidī
Ḥammām = al-Kayyālī
Ḥamza
al-Ḥamzāwī = Ḥamza
Ḥannāwī
al-Ḥarākī
al-Ḥarbalī
al-Ḥarīrī
al-Ḥashā
Hāshim in Damascus.
Hāshimī in Homs, share an ancestor with the Iskāf, ʿAbd al-Ṣamad and Tawakkul.
al-Ḥasībī
Ḥawāmda
al-Ḥawāṣlī
Ḥaydar
al-Ḥazzūrī
al-Hibrāwī
al-Ḥijāzī
al-Ḥimrān
al-Ḥiṣnī
al-Hud-hud
al-Ḥūrānī
al-Ḥūrī Ṭulaymāt
Ḥusayn Āghā
al-Ḥusaynī
Ḥūsū
al-Ḥūt
al-Ījī
al-ʿĪsā in Qāmushlī, al-Ḥasaka.
al-Isḥāqī
Iskāf
ʿIyāḍ in Ḥūrān
ʿIzz al-Dīn
Jabr al-Shidda
al-Jadhba = al-Kayyālī
Jalāl al-Dīn
al-Jalūf
al-Jamal = Qarāja
Jamāl al-Dīn
al-Jamālī
Jamīl
Jamjūm
al-Jamlān
Jandal
Jandal al-Rifāʿī
al-Jandalī = Jandal
al-Jawādī
al-Jayjaklī
Jihān
al-Junayd
Kabbāra of Tripoli, Rifāʿīs.
al-Kabīr = Kabbāra
al-Kakhan in Palestine.
al-Katkhudā [from the Ottoman title Kethüda] in Aleppo.
al-Kawākibī
Kʿayṭ in al-Ḥasaka.
al-Kayyāl =al-Kayyālī
al-Kayyālī, a worldwide family of Rifāʿī lineage.
al-Kāẓim
Khalaf
Khalīl
al-Khalīlī
al-Khamra
al-Khārūf
al-Khaṣāwnah
al-Khaṭīb = al-Faqīh al-Khaṭīb
Khayr Allāh
al-Khayyāṭ
Khizām
al-Khizāmāt
al-Kimyān
al-Kūsā
al-Laḥḥām
Laḥlūḥ
Laqqāṭa
al-Madāhīsh
al-Mad-hūn
al-Maḥāmīd
al-Mahdī are prt of the many subtribes of the Rifāʿīs, among them the Bayk of Aleppo.
al-Maḥfal
al-Maḥjūb, sharing same origin as Ḥājj Ḥusayn Aghā of Aleppo.
al-Maḥlūl
al-Majdhūb
al-Makānsī = al-Maknāsī
al-Maknāsī in Aleppo, descendants of Aḥmad Suwaydān.
al-Māliḥ, said to be of the Rifāʿī Ḥusaynīs.
al-Mallāḥ of Damascus, sharing the same grandfather as the Qabbānī.
al-Maʾmūn
al-Māniʿ
al-Maʿṣarānī

al-Maṭāyira
Maʿtūq
Mazʿal in Ḥūrān, of Rifāʿī descent.
Muḥammad of the Kayyālī Rifāʿīs of Idlib and Sarmīn.
Muḥsin in al-Quds and Jordan.
Muḥyī al-Dīn, the same as the Muḥammad.
al-Mullā in Idlib and Sarmīn, sharing the same root as the Kayyāl Rifāʿīs.
al-Munayyir
al-Munlā = al-Mullā
al-Mūmanī
al-Mūqaʿ
al-Murādī
Murtaḍā
al-Mushāhada in Dayr al-Zūr and al-Ḥasaka.
Mushrif
Muṣṭafā
al-Muṣṭū
al-Muṭīʿ
Nabhān in Hama, descendants of Sulaymān al-Sabsabī.
al-Naḥḥās, Beirut Ḥusaynīs.
al-Naʿīm, a very large tribe covering all of Syro-Palestine and Iraq.
al-Naʿīmī = al-Naʿīm
Najjār in Homs, descendants of al-Sabsabī.
Najm, Rifāʿīs of Jhān Shaykhūn.
al-Naqīb
Naʿsān in Aleppo and its vicinity.
al-Nāṣīf in Syria, descendants of Ismāʿīl al-Ṣāliḥ al-Akhḍar the brother of Aḥmad al-Rifāʿī al-Kabīr.
Nāṣir in Beirut originally of the Zantūt family.
al-Nāṣir of the Rifāʿīs of Qāmushlī (al-Ḥasaka).
Naṣrī of Damascus.
Naṣrī al-Ḥuṣarī also in Damascus.
Naṣrī Shaykh al-Buzūriyya also in Damascus.
Naṣṣār in al-Khalīl and Sidon.
al-Nawāṣira = al-Nāṣir
Nawfal
Niẓām al-Dīn
al-Qabbānī of Beirut, Sidon and Palestine, originally from Egypt. There is also a different Ḥusaynī branch in Damascus.
al-Qadda
al-Qāḍī in Aleppo, Rifāʿī descent unrelated to the Qāḍīs of the Shūf mountain in Lebanon.
al-Qāḍī al-Rifāʿī of Homs. They share the same root as the Jandal and Ḥajjū.
al-Qādirī al-Ḥusaynī
al-Qaḍiyya of al-Ḥasaka
al-Qāq
Qarājah
al-Qawāsima
al-Quḍāt
al-Qudsī
al-Qunayʿ
Qunūt
Quṣaybātī of Damascus.
al-Rabaʿī
Rajab
al-Rāwī of the Rifāʿīs of Shām and Iraq
al-Rifāī
al-Rifāʿiyya
al-Ruḥaybātī
al-Rukābī
al-Rukhmān
Saʿāda
Sabʿa
al-Ṣabbāgh
al-Sabsabī
al-Sakkāf = Iskāf
al-Ṣalāḥī
al-Salqīnī
al-Ṣammādī in Damascus and ʿAjlūn.
al-Sammān
al-Sandarūsī
Ṣandūq
Ṣannūfah
al-Saqqāf
Ṣaqr in Beirut.
al-Sawwāḥ
al-Sayrawān
al-Ṣayyād
al-Ṣayyādī = al-Ṣayyād
Sayyāj
al-Sayyid in Idlib and Sarmīn.
Shāhīn
al-Shalḥāwī = al-Sabsabī
Shamāʿa in Sidon and Beirut.
al-Shāmī in Beirut.
al-Shammāʿ = Shamāʿa
Shammūṭ
al-Shaqqān
Sharaf al-Dīn
al-Sharbātī = ʿAlwān al-Ḥusayniyyīn
al-Sharīf
al-Shaykh = Fatḥ Allāh
al-Shaykh in Salqīn, Rifāʿī descendants of Ismāʿīl al-Kayyāl
al-Shaykh Khalīl in Palestine.
al-Shaykh Mūsā in Maʿarrat al-Nuʿmān.
al-Shaykh Sulaymān = Qarājah
Shaykh Yāsīn in Palestine.
al-Shaykhān
Shḥāda in al-Khalīl.
Shḥūd al-Qāsim
al-Shuwaykī
al-Shuyūkh
Ṣibyān
Sukkar in Damascus and Beirut of the Rifāʿīs.
al-Sukkarī
Sulaymān = Qarājah
al-Sulaymān in al-Ḥasaka, of the Rifāʿīs.
Sulṭān
Sulṭān al-Ḥusaynī = Sulṭān
Suwaydān in Aleppo, originally from Homs.

Ṭa Ha
Ṭabbāra
Taghlib = Taghlibī
al-Ṭaḥḥān
Tāj al-Dīn
Taqī
Taqī al-Dīn
Tawakkal
Ṭayfūr = al-Sabsabī
al-Ṭayyār
al-Tūblis
Tuffāḥa
Ṭulaymāt
Ṭumayza
al-'Ubaysī in Aleppo and Hama
al-'Ujayl
'Ukāsha in Ḥūrān, Rifā'ī descendants.
al-'Ulmā
al-Unsī
al-'Uqaydāt
al-'Uṣaylāt = al-Bū Jamīl
al-'Uwayshāt
al-Uwaysī
al-Wafā'ī in Aleppo and Beirut.
al-Wahbān in Idlib and Aleppo.
al-Waqfī = Qarājah
Waysāt = al-Uwaysī
al-Yāfī in Damascus, Beirut and Homs, originally from Yāfā.
Yaḥyā
al-Yasāwī
al-Yāsīn in Ḥūrān.
al-Yāsīn al-Ṣabbāgh = al-Ṣabbāgh
al-Zāhid
Zahra
Zahrān
Zahrāwī
al-Zanābīlī
Zantūt
al-Za'tarī
al-Zawātina
al-Zayādina = al-Bū Jamīl
al-Zayn
Zayn al-'Ābidīn
al-Zayr
al-Zaytāwī

27
Some of our Liege-lord ʿAlī's Sayings

Among 'Alī's sayings narrated by Abū Nu'aym and others:

- From al-Ḥusayn b. 'Alī: "The most sincere of people in their actions and the most knowledgeable of Allah are those who are strongest in their love and awe for the sanctity of the people of *lā ilāha illallāh*"
- From 'Abd Khayr: "Goodness does not consist in having much property and children, but in doing many good deeds, increasing your gentle character, and adorning yourself before people with the worship of your Lord. Then, if you do well, glorify Allah; if you do ill, ask forgiveness of Him. There is no good in the world except for two types of people: someone who sins and then follows up with repentance, and someone who races to do good deeds. What is done in Godwariness is never little, and how can something be little if accepted by Allah?"
- From Abū al-Zaghl: "Remember five instructions from me in following which you shall sooner exhaust your camels than run out of their benefit: let no servant hope for anything except from his Lord; let him not fear anything except his own sin; let no ignorant person feel ashamed to ask about what he knows not; let no knowledgeable person, if asked about what he knows not, feel ashamed to say Allah knows best; and patience is in relation to belief like the head to the body, one has no belief if he has no patience."
- From Muhājir b. 'Umayr: "What I fear most is the hankering after idle desires and long hopes. The former blocks one from the truth and the latter causes forgetfulness of the hereafter. In truth the world has gone its way out, in truth the hereafter has come journeying to us – and each of the two has its own sons. Therefore be a son of the hereafter and do not be a son of the world! Today there are deeds without accounts, and tomorrow, accounts without deeds."
- From Abū Arāka, after praying the dawn prayer behind our liege lord ʿAlī, saw him pensive and sad, then he heard him say: "I have seen a remnant of the Companions of the Messenger of Allah ﷺ. I see no one who resembles them now. By Allah! They used to rise in the morning disheveled, dust-covered, pale, with something between their eyes like a goat's knee, having spent the night chanting the Book of Allah, turning and returning from their feet to their foreheads. When Allah ﷻ was mentioned they swayed the way trees sway on a windy day, then their eyes poured out tears

until – by Allah! – they soaked their clothes. By Allah! Folks today are asleep, heedless."[668] This is a famous report from our liege lord 'Alī, whose narrators add that after telling this story he was never seen smiling again until the enemy of Allah slew him.

- From al-Ḥasan b. 'Alī: "Blessed is the servant that cries constantly to Allah, who has known people [for what they are] while they have not known him, and Allah has marked him with His contentment. These are the true beacons of guidance. Allah repels from them every wrongful dissension and shall enter them into His own mercy. They are not the wasteful tale-bearers[669] nor the ill-mannered self-displayers."[670]
- From 'Āṣim b. Ḍamura: "The true, the real *faqīh* is he who does not push people to despair from the mercy of Allah ﷻ, nor lulls them into a false sense of safety from His Punishment, nor gives them licenses to disobey Allah, nor leaves the Qur'ān for something else. There is no good in worship devoid of knowledge, nor

[668]Ibn Abī al-Dunyā, *Tahajjud wa-Qiyām al-Layl* (pp. 271-272 §205); Abū Nu'aym, *Ḥilya* (1:76 and 10:388); al-Khaṭīb, *Muwaḍḍiḥ* (2:330-331), Ibn 'Asākir (42:492) cf. Ibn Kathīr, *Bidāya* (8:6-7=11:111); Zabīdī, *Itḥāf* (10:130). Abū Nu'aym narrates this report through two chains in the *Ḥilya*: [1] Abū Hishām Muḥ. b. Yazīd, from al-Muḥāribī, from Mālik b. Mighwal, "from a Ju'fī man," from al-Suddī, from Abū Arāka from 'Alī and [2] Ḥusayn b. Muḥ b. Ghufayr *(thiqa)* from [Abū 'Alī] al-Ḥasan b. 'Alī [b. 'Īsā] al-Saysarī [al-Qūhustānī] (a friend of Ibn Rāhūyah), from Khalaf b. Tamīm *(thiqa),* from 'Amr or 'Umar b. al-Raḥḥāl [al-Ḥanafī al-Kūfī] from al-'Alā' b. al-Musayyib *(thiqa)* from 'Abd Khayr *(thiqa)*, from 'Alī. Nāṣir al-Albānī claimed in *al-Silsila Ṣaḥīḥa* (3:307): "This is a weak, pitch-dark chain, I do not know Abū Arāka and I found no one who mentions him, only a certain Abū Arāk narrating from 'Abd Allāh b. 'Amr in al-Dūlābī's *Kunā*; the Ju'fī man is not named as you see; and of Muḥammad b. Yazīd, al-Bukhārī said they all agreed on his weakness." All this is spoken in haste and incorrect as is his habit, since Abū Arāka is found thus named in all the above chains and in Ibn Abī Ḥātim's *al-Jarḥ wal-Ta'dīl* (9:336 §1489) while in al-Dūrī's narration of *Tārīkh Ibn Ma'īn* (3:562 §2759) the latter asserts that the narrator from Abū Arāka is 'Amr b. Shimr, as does Ibn Abī al-Dunyā also name him in his chain (which does not contain Muḥ. b. Yazīd); also in Ibn Ḥibbān's *Thiqāt* (5:584 §6402) where the latter says: "Abū Arāka narrates from 'Alī b. Abī Ṭālib and from him narrates al-Suddī." Ibn Ḥajar in the *Iṣāba* (6:273) mentions Abū Arāka al-Kūfī in the entry on his father the Companion Mālik b. 'Āmir b. 'Amrūn al-Bajalī and refers to the report of 'Alī obliquely. Furthermore from him also narrates al-Minhāl b. 'Amr as in Ibn 'Asākir (41:338) cf. Ibn Kathīr's *Tafsīr* (4:150), where he narrates from 'Abd Allāh b. 'Amr. Furthermore, al-'Uqaylī (5:238) cites a chain with al-Suddī's father in between al-Suddī and Abu Arāka, from 'Alī, from the Prophet ﷺ: "O 'Alī, Allah has written on His Throne, 'I am Allah, Muḥammad is My Messenger.'" Ibn al-Jawzī includes Abū Arāka in *Ṣifat al-Ṣafwa* (1:331). The "Ju'fī man" is named by al-Khaṭīb who adduces the entire chain and report in *Muwaḍḍiḥ Awhām al-Jam' wal-Tafrīq* (2:330-331), then he adduces a different chain leading up to al-Suddī and he narrates the report, in the process identifying the narrator of this report from Ismā'īl al-Suddī, as 'Amr b. Shimr al-Ju'fī. The latter is discarded and through him the grading of this report would be very weak. However, as we already mentioned, Abū Nu'aym narrates it through a second chain of apparently stronger status, and Allah knows best.

[669]Those who fanned dissension between 'Alī and the other Companions.

[670]The Khawārij.

in knowledge devoid of understanding, nor in inattentive recitation." This is comparable to al-Ḥasan al-Baṣrī's own definition: "Have you ever seen a *faqīh*? The *faqīh* is he who has renounced the world, longs for the hereafter, possesses insight in his Religion, and worships his Lord without cease."[671]

- From 'Amr b. Murra: "Be wellsprings of the Science and beacons in the night, wearing old clothes but possessing new hearts for which you shall be known in the heaven and remembered on the earth."
- From 'Iyāḍ b. Khalīfa who heard 'Alī say in Ṣiffīn: "The mind *(al-'aql)* is in the heart; mercy *(al-raḥma)* is in the liver; pity *(al-ra'fa)* is in the pancreas; and the animus *(al-nafs)* is in the lungs."[672]
- "This world lasts for an hour: Spend it in obedience."[673]
- "Thus does Knowledge die: when those who possess it die. By Allah, I do swear it! The earth will never be empty of those who establish the proofs of Allah so that His proofs and signs never cease. They are the fewest in number, but the greatest in rank before Allah. Through them Allah preserves His proofs until they bequeath it to those like them (before passing on) and plant it firmly in their hearts. By them knowledge has taken by assault the reality of things, so that they found easy what those given to comfort found hard, and found intimacy in what the ignorant found desolate. They accompanied the world with bodies whose spirits were attached to the highest regard. Ah, ah! How one yearns to see them!"[674]
- "There shall come a time when people have energy only to fill their bellies; their pride will be in their possessions; their *qibla* will be their women; their religion will be silver and gold. Those are the most evil of creatures, and they shall have no share [of the Hereafter] in the presence of Allah."[675]
- "He ﷻ spoke to Mūsā directly *(taklīman)* without limbs, without organs, without lips, and without uvula! Glorified is He above the

[671]As cited by al-'Aynī in *'Umdat al-Qārī*, Book of *'Ilm*, in his commentary on the ḥadīth: "He for whom Allah desires great good, He grants him understanding in the Religion". Cf. Ibn al-Jawzī, *Manāqib al-Ḥasan al-Baṣrī* (p. 16). See also Imām Mālik's definition of wisdom, al-Shāfi'ī's, al-Tustarī's, and Ibn Ḥibbān's definitions of knowledge in our *Four Imams and Their Schools*, and those of reason. For the superior merit of *'ilm* and the Ulema see Ibn 'Abd al-Barr's *Jāmi' Bayān al-Ilm wa Faḍlih* and Imām al-Baghawī's *Sharḥ al-Sunna* (1:272-282).
[672]Narrated by al-Bukhārī in *al-Adab al-Mufrad* (p. 192) and al-Bayhaqī in the *Shu'ab* (4:161).
[673]Cited by Ibn al-Jawzī in his chapter on 'Alī in *Ṣifat al-Ṣafwa.*
[674]Ibn al-Jawzī, *Ṣifat al-Ṣafwa* 2(4):10 (§570) and 1(2):203 (§254); Abū Nu'aym, *Ḥilyat al-Awliyā'* (6:155) and in the chapter titled "Abū Hāshim."
[675]Narrated by al-Sulamī as cited in *Kashf al-Khafā* and *Kanz al-'Ummāl.*

imposition of modality by attributes. Whoever claims that our God has boundaries is ignorant of the Creator Who is worshipped. Whoever says that locations encompass Him is inevitably heading for perplexity and confusion."[676]

[676]Narrated from Muḥammad b. Isḥāq, from al-Nuʿmān b. Saʿd by Abū Nuʿaym in *Ḥilyat al-Awliyā'* (1997 ed. 1:114-115 §227=1985 ed. 1:73). Abū Nuʿaym said: "This narration is single-chained and narrated only by al-Nuʿmān, and Ibn Isḥāq narrated it from him with a missing link *(mursal)*.

28
Did al-Ḥasan al-Baṣrī Narrate from ʿAlī?

The consensus of the early Imams of Hadith is that al-Ḥasan did not hear anything directly from ʿAlī, or from Ibn ʿAbbās, or from Abū Hurayra as stated by Qatāda, Shuʿba, Ayyūb al-Sakhtiyānī, Ibn al-Madīnī, Abū Zurʿa, ʿAlī b. Ziyād, Yaḥyā b. Maʿīn, Abū Ḥātim, Ibn Abī Ḥātim, al-Tirmidhī and Bahz b. Asad, and that such chains are *mursal.*[677] Yet, according to one narration from Imām Aḥmad, the latter reportedly said that al-Ḥasan did narrate from ʿAlī[678] and it is indeed related that he said: "ʿAlī told me…" and "ʿAlī led us in prayer" but either such reports are inauthentic or in reality they are spoken by his son al-Ḥasan b. ʿAlī b. Abī Ṭālib. ʿAbd al-Razzāq's narration that ʿAlī once followed al-Ḥasan's recommendation in a judicial case[679] is an anachronism in view of al-Ḥasan's adolescent age when he last saw our liege lord ʿAlī, at the time the latter left Medina for al-Kūfa.[680]

Among later scholars, al-Suyūṭī in *Ta'yīd al-Ḥaqīqat al-ʿAliyya wa-Tashyīd al-Ṭarīqat al-Shādhiliyya* (The Support of the Higher Truth and the Strengthening of the Shādhilī Path) and *Itḥāf al-Firqa bi-Rafwi al-Khirqa* (The Gift to the Group in the Mending of the Cloak) printed in *al-Ḥāwī lil-Fatāwī*, as well as Aḥmad al-Ghumārī in *al-Burhān al-Jalī fī Taḥqīq Intisāb al-Ṣufiyyati ilā ʿAlī* (The Glaring Proof in Verifying the Connection of the Sufis to ʿAlī) adduced narrative chains of transmission to prove the narration of al-Ḥasan al-Baṣrī from ʿAlī,none of them conclusive. The *Iḥyā'* and al-Ṭurṭūshī in *al-Ḥawādith wal-Bidaʿ* mention the account that "ʿAlī brought out the story-tellers from the mosque of al-Baṣra but he did not bring out al-Ḥasan because the latter spoke of the knowledge of the hereafter." Regardless of the authenticity of this report, it provides no indication of any narration of al-Ḥasan from ʿAlī. Al-Mizzī cites a report in which al-Ḥasan affirms that he narrates from ʿAlī, but the wording does not suggest directness, so he could be referring to his ultimate source, not his direct source.[681] Ibn Ḥajar said: "The Imāms of ḥadīth did not deem authen-

[677]Narrated by al-Dhahabī in the *Siyar* (Arnā'ūṭ ed. 4:566). Cf. Ibn Ḥajar, *Ta'rīf Ahl al-Taqdīs* (p. 56 §40). See also al-ʿAlā'ī's *Jāmiʿ al-Taḥṣīl*, Walī al-Dīn al-ʿIrāqī's *Tuḥfat al-Taḥṣīl* and al-Sakhāwī's words in his *Maqāṣid*, in the entry *khirqa*. Al-Bazzār in his *Musnad* – at the end of the section devoted to the narrations of Saʿīd b. al-Musayyab from Abū Hurayra – listed the Companions from whom al-Ḥasan narrated and those from whom he did not narrate. This list was reproduced by al-Zaylaʿī in *Naṣb al-Rāya*, first section *(Ṭahāra)*.
[678]Ibn Abī Yaʿlā, *Ṭabaqāt al-Ḥanābila* (1:192): "My blessed father (Abū Yaʿlā) related to me in writing: ʿĪsā b. Muḥammad b. ʿAlī narrated to us: I heard ʿAbd Allāh b. Muḥammad (Abū al-Qāsim al-Baghawī) say: I heard Abū ʿAbd Allāh Aḥmad b. Muḥammad b. Ḥanbal say: 'al-Ḥasan did narrate *(qad rawā)* from ʿAlī b. Abī Ṭālib.'"
[679]As narrated by ʿAbd al-Razzāq (7:412). Cf. al-Qalʿajī, *Mawsūʿat Fiqh al-Ḥasan al-Baṣrī* (1:21).
[680]Cf. al-ʿAlā'ī, *Jāmiʿ al-Taḥṣīl* (p. 162) and al-ʿIrāqī in *Tuḥfat al-Taḥṣīl* (p. 67).
[681]Al-Mizzī, *Tahdīb* (6:124).

tic that al-Ḥasan ever even heard anything from ʿAlī." Al-Sakhāwī mentions this in his entry on "the Ṣūfī *khirqa*" in the *Maqāṣid* and adds:

> Our Shaykh [i.e. the arch-Hadith master Ibn Ḥajar al-ʿAsqalānī] was not the only one to say this but was preceded by a number of Scholars who said the same... such as al-Dimyāṭī, al-Dhahabī, al-Hakkārī, Abū Ḥayyān, al-ʿAlā'ī, Mughulṭāy, al-ʿIrāqī, Ibn al-Mulaqqin, al-Anbāsī, al-Burhān al-Ḥalabī, Ibn Nāṣir al-Dīn, and others of those who passed away among our colleagues. I clarified all this together with my own chains of transmission to it in a monograph [*al-Jawāhir al-Mukallala*].[682]

A further complication is that a studied avoidance of the risk of persecution motivated al-Ḥasan to conceal his narrations of any report mentioning 'Alī. The Sharif al-Murtaḍā Abū al-Barakāt Muḥammad b. Aḥmad b. Muḥ. al-Ḥusaynī said in his book *al-Ghurar wal-Durar* [in Persian cf. Ḥajjī Khalīfa]: "Al-Ḥasan al-Baṣrī, in the time of the Banū Umayya, whenever he narrated from 'Alī b. Abī Ṭālib, would say, *qāla Abū Zaynab*."[683]

[682]In print. See a study of this work in Arberry's *Sakhawiana*.
[683]In Ibn Ḥajar, *Nuzhat al-Albāb fil-Alqāb* (2:263).

29
Nahj al-Balāgha and Other Forged Attributions to 'Alī

Our liege lord 'Alī is the subject of the largest amount of lies ever forged about any Companion. One example is the alteration of the authentic narration reported from Ibn Mas'ūd: "The Qur'ān was revealed in seven dialects *(aḥruf)* and each dialect has an inner aspect *(baṭn)* and an outer aspect *(ẓahr)*"[684] to which forgers added, "and the knowledge of all of that is with 'Alī b. Abī Ṭālib, both the inner and the outer knowledge."[685]

Another example is the spurious collection of speeches and sayings – including "Woman is all bad but the worst part of her is that she is indispensable,"[686] a goliardic rather than Islamic notion – attributed to 'Alī in *Nahj al-Balāgha* (Peak of Eloquence), concerning which al-Dhahabī said:

> Al-Murtaḍā Abū Ṭālib 'Alī b. Ḥusayn b. Mūsā al-Mūsawī (355-436) is the compiler of the book *Nahj al-Balāgha*, the words of which are attributed to Imām 'Alī – and no chains of transmissions exist for such an attribution! Some of it is falsehood and it contains some truth, however, there are in it forgeries of which the Imām is completely innocent and which he never said – but where is he that judges fairly? It is also said that the compiler is his brother, al-Sharīf al-Raḍī.[687]

[684]Narrated from Ibn Mas'ūd by al-Ṭabarānī in *al-Awsaṭ*, Abū Ya'lā, and al-Bazzār with trustworthy narrators as stated by al-Haythamī, *Majma' al-Zawā'id* (7:152).

[685]Narrated from Ibn Mas'ūd by Abū Nu'aym, *Ḥilya* (1985 ed. 1:65) through Muḥ. b. Marwān al-Suddī who is discarded *(matrūk)* and accused of forgery.

[686]A medieval European misogynistic cliché based on the Judeo-Christian constructs of "original sin" and "the evil that is woman." If "woman is totally bad and the worst part is that you cannot do without her" it would follow that men are even more so, since Allah ﷻ said that *He created from one soul its match* (4:1, 7:189, 39:6). More proofs that the above is a forgery are the sound Prophetic sayings: "Beloved to me in the world are perfume and women" [on this ḥadīth see Haytamī's *Fatāwā Ḥadīthiyya* (p. 277)]; "Celibacy is not of Islam. He is not one of us who shuns marriage"; and "the best temporary possession in the world is a righteous wife." Allah mentions women also as one of His most prized rewards in Paradise and mothers are the chief means by which, according to mass-transmitted evidence, the Prophet ﷺ shall pride himself of the abundance of this Umma before other Communities at that time. For more such forgeries see our introduction to al-Qārī's *Encyclopedia of Forgeries*.

[687]Dhahabī, *Siyar* (Dār al-Fikr 1997 ed. 13:383 §4008), cf. *Mīzān* (3:124): "He is the one blamed for forging the book *Nahj al-Balāgha*." However, he and a few other Shī'īs declare *kāfir* whoever holds that the Qur'ān has been tampered with. Nevertheless the *Nahj* is skillfully defended by Abū al-Ḥasan al-Nadwī in his *Sīra* of 'Alī entitled *al-Murtaḍā*, 2nd ed. (Damascus: Dār al-Qalam, 1419/1998) p. 201 n.

30
The Earthquake Prayer

Al-Shāfiʿī in *al-Umm* and Bayhaqī in the *Sunan* narrated from ʿAlī b. Abī Ṭālib–may Allah honor him–that he prayed in congregation at the time of an earthquake [two prayer cycles totalling] six *rukū*ʿs (bowings) and four prostrations. Namely, in the first *rakʿa*, five *rukū*ʿs and two prostrations, and in the second *rakʿa* one *rukū*ʿ and two prostrations. Shāfiʿī said, "Were it established from ʿAlī we would say to do it." Our teacher Nūr al-Dīn ʿItr said in his book on the special prayers, "this is an indication that he did not consider it established."[688] However al-Bayhaqī said: "It is well-established on the part of Ibn ʿAbbās… as his ijtihad," and he adduced its chain and text whereby Ibn ʿAbbās prayed (i) the earthquake prayer (ii) in congregation (iii) the morning directly after the night in which the earthquake had taken place.[689] Saʿīd b. Manṣūr also narrated in his own *Sunan* that Ibn ʿAbbās prayed it as imam and he made *takbīr* then recited, bowed, then raised his head and recited, then bowed, then raised his head and recited, then bowed, then raised his head and recited, then bowed, [etc.] after which he prostrated, whereby his prayer consisted in six bowings and two prostrations."[690] Another modality of a total of four bowings (3+1) is also reported.[691]

It was also narrated with a sound chain from ʿĀʾisha – Allah be well-pleased with her – that the Prophet – upon him the blessings and peace of Allah – prayed this exact modality during an eclipse. She added, "The prayer of the great signs of Allah is six bowings with four prostrations"[692]

The righteous caliph ʿUmar b. ʿAbd al-ʿAzīz ordered such a prayer upon earthquakes in his time as well as repentance and massive alms-giving. Al-Suyūṭī mentioned all of the above in his *Kashf al-Ṣalṣala ʿan Waṣf al-Zalzala* (The Piercing Alarm Disclosing the Description of Earthquakes).[693]

[688] ʿItr, *Hady al-Nabī –ṣallā Allāhu ʿalayhi wa-ʿalā Ālihi wa-Sallam– fīl-Ṣalawāt al-Khāṣṣa*, 3rd ed. (Damascus: Dār al-Fikr, 1422/2001) p. 275.
[689] "Ibn ʿAbbās prayed it [=the earthquake prayer] the morning after, so his rule [as opposed to the Shāfiʿī school] is probably that temporary-cause prayers can be made up later, as is the position of a group of the scholars" per al-Suyūṭī, *Kashf al Salsala ʿan Waṣf al-Zalzala*, ed. ʿAbd al-Raḥmān b. ʿAbd al-Jabbār al-Faryawāʾī (Medina: Maktabat al-Dār, 1404/1984) p. 53.
[690] al-Shāfiʿī, *Umm* (1:218); Ibn Abī Shayba (2:115); Bayhaqī, *Sunan* (3:343 *isnād ṣaḥīḥ*), *Maʿrifat al-Sunan*; Nawawī, *Majmūʿ* (5:58-59); Ibn Ḥajar, *Talkhīṣ al-Ḥabīr*.
[691] ʿAbd al-Razzāq, *Muṣannaf* (3:101); Ibn al-Mundhir, *Awsaṭ* (5:314); Ibn Ḥazm, *Muḥallā* (5:99). Cf. Qalʿahjī, *Mawsūʿat Fiqh Ibn ʿAbbās* (p. 471).
[692] Muslim (*Kusūf*); Ibn Abī Shayba (2:470-471 reciting al-Baqara and Āl ʿImrān).
[693] al-Suyūṭī, *Kashf al-Ṣalṣala* (pp. 47-49, pp. 52-53).

31
Imam al-Nawawī's Patrilineal Pattern-Chained Ḥadīth From 'Alī

Imām al-Nawawī narrated a remarkable patrilineal chain for a ḥadīth going back to 'Alī: "Among the best of the narrations of the type 'sons from fathers' is that of al-Khaṭīb with a chain going back to 'Abd al-Wahhāb b. 'Abd al-'Azīz b. al-Ḥārith b. Asad b. al-Layth b. Sulaymān b. al-Aswad b. Sufyān b. Yazīd b. Akīna al-Tamīmī who said: I heard my father (Yazīd) say: I heard my father (Sufyān) say: I heard my father (al-Aswad) say: I heard my father (Sulaymān) say: I heard my father (al-Layth) say: I heard my father (Asad) say: I heard my father (al-Ḥārith) say: I heard my father ('Abd al-'Azīz) say: I heard my father ('Abd al-Wahhāb) say: I heard 'Alī b. Abī Ṭālib ﷺ say: 'The affectionate one *(al-ḥannān)* is he who comes to the one who had shunned him. The granter of favor *(al-mannān)* is he who extends the favor before he is asked for it."[694]

Main sources: Abū Nu'aym, *Ḥilya* 1:100-128 §4; al-Dhahabī, *Siyar* 1/2:615-660 §5; Muḥibb al-Dīn al-Ṭabarī, *al-Riyāḍ al-Naḍira.*

[694]Al-Nawawī narrates it in his condensed treatise on the science of ḥadīth entitled *al-Taqrīb wal-Taysīr* (p. 101). See also Ibn al-Jawzī, *al-Muntaẓam* (9:88).

Bibliography

ʿAbd Allāh b. Aḥmad b. Ḥanbal. *Faḍāʾil al-Ṣaḥāba*. See Aḥmad b. Ḥanbal, *Faḍāʾil al-Ṣaḥāba*.

ʻAbd b. Ḥumayd. *Musnad*. Eds. Subḥī al-Badrī al-Sāmirā'i and Maḥmūd al-Sa'īdī. Cairo: Maktabat al-Sunna, 1988.

ʻAbd al-Razzāq. *al-Muṣannaf*. 11 vols. Ed. Ḥabīb al-Raḥmān al-A'ẓamī. Beirut: al-Maktab al-Islāmī, 1983. With Ma'mar b. Rāshid's *Kitāb al-Jāmiʿ* as the last two volumes.

Abū Dāwūd. *al-Marāsīl*. Ed. Shu'ayb Arnā'ūṭ. Beirut: Mu'assasat al-Risāla, 1988.

———. *Sunan*. 3 vols. Ed. Muḥammad Fu'ād 'Abd al-Bāqī. Beirut: Dār al-Kutub al-'Ilmiyya, 1996. See also al-'Aẓīm Ābādī, *'Awn al-Ma'būd*.

Abū Nu'aym al-Aṣfahānī. *Tārīkh Aṣbahān* (*Dhikr Akhbār Aṣbahān*). Ed. Sayyid Kisrawī Ḥasan. 2 vols. Beirut: Dār al-Kutub al-ʿIlmiyya, 1410/ 1990.

———. [*al-Muntakhab min*] *Dalā'il al-Nubuwwa*. Eds. Muḥammad Rawwās Qal'ajī and 'Abd al-Barr 'Abbās. Beirut: Dār al-Nafā'is, 1999^{4}.

———. *Ḥilyat al-Awliyā' wa Ṭabaqāt al-Asfiya'*. 12 vols. Ed. Muṣṭafā 'Abd al-Qādir 'Aṭā. Beirut: Dār al-Kutub al-'Ilmiyya, 1997.

———. *Tasmiyatu mā Intahā ilaynā min Ruwāt Sa'īd b. Manṣūr*. Ed. 'Abd Allāh Yūsuf al-Jadya'. Ryadh: Dār al-'Āṣima, 1989.

Abū Ṭālib al-Qāḍī. *'Ilal al-Tirmidhī al-Kabīr*. Ed. Ṣubḥī al-Sāmirā'ī, Abū al-Ma'āṭī al-Nūrī, and Maḥmūd al-Sa'īdī. Beirut: 'Ālam al-Kutub, 1989.

Abū Ya'lā al-Mawṣilī. *Musnad*. 13 vols. Ed. Ḥusayn Salīm Asad. Damascus: Dār al-Ma'mūn līl-Turāth, 1984.

al-Aḥdab, Khaldūn. *Zawā'id Tārīkh Baghdād 'alā al-Kutub al-Sitta*. 10 vols. Damascus: Dār al-Qalam, 1996.

Aḥmad b. Ḥanbal. *Faḍā'il al-Ṣaḥāba*. 2 vols. Ed. Waṣī Allāh Muḥammad 'Abbās. Beirut: Mu'assasat al-Risāla, 1983.

———. *al-Musnad*. 20 vols. Ed. Aḥmad Shākir and Ḥamza Aḥmad al-Zayn. Cairo: Dār al-Ḥadīth, 1995.

———. *al-Musnad*. 50 vols. Ed. Shu'ayb Arnā'ūṭ. Beirut: Mu'assasat al-Risāla, 2000-2001.

———. *al-Zuhd*. Beirut: Dar al-Kutub al-'Ilmiyya, 1978.

al-'Ajlūnī. *Kashf al-Khafā*. 2nd ed. 2 vols. Beirut: Dār Iḥyā' al-Turāth al-'Arabī, 1932.

al-Ājurrī. *al-Sharī'a*. Ed. 'Abd al-Razzāq al-Mahdī. Beirut: Dār al-Kitāb al-'Arabī, 1996.

al-Baghawī. *Sharḥ al-Sunna*. 8 vols. Eds. Shu'ayb Arnā'ūṭ and Zuhayr al-Shāwīsḥ Beirut: al-Maktab al-Islāmī, 1971.

al-Bayhaqī. *al-Asmāʾ wal-Ṣifāt*. Ed. ʿAbd Allāh al-Ḥāshidī. 2 vols. Jeddah: Maktabat al-Sawādī, 1413/1993.

———. *Dalāʾil al-Nubuwwa wa Maʿrifat Aḥwāl Ṣāḥib al-Sharīʿa*. 7 vols. Ed. ʿAbd al-Muʿṭī Amīn Qalʿajī. Beirut: Dār al-Kutub al-ʿIlmiyya, 1985.

———. *al-Iʿtiqād ʿalā Madhhabi al-Salaf Ahl al-Sunna wa al-Jamāʿa*. Beirut: Dār al-Afāq al-Jadīda, 1981; Dār al-Kutub al-ʿIlmiyya, 1986[2].

———. *al-Madkhal ilā al-Sunan al-Kubrā*. Ed. Muḥammad Ḍiyāʾ al-Raḥmān al-Aʿzami. Kuwait: Dār al-Khulafāʾ līl-Kitāb al-Islāmī, n.d.

———. *Maʿrifat al-Sunan wal-Āthār*. Ed. ʿAbd al-Muʿṭī Amīn Qalʿajī, 15 vols. Aleppo and Cairo: Dār al-Waʿī, 1411/1991.

———. *Shuʿab al-Īmān*. 8 vols. Ed. Muḥammad Zaghlūl. Beirut: Dār al-Kutub al-ʿIlmiyya, 1990.

———. *al-Sunan al-Kubrā*. 10 vols. Ed. Muḥammad ʿAbd al-Qādir ʿAta. Mecca: Maktabat Dār al-Baz, 1994.

al-Bazzār. *Musnad*. [*al-Baḥr al-Zakhkhār*.] 18 vols. Ed. Maḥfūẓ al-Raḥmān Zayn Allāh et al. Beirut: Muʾassasat ʿUlūm al-Qurʾān; Medina: Maktabat al-ʿUlūm wa al-Ḥikam, 1988-2009.

———. *Mukhtaṣar al-Musnad*. See Ibn Ḥajar, *Mukhtaṣar Zawāʾid Musnad al-Bazzār*.

al-Bukhārī. *Ṣaḥīḥ*. Ed. Aḥmad ʿAlī al-Siharanfūrī. 1272/1856.

———. *Ṣaḥīḥ*. 8 vols. in 3. Ed. Muḥammad al-Zuhrī al-Ghamrāwī. Bulāq: al-Maṭbaʿat al-Kubrā al-Amīriyya, 1314/1896. Repr. Cairo: al-Maṭbaʿat al-Maymūniyya [Muṣṭafā Bābā al-Ḥalabī *et al.*], 1323/1905.

———. *Ṣaḥīḥ*. See Ibn Ḥajar, *Fatḥ al-Bārī*.

———. *al-Tārīkh al-Kabīr*. 8 vols. Ed. al-Sayyid Hāshim al-Nadwī. Beirut: Dār al-Fikr, n.d.

al-Būṣīrī. *Miṣbāḥ al-Zujāja fī Zawāʾid Ibn Mājaḥ* 2nd ed. 4 vols. Ed. Muḥammad al-Muntaqā al-Kashnawī. Beirut: Dār al-ʿArabiyya, 1983.

al-Dāraquṭnī. *al-ʿIlal*. 9 vols. Ed. Maḥfūẓ al-Raḥmān Zayn Allāh al-Salafī. Ryad: Dār Tiba, 1985.

———. *Sunan*. 4 vols. in 2. Together with Muḥammad Shams al-Ḥaqq al-ʿAẓīm Ābādī's *al-Taʿlīq al-Mughnī*. Ed. al-Sayyid ʿAbd Allāh Hāshim Yamānī al-Madanī. Beirut: Dār al-Maʿrifa, 1966. Repr. Beirut: Dār Ihyā al-Turāth al-ʿArabī, 1993.

Daḥlān, Aḥmad Zaynī. *al-Fatḥ al-Mubīn fī Faḍāʾil al-Khulafāʾ al-Rāshidīn wa-Ahl al-Bayt al-Ṭāhirīn*. Ed. Rabīʿ b. Ṣādiq Daḥlān. Beirut: Dar al-Fikr, 1426/2005.

al-Dārimī. *Musnad* [*Sunan*]. 2 vols. Ed. Fuʾād Aḥmad Zamarlī and Khālid al-Sabʿ al-ʿIlmī. Beirut: Dār al-Kitāb al-ʿArabī, 1987.

al-Dhahabī. *Mīzān al-Iʿtidāl*. 4 vols. Ed. ʿAlī Muḥammad al-Bajawī. Beirut: Dār al-Maʿrifa, 1963.

———. *Mīzān al-Iʿtidāl*. 8 vols. Eds. ʿAlī Muḥammad Muʿawwaḍ and ʿĀdil Aḥmad ʿAbd al-Mawjūd. Beirut: Dār al-Kutub al-ʿIlmiyya, 1995.

———. *al-Mughnī fīl-Ḍuʿafāʾ*. 2 vols. Ed. Nūr al-Dīn ʿItr. Qatar: Idara Iḥyāʾ al-Turāth al-Islāmī, 1987.

———. *Siyar A'lām al-Nubalā'*. 19 vols. Ed. Muḥibb al-Dīn al-'Amrāwī. Beirut: Dār al-Fikr, 1996.

———. *Siyar A'lām al-Nubalā'*. 23 vols. Ed. Shu'ayb Arnā'ūṭ and Muḥ. Na'īm al-'Araqsūsī. Beirut: Mu'assasat al-Risāla, 1992-1993.

———. *Tadhkirat al-Ḥuffāẓ*. 4 vols. in 2. Ed. 'Abd al-Raḥmān b. Yaḥyā al-Mu'allimī. A fifth volume, titled *Dhayl Tadhkirat al-Ḥuffāẓ*, consists in al-Ḥusaynī's *Dhayl Tadhkirat al-Ḥuffāẓ*, Muḥammad b. Fahd al-Makkī's *Laḥẓ al-Alḥāẓ bi Dhayl Tadhkirat al-Ḥuffāẓ*, and al-Suyūṭī's *Dhayl Ṭabaqāt al-Ḥuffāẓ*. Ed. Muḥammad Zāhid al-Kawtharī. Beirut: Dār Iḥyā' al-Turāth al-'Arabī and Dār al-Kutub al-'Ilmiyya, n.d. Reprint of the 1968 Hyderabad edition.

———. *Tārīkh al-Islam wa Wafayāt al-Mashāhīr wal-A'lām*. 52 vols. Ed. 'Umar 'Abd al-Salām Tadmurī. Beirut: Dār al-Kitāb al-'Arabī, 1989-2000.

———. *Tartīb al-Mawḍū'āt li-Ibn al-Jawzī*. Ed. Kamāl b. Basyūnī Zaghlūl. Beirut: Dār al-Kutub al-'Ilmiyya, 1994.

al-Dūlābī al-Rāzī, Abū Bishr Muḥammad b. Aḥmad b. Ḥammād b. Sa'īd al-Anṣārī. *al-Kunā wal-Asmā'*. Ed. Naẓar al-Faryābī. 3 vols. Beirut: Dār Ibn Ḥazm, 1421/2000.

al-Ghumārī, Aḥmad b. Muḥammad b. al-Ṣiddīq. *al-Burhān al-Jalī fī Taḥqīq Intisāb al-Ṣūfiyya ilā 'Alī*. With *Fatḥ al-Malik al-'Alī bi-Ṣiḥḥat Ḥadīth Bāb Madīnat al-'Ilmi 'Alī*. Ed. Aḥmad Muḥ Mursī al-Naqshbandī. Cairo: Maṭba'at al-Sa'āda, 1969.

———. *al-Mudāwī li 'Ilal al-Jāmi' al-Ṣaghīr wa Sharḥay al-Munāwī*. 6 vols. Ed. Muṣṭafā Ṣabrī. Cairo: al-Maktaba al-Makkiyya, 1996.

Haddad, Gibril Fouad. *The Excellence of Syro-Palestine–al-Shām–and Its People: Forty Hadiths*. Damascus: Maktabat al-Aḥbāb, 2002. 2nd ed. Birmingham, UK: Remembrance Publications, 2016.

_______. *The Four Imams and Their Schools: Abū Ḥanīfa, Mālik, al-Shāfi'ī, Aḥmad b. Ḥanbal*. London: Muslim Academic Trust, 2007.

_______. *The Muhammadan Light in the Qur'ān, Sunna and Companion-Reports*. London: Centre for Spirituality and Cultural Development, 2012.

———. *The Musnad of Ahl al-Bayt: Forty full-chained Hadiths on the Family of the Prophet narrated from forty of his descendants out of forty books*. Third Arabic edition and first English translation. Fenton, Michigan: Institute for Spiritual and Cultural Advancement, 2022.

———. *Sunna Notes I: Hadith History and Principles*. Birmingham: al-Qur'an wal-Sunna Association, 2005.

———. *Sunna Notes II: The Excellent Innovation in the Qur'ān and Hadith* Birmingham: al-Qur'an wal-Sunna Association, 2006.

_______. *Sunna Notes III: The Binding Proof of the Sunna*. Birmingham: al-Qur'an wal-Sunna Association, 2010.

al-Ḥākim. *al-Madkhal ilā Ma'rifati Kitāb al-Iklīl*. Ed. Mu'tazz 'Abd al-Laṭīf al-Khaṭīb. Damascus: Dār al-Fayḥā', 2000.

———. *al-Madkhal ilā al-Ṣaḥīḥ*. Ed. Rabī' Hādī al-Madkhalī. Beirut: Mu'assasat al-Risāla, 1984.

———. *al-Mustadrak 'alā al-Ṣaḥīḥayn*. With al-Dhahabī's *Talkhīṣ al-Mustadrak*. 5 vols. Indexes by Yūsuf 'Abd al-Raḥmān al-Mar'ashlī. Beirut: Dār al-Ma'rifa, 1986. Reprint of the 1334/1916 Hyderabad edition.

———. *al-Mustadrak 'Ala al-Ṣaḥīḥayn*. With al-Dhahabī's *Talkhīṣ al-Mustadrak*. 4 vols. Annotations by Muṣṭafā 'Abd al-Qādir 'Aṭā'. Beirut: Dār al-Kutub al-'Ilmiyya, 1990.

al-Ḥakīm al-Tirmidhī. *Khatm al-Awliyā'*. Ed. 'Uthmān Ismā'īl Yaḥyā. Institut de lettres orientales de Beyrouth. Beirut: Imprimerie Catholique, n.d. Translated as *The Concept of Sainthood in Early Islamic Mysticism*.

———. *Nawādir al-Uṣūl*. Beirut: Dār Sadir, n.d. Repr. of Istanbul ed.

al-Ḥārith b. Abī Usāma. *Musnad*. [*Bughyat al-Bāḥith 'an Zawā'id Musnad al-Ḥārith*]. 2 vols. Ed. Ḥusayn Aḥmad Ṣāliḥ al-Bakirī. Medina: Markaz Khidmat al-Sunna wa al-Sīra al-Nabawiyya, 1992.

al-Haythamī, Nūr al-Dīn. *Majma' al-Zawā'id wa Manba' al-Fawā'id*. 10 vols. in 5. Cairo: Maktabat al-Qudsī, 1932-1934. Repr. Beirut: Dār al-Kitāb al-'Arabī, 1967, 1982, and 1987.

Ibn 'Abd al-Barr. *al-Istī'ab fī Ma'rifat al-Aṣḥāb*. 4 vols. Ed. 'Alī Muḥ. al-Bījāwī. Cairo: Maktabat Nahḍat Miṣr, 1380?/1960?. Rept. Beirut: Dār al-Jīl, 1412/1992.

_______. *Jāmi' Bayān al-'Ilm wa-Faḍlih*. Ed. Abū al-Ashbāl al-Zuhayrī. 2 vols. Dammam: Dār Ibn al-Jawzī, 1414/1994.

———. *al-Tamhīd limā fil-Muwaṭṭa' min al-Ma'ānī wal-Asānīd*. 22 vols. Eds. Muṣṭafā b. Aḥmad al-'Alawī and Muḥammad 'Abd al-Kabīr al-Bakrī. Morocco: Wizarat 'Umūm al-Awqāf wal-Shu'ūn al-Islāmiyya, 1967-1968.

Ibn Abī 'Āṣim. *al-Āḥād wal-Mathānī fī Faḍā'il al-Ṣaḥāba*. 6 vols. Ed. Bāsim Fayṣal al-Jawābira. Ryad: Dār al-Raya, 1991.

———. *al-Sunna*. Ed. M. Nāṣir al-Albānī. Beirut and Damascus: al-Maktab al-Islāmī, 1993.

Ibn Abī al-Dunyā. *al-Ṣamt wa Ādāb al-Lisān*. Ed. Najm 'Abd al-Raḥmān Khalaf. Beirut: Dār al-Gharb al-Islāmī, 1986.

———. *al-Ṣamt wa Ādāb al-Lisān*. Ed. Abū Isḥāq al-Ḥuwaynī. Beirut: Dār al-Kitāb al-'Arabī, 1990.

———. *al-Wara'*. Ed. Abū 'Abd Allāh Muḥammad Ḥamd al-Ḥammūd. Kuwait: al-Dār al-Salafiyya, 1988.

Ibn Abī Khaythama. *al-Tārīkh al-Kabīr*. Ed. Ṣalāḥ b. Fatḥī Hilāl. 4 vols. Cairo : al-Fārūq al-Ḥadītha, 1427/2006.

Ibn Abī Shayba. *al-Muṣannaf*. 7 vols. Ed. Kamāl al-Ḥūt. Ryadh: Maktabat al-Rushd, 1989.

Ibn 'Adī. *al-Kāmil fī Ḍu'afā' al-Rijāl*. 7 vols. Ed. Yaḥyā Mukhtār Ghazawī. Beirut: Dār al-Fikr, 1988.

Ibn al-'Arabī, Abū Bakr. *al-'Awāṣim min al-Qawāṣim fī Taḥqīq Mawāqif al-Ṣaḥāba ba'da Wafāt al-Nabī* ﷺ. Ed. Muḥibb al-Dīn al-Khaṭīb. Cairo: al-Maṭba'at al-Salafiyya, 1952.

Ibn 'Asākir, Abū al-Qāsim. *Tārīkh Dimashq*. 70 vols. Damascus: Dār al-Fikr, 2000.

Ibn al-Athīr al-Jazarī (d. 630). *al-Kāmil fīl-Tārīkh*. 20 vols. Beirut: Dār Ṣādir, 1979.

———. *al-Kāmil fīl-Tārīkh*. 10 vols. Ed. Abu al-Fidā' 'Abd Allāh al-Qāḍī. Beirut: Dār al-Kutub all-'Ilmiyya, 1995.

———. *al-Nihāya fī Gharīb al-Athar*. 5 vols. Eds. Ṭāhir Aḥmad al-Zāwī and Maḥmūd Muḥammad al-Ṭabbākhī. Beirut: Dār al-Fikr, 1979.

Ibn Balbān. *Tuḥfat al-Ṣiddīq fī Faḍā'il Abī Bakr al-Ṣiddīq*. Ed. Muḥyī al-Dīn Mustū. Damascus: Dār Ibn Kathīr and Medina: Maktaba Dār al-Turāth, 1988.

Ibn Ḥajar. *Fatḥ al-Bārī Sharḥ Ṣaḥīḥ al-Bukhārī*. 13 vols. Ed. Muḥammad Fu'ād 'Abd al-Bāqī and Muḥibb al-Dīn al-Khaṭīb. Beirut: Dār al-Ma'rifa, 1959-1960.

———. *Ibidem*. Cairo: al-Maṭba'at al-Bahiyya, 1348/1929-1930.

———. *al-Iṣāba fī Tamyīz al-Ṣaḥāba*. 8 vols. Calcutta, 1269/1853.

———. *al-Iṣāba fī Tamyīz al-Ṣaḥāba*. 8 vols in 4. Ed. 'Alī Muḥammad al-Bijāwī. Beirut: Dār al-Jīl, 1992.

_______. *al-Kāfī al-Shāf fī Takhrīj Aḥādīth al-Kashshāf*. With Muḥibb al-Dīn Afandī. *Tanzīl al-Āyāt 'alā al-Shawāhid min al-Abyāt*. Beirut: Dār Iḥyā' al-Turāth al-'Arabī, 1418/1997.

———. *Lisān al-Mīzān*. 7 vols. Hyderabad: Dā'irat al-Ma'ārif al-Ni$āmiyya, 1329/1911. Repr. Beirut: Mu'assassat al-A'lamī, 1986.

———. *al-Maṭālib al-'Āliya*. 4 vols. Kuwait, 1973.

———. *Mukhtaṣar Zawā'id Musnad al-Bazzār*. 2 vols. Ed. Sabri 'Abd al-Khāliq Abū Dharr. Beirut: Mu'assasat al-Kutub al-Thaqāfiyya, 1993.

———. *Natā'ij al-Afkār fī Takhrīj Aḥādīth al-Adhkār*. Ed. Ḥamdī al-Salafī. 2nd ed. 5 vols. Damascus and Beirut: Dār Ibn Kathīr, 1429/ 2008.

———. *Tahdhīb al-Tahdhīb*. 14 vols. Hyderabad: Dā'irat al-Ma'ārif al-Ni$āmiyya, 1327/1909. Repr. Beirut: Dār al-Fikr, 1984.

———. *Taḥrīr Taqrīb al-Tahdhīb*. 4 vols. By Bashshar 'Awwād Ma'rūf and Shu'ayb Arnā'ūṭ. Beirut: Mu'assasat al-Risāla, 1997.

———. *Talkhīṣ al-Ḥabīr*. 4 vols. Ed. Sayyid 'Abd Allāh Hashim al-Yamānī. Medina, 1964. Repr. 4 vols. in 2, Cairo: Maktabat al-Kulliya al-Azhariyya, 1979.

———. *Taqrīb al-Tahdhīb*. Ed. Muḥammad 'Awwāma. Aleppo: Dār al-Rashid, 1997.

Ibn Ḥibbān. *Ṣaḥīḥ Ibn Ḥibbān bi-Tartīb Ibn Balbān*. 18 vols. Ed. Shu'ayb Arnā'ūṭ. Beirut: Mu'assasat al-Risāla, 1993.

Ibn al-Jawzī. *al-'Ilal al-Mutanāhiya fīl-Aḥādīth al-Wāhiya*. 2 vols. Ed. Shaykh Khalīl al-Mays. Beirut: Dār al-Kutub al-'Ilmiyya, 1983.

———. *al-Mawḍū'āt*. 3 vols. Ed. 'Abd al-Raḥmān Muḥammad 'Uthmān. Medina: al-Maktabat al-Salafiyya, 1967. See also al-Dhahabī's *Tartīb al-Mawdū'āt*.

———. *al-Quṣṣāṣ wa al-Mudhakkirīn*. Ed. Muḥammad Basyūnī Zaghlūl. Beirut: Dār al-Kutub al-'Ilmiyya, 1986.

———. *Ṣifat al-Ṣafwa*. 4 vols. 2nd ed. Eds. Maḥmūd Fākhūrī and Muḥammad Rawwās Qal'ajī. Beirut: Dār al-Ma'rifa, 1979.

Ibn Kathīr. *al-Bidāya wa al-Nihāya*. 15 vols. Ed. Editing Board of al-Turāth. Beirut: Dār Iḥyā' al-Turāth al-'Arabī, 1993.

———. *Ibid.* 14 vols. Beirut: Maktabat al-Ma'ārif, n.d.

———. *Tafsīr al-Qur'ān al-'A$īm*. 4 vols. Beirut: Dār al-Fikr, 1981.

Ibn Khuzayma. *al-Ṣaḥīḥ*. 4 vols. Ed. Muḥammad Muṣṭafā al-A'$amī. Beirut: al-Maktab al-Islāmī, 1970.

Ibn Mājah. *Sunan*. See al-Suyūṭī *et al.*, *Sharḥ Sunan Ibn Mājah.*

Ibn al-Mubārak. *al-Zuhd*. Ed. Habib al-Raḥmān al-A'zami. Beirut: Dār al-Kutub al-'Ilmiyya, n.d.

Ibn Nuqṭa, *Takmilat al-Ikmāl*. 4 vols. Eds. 'Abd al-Qayyūm 'Abd Rabb al-Nabī and Muḥammad Ṣāliḥ al-Murād. Mecca: Jāmi'at Umm al-Qurā, 1988-1990.

Ibn Qāḍī Shuhba. *Ṭabaqāt al-Shāfi'iyya*. 2 vols. Ed. 'Abd al-'Alīm Khān. Beirut: Dār al-Nadwa al-Jadīda, 1987.

Ibn Qāni'. *Mu'jam al-Ṣaḥāba*. 3 vols. Ed. Ṣalāḥ b. Sālim al-Miṣrātī. Medina: Maktabat al-Ghurabā' al-Athariyya, 1998.

Ibn Qudāma, Najm al-Dīn. *Mukhtaṣar Minhāj al-Qāṣidīn li Ibn al-Jawzī*. Ed. M. Aḥmad Ḥamdān and 'Abd al-Qādir Arnā'ūṭ. 2nd. ed. Damascus: Maktab al-Shabab al-Muslim wa al-Maktab al-Islāmī, 1961.

Ibn Rajab. *Jāmi' al-'Ulūm wal-Ḥikam*. 2 vols. Ed. Wahbat al-Zuḥaylī. Beirut: Dār al-Khayr, 1996^2.

———. *Jāmi' al-'Ulūm wa al-Ḥikam*. Ed. Shu'ayb al-Arnā'ūṭ. Beirut: Mu'assasat al-Risāla, 1998^7.

———. *Laṭā'if al-Ma'ārif fī-mā lil-Mawāsim min Waẓā'if*. Ed. Yāsīn al-Sawwās. 5th ed. Damascus and Beirut: Dār Ibn Kathīr, 1420/ 1999.

Ibn Sa'd. *al-Ṭabaqāt al-Kubrā*. 9 vols. Beirut: Dār Sadir, 1957-1960.

al-Kattānī, Muḥammad b. Ja'far. *Na$m al-Mutanāthir fīl-Ḥadīth al-Mutawātir*. Ed. Sharaf Ḥijāzī. Cairo: Dār al-Kutub al-Salafiyya, n.d. and Beirut: Dār al-Kutub al-'Ilmiyya, 1980.

al-Khalīlī. *al-Irshād fī Ma'rifati 'Ulama' al-Ḥadīth*. 3 vols. Ed. Muḥammad Sa'īd 'Umar Idrīs. Ryad: Maktabat al-Rushd, 1989.

al-Khaṭīb al-Baghdādī. *al-Jāmi' li-Akhlāq al-Rāwī wa-Ādāb al-Sāmi'*. Ed. Muḥ. 'Ajāj al-Khaṭīb. 2 vols. Beirut: Mu'assasat al-Risāla, 1412/1991.

———. *Muwaḍḍiḥ Awhām al-Jam' wa al-Tafrīq*. 2 vols. Ed. 'Abd al-Mu'ṭī Qal'ajī. Beirut: Dār al-Ma'rifa, 1987.

———. *Sharaf Aṣḥāb al-Ḥadīth*. Ed. Muḥammad Sa'īd Ūghlī. Ankara: Dār Iḥyā' al-Sunnat al-Nabawiyya, [1971].

———. *Tārīkh Baghdād*. 14 vols. Medina: al-Maktabat al-Salafiyya, n.d. See also al-Aḥdab, *Zawā'id Tārīkh Baghdād.*

al-Khaṭṭābī. *Ma'ālim al-Sunan Sharḥ Sunan Abī Dāwūd*. 4 vols. in 2. Ed. 'Abd al-Salām 'Abd al-Shāfī Muḥammad. Beirut: Dār al-Kutub al-'Ilmiyya, 1996.

Mālik b. Anas. *al-Muwaṭṭa'*. 2 vols. Ed. Muḥammad Fu'ād 'Abd al-Bāqī. Beirut: Dār al-Kutub al-'Ilmiyya, n.d.

al-Maqdisī. *al-Aḥādīth al-Mukhtāra*. 10 vols. Ed. 'Abd al-Mālik b. 'Abd Allāh b. Duhaysh. Mecca: Maktabat al-Nahḍat al-Ḥadītha, 1990.

al-Mizzī. *Tahdhīb al-Kamāl*. 35 vols. Ed. Bashshār 'Awwād Ma'rūf. Beirut: Mu'assasat al-Risāla, 1980.

al-Mubārakfūrī. *Tuḥfat al-Aḥwadhī bi-Sharḥ Jāmi' al-Tirmidhī*. 10 vols. Beirut: Dār al-Kutub al-'Ilmiyya, 1990. Includes al-Tirmidhī's *Sunan*.

al-Munāwī. *Fayḍ al-Qadīr Sharḥ al-Jāmi' al-Ṣaghīr*. 6 vols. Cairo: al-Maktaba al-Tijāriyya al-Kubrā, 1356/1937. Repr. Beirut: Dār al Ma'rifa, 1972.

al-Mundhirī. *al-Targhīb wa al-Tarhīb*. 4 vols. Ed. Ibrāhīm Shams al-Dīn. Beirut: Dār al-Kutub al-'Ilmiyya, 1997.

Muslim. *Ṣaḥīḥ*. 5 vols. Ed. M. Fu'ād 'Abd al-Bāqī. Beirut: Dār Iḥyā' al-Turāth al-'Arabī, 1954. Also see al-Nawawī, *Sharḥ Ṣaḥīḥ Muslim*.

al-Muttaqī al-Hindī al-Burhānfūrī, 'Alā' al-Dīn 'Alī al-Muttaqī b. Ḥusām al-Dīn. *Kanz al-'Ummāl fī Sunan al-Aqwāl wal-Af'āl*. Ed. Bakrī Ḥayyānī and Ṣafwat al-Saqqā. 18 vols. 5th ed. Beirut: Mu'assasat al-Risāla, 1405/1985.

al-Nasā'ī. *'Amal al-Yawm wa al-Layla*. 2nd ed. Ed. Fārūq Ḥammāda. Beirut: Mu'assasat al-Risāla, 1986.

———. *Sunan*. See al-Suyūṭī, *Sharḥ Sunan al-Nasā'ī*.

———. *al-Sunan al-Kubrā*. 6 vols. Eds. 'Abd al-Ghaffār Sulaymān al-Bandari and Sayyid Kisrawi Ḥasan. Beirut: Dār al-Kutub al-'Ilmiyya, 1991.

al-Nawawī. *Fatāwā al-Imām al-Nawawī al-Musammāt bil-Masā'il al-Manthūra*. Ed. Muḥ. al-Ḥajjār. Aleppo: al-Maṭba'at al-'Arabiyya, 1391 /1971.

———. *Tahdhīb al-Asmā' wa al-Lughāt*. 3 vols. Cairo: Idārat al-Ṭibā'at al-Munīriyya, [1927?]. Rept. Beirut: Dār al-Kutub al-'Ilmiyya, 1977.

Nu'aym b. Ḥammād al-Marwazī. *Kitāb al-Fitan*. 2 vols. Ed. Samīr Amīn al-Zuhrī. Cairo: Maktabat al-Tawḥīd, 1992.

al-Qārī, Mullā 'Alī. *Encyclopedia of Hadith Forgeries:* al-Asrār al-Marfū'a fīl-Akhbār al-Mawḍū'a. *Sayings Misattributed to the Prophet Muḥammad* صلى الله عليه وآله وصحبه وسلم. Transl. Gibril Fouad Haddad. London: Beacon Books, 2013.

al-Qurṭubī. [*Tafsīr.*] *al-Jāmi' li-Aḥkām al-Qur'ān*. 2nd ed. 20 vols. Ed. Aḥmad 'Abd al-'Alīm al-Bardūnī. Cairo: Dār al-Sha'b and Beirut: Dār Iḥyā' al-Turāth al- 'Arabī, 1952-1953. Reprint.

al-Rāzī, Fakhr al-Dīn. *Mafātiḥ al-Ghayb* [*al-Tafsīr al-Kabīr*] with Abū al-Su'ūd's *Tafsīr*. 7 vols. Cairo: al-Maṭba'at al-'Āmira, 1308/1891.

Sa'īd b. Manṣūr. *Sunan*. 2 vols. Ed. Ḥabīb al-Raḥmān al-A'$amī. India: al-Dār al-Salafiyya, 1982.

al-Sakhāwī, Muḥammad b. 'Abd al-Raḥmān. *al-Jawāhir wa al-Durar fī Manāqib Shaykh al-Islam IbnḤajar*. Ed. Ḥāmid 'Abd al-Majīd and Ṭāha al-Zaynī. Cairo: Lajnat Iḥyā' al-Turāth al-Islāmī, 1986.

———. *al-Maqāṣid al-Ḥasana*. Ed. Muḥammad 'Uthmān al-Khisht. Beirut: Dār al-Kitāb al-'Arabī, 1985.

al-Suyūṭī, Jalāl al-Dīn. *al-Durr al-Manthūr fīl-Tafsīr al-Ma'thūr*. 8 vols. Beirut: Dār al-Fikr, 1994.

———. *al-Ḥāwī lil-Fatāwī*. Ed. 'Abd al-Laṭīf Ḥasan 'Abd al-Raḥmān. 2 vols. Beirut : Dār al-Kutub al-'Ilmiyya, 2000.

———. *al-Khaṣā'iṣ al-Kubrā aw Kifāyat al-Ṭālib al-Labīb fī Khaṣā'iṣ al-Ḥabīb* ﷺ. 2 vols. Hyderabad al-Dakn: Dā'irat al-Ma'ārif al-Ni$āmiyya, 1901-1903. See also below, *Tahdhīb al-Khaṣā'iṣ*.

———. *Sharḥ Sunan al-Nasā'ī*. 9 vols. Ed. 'Abd al-Fattah Abū Ghudda. Aleppo: Maktab al-Maṭbū'āt al-Islāmiyya, 1986. With Nasā'īs' *Sunan*.

———. *Ṭabaqāt al-Ḥuffā$*. Ed. 'Alī 'Umar. Cairo: Maktabat Wahba, 1973.

———. *Tahdhīb al-Khaṣā'iṣ al-Nabawiyya al-Kubrā*. 2nd ed. By 'Abd Allāh al-Talīdī. Beirut: Dār al-Bashā'ir al-Islāmiyya, 1990.

———. *Tanwīr al-Ḥawālik bi-Sharḥ Muwaṭṭa' Mālik*. 2 vols. Cairo: al-Maktabat al-Tijāriyya al-Kubrā, 1969.

———. *Tārīkh al-Khulafā'*. Ed. Raḥāb Khiḍr 'Akkāwī. Beirut: Mu'assasat 'Izz al-Dīn, 1992.

———, 'Abd al-Ghanī al-Dihlawī, and Fakhr al-Ḥasan al-Gangohi. *Sharḥ Sunan Ibn Mājah*. Karachi: Qadimi Kutub Khana, n.d. Includes Ibn Mājah's *Sunan*.

al-Ṭabarānī. *al-Mu'jam al-Awsaṭ*. 10 vols. Eds. Ṭāriq b. 'Awaḍ Allāh and 'Abd al-Muḥsin b. Ibrāhīm al-Ḥusaynī. Cairo: Dār al-Ḥaramayn, 1995.

———. *al-Mu'jam al-Kabīr*. 20 vols. Ed. Ḥamdī b. 'Abd al-Majīd al-Salafī. Mosul: Maktabat al-'Ulūm wa al-Ḥikam, 1983.

———. *al-Mu'jam al-Saghīr*. 2 vols. Ed. Muḥammad Shakūr Maḥmūd. Beirut and Amman: al-Maktab al-Islāmī, Dār 'Ammār, 1985.

———. *Musnad al-Shāmiyyīn*. 2 vols. Ed. Ḥamdī b. 'Abd al-Majīd al-Salafī. Beirut: Mu'assasat al-Risāla, 1984.

al-Ṭabarī, Muḥammad b. Jarīr. *Jāmi' al-Bayān fī Tafsīr al-Qur'ān*. 30 vols. Beirut: Dār al-Ma'ārif, 1980; Dār al-Fikr, 1985.

_______. *Tahdhīb al-Āthār: al-Juz' al-Mafqūd*. Ed. 'Alī Rīḍā b. 'Abd Allāh b. 'Alī Riḍā. Damascus and Beirut: Dār al-Ma'mūn lil-Turāth, 1416/1995.

_______. *Tahdhīb al-Āthār wa-Tafṣīl al-Thābit 'an Rasūl Allāh min al-Akhbār*. Ed. Maḥmūd Muḥ. Shākir. 6 vols. Cairo: Maṭba'at al-Madanī, 1402/1982.

al-Ṭabarī, Muḥibb al-Dīn. *al-Riyāḍ al-Naḍira fī Manāqib al-'Ashara*. 2 vols. Ed. 'Īsā al-Ḥimayrī. Beirut: Dār al-Gharb al-Islāmī, 1996.

al-Ṭaḥāwī. *Mushkil al-Āthār*. 4 vols. Hyderabad: Dā'irat al-Ma'ārif al-'Uthmāniyya, 1915. Repr. Beirut: Dār Sadir, n.d.

———. *Sharḥ Ma'ānī al-Āthār*. 4 vols. Ed. Muḥammad Zuhrī al-Najjār. Beirut: Dār al-Kutub al-'Ilmiyya, 1979.

———. *Sharḥ Mushkil al-Āthār*. 16 vols. Ed. Shu'ayb al-Arnā'ūṭ. Beirut: Mu'assasat al-Risāla, 1994.

al-Ṭanṭāwī, 'Alī and Nājī al-Ṭanṭāwī. *Akhbār 'Umar wa-Akhbār 'Abd Allāh b. 'Umar*. 8th ed. Beirut: al-Maktab al-Islāmī, 1403/1983.

al-Tirmidhī. *al-'Ilal*. See Abū Ṭālib al-Qāḍī's *'Ilal al-Tirmidhī al-Kabīr*.

———. *al-Sunan*. See al-Mubārakfūrī, *Tuḥfat al-Aḥwadhī*.

al-Wāḥidī. *Asbāb al-Nuzūl*. Ed. Ayman Ṣāliḥ Sha'bān. Cairo: Dār al-Ḥadīth, 1996.

———. *al-Wajīz fī Tafsīr al-Kitāb al-'Azīz*. 2 vols. Ed. Ṣafwān 'Adnān Dāwūdī. Damascus and Beirut: Dār al-Qalam and al-Dār al-Shamiyya, 1995.

al-Zabīdī, *Itḥāf al-Sādat al-Muttaqīn bi Sharḥ Asrār Iḥyā' 'Ulūm al-Dīn*. Printed together with the text of the *Iḥyā'* in the margins. Also with 'Abd al-Qādir b. 'Abd Allāh al-'Aydarūs Bā 'Alawī's *Ta'rif al-Aḥyā' bi Faḍā'il al-Iḥyā'* and al-Ghazali's *al-Imlā 'an Ishkālāt al-Iḥyā*. 10 vols. Cairo: al-Maṭba'at al-Maymuniyya, 1311/1893.

al-Zarkashī. *al-Tadhkira fīl-Aḥādīth al-Mushtahara*. Ed. Muṣṭafā 'Abd al-Qādir 'Aṭā. Beirut: Dār al-Kutub al-'Ilmiyya, 1986.

al-Zayla'ī. *Naṣb al-Rāya li-Aḥādīth al-Hidāya*. 4 vols. Ed. Muḥammad Yūsuf al-Binūrī. Cairo: Dār al-Ḥadīth, 1357/1938.

al-Zurqānī. *Sharḥ al-Muwaṭṭa'*. 4 vols. Beirut: Dār al-Kutub al-'Ilmiyya, 1981.

Milton Keynes UK
Ingram Content Group UK Ltd.
UKHW032210260724
446191UK00003B/10

9 781938 058691